*Suspicious Readings of Joyce's* Dubliners

# Suspicious Readings of *Joyce's* Dubliners

Margot Norris

**PENN**

University of Pennsylvania Press
Philadelphia

10   9   8   7   6   5   4   3   2   1

Published by
University of Pennsylvania Press
Philadelphia, Pennsylvania 19104-4011

Library of Congress Cataloging-in-Publication Data
Norris, Margot.
   Suspicious readings of Joyce's Dubliners / Margot Norris.
   p.   cm.
   ISBN 0-8122-3739-0 (acid-free paper)
   Includes bibliographical references and index.
   1. Joyce, James, 1882–1941. Dubliners.   2. Dublin (Ireland)—In literature.   I. Title
PR6019.O9 D8766   2003
823'.912—dc21                                        2003051247

*To the international community of scholars of Joyce, who make colleagues feel like family and meetings feel like a party*

# Contents

# Abbreviations

References to Joyce's works are cited parenthetically within the body of the text, without abbreviation, if the context identifies the text, but otherwise using the following abbreviations.

| | |
|---|---|
| *CW* | Joyce, James. *The Critical Writings of James Joyce*. Ed. Ellsworth Mason and Richard Ellmann. Ithaca, N.Y.: Cornell University Press, 1989. |
| *D* | Joyce, James. *Dubliners: Text and Criticism*. Ed. Robert Scholes and A. Walton Litz. New York: Penguin Books, 1996. |
| *FW* | Joyce, James. *Finnegans Wake*. New York: Penguin Books, 1976. |
| *JJII* | Ellmann, Richard. *James Joyce*. New York: Oxford University Press, 1983. |
| *JJA* | *The James Joyce Archive*. Ed. Michael Groden et al. New York and London: Garland Publishing, 1977–1979. |
| *Letters I, II, III* | *Letters of James Joyce*. Vol. I. Ed. Stuart Gilbert. New York: Viking Press, 1957, reissued with corrections 1966. Vols. II, III. Ed. Richard Ellmann. New York: Viking Press, 1966. |
| *P* | Joyce, James. *A Portrait of the Artist as a Young Man*. New York: Penguin Books, 1976. |
| *SL* | Joyce, James. *Selected Letters of James Joyce*. Ed. Richard Ellmann. New York: Viking Press, 1975. |
| *U* | Joyce, James. *Ulysses*. Ed. Hans Walter Gabler et al. New York: Random House, 1986. |

# Introduction

Why do we remain enthralled, at the beginning of the twenty-first century, with *Dubliners*, James Joyce's stories of ordinary people and ordinary life set in Dublin at the last century's beginning? Those of us who call ourselves "modernists" or "twentieth-century" scholars have newly taken on the role once held by the Victorians, as critics of a previous century, a bygone era that passed from contemporaneity for the older among us into a time increasingly historical and historiographed. *Dubliners*, with its obsessive specification of turn-of-the century shop names, streets, train stations, bridges, books, songs, personages, and events, should appeal precisely to our newly minted status as antiquarians. Yet curiously—while the stories' historical and topical specificity becomes more, rather than less, necessary for interpretation—our collective fascination with *Dubliners* is as contemporary as today. This earliest of Joyce's literary productions, with its tortured and difficult journey to publication, was not always thought destined for such an honored longevity. Garry Leonard reminds us that at the time the stories were published an early, anonymous review declared that "at least three would have been better buried in oblivion" (1). James Fairhall points out that *Dubliners* was largely ignored until 1956, when American critics rediscovered the collection, which had never sold well and received little early distinguished attention. "Writing separately, Brewster Ghiselin, Hugh Kenner, and Marvin Magalaner and Richard Kain all discerned in the stories a remarkable formal unity whose key is the theme of paralysis," he writes (*James Joyce* 65). Yet fourteen years later, in 1969, Warren Beck still lamented the volume's marginalization. "Strong drifts of relative interest in Joyce's various works have followed the extraordinary turns they took," Beck wrote in his influential *Joyce's "Dubliners": Substance, Vision, and Art*. He goes on to say, "to some minds the 'fame' which came to Joyce twixt Molly Bloom's sleep and Finnegan's wake has relegated *Dubliners* almost to the status of juvenilia" (1). Still, three collections of essays on *Dubliners* appeared within a year or two of Beck's book and the stories' popularity has quickened over time. There are now a dozen or more books, collections of critical essays, and special journal issues on *Dubliners*, including significant monographs and works by single authors who approach the collection alone or along with Joyce's later works. These include, in addition to Warren Beck's, studies by Garry Leonard, Donald Torchiana, Earl Ingersoll, Craig

Hansen Werner, Bernard Benstock, R. B. Kershner, and the intriguing recent study by Tanja Vesala-Varttala.[1] These single author books follow or accompany the various volumes of collected essays including Peter Garrett's 1968 edition of *Twentieth Century Interpretations of "Dubliners"*, the 1969 *James Joyce's "Dubliners": A Critical Handbook,* edited by James Baker and Thomas Staley, and *James Joyce's Dubliners: Critical Essays,* edited in 1969 by Clive Hart. More recently, Rosa M. Bolletieri Bosinelli and Harold F. Mosher, Jr. have expanded a special issue that the journal *Style* had devoted to the stories in 1991 into a volume entitled *ReJoycing" New Readings of "Dubliners"*. Special *Dubliners* issues were published by the venerable *James Joyce Quarterly* in 1991 and in 1999/2000, and by *Studies in Short Fiction* in 1995. In their introduction to *New Perspectives on Joyce's "Dubliners"*, Mary Power and Ulrich Schneider asked, "Is a rationale needed for another critical book on *Dubliners*? We feel that it is appropriate to look at these stories as the millennium nears in the light of new information and critical theories that are available to us. We also feel that the text of these stories is so rich, allusive and unexpected that it almost compels further study and commentary" (i). Writing thirty years after Beck's lament, Power and Schneider firmly assert, "It is also clear that *Dubliners* is not to be dismissed as juvenilia, but is as distinguished as Joyce's later fiction" (i).

Needless to say, I concur completely with this judgment, and am eager to explore in some detail the text's ability to continue to fascinate us. But although I will offer my own more specific meditation on the text's status a little later, a more general answer may lie in the way the *Dubliners* stories have responded rewardingly to the varied and shifting theoretical approaches that have dominated critical practice in the last several decades. This is not to ignore the lively controversies and methodological arguments that engaged, and sometimes vexed, early critics of the volume.[2] Warren Beck fulminates against Richard Levin's and Charles Shattuck's "First Flight to Ithaca," as though he had to blow away what he called their "analogical-archetypal vaporings" (7) before his own flexible and expansive humanistic approach could breathe critical air. Even early on, the *Dubliners* stories bothered people; they demanded some sort of critical activity to make them meaningful, whether it was deciphering them as allegories or as mythical analogues or, as Beck astutely does, dilating Joyce's "adaptation of narrative modes to socio-psychological subjects" (10). The long perdurance of "the epiphany" as the key to illumination of the stories is another evidence of this interpretive urgency.[3] If we recall Leonard Albert's discovery that the ancient Greek meaning of "gnomon" was "model, criterion, or standard" (355), then *Dubliners* has been "gnomonic" in two senses of the word. I will discuss the more familiar notion in the chapter on "The Sisters"—that is, the sense that all the stories are incomplete and require interpretive activity to complete them. James Buzard imputes this discovery to the consequence of Colin MacCabe's "notorious salvo of the culture wars, *James Joyce and the Revolution of the Word*." He writes, "Since then we have grown accustomed to hearing of the many gaps, fissures, silences, and lacunae of the Joycean text" (43). Yet Warren Beck, writing before MacCabe, heard the sound of silence in the stories, even without benefit of theory. "The restrained voice comes to no emphatic climax but simply ceases and does not resume. The whole story is not to be told, and the gist of it, its human source and its indications, cannot be spoken at all but only shadowed forth" (31). Even before the gaps and silences were theorized, Warren Beck intuited them. But even without recourse to gaps and silences, the seeming simplicity of the stories early began to dissolve into complexity, and it may have been the lure of their elaborate crafting that enticed the New Critics to rediscover them. James Fairhall writes, "Joyce's fictions at once resist and lend themselves to formal analysis . . . the formalists rose to the challenge of his increasingly elaborate texts and turned out a body of interpretation that, at its best, thoroughly maps the internal cross-relations of these texts and the techniques used to create them" (67).

The second, even more intriguing possibility of seeing *Dubliners* as gnomonic is to consider that the collection may function as something like a "model organism" in biology. My husband, Rowland Davis, is a geneticist who studied cell metabolism through an inconspicuous mold few of us have ever seen called *Neurospora*. However, this seemingly trivial little fungus served as a "model organism" during a crucial phase of the history of modern molecular biology. It was chosen as a genetically simple life form that nonetheless displayed universal features of cell metabolism. In this context it is extremely interesting to recall some of the early scholarly exercises that used *Dubliners* to test new theories that were then changing our analyses of how fictional texts worked. In a special 1978/79 Structuralist/ Reader Response issue of the *James Joyce Quarterly*, for example, Robert Scholes used "Eveline" to illustrate a semiotic approach that systematically draws on the work of Tzvetan Todorov, Gérard Genette, and Roland Barthes. A couple years later, the MURGE project, which stood for "Miami University Research Group Experiment," under the direction of James Sosnoski, tested the principles of Seymour Chatman's *Story and Discourse* by conducting a rigorous analysis of "Araby." None of these essays justifies why a *Dubliners* story was specifically chosen for their experiment, and, to be sure, other scholarship used other Joyce texts—and other literatures—as models for testing new theories.[4] But even if they are not alone in this distinction, the stories of *Dubliners* seemed to inspire the tacit assumption that they are somehow able to stand in for fiction in general in their ability to make manifest the structure and function of textuality itself. This tacit assumption—

that the stories somehow make the operation of texts explicit and visible—may also account for the stories' extraordinary popularity on the syllabi of introductory fiction courses.[5]

Yet thinking of *Dubliners* as a *model* for the study of study of fiction fails to do justice to the role that critical theory itself may have played in endowing the stories with their ability to demonstrate how texts work. In other words, the stories' fictional exemplarity has itself been abetted by the theoretical approaches brought to them. This is certainly true of the fine political studies of the stories that in recent years have greatly illuminated, with post-colonial sophistication, the way *Dubliners* speaks to Ireland's colonial status and its struggles for independence.[6] But because these studies generally devote themselves to *Dubliners* in parts rather than comprehensively, a better example may be found in R. B. Kershner's groundbreaking 1989 study, *Joyce, Bakhtin, and Popular Literature: Chronicles of Disorder*, which devotes about half of its length to a systematic treatment of the stories. Kershner's book provides an excellent example of how a theoretical vantage, in this case the recognition borrowed from M. M. Bakhtin that makes of fiction a dialogical enterprise, opens up each *Dubliners* story as a matrix of competing and conflicting discourses in which the voice of popular literary genres plays a particularly interesting role. This allows Kershner to generally resist interpreting the stories in favor of overhearing the ideological echoes of the culture in the speech of the narrators and figures in the stories. For Kershner the *Dubliners* texts are significantly *performative*; that is, they don't just *say* things but *act* in certain ways by the things they say and the way they say them. In his explorations the reader becomes more than anything a listener to the various cultural discourses in the stories and the ideological effects they produce. "Its focus," Kershner says of his study, "has been upon *what the text is doing* rather than *what Joyce is saying*" (298).

A different example of how theory reshapes the stories may be found in Garry Leonard's 1993 *Reading "Dubliners" Again: A Lacanian Perspective*. Leonard also listens to the competing and conflicting discourses in the stories, but with specific attention to their effect on what they do to the protagonists' and characters' sense of themselves. His formulation of the stories' discourses is also performative, in the sense that they shape the way individuals live, psychologically and socially, in their worlds. Leonard is thereby able to add to his analysis the possibility that the *Dubliners* stories can have a transformative effect on the reader. He writes, "One of the points I argue in this book is that the readers of *Dubliners* are encouraged by Joyce to enjoy transcending the limited perspective of the fictional selves (characters) in the stories but only at the price of becoming uneasily aware that the stories of their own lives also operate as texts that maintain their unity and coherence by forgetting, excluding, or marginalizing whatever contradicts the myth of the self" (3). The Lacanan reading Leonard performs on the stories makes visible and palpable the invisible symbolic universe in which Joyce's Dubliners live, with the mysterious values and significances that are attached to all their social transactions. He makes of *Dubliners* a compelling laboratory for exploring the perils to the self—a matter that because it dilates the conditions for oppression and repression is frequently ethically suggestive, and therefore anticipates the ethical criticism of Tanja Vesala-Varttala and Joseph Valente.

Although ethical reading of *Dubliners* as an explicit enterprise is a relatively recent phenomenon in Joyce criticism, the various feminist, political, post-structural, and cultural studies over the last decade or two have certainly addressed questions of power and oppression in ways that have been at least implicitly ethically probing. But as the subtitle of Tanja Vesala-Varttala's *Sympathy and Joyce's "Dubliners": Ethical Probing of Reading, Narrative, and Textuality* makes clear, she brings an explicit attention to responsible interactions of reading, narrative, and text. Like Garry Leonard, she too endows the interpretive process with a self-reflective dimension. Her insightful and rigorous readings test her premise that "the most productive way of relating to the other in the course of reading is to acknowledge the self's connectedness with mediation and otherness. This necessitates a change in the reader's perception of 'character,' both in the sense of the literary character and the character of his/her own reading self" (31). These three studies—Kershner's, Leonard's, and Vesala-Varrtala's—are only several of many critical works that bring a transformative theory to the stories and thereby make the workings of fiction in *Dubliners* visible in a more highly dynamic and contextual way than was possible with the earlier formalistic approaches. I single them out chiefly because in their attention to textual effects, and particularly to the possibility of textual effects on the reader, they have greatly influenced my own approach to the stories. This attention to textual effects is one I hope to augment and intensify in my readings in this volume.

My own fascination with *Dubliners* emerged from the unlikely genesis of my 1976 book, *The Decentered Universe of "Finnegans Wake": A Structuralist Analysis*, when I found in *Dubliners* a key for understanding many of the mysterious scenarios in the *Wake*. While trying to read *Finnegans Wake* as an open, pluri-signifying writing that refused to allow any singularities of character, voice, event, or meaning to consolidate, strange echoes and resonances in some of its most surrealistic scenes sent me back to *Dubliners* as though along a clew or guiding thread. It was a rewarding exercise that gave me a kind of "manifest content"—to use a term from Freudian dream theory—to scenes like the strange vigil around a corpse in Book I or the provocative and puzzling children's games in Book II.⁷ My reading of Joyce's highly avant-garde last work through *Dubliners* may have been a patently domesticating strategy, but while it domesticated the *Wake* for me, it simultaneously made *Dubliners* much more wild and strange and defamiliarized. But of course I was then unaware of the sort of plea Warren Beck was concurrently making, that *Dubliners* should be embraced as a "primary work entire and sui generis, uncolored by cross-lights from the differing creations that followed" (16). Importing the vantage of openness from a decentered text like *Finnegans Wake* to the fictions of *Dubliners* does indeed alter the way we perceive the stories themselves, but it can do so in a highly productive rather than a reductive way. Christine Van Boheemen alluded to this in her 1985 essay presented at the Philadelphia Joyce Conference and published in *New Alliances in Joyce Studies*. "Reading *Dubliners* with the insights gained from *Finnegans Wake*, we suddenly discover affinities between the two works which reveal a new complexity in the apparent realism of the earliest epiphanies, and, to use Roland Barthes's terms, note 'writerly' qualities in a 'readerly' text" (35). Since that time *Dubliners* has begun to seem more and more 'writerly' in the sense that the stories appear to function less as product than as process, to gloss Roland Barthes's sense in *S/Z*. We have more and more that sense that in the process of reading the text we are completing it, producing new versions of it, writing it anew; "the writerly text is *ourselves* writing," Barthes says (5).

This is very much how my own work on *Dubliners* has evolved over a twenty-year period: as a re-reading that gradually turned into a *re-writing*—one that made me sharply reflective of what I was doing as a reader. In this I realize I merely join other producers of revisionary readings like the ones I've just discussed. But I use the presumptuous claim of a kind of *re-writing* advisedly because so many of my readings produced a version so completely at odds with the manifest spirit of the stories' narration that they could be called a speculative counter-narrative. Before explaining my interpretive procedure, I should point out that I bring less a specific theoretical perspective or approach to the stories than a more generalized disposition produced by many years of wide theoretical reading. This has included not only contemporary theorists but also the array of modern prolegomenal thinkers (Hegel, Nietzsche, Freud, and Heidegger, among others) who inform twentieth-century theory. It may be from Freud and Nietzsche that I acquired an instinct for suspicious reading of the kind generally associated with Paul Ricoeur as a "hermeneutics of suspicion." Given my own backward trajectory from a Freudian reading of *Finnegans Wake* as a dream text—a text in which every sentence, every line, every discourse contains multiple and generally contradictory meanings—my own approach to *Dubliners* was conditioned in advance by a predisposition toward suspicion and skepticism in the face of story-telling. That Joyce had also read Freud and Nietzsche, and had therefore also been exposed to their hermeneutics of suspicion, need not be discounted as a possible factor in his creation of a fiction possibly designed, with infinite subtlety, to arouse suspicion. At the same time, I would be reluctant to posit authorial intention behind whatever it is that arouses suspicion and resistance in the process of reading the stories. When a narration can be caught in a confusion, disjunction, contradiction, or even a lie, it is—to be sure—worthwhile to assume that the problem is intentional and to speculate on Joyce's strategic function or purpose in creating a narrational disruption. But suspicion and interpretive unease may be provoked by many operations of the *Dubliners* text—by style or aesthetic effects, for example—that may be indeterminate with respect to authorial control.

Reading *Dubliners* against its silences has been practiced for years, of course, both with and without theory as the impetus—by Jean-Michel Rabaté in his deconstructively inflected essay on "The Silences of *Dubliners*," for example, in Fritz Senn's intuitive sense of the stories' misdirections and dislocutions, and in Phillip Herring's *Joyce's Uncertainty Principle*. I will turn to these gaps and silences in a moment, after exploring a bit further the effects that readerly skepticism has on the perception of narrative. My own suspicious reading practice perhaps more than some others puts the narration into either collusion or conflict with one or another figure in the story, obliging the narrator to play an interpretive role that frequently has an ethical dimension. In this respect, my emphasis pulls in a somewhat different direction than that marked in Sonia Bašić's persuasive narratological focus on "narratorial 'invisibility' " (18), the "undecidability of free indirect style" (19), and the "lack of narrative intervention and guidance" (17) to which she attributes the interpretive uncertainties in the stories. I find that the seeming neutralities of many of the narrative discourses are propelled by pressures that influence what is finally of ethical moment in the stories, that is, the distribution of justice in the form of censure, esteem, sympathy, opprobrium, and a host of other judgments. Narratology, speech act theories, and reader-response theories have given us an array of conceptual tools for exploring the workings of discursive and interpretive process, and have therefore complicated our more traditional ways of thinking about the operation of stories. The narrator or narrative voice, for example, is not consistent in the stories—as John Paul Riquelme and R. B. Kershner note repeatedly—and it is a problematic matter whether or not to personify or gender that story-telling voice, or merely endow it with a function. The configuration of the narrative voice varies from story to story, which necessitates various solutions to whether or not, and how, to personify it. In my own practice, for example, I consider the narrative voice of "Clay" a hypothetical voice, a *language of desire* that represents Maria's sense of how a refined idiom might flatter her rather than a voice that could be identified with any plausible speaker in Maria's world. On the other hand, I construe the narrator of "After the Race" as in homosocial league with the Continentals defrauding the young Irish scion, and therefore capable of being figured as young, male, and working in opposition to Jimmy Doyle. Occasionally I find the narrative voice as exercising a patently political function, as in "A Mother," when it takes upon itself responsibility for discrediting in advance a feminist protest against a perceived injustice with its characterization of Mrs. Kearney. The narrator or narrative voice is therefore always *discursive* in my readings in the sense that it has an interest or an agenda in communicating events in which the figures in the story as well as the reader also have an interest. Put differently, narration in *Dubliners* is, to my mind, not only intersubjective but also social and ideological. What it reports *matters* to the characters, and *matters to it*—whoever or whatever *it* is. In my reading of the narrations of *Dubliners*, cultural norms and values are mobilized in a variety of rhetorical practices that speak to readers configured in certain relations to the narration and to the other figures in the story.

My interpretive suspicion therefore frequently configures the narrators or narrative voices of *Dubliners* as *unreliable*. But I mean this in a sense that departs considerably from its original definition by Wayne Booth. Ansgar Nünning cites Booth's definition in an extremely interesting piece on the unreliable narrator: "I have called a narrator *reliable* when he speaks for or acts in accordance with the norms of the work (which is to say the implied author's norms), *unreliable* when he does not" (64). For one thing, I make no appeal to an "implied author" as the standard to whose norms the narrator has an obligation to be faithful. For another, my suspicions extend beyond first-person narrators to the more ambiguous omniscient or variously focalized narrators of the stories after the first three. Also I use the notion of unreliability in a much looser sense, to refer to a story-telling voice *not to be trusted to be as objective, impartial, or faithful to the events narrated as it appears to be*, than would be found in the more rigorously technical formulations of narratology.[8] However, my approach shares with more traditional narratology the effect that, once the narrative voice arouses suspicion, it focuses attention on itself and foregrounds itself. But I am inclined to go farther than Nünning, who describes this redirected focus as pointed toward the "peculiarities of the narrator's psychology" (69), for I would interrogate also its ideological agenda and social motives. For example, we are obliged to consider what the narrative voice of "The Dead" is up to when we catch it in either an inexcusable ignorance or a deliberate lie. Why would it tell us that Julia Morkan, "though she was quite grey, was still the leading soprano in Adam and Eve's," when we will learn from her sister Kate that the papal *Motu proprio* has, in fact, expelled Julia from the choir? Why would the narrative voice

give a description of a character that will be factually disputed, in public, by another character? There are many possible explanations for this disjunction,
most of which will point in the same general direction. The narrative voice
seems to promote a highly complacent representation of turn-of-the-century
bourgeois Dublin life that papers over all manner of conflict, oppression, unhappiness, and injustice—and is therefore in league with Gabriel Conroy and
several other figures in the story. This is less a psychological than a socio-political
or ideological interpretation of how the reader may be expected to construe the
narrator's foregrounding. Elsewhere, of course, the narrative unreliabilities may
indeed be psychological—for example, in "An Encounter." We can readily impute repression to the adult narrator's ellipsis in not telling us the meaning that
"green eyes" held for him as a boy. He may be unable to say because he cannot
remember, because the answer was—or has become—too painful or embarrassing to recollect. But the elision could also signify a refusal rather than a repression, a censorship rather than an amnesia, holding back something that
might make him, and the boy he once was, less innocent than he wants himself
to appear. Sonia Bašić is much more inclined to let the narrative indeterminacies of the stories stand as their point, their lesson, their moral. "What exactly
did the boy in 'An Encounter' see?" she asks. "We do not know, but Joyce also
seems to indicate that we need not know the precise answers or even ask such
questions, because in literature characters, events, and motivations are fluid and
finally unfathomable just as they are in life" (17). But although I also cannot resolve the indeterminacies, I generally feel impelled to press for less cosmic and
more specific rationales for them.

In reading *Dubliners* it is as important to attend to everything that is outside the narration—outside it in a determinate rather than an indeterminate
sense—and to treat these extra-narrational elements as expressive and, therefore, as silent discourses that supplement, interrogate, and frequently, dispute
the narration. These include the famous elisions ("had any of them green eyes
for I had some confused notion . . ." [23]) and the *marked* gaps in the narration,
such as the unremembered ending of the dream reported in "The Sisters." They
include also such *unmarked* gaps as conversations that are reported but not described (in "The Boarding House" and "A Painful Case"), letters that are mentioned but not cited ("Eveline" and "The Dead"), mistakes that are noted but
not explained ("Clay" and "After the Race"). Sometimes the silent discourse is
no more than the pressure of a rhetoric that invites us to consider its obverse, to
wonder if the story couldn't be otherwise, or at least be told in another way.
What the narrators fail or refuse to tell, as well as how they tell things, is always
significant because it opens a silent counter-discourse that presses the possibility of an interpretation in opposition to that prompted by the narrative voice.

Ross Chambers, who is a major theoretical inspiration to Tanja Vesala-Varttala's ethical readings, proposes a narratological model of "oppositionality" that organizes narrative and extra-narrative elements into a discursive split in his book *Room for Maneuver: Reading the Oppositional in Narrative.* "Oppositionality," Chambers writes, "takes the form, precisely, of a split between the 'narrative' and the 'textual' functions of discourse such that the 'narrative function,' as the site of an address to the narratee in the position of power, comes to be relativized—or, more technically, ironized—by a 'textual function' that distances the reader from the narratee position and requires the 'narrative function' to become part of the text as an *object of interpretation*" (43). What I find particularly interesting in this model is that it also addresses the shift in the reader that the "narrative" and "textual" split of the fictional discourse obliges, and thereby explains the transformation the reader undergoes in the exercise of oppositional reading. Reader "suspicion" or "distrust" of the narration is produced precisely by unease or dissatisfaction with what I would call *narrational prompts*—cues that the narration gives us in order to lead us (that is, the implied interlocutor of the story or its narratee) to one or another interpretation. By resisting these prompts or cues, "we" readers are transformed from narratees into critics, in the sense that, instead of passively following the narrational lead toward certain judgments of the characters and events in the story, we begin to objectify and evaluate the narrational practice itself. One could take the implications of this shift or split in the reader even further by locating in it the transformation of a consumptive reading into an ethical reading. If the reader begins rather naively by occupying the position of a narratee who more or less figuratively *swallows* the narrative line, then the turn toward questioning the way the story is told and resisting the interpretations it prompts also makes the reader objectify and interrogate her or his own reading practice and the bases of her or his own judgment. This confrontation with reader implication or incrimination in judgments produced by reading has potential as an ethical act. When the stories of *Dubliners* are subjected to suspicious reading, they tend to turn judgment self-reflexively on the reader herself.

My own sense of the "text" constructs it as the narration supplemented by the questions and disputes produced by its elisions, gaps, and silences, which point up alternative representations or narrative versions that create interpretive dilemmas, and sometimes interpretive crises for the reader. In other words, the "text" of the *Dubliners* stories is to my mind a dynamic discursive field in which what is not spoken or said nonetheless "speaks" in the story, in the sense that a speculative reconstruction of the gap or silence can be recreated. But it is always important to ask *why* the gap is there in the first place. This requires that the conjectured or speculative version it produces must be put into interpretive play with the narration in a way that reveals various hidden psychological or ideological agendas at work in the narrational prompts or cues we have been given. In a sense, all narrations could be thought of as *twice-told* events in the sense that they are grounded in a kind of imaginative prior interpretation—an imagined interlocution in which the narrator is an imagined narratee hearing in the mind's ear, as it were, events put together as a story for further retelling. In the hidden interpretive exercise that precedes the narration of the story lies some point of interest, some stake that will appear to matter to the narrative voice and will therefore direct the rhetoric, the supply and deprivation of information, the ambiance of the story. Sometimes what appears to be a description is transformed into a speech act, an evaluation or judgment—as in the tropes that make Mrs. Kearney rigid and spiteful and that render Farrington's body gross. In other cases it is the aesthetic or poetic element of the language that plays an extremely important and often highly ambiguous role in the text. When the language draws attention to itself with some arresting trope (the harp in "Two Gallants"), some gorgeous melody (Gabriel's memories of courting Gretta in "The Dead"), some unmistakeable aesthetic self-display (the prose of "Araby"), we ought to expect that something is going on, that the narrative voice is *doing* something rather than just *saying*. The miraculously clean and precise and taut prose of the stories may be at work seducing or distracting or mimicking rather than just plain being beautiful. Language has itself a *body language*, as it were, a mode of expression superimposed on its mode of expression that is itself potentially meaningful, and can itself be read. Even in the absence of gaps—in "A Little Cloud," for example—this stylistic *body language* of the narration plays a "textual" role inviting interpretation. This nonformalistic way of attending the style or poetics of the stories can alter our sense of the stories' "modernism" by politicizing its aesthetics. My own prior exercise of this in *Joyce's Web* has been to see in the most aesthetic and most "modernistic" moments of Joycean writing an immanent *self-critique* of Modernism itself.

The theoretical genealogy of a layered textual model such as the one I have been sketching out is inevitably heterogeneous and reminds us of the propensity of theories to infect and inflect each other as they cross disciplines and intellectual fields. Somehow underlying many of the theoretical approaches to *Dubliners* we can divine the deconstructive language of presence and absence, and its interplay in meaning production. In what Craig Hansen Warner calls "the least compromising post-structuralist essay on *Dubliners* to have appeared in English" (21), Jean-Michel Rabaté's "Silences in *Dubliners*" preserves the antirealist premises of deconstruction most rigorously. In somewhat different registers both Sonia Bašić and Derek Attridge argue against the interpretation of gaps and mysteries, Bašić to preserve their power to subvert and Attridge in the interest of ethics. Arguing against my assorted efforts to make sense of the "clay" in the children's game, Attridge holds that the story may "remind us of the need, in acts of responsible interpretation, to respect the other as other. Although 'Clay' demands, more insistently than most stories, intense interpretive activity, it also reminds us that there is sometimes a virtue in not interpreting, that responding fully to a text can mean allowing its otherness to remain other, unassimilable, unconceptualizable, irreducible, resistant" (51). But the otherness produced by absences in the stories can be treated responsibly otherwise in both psychoanalytical and ethical criticism. In its Lacanian formulation, presence and absence can be found to form the interplay of what Lacan calls the full word (*parole pleine*) and the empty word (*parole vide*) in the analytical situation. What is actually said, the versions or feelings or explanations that the patient offers in the session with the analyst, is actually not as expressive as what that discourse reveals to have been unsaid or censored. Thus, instead of accepting the narrative prod to interpret the solecisms of Eliza Flynn as signs of ignorance, Garry Leonard will pay specific attention to them as revelations. "I turn now to Eliza's famous verbal slips ('*Freeman's general*' for *Freeman's Journal* and 'rheumatic wheels' for pneumatic wheels), which may be seen as further examples of full speech subverting empty speech" (44). Leonard is thereby able to *read* in Eliza's slips of the tongue a hidden story of resentments and resistances to her brother of which she may be quite unaware, and which the narrator may transmit to us without himself comprehending them.[9] A different function is given to presence and absence in the Lyotardian *differend*, which Joseph Valente explores to such insightful effect in *James Joyce and the Problem of Justice*. Valente writes "the *differend* may be classified as an unstable state or instance of specifically moral or judicial discourse, wherein a claim, grievance, or point of view that needs to be registered cannot be registered, at least not effectively. 'In the *differend*,' Lyotard writes, 'something asks to be put into phrases and suffers the wrong of not being able to be put into phrases' " (8). It is not difficult to see the affinities of this political formulation with the psychoanalytic model, where the self, in a sense, suffers the wrong of not having the thing it needs to have registered put into phrases, except as slips, mistakes, gaps, and silences. But the Lyotardian model of the *differend* brings into focus social, cultural, and generic contexts in interpretation and judgment—of both nonliterary and literary texts. This formulation is particularly helpful in addressing the difficulty of adjudicating the stakes of some of the stories of public life in *Dubliners*, as we see in Joseph Valente's exploration of the sexual politics in "A Mother." I use a somewhat different sense of the *differend* to come to terms with the politics of "Ivy Day in the Committee Room" as a problem of genre.

These are only some of the ways in which varieties of theoretical approaches to *Dubliners* echo, reinforce, and vary each other. I bring them up to clarify the apparent eclecticism of my own approach, my resort to theory in a rather ad hoc fashion, like a *bricoleur* taking this or that tool as it comes to hand and as it fits the purpose for reading whatever story is before me. Although I appear to privilege a narratological approach at this time, this approach is itself undergirded by a range of other intersecting and overlapping theories that have informed my reading of the stories over a period of many years. Nonetheless, my theoretical inspirations have not been random or accidental. They have in common an oppositional, or dialectical, or dialogical logic that I find necessary for reading the stories *otherwise* rather than simply as reinforcements or paraphrases of the narrations themselves. In this way we have come back to Joyce's initial announcements at the beginning of his career that he intended for the stories to have some didactic function, some moral purpose, to represent "a chapter of the moral history of my country" (*SL* 83). The difficulty is that each story offers not only the possibility of an ethical reading and other readings, but the possibility of conflicting ethical readings. Is "A Mother" a parable whose moral is that greed and willfulness will backfire or a parable whose moral is that narrations and reviews of the arts can be warped by prejudice and misogyny? Does "Counterparts" stimulate our revulsion by a vicious domestic abuser or our sympathy for the systematic degradation of a working man? Is "An Encounter" a cautionary tale to keep children out of the clutches of pederasts or a parable about the effects of homosexual panic? Each of these proposed morals puts the reader or interpreter at ethical risk because, however we adjudicate the moral conundrum posed by each story, our resolutions and interpretations of the stories will remain unauthorized. I mean this in both senses—that we are obliged to make judgments without imprimatur of the author and that our difficulty in verifying or confirming our interpretations makes them vulnerable to charges of subverting conventional morality, on the one hand, and colluding with political and social oppressions, on the other.[10] But an even more rigorously ethical stance may judge the pressure to interpret, to judge or take a side at all, as itself an ethically dubious maneuver, a reaching toward a morally superior stance that is itself potentially oppressive. And yet a theoretically principled refusal to delve into the moral dilemmas posed by the stories in the interest of eluding a humanistic entanglement with their matter, strikes me as loss of an opportunity to sharpen our ability to discriminate finely, to consider alternative possibilities to versions of things, to imagine the feelings or conditions of others when these are not directly represented. And this brings me to the place where, I suspect, all critics of *Dubliners* invest a fond hope, and that is that their readings may find some useful place in the teaching of literature.

Since I often come down on one or another side of an undecidable issue in my readings of *Dubliners*, I can't claim to adhere rigorously to J. Hillis Miller's own protocol for ethical reading. Yet I nonetheless want to appeal to Miller's *The Ethics of Reading* to explain what I would hope to have my readings of *Dubliners* accomplish in the classroom. He writes, "An understanding of ethics as a region of philosophical or conceptual investigation depends, perhaps surprisingly, on mastery of the ability to interpret written stories, that is, on a kind of mastery usually thought to be the province of the literary critic" (3). In its broadest, most general sense, I take this to suggest that learning to reflect on what we do when we interpret a story may help us to reflect on what we do when, in real life, we are obliged to make judgments in situations that are not easily decidable. We may have to serve on a jury in a case with ambiguous or insufficient evidence, or figure out how to respond, as newspaper readers and as voters, when a political scandal breaks out. I would like to think that learning how to read *Dubliners* oppositionally could enhance student skill and confidence in dealing with situations where there are limitations to their knowledge, and yet where they may be obliged to act. The *Dubliners* stories are easy for freshmen and sophomores to read, because they appear quite simple. But they are, of course, *deceptively* simple, and their deception resides precisely in the fact that, beyond their narrative unreliability, there is much complex signifying activity going on in each story, and this *in and of itself* requires interpretation. For getting students to go beyond considerations of theme, and beyond considerations of style, even, to think about how textuality itself works, it would be difficult to find a better curriculum than *Dubliners*. The stories can be taught in a way that makes narration opaque rather than transparent to them and obliges them to interpret the narrative operation itself. The stories can help them see fiction as a text, as a bundle of dynamic meaning-producing strategies that put various possible, and often conflicting, interpretations into destabilizing and productive play. And the stories can help students to read self-reflectively, to think about how the text positions them as readers and provides them with prompts or invites their resistance. *Dubliners* can lead students into the act of reading as a meaning-producing *process* rather than as merely confrontation with a meaning-laden *product*.

My readings address the literary critic rather than speaking to the student directly, and they draw upon the conventional panoply of scholarly sources, secondary literature, and occasional archival material to construct (hopefully) a convincing and sophisticated support for my sometimes unconventional argument. But I have been mindful, in unfolding my argument, of structuring my interpretive procedure in ways that could be adapted to the methodologies of the classroom. In particular, many of my analyses depend upon a recreation of what I call a 'virgin' reading of the story, reading the story as though we had never read it before and had no idea how it would unfold. This intriguing property of the fiction—that it can produce certain effects of shock only once, upon a first reading—offers teachers of the story an extraordinary opportunity to relive the 'virgin' reading experience of *Dubliners* in a setting that makes students a genuinely valuable resource to the critical and interpretive production. The outcome of such 'virgin' readings of self-disputing texts can be to demonstrate that the production of conflicting interpretations is an integral aim of the textual project, one that is already staged in the writing itself. While privileging one interpretation over another in my analyses, I too am conscious that the critical traditions with which I am perforce engaged in dialogue represent alternative interpretations as scripted into *Dubliners* as my own. In the end, it is never we who read *Dubliners* as much as it is *Dubliners* that reads us.

## Chapter 1
# *The Gnomon of the Book: "The Sisters"*

Among the stories in *Dubliners*, the gaps, ellipses, and silences in "The Sisters" have engrossed critics for decades, and have received such illuminating attention that their dilation of the story's interpretive possibilities has been extensively explored. This is clearly no accident, for I believe (along with other critics) that Joyce made the figure and function of the gap, the silence, and the figure of incompletion an inescapably foregrounded trope in the story. By doing so he guaranteed that it could not be missed, and would therefore serve as a clew and a clue, a guiding thread and key to the entire volume's hermeneutical enigma. No reader of "The Sisters" can get past that arresting sentence on the first page of the story—and of *Dubliners*—when the narrative voice invests a quite ordinary word with the sound of strangeness ("I said softly to myself the word *paralysis*. It had always sounded strangely in my ears" [9]), and then multiplies that strangeness with the sound of two even stranger words, "like the word *gnomon* in the Euclid and the word *simony* in the Catechism" (9). When the narrative voice confesses its fascination with these strange bookish words, it simultaneously invites the reader to look into the abyss of stories that are marked by incompletion, by insufficient information, by chunks missing from them, gaps and silences that render them undecidable. Their indecidability also renders them, in a sense, unreadable, albeit unreadable in quite determinate ways.

The evidence for the function of these mysterious words as a hermeneutical signal was made available quite early in the tradition of *Dubliners* criticism, and nowhere more clearly or persuasively than in Florence Walzl's 1973 *James Joyce Quarterly* essay examining Joyce's draft revisions of "The Sisters." Walzl stressed the relentlessly realistic, though not entirely unambiguous, representational mode of the first version of the story that Joyce wrote for the August 13, 1904 *Irish Homestead*. At the same time she makes it clear that the strangely resonant figures of paralysis, gnomon, and simony were later additions—"there is no mention of paralysis and no detail that can be specifically pinpointed hemiplegia (a unilateral paralysis), let alone total paralysis. There are also no suggestions of immoral conduct. And in this description there are no mysterious gnomons, no inferences of simony, and no hints of sodomy" (379). Walzl infers that the function of these additions and revisions was to allow "The Sisters" to serve as introduction and overture to the volume as a whole: "Examination of the final versions indicates that 'The Sisters' had been gradually redesigned to act as introduction to *Dubliners'* main themes and motifs" (376). By 1985, when Thomas F. Staley wrote "A Beginning: Signification, Story, and Discourse in 'The Sisters,' " he was able to call this notion—that the opening paragraph of the story was intended to function as an overture for the themes, conflicts, and tensions of the entire volume—a "critical commonplace" (181). He was also able to describe that function in terms of new theoretical concepts and a new theoretical language: "With 'The Sisters' Joyce had just begun a deconstructive process, and the title is the first announcement of a new awareness of the potentiality of language" (181).

We can take this point even further in the direction of Jean-Michel Rabaté's formulation of the function of silence in *Dubliners*, arguing that it allows the volume to produce a "theory of its own interpretation, of its reading, of its possible metadiscourses about textuality" (46). In this sense "The Sisters" can be thought of as that which makes of *Dubliners* a gnomon—by serving as a synecdoche or miniature representation of the whole collection. Walzl gives a Webster's dictionary definition of a gnomon as "the remainder of a parallelogram after the removal of a similar parallelogram containing one of its corners" (389). Much later Leonard Albert offered a diagram of a gnomon to illustrate the story's "gnomonology." He also pointed out its possibilities as a genealogical trope, as a geometric version of the colloquial description of a son as "a chip off the old block" (355): "we are being shown, in effect, two parallelograms with congruent angles, that is, of the same shape, different only in size, the smaller being the offspring, so to speak, of the larger or parent figure" (355). Albert uses this insight into the generational relationship inherent in the gnomonic structure by which a "parent parallelogram" produces a gnomon through the removal or separation of a "scion parallelogram" (356) to look at the relationship between the priest and the boy. More accurately, gnomon as a generational trope would point to a parent who has lost a same-sex child: Leopold Bloom would be a human gnomon, as would the mythical figure of Daedalus. But a child is itself a gnomonic figure, a figure of incompletion, and a dead child becomes an unreadably gnomonic figure, since its destiny, its hypothetical completion as a human being, is rendered eternally unknowable by the truncation of its life. One way of reading "The Sisters," in this light, would be to place the adult narrator and his boy-self into a gnomonic genealogical relationship. This would allow us to explore whether the adult narrator is the *father*, as it were, of a boy-self who suffered a trauma that left him *un-whole*, and that subsequently produced an adult with a missing piece. The narrator would be missing a part of childhood that can't be remembered or articulated, and his telling of a story of his boyhood would be necessarily left unfinished and therefore unreadable.[1] I plan later to explore not only the triangulated relationship between the reader, the "adult" narrator, and the narrated-narrating boy, but to stretch that triangle into a gnomonic parallelogram by configuring it to include the fourth figure of the titular sisters.[2]

Before moving inside the story, however, I would like to consider how "The Sisters" functions gnomonologically for the entire collection of *Dubliners*, and for the Joycean oeuvre as a whole. If we translate what Albert calls the "scion" parallelogram or "chip off the old block" into a rhetorical figure, we could say that "The Sisters"—with its gaps and silences—functions as a synecdoche, not for the book *as a whole*, but precisely for the book *as an un-whole*, a volume of incompletion, a collection of stories each of which is riddled by gaps and silences that afflict it with incompletion. In other words, in its status as a fiction without wholeness, "The Sisters" serves as a synecdoche for a collection of fictions without wholeness. This sense of "The Sisters" ' relationship to the rest of the stories would also encompass Leonard Albert's recollection of gnomon's Greek root—"Unchanged from ancient Greek . . . the basic meaning of gnomon is 'model, criterion, standard' " (355). What "The Sisters" performatively announces in its function as a model or standard for the rest of the collection is that the remaining stories will be as fragmented, as full of gaps and ellipses and mysteries, as it is itself. I would go further to give a moral resonance to "The Sisters" as the un-whole model of a collection of *un-whole* stories by suggesting that its state of *un-wholeness* opens the possibility that its gaps and ellipses will open into a moral universe of *unwholesomeness*, an unwholesomeness at the heart of all the stories that points to what Joyce himself in his October 15, 1905 letter to Grant Richards called "the special odour of corruption which, I hope, floats over my stories" (*Letters* II, 123).

The critical readings that have been performed on "The Sisters" have been among the most sophisticated and inventive in the entire canon of *Dubliners* criticism precisely because they have delved into the gaps and silences. Perhaps because Joyce posed the narrative mysteries so pointedly in the story's disjointed narration, the kinds of undecidable speculation and inference readers would normally be reluctant to make were hazarded even at the beginning of the story's critical history. Florence Walzl remembers Joyce reporting a conversation with his editor George Roberts, "He asked me very narrowly was there *sodomy* also in 'The Sisters' and what was 'simony' and if the priest was suspended only for the breaking of the chalice" ("Joyce's 'The Sisters' " 392). Walzl not only refused to shy away from the startling speculation that Father Flynn's sin might have been of a sexual nature, but she went further. In an essay coauthored with a medical physician, she linked the priest's breakdown and death to this sin by diagnosing his paralysis as syphilitic paresis, also known as "general paralysis of the insane" (Torchiana 20). The argument is not unconvincing, particularly given Joyce's early admiration of Ibsen—the author who dared make syphilis and its concealment the subject of the drama *Ghosts*. Stanislaus Joyce's 1904 diary entry notes that his brother James "talks much of the syphilitic contagion in Europe, is at present writing a series of studies on it in Dublin, tracing everything to it" (*Complete Dublin Diary* 51). Walzl nonetheless ascribes chiefly symbolic significance to the syphilis, treating it as a medical figure for the spiritual condition of the Irish people.

The holes in the *Dubliners* stories open up the possibility of transgressive reading in two senses or layers. First, the reader (like the characters, on occasion) entertains the suspicion that the gaps and ellipses in the narration hide or occlude evidence of transgression. Second, this suspicion itself becomes a form of readerly transgression by implicating the reader in imagined transgressive knowledge. Tanja Vesala-Verttala argues that all readers share a characteristic *vulnerability* with the child-protagonists, or what she calls the "child interpreter," of Joyce's stories (123). In this way the reader confronted by the gaps and ellipses of "The Sisters" shares the vulnerability of the boy who risks a loss of innocence by the very fact that he must confront gnomonic language. As soon as a text is recognized as *un-whole* it threatens the reader with the specter of the *unwholesome*, and the risk of engaging in an *unwholesome* interpretive experience. This phenomenon has both a psychoanalytical and a political explanation. Psychoanalytically, we can conjecture that an epistemological gap or a missing piece of knowledge (as opposed to a random absence) must have a negative psychological origin in repression motivated by fear, a sense of danger, or a reluctance. Politically, we know that textual censorships are motivated by the need to suppress an injurious disclosure, a dangerous knowledge, or a threat against authority. The boy protagonist in "The Sisters" is confronted by ellipses in adult conversations—particularly those of Mr. Cotter and Eliza Flynn—whose reading has threatening implications for him ("When children see things like that, you know, it has an effect . . ." [11]). Cotter's conversational gaps imply that the boy had unwittingly entered into a relationship with an unwholesome priest. But the narrative also implies that the boy is himself scrutinized for agitations that might betray his recognition of this unwholesomeness ("I felt that his little beady black eyes were examining me but I would not satisfy him by looking up from my plate" [10]). The boy is vulnerable both as an interpreter and as object of interpretation—and so, presumably, is the adult narrative voice of the boy, telling his retrospective story. Kershner points out that the two voices of the narrator-protagonist—"the voice of immediate (child's) experience and the voice of retrospection (from some indeterminate distance in time)" are curiously "mixed": "the boy seems in some respects to be a disguised adult—he is almost preternaturally sensitive, suspicious, and evasive. To what extent are we to attribute the boy's expressions of suspicion, hostility, and general free-floating anxiety to a later retrospection, and to what extent may they be directly attributed to the child's immediate experience?" (24). Indeed, virtually every figure in "The Sisters" is placed in an anxious interpretive position: the boy, his aunt and uncle, Father O'Rourke, and the priest's sisters, Eliza and Nannie Flynn. Even Mr. Cotter, the only person who seems comfortable with his suspicion of unwholesomeness, is put into an uncomfortable narrative position, as he realizes that his imputations will be met with skepticism and resistance, and denied corroboration by the boy. No wonder then that the adult narrator, in telling his story of anxious interpreters and uncomfortable narrators, transfers his own performative unease—symptomatized in the fragmented and elliptical conversations he reports and in his own unremembered and unfinished dreams and confessions—onto the reader.[3]

What seems to be at stake for the adult narrator in telling this riddled story of his youth is his own interpretation—or rather his refusal to interpret—whether the childhood experience he narrates is innocent or guilty. And here, it seems, may be the nub of the problem: that an interpretation of innocence can itself be culpable as a denial of transgressive knowledge, as a refusal to confront and tell a truth, while a suspicion of guilt can itself be culpable as a potential betrayal and sullying of innocence. Is the boy guilty of something because he acquired or confronted a guilty knowledge about the priest, or because he studiously refused to confront the mysteries that surround him? Is the adult narrator reenacting precisely the same mystified stance as the boy, or is he recreating for the reader the suspicious discourse of innuendo that surrounds the boy? Is the boy infected by the adult whisperings into imagining himself as guilty of a desire for guilty knowledge, or is he repressing or withholding guilty secrets that he knows and finds, to his discomfiture, betrayed to the outside world? When the narrative voice tells us of his childhood fascination with the word *paralysis*—"But now it sounded to me like the name of some maleficent and sinful being. It filled me with fear, and yet I longed to be nearer to it and to look upon its deadly work" (9)—it appears to be confessing something that it will spend the remainder of the story concealing. As Tanja Vesala-Varttala writes, "What the child as a figure for reading demonstrates is that it is never possible to read innocently" (129).

The fractured sequence of narrative disclosure further functions more like a symptom of a moral and psychological splintering of knowledge than like a willing revelation or confession. The boy's morally charged meditations on the

word "paralysis" are reported as preceding the priest's death and its announcement by Mr. Cotter. His thoughts could therefore be construed as a desire for
transgressive knowledge that precedes the creation of its object by Mr. Cotter's ellipses ("I puzzled my head to extract meaning from his unfinished sentences" [11]). The boy is reported as filling in the puzzle with the image of the
paralytic's "heavy grey face," which he tries unsuccessfully to banish by ducking
under his covers and thinking of Christmas. But not only does the face reintrude
into his thoughts, it now comes accompanied by a murmuring, confessing voice
issuing from an increasingly corporeal and vividly imagined smiling mouth
whose "lips were so moist with spittle" (11). Is the boy conflating his own supplement to Mr. Cotter's innuendo with a sexual fantasy ("I felt my soul receding
into some pleasant and vicious region" [11]) or with a remembered experience?
The puzzle is clarified no better when this sequence—Mr. Cotter's innuendo
and the dream it produces—is recapitulated in reverse as the boy is pictured
walking past the priest's house on the sunny side of the street on the following
morning. The heavy grey face of the priest is now remembered in daylight—still
with vivid attention to an enlarged corporeal smiling mouth ("When he smiled
he used to uncover his big discoloured teeth and let his tongue lie upon his
lower lip" [13]). This image recalls Cotter's words and a part of the boy's dream
that was elided in the reportage of the previous night, "As I walked along in the
sun I remembered old Cotter's words and tried to remember what had happened afterwards in the dream. I remembered that I had noticed long velvet
curtains and a swinging lamp of antique fashion. I felt that I had been very far
away, in some land where the customs were strange—in Persia, I thought. . . .
But I could not remember the end of the dream" (13).[4] Presumably the adult
narrator, remembering his inability, as a boy, to remember the end of a dream,
still fails to remember it. As an auto-parental gnomon, the adult narrator harbors a psychologically gnomonic scion-self.

The story of "The Sisters" ends with an ellipsis in Eliza's story about the
priest laughing in the confession box—an ellipsis that forecloses the revelation
at the heart of the story, "there was something gone wrong with him . . ." (18).
The adult narration still does not, and perhaps cannot, tell us what had gone
wrong with the priest, and what the boy knew of what had gone wrong with the
priest. The trail of signifiers, however, is sufficiently ample by this time that it
can be suggestively linked into a hidden guilty narrative of the priest's sexual
molestation of a complicit child. One could reconstruct from the adult narration a sense that the boy already knows, at the opening of the story and before
he learns of his death, the sin the laughing priest confesses to himself in the
confession box of the empty chapel. We can conjecture that it informs his fascination with paralysis, gnomon, and simony, and that he already knows what

Cotter is talking about, and what he fears Eliza and Nannie will betray to his aunt. The narrator tells of the unfinished dream in two parts. But if we put the parts together, and juxtapose the dreamed confession of the moist-lipped priest with the Persian velvet curtains and antique lamp, we have an image that gestures toward the laughing priest in the dark chapel and the confession box. Yet the boy will not hear about the confession-box incident until the evening of the next day, when Eliza tells her incomplete story. What are we to make of the equanimity with which the narrative reveals the boy's repeated attention to the priest's lower face, the great snuff-filled nostrils, the smiling or laughing mouth with its large teeth, moist lips, and protruding tongue? The memory suggests not sodomy but some less invasive intimacy of a more or less guilty kind. The vision may be simply a child's vantage of a towering figure seen from below. But it may also suggest a connection between the discursive intimacy between priest and boy, the teaching and telling and confessions, to an intimacy with its source in the priest's corporeal mouth.[5]

The construction of this guilty reading of the story is itself culpable, however, if the story is innocent. What if the priest is merely a lonely and kind old man who gratefully repays a boy's charitable visits and gift of snuff by talking to him, and teaching him things? Then the guilty interpretation becomes itself a species of the kind of vicious innuendo with which a dirty-minded Cotter besmirches the reputation of an innocently demented and stroke-palsied priest. In that case, the adult narrator's tale both tells and performs the way in which the libeling of the priest also victimizes the boy, and victimizes the adult the boy becomes. The gaps in knowledge at each level of the story—in the childhood experience and the adult retelling—makes a measure of guilt and victimization inevitable, and intensifies it by its unlocatability and unverifiability. The story entraps the reader as surely as it entraps all of the story's figures, and especially the protagonist, in a cloud if ethical incertitude that also victimizes the reader. Brian Bremen's discussion of *scupulosity* in relation to the story sheds an important light on the reader's ethical dilemma. He cites the *New Catholic Encyclopedia*'s definition of scruples—"Scruples render one incapable of making with finality the daily decisions of life. The psychic impotence, providing a steady source of anxiety and indecisiveness, is especially prevalent in ethical and pseudoethical areas" (63). With this definition, Bremen gives our interpretive paralysis in the face of an impossible ethical adjudication a new, or rather, an old name: "The Sisters" afflicts us with inescapable scruples. The story poses to us the kind of moral conundrum posed by the priest to the boy: "Sometimes he had amused himself by putting difficult questions to me, asking me what one should do in certain circumstances or whether such and such sins were mortal or venial or only imperfections" (13). The need to make difficult moral adjudications places the reader in a scrupulous situation, like that of the boy, who responds to the priest's "intricate questions" by telling us, "I could make no answer or only a very foolish and halting one" (13).

I wish, however, to compound this mystery of the priest's breakdown and potential hidden sin and its implications for the boy, by linking it to the more prosaic textual problem of the story's title. Peter Spielberg is given credit for first drawing serious attention to the story's title as one of its enigmas—" 'The Sisters' still presents the reader with a major and tantalizing riddle: *the title*" (Albert, 354). Fritz Senn gives nuance to this problem when he links it to the other strangenesses of "a story as intricately layered, as bifocal, as off-center, as oddly titled as 'The Sisters' " (17). Are the sisters of the title signposts of misdirection or red herrings? Are they central chiefly as a generalized stand-in for the paralytic Irish people, as many critics suppose? Or must the mystery of the title be brought into some direct link with the mystery of the boy and the priest. Do the sisters belong to the general gnomonology of "The Sisters" as a story, and to the gnomonology of the book? One critic who has made such a link is Leonard Albert. He makes the title coincide with the relationship of boy and priest by arguing that with its connotation of effeminacy, as in the diminutive "sissy," the word "sisters" serves as a code for homosexuality—" 'The Sisters' therefore has a meaning akin to 'the odd couple,' or in today's phrase, 'the gay couple' " (363). I find this argument, which totally extrudes the literal sisters from the story's drama, intriguing but finally too extreme. Reluctant to abandon the story's literal sisters, I would take the problem of this story of a boy, a priest, and his sisters, in a different direction, by reading it backwards from my own later reading of another pair of spinster sisters in "The Dead." As I argue later in this volume, I believe that the lives of the Morkan sisters in "The Dead" are represented in the story as a narratively occluded feminist tragedy. One can show that Joyce slipped a hidden dimension as artist and protester behind the insignificant exterior of the sisters, one that the narrator and the other figures in the story manage to stifle. Perhaps, we should look at Nannie and Eliza Flynn as possible figures of occlusion that also hide eloquent silences they cannot speak.

I begin with the view, already explored above, that the question of the priest's (and the boy's) sin or innocence is absolutely undecidable by the reader, and that there is simply insufficient evidence to do more than create the conditions for an overdetermined skepticism or doubt. Although this skepticism taints any possibility of an "innocent" reading, it is nonetheless heuristically useful to construct both "innocent" and "transgressive" hypothetical readings of the priest and the boy against its implications for, and effects on, Eliza and Nannie Flynn, the sisters. The "innocent" reading produced by rigorously limiting our interpretation to what the boy reveals about his intimacy with Father Flynn, proposes that the boy simply delivered packets of High Toast snuff to the priest on behalf of his aunt. In return for this gift, or the gift of his visit, he received an ongoing, informal tutorial in clerical and theological lore from the house-bound paralytic. The priest's innocent motive, in this case, is his construction of the boy's fascination with this religious instruction into "a great wish" (10)— presumably for a religious vocation. Yet in this "innocent" reading, the sisters remain subject to varying and contradictory interpretations. William Johnsen, for example, discusses the priest's sisters as powerful and vulgar figures who have enslaved their helpless and intellectually superior brother in the "sordid tide" of Dublin life, which will again engulf the boy upon the priest's death. Johnsen shares the boy's "disdain" for these common women: "This is the crux of the story. The grotesque ministrations to the corpse makes apparent a condition which has always existed: the paralytic's enslavement to the patronage of the sisters" (11). But we can as easily construct a much more sympathetic version of "The Sisters" as a naturalistic tale of poverty, ignorance, and sadness that betrays the politics of gender differences. The story of Nannie and Eliza Flynn may well concern two very poor women from the slums of Irishtown (Gifford, 30) who never married and rose to little more than a meager draper's business in Dublin. Indeed, at the time of the priest's death, Eliza Flynn still characterizes herself and her sister as "poor as we are" (16). Meanwhile, their brother managed to receive an education and travel to Rome to attend the Irish college there (Gifford, 31). Yet instead of transferring the respectability and benefits of this vocation to his sisters, the outcome of their brother's ecclesiastical career was unhappiness, disappointment, and a final dementia that now threatens to further cloud their lives.[6]

Garry Leonard, ever sensitive to the onto-psychological nuances of gender implication, also produces an "innocent" reading of the story that foregrounds the victimization of the sisters by their brother's life and fall. He finds that the symptoms of Eliza Flynn's "empty" speech (in the Lacanian sense) and the "full" speech of her slips of the tongue (the famous "rheumatic" tires, for example) betray her hidden and bitter feelings about her own and her sister's disappointed and crossed lives. Leonard conjectures that in their bitterness at having been disgraced by the scandal of their brother's final madness, Eliza and her sister may have resisted a return to Irishtown, to the origin and site of their poverty: "Eliza's empty speech presents the failure to visit Irishtown as one more unfortunate disappointment in the life of a disappointed man. But once again something is insisting from beyond her discourse. Her full speech, the slip of her tongue, betrays something else: a determined woman who frustrates a dying man's wish in her bitter attempt to hold together the appearance of normalcy and propriety he has so incomprehensively compromised" (47).

Garry Leonard's reading takes us a long way to a more nuanced and precise observation of the sisters than the typological function assigned to them since Florence Walzl's day.[7] As "representative of Ireland," the two ignorant old women, in Walzl's view, "have neither the boy's sharp view of reality nor his fortitude." As drapers, they "clothe their apprehension" in comforting clichés, Walzl suggests (417). Even such an astute and interesting analysis as James Wohlpart's 1993 essay, makes exactly the same point about the sisters. "The sisters become the central figures of the story, deserving the title role," he writes, "for just as they represent the enforcement of silence and the tradition of the Irish Catholic Church that has paralyzed Father Flynn, they also represent the Irish people, the people who are truly paralyzed" (416). Instead of this purely typological reading, Leonard situates the Flynn sisters in a sociologically specific space in the Ireland of their day. He endows their plight with its own poignancy, in their compromised rescue from the acute poverty of their origins. Such a reading allows us to notice that even at the time of the story, the flowers and candlesticks for their brother's coffin had to borrowed from the chapel. We notice too the difference between the overworked dogsbody, Nannie, and the bitter and determined Eliza. And Leonard's reading gives Eliza's speech a complicated managerial function in dealing discursively with her brother's embarrassing end. I would only add to this reading, that seen in this light, Eliza's handling of the delicate issue of her brother's madness under the scrutiny of curious friends and neighbors can be seen as far more skillful and shrewd than the ignorance of her malapropisms and solecisms would suggest.

A question remains even after Leonard's sophisticated version of an "innocent" reading gives the sisters a dramatic, rather than a purely symbolic or figural, function in the story. How does Eliza and Nannie Flynn's negotiation of their brother's scandal fit into what is finally the story's more central preoccupation with the consciousness of the boy? This question draws our attention to the fragmentary information we receive about the priest's decline. "There was no hope for him this time: it was the third stroke" (9), we learn through the "mixed" adult/boy narrative voice in the first line of the story. But we never learn when the two previous "strokes" occurred, when the boy learned of them, or why Eliza makes no mention of them in her account of her brother's "crossed" life. Indeed, her narrative of her brother's decline works curiously in reverse. She begins by conceding, "I noticed there was something queer coming over him latterly" (16). This observation of his breviary fallen to the floor and his doze with open mouth is followed by a more general characterization of James's disappointed life. After a long silence, in which Eliza has seemingly "fallen into a deep revery," she finally offers the explanation of the broken chalice as the beginning of James's queerness. "That affected his mind" (17) she tells the boy and his aunt, before giving final testimony of his dementia in his dis-covered laughing in the confession box of the dark and locked chapel. Clearly, the queer thing that had come over Father Flynn had come over him not lately at all, but in stages that could, arguably, be correlated with the two previous "strokes." Or had the three strokes occurred in relatively rapid succession at the end—but still far enough apart that word had been circulated widely enough for the boy to have learned of them. If James had been acting queer since the time of the broken chalice ("he began to mope by himself, talking to no one and wandering about by himself" [17]), why had the boy noticed nothing odd about him, except that his hands trembled when he took snuff and that his tongue protruded when he smiled? We never learn whether the chalice was broken publicly, perhaps during a Mass, since an acolyte may have been implicated ("They say it was the boy's fault" [17]), or privately, in the sanctuary, before or after a service, since the chalice was empty. What is the broken chalice a symp-tom of, to paraphrase Gabriel Conroy? One of the priest's strokes? Or the dis-covery of some misconduct on his part with an altar boy? The holes in the innocent readings continually open up the possibility of the unwholesome. However, the priest had clearly remained clerically active after the incident of the broken chalice, since he remained "on call" ("So one night he was wanted for to go on a call" [27]) to attend to such religious emergencies as the adminis-tration of last rites. Was he retired on disability, as it were, or was he informally defrocked? "And was that it? said my aunt. I heard something. . . ." (17). The nar-rator describes Eliza Flynn as opening the discussion of her brother's condition "shrewdly" (16). She has certainly produced an "innocent" reading of the priest's queerness both for the boy and his aunt, and for our own consumption—regardless of what we assume to be the truth.

So, what if we assume the transgressive scenario that has been a staple of "Sisters" criticism since the beginning, and believe that the priest is syphilitic, and perhaps even guilty of molesting or sodomizing the boy? The truly horrify-ing implications of this scenario have rarely been fully confronted—the im-morality of broken clerical vows with diseased sexual partners compounded with the criminality of a priest preying on, and perhaps fatally infecting, a kindly child. The unreliability of the boy's narration in this case takes on mon-strous and tragic proportions as his shielding of a dreadful man, and his con-cealment of a dreadful experience, either through denial produced by his own feared complicity, or through a kind of occlusion or amnesia produced by trauma. The function of the reader in this case becomes highly problematic as well, as the undecidabilities produced by the boy's willful or unconscious cover-up prevent us from exonerating him from complicity even as we recognize that he must not be blamed. We too are rebuffed as prying and tiresome old imbeciles, like Mr. Cotter, scrutinizing a boy with secrets he refuses to reveal. Wohlpart proposes that Father Flynn's legacy to the boy is "that he must seek out the tales of the people so that they can be incorporated in a new form of confession, a form which might purge the conscience of Ireland" (413). If so, then "The Sisters" is the very opposite of such a confession, an adult tale designed to divert, mislead, and mystify, leaving readers with no possibility of determining a truth, and with no way to purge their everlasting unease.

What of the sisters, if we assume the priest's guilt of syphilis and sodomy? Their role in the story then becomes far more sinister, incriminated, and tragic. To speculate about their role, we need to return to that strange supper conversation in which the aunt insists on pressing Mr. Cotter to clarify his insinuations that the boy ought not to have been allowed to spend time with the old priest. "How do you mean, Mr Cotter?" (10), she asks him, "But why do you think it's not good for children, Mr Cotter?" (11). Leonard suggests that old Cotter is "as suspicious of the boy as he is of Father Flynn" (37), going so far as to say, "one of Old Cotter's unfinished sentences implies that it is the boy who has been suspiciously aggressive in courting the attention of Father Flynn" (38). But Fritz Senn stays with the aunt, and her unanswered question: "The aunt may be irritating and intrusive to her husband and Mr. Cotter, but she asks the right question, and has an inquisitive mind. The visit to the house of mourning owes something to her curiosity" (2). Senn's suggestion, that the aunt's visit to the Flynn home with the boy is an investigative mission, casts her mourning platitudes into a much more ambiguous light. "Did he . . . peacefully?" (15) leaves the discursive door open to a possible deathbed confession, as does the unfinished "And everything . . . ?" (15). But the aunt appears mollified by news that the priest took the last rites while still conscious, perhaps satisfied that anything of a scandalous nature would have erupted on his deathbed. Yet her unease returns when Eliza edges into her confession that "there was something queer coming over him latterly" (16) and tells the story of the broken chalice. " 'And was that it? said my aunt, I heard something. . . .' " (17). The aunt has not pressed for an explanation; Eliza has volunteered it, though she may have done so knowing that everyone, like the aunt, has "heard something."

The aunt receives little more than the story of the missing priest found laughing softly to himself in the confession box. But what if Eliza and her sister know more than this, more than they let on? What if these women who confuse "pneumatic" with "rheumatic" nonetheless have an inkling about the syphilitic paresis, and suspect that their brother's crossed ways and disappointments reflect a violated celibacy. The honor Eliza imputes to him—"He was too scrupulous always" (17)—then becomes a highly ironic and mendacious mask. It seems almost monstrous to imbue this elderly spinster, with her imperfect grasp of language, with the ability to have perceived vice and violation in her brother and in her home. The time sequence of the story remains obscure, but the boy's intimacy with the priest seems to have been confined to that back room, the very one in which the boy and his aunt are conversing with Eliza and the nodding Nannie at the story's end. How could Eliza and Nannie have failed to notice something, suspect something, register something going on in that back room in their home when the boy visited his friend? We might say that they were, after all, working in their draper's shop, recovering old umbrellas and such, and not capable of monitoring the activities in their house. But such alibis smack of resistant disavowal, recalling the resistance that Freud encountered in arguing to a shocked world that children are sexualized beings with sexual fantasies and desires, and with misprised knowledge of the life and passions that go on around them. If children know more than we want to believe they know, why not two elderly spinsters?

It is fatuous, I would argue, to maintain Eliza and Nannie's perfect innocence once one posits their brother's vice and the boy's complicity or victimization. Even if we adopt the most moderate view of an improper relationship between priest and boy—that it was discursive and confined to spoken confidences and confessions rather than corporeally enacted—there is still an inescapable ethos of suspect intimacy that the sisters would have had the opportunity to register. What do we make of the sisters once we impute to them a knowledge however fragmented, imperfect, and repressed, of a brother who crossed into transgression and who initiated a child into "a pleasant and vicious region" (11) of smiling exchange and fantasy? I believe the sisters then become figures of the boy and of the reader: figures not of blindness and cowardice, as Walzl supposes, but of tormented uncertainty and troubled incrimination in a moral universe not of their making that nonetheless entrains them in unwanted moral risks and responsibilities. What could or should they have done? Should they have reported their brother's friendship with the boy to Father O'Rourke, the trusted friend ("a body can trust" [16]) who helped them with their arrangements and the insurance? Perhaps Father O'Rourke need not be told since he was one of the three men who found Father Flynn in the confession box laughing to himself? Should they have confessed what they knew, or feared, to the boy's aunt?

Certainly they could not have done so in the boy's presence. William Johnsen takes the boy's judgment of the sisters at face value—"With scrupulous meanness he notes Nannie's commonness. He fancies a conspiratorial smile from the priest, confirming his disdain for these trolls" (11). Johnsen assumes that the reader will share the boy's judgment of the aunts as trolls. But the boy's strange fixation on the *material* during his vigil, his observation of the badly hooked skirt and down-trodden heel, of poured sherry and sips and sighs, could betoken something quite different than mere disdain. Is the boy determined to distract himself from his fear that he will find himself betrayed, that the sisters have observed him with the priest and will, like Old Cotter, try to air their suspicions to his aunt? As it happens, he remains quite safe, perhaps because the priest was innocent and there was nothing for the sisters to tell except that their invalid brother went mad. But perhaps Eliza, knowing there were rumors, made her own decision to squelch them with a story of ecclesiastical breakdown. Imagining the sisters with a painful dilemma in telling allows us to see them as the mirror of our painful dilemma in reading, veering from possibly innocent blindness to possibly prurient and self-incriminating suspicion.

I am suggesting then that Joyce opens his fictional career with a story that alerts us to pay attention to marginalized and stereotyped figures. The story's title may prod us to consider that all Dubliners, even its seemingly ignorant old women, enjoy the dignity of complex inner lives, moral dilemmas, and, in their later incarnation in "The Dead," political tragedies. Joyce's early fiction seems to privilege the figure of the sensitive boy in the initiation narrative—not only in the first three *Dubliners* stories, but in *Portrait of the Artist as a Young Man* as well. Yet impoverished sisters with no prospects, and aging spinsters with few resources, live on the margins of Joyce's fiction just as they live on the margins of society's awareness of them. Their frustrated hopes and dreams are hidden and suppressed as they watch their brothers go off to Rome or Paris to study while they stay behind covering umbrellas or embroidering scenes of Shakespeare in wool or buying a French primer with money needed for food. Not only is "The Sisters" the gnomon for the collection, but the sisters in "The Sisters" are themselves as gnomonic in the story as they are in the remainder of Joyce's oeuvre.

## Chapter 2
## A Walk on the Wild(e) Side:
## "An Encounter"

Like many of the stories in *Dubliners*, Joyce's "An Encounter" functions as an enigmatic provocation to problematized ethical reading. Consider
the shift in ethical assumptions inscribed in the historical arc of the questions
that were asked of the story when it was written ("Is this an immoral text?") and
those we might ask now ("Is this a homophobic text?"). Yet the puzzling and
ambiguous gestures of both the story's writing and its telling—enigmas of both
text and narration—further complicate these questions of Joyce's own time and
our present moment. Grant Richards first underreacted, then overreacted, to a
story whose 'enormity' no one in the publishing establishment recognized until
Joyce drew their attention to it—"The more subtle inquisitor will denounce *An
Encounter*, the enormity of which the printer cannot see because he is, as I said,
a plain blunt man" (*SL* 83). What, precisely, is that "enormity," and what is its
ethical status if the story's publication depends on, and the author relies on, its
expected and desired invisibility? "Many of the passages and phrases over which
we are now disputing escaped you: it was I who showed them to you," Joyce
wrote Richards. "And do you think that what escaped you (whose business it is
to look for such things in the books you consider) will be surely detected by a
public who reads the books for quite another reason?" (*SL* 88). Is Joyce positing
a double readership—vulgar and cultivated—with different cognitive and
moral horizons? If so, how is the text written to conceal itself to one and expose
itself to the other? To put it differently, is the text's 'enormity' its function as a
homosexual text that is both in and out of the closet depending on the gender
positioning (what I will later call the "implication") of the reader? By considering the implications of having readers trope the story as a "homosexual text,"
one raises questions about the explicitness of its content and that content's
recognition—which Joyce's friend Thomas Kettle is reported to have considered
"beyond anything in its outspokenness he had ever read" (*JJII* 329). I will argue
that the text's outspokenness in describing the pervert masks a deeper male reticence about speaking feelings and desires in relation to boys and men.

The best precedent for translating the story's moral perils into political and ideological problems is provided by Joyce himself, in his writings on Oscar Wilde. The case of Wilde prompts a heuristic interrogation of Joyce's intention. Why would Joyce—who in his 1909 review of "Salome" excoriated, with insight and sympathy, the homophobic events of Oscar Wilde's arrest and imprisonment—have written a story in 1905 in which the homosexual is figured as a sinister and sadistic predator of young boys? Joyce's 1909 essay—timely in its insertion between his writing of "An Encounter" in 1905 and its publication controversies in 1912—serves as a useful lens (or cracked looking-glass) for exploring the relationship between homosexuality, homophobia, and textuality in "An Encounter." The essay may be seen as a constructivist antidote to the essentialized version of its origin promoted by Richard Ellmann. Ellmann grounds Joyce's story in a real boyhood experience: "Joyce pointed out that he had actually taken part in the events described in such a story as 'An Encounter,' and Kettle granted, with reference to the homosexual in that story, 'Yes, we have all met him' " (*JJII* 329). But the collapse of the homosexual and the pervert into a universal immoral type fits neither Joyce's treatment of Wilde nor, as I will point out later, Stanislaus Joyce's account of the original "encounter." In his essay, Joyce explicitly acquits Wilde of being a "perverted monster" (*CW* 204). He further constructs etiologies for Wilde's homoeroticism that Richard Brown calls "provocatively tolerant" for their time (80).[1] "An Encounter," I will argue, performs a more sophisticated anatomy and enactment of the textual constructedness of the homophobic object by engaging and arousing what Eve Sedgwick calls "homosexual panic" (19).

Joyce, who chiefly nationalized the sexual scandals that threatened and destroyed Irish writers and politicians,[2] may nontheless have perceived an attenuated "homosexual panic" as the parallel condition for the censure of Oscar Wilde and the censorship of "An Encounter." Grant Richards's impulsive and dramatic reversal on the inclusion of the story after Joyce had pointed out its 'enormity' has the marks of that aggressive fright of *recognition*—the fear that one's own knowledge of transgressivity exposes itself and therefore requires a powerful disassociative act. George Lidwell, Joyce's solicitor in his publishing disputes, most vividly conveys the rhetorical manifestation of the violently dissociative gestures that characterize homosexual panic when he invokes Gibbon's *The History of the Decline and Fall of the Roman Empire* to characterize his response to "An Encounter"—

As to the last paragraphs in the Chapter under the head of "An Encounter," the matter is different. . . . I might quote Gibbon's "Decline and Fall" to show how much the subject is loathed "I touch with reluctance and dispatch with impatience this most odious vice of which modesty rejects the name and nature abominates the idea." (*JJII* 330)

In contrast, Joyce had no trouble recognizing the homosexual theme of Wilde's *The Picture of Dorian Gray.* "It is not very difficult to read between the lines," he wrote to Stanislaus, and he lauded what he recognized as Wilde's attempt to 'come out' ("Wilde seems to have had some good intentions in writing it— some wish to put himself before the world"). He complained only that Wilde failed to be sufficiently explicit ("If he had had the courage to develop the allusions in the book it might have been better" [*SL* 96]). Three years later, in his review of *Salome,* Joyce attributed the "howl of puritanical joy" with which Wilde was persecuted to a hypocrisy tinged with features of clinical homosexual panic. To Joyce, Wilde predicted the mechanism—"Oscar Wilde's own defence in the *Scots Observer* should remain valid in the judgment of an objective critic. Everyone, he wrote, sees his own sin in Dorian Gray (Wilde's best-known novel). What Dorian Gray's sin was no one says and no one knows. Anyone who recognizes it has committed it" (*CW* 204). In other words, Joyce appeared to recognize that aggressive homophobia might function as a violent dissociation triggered by fears of incrimination and identification. These are the fears implicit in what Eve Sedgwick identifies as the "psychiatric classification '*homosexual* panic,' " which "refers to the supposed uncertainty about his own sexual identity of the perpetrator of the antigay violence' " (20).

Homophobic anxiety produces culturally regulated protocols of reading with highly disruptive consequences. Joyce finds this in the judicial use made of *Dorian Gray* to criminalize Oscar Wilde. "I can imagine the capital which Wilde's prosecuting counsel made out of certain parts of it," he wrote to Stanislaus (*SL* 96). But the same protocol may have prompted the proposed editorial excision of "An Encounter, " reducing it to an indexed gap or blank spot in the published volume of *Dubliners.* (Joyce agreed to accede to George Roberts's demanded omission of the story if "the following note be placed by me before the first story: *This book in this form is incomplete. The scheme of the book as framed by me includes a story entitled* An Encounter *which stands between the first and second stories in this edition*" [*JJII* 331]). But the implications of these intersections of reading and violence are themselves thematized in "An Encounter" in ways that illuminate the story's own power to arouse homosexual panic. The story's own thematized commentary on canonicity, and on the duplicity of canonical and noncanonical texts, serves the heuristic function of demonstrating under what conditions the homosexual text seduces, incriminates, and invites punishment. I will argue then that "An Encounter" is a doubled text that conceals a homosocial fantasy whose desirous homosexual undercurrents affright it, and oblige it to mask itself as a canonical cautionary tale of imperiled innocence. This doubled text further internally comments on, thematizes, and betrays its own devious duplicity.

To pursue this argument I will need to move in and out of the narration, and in and out of the text (the *text* as the narration modified by its silences and gaps, and supplemented by tacit and implicit information and knowledge). My aim is to show that the narrative is textually constructed (Kershner writes, "The two boys who skip school are both enacting popular literary plots" [36]), and textually operative as "kinetic" rather than "static" writing. The narration of "An Encounter" is not innocent, I will argue, even as it constructs the figure of the sadistic homosexual pervert in order to warrant its innocence, and the innocence of its addressee or reader.

Before turning to the thematized perversion of bibliophilia in the story—the "queer old josser" 's abuse of the library to seduce and incriminate the young boy—consider certain provocative similarities in the rhetorical strategies of the pervert and the narrator. We might remember, or imagine, that the initial or 'virgin' reader who encounters "An Encounter" for the first time is stimulated, like the boy, to seek a reading adventure "abroad," as it were. The story's "abroad" is an open-ended and generically uncertain narrative terrain that gives little indication of where it is going, what to expect, or what risks it entails. The story's opening is not wholly indeterminate: we might expect a *Bildungsroman*, a romantic quest, a modern fairy tale, a pastoral idyll, modern urban naturalism, escapist nostalgia, or an initiation narrative. But there is no preparation for a pornographic outcome to the adventure. Only in retrospect, once the 'virgin' reading is irremediably past, do the similarities in the discursive strategies of the narrator and the old pervert become apparent. We realize, then, that we too were bored with banal and benign remarks on the weather, school, and books, social differences and cultural regulation, before the complacent lull of the story—delivered with the misleading reassurance of a "good" accent—is jolted by an indecent exposure. This disturbing discursive surprise has a similar effect on the young boy and the reader: a feeling of betrayal, anger, and resentment at having been manipulated into complicity, verbally assaulted, and subjected to a form of sexual aggression. The troublesome ethical locus of the story thereby becomes the shadowy figure of the boy grown up, the "adult" story-teller [3] who knows the adventure's outcome in advance, and understands the "enormity" of its possible impact, yet who deliberately defers information that would have protected us against shock and trauma.

This perverse construction of the narrator as the perverse double of the "queer old josser" in the story is meant to serve as a provisional difference intended to dilate the more conventional constructions of the narration's rhetorical and ethical strategies. My speculative demonization of the narrator as a sexual adept is intended to interrogate the story's rhetorical construction of the narratee or "reader" as innocent, as possessing a presexual innocence antecedent to heterosexuality. This innocence threatens to remain a constant outcome of the story's various alternative readings. Whether the story's narrative function is therapeutic (a psychoanalytic rememoration of a juvenile trauma for psychic relief), or testimonial (the authority of a victim serving prophylaxis, to protect future children from pederasts), the reader is situated in the ethical space of the inexperienced child. This remains true for the interpretive scenario in which the narrator uses the figure of the pederast to define himself as heterosexual within the overdetermined homosocial milieu of the story's setting. However, the version of this story that unsettles its ethical dynamics most profoundly belongs to the *ur*-narrative I alluded to earlier—Stanislaus Joyce's version of the brothers' truant encounter with a putative pederast:

In "An Encounter," my brother describes a day's miching which he and I planned and carried out while we were living in North Richmond Street, and our encounter with an elderly pederast. For us he was just a "juggins." Neither of us could have any notion at the time what kind of "juggins" he was, but something funny in his speech and behaviour put us on our guard at once. We thought he might be an escaped madman. (62)

In this encounter, the old man is a "juggins," a harmless, if peculiar, simpleton whose gestures fail to overly worry, menace, or frighten the young Joyces. The suspicion that the old man was "an escaped madman" appears a romantic elaboration of their initial perception of his mild idiocy. There is no report of an explicit erotic overture, nor of the old man's cunning and elaborate conversation that becomes the climax of the written story. The salient point of the biographical encounter is the boys' ability to read a sexual semiotics inscribed in the man's speech and gestures that "put us on our guard" against a homosexual advance. "An Encounter" thus transformed a defensive presexual experience, in which the boys "knew" something of the old man's sexuality without quite understanding what they "knew," into an offensive assault in which they are refunctioned as innocent asexual victims. Joyce patently seems to have invented the pornographic discourse that criminalizes the "juggins" while at the same time sanitizing the boys' minds to an improbable purity. He thereby supplied his and Stanislaus's mild homosexual panic with the full-blown fantasy of a monstrous sexual bogy.

Joyce's transformation of a boyhood encounter into the fictional "Encounter" could usefully, if paradoxically, exemplify some aspects of the problematical power that the authority of personal experience brings to the workings of "identity politics"—which Diana Fuss sums up as "personal consciousness, individual oppression, lived experience" (113). Personal experience becomes an index of oppression with truth value—a signifier of privileged knowledge—

which is exposed in the Joyce anecdote for its counter-oppressive potential. The boys (in a logic resembling that of the creation of witches from women) transform a figure of extreme social marginalization into an inchoate sexual predator. A putative *experience* of victimization becomes the authorization for a self-masking *exercise* of victimization. A major philosophical problem with the privileging of experience as the signifier of identity is articulated by Fuss when she glosses Derrida—"while experience may be underwritten by a metaphysics of presence, this does not mean experience is necessarily present to us—in the form of an unmediated real" (114). In Stanislaus Joyce's memory of boyhood experience, the boys "read" an old man according to some tacit prior cultural coding of the homosexual or the pederast that interprets their experience according to preexisting homophobic conventions. In transforming the experience to fiction, Joyce makes the source of the cultural code visible as pornographic discourse, as a literature- and language-generated knowledge of perversity. The old man's ability to deliver a sexually charged narration—"He described to me how he would whip such a boy" (27) participates in the specific rhetorical conventions of pornography. These conventions (the program, the demonstration, the speculation, etc.) provoke such theorists of pornological writing as Deleuze and Barthes to stress that masochism and sadism should be treated as discourse or text rather than as forms of behavior. As perversions with their origins in texts and with names conferred by authors, sadism and masochism are theoretically construed as literary or textual phenomena. The encounter with a pederast, by the young Joyces or by the fictional boy narrator, is an encounter mediated by the literary discourses and conventions that construct and produce the figure of the pervert and his language. These boys experience not so much an encounter as the construction of an encounter.

The logic of textual mediation is, of course, the foregrounded donnée of the opening of the story. The opening line, "It was Joe Dillon who introduced the Wild West to us," (19) may suppress the mediation of the book metonymically, but not logically. It was Joe Dillon's library—"He had a little library made up of old numbers of *The Union Jack, Pluck,* and *The Halfpenny Marvel*" (19)—that introduced the boys not to the Wild West, but to literary constructions of the American West. The boys encounter fantasy texts designed to domesticate the exotic people and bloody history of the New World into scripts that they can mimic. The boys transform text into enactment, into the "mimic warfare" of juvenile play—"He looked like some kind of an Indian when he capered round the garden, an old tea-cosy on his head, beating a tin with his fist and yelling:—Ya! yaka, yaka, yaka!" (19). Kershner's historical elaboration of the substance and significance of the "chronicles of disorder" supplies the extratextual knowledge that the story's contemporary readers had readily available for intertextual interpolation. Kershner's ideological analysis of the unstable moral categorizations of the shifting literary and commercial productions of children's literature and boys' magazines in the late nineteenth century gives us a better estimation of the function and power of their regulation. Popular children's literature's willingness to appeal to youngsters through titillation and sensationalism allowed reading to become contested moral and ideological terrain inviting critical, and often hypocritical, gestures of denunciation. "Ironically for a magazine generally regarded as cheaply sensational," Kershner writes of *The Halfpenny Marvel*, "it claimed the intent of counteracting the influence of unhealthy sensationalism aimed at children. . . . Soon *The Marvel* began printing testimonials such as that of the Reverend C. N. Barham expressing pleasure that the magazine was so 'pure and wholesome in tone.' On the front cover of that issue was a man being tortured" (33).

The sadomasochistic "knowledge" that the boys in "An Encounter" bring to their "encounter" with the queer old josser is presumably already inscribed in their truant reading, but without moral or psychological indexing of its prurience. As Kershner explains, "The sadomasochistic element in boys' periodicals was far less visible to the adults of the late nineteenth century than to ourselves; as will become apparent in the discussion of school stories below, it was an accepted, relatively transparent aspect of the ideology of bourgeois schooling" (33). Yet at stake in the regulation of transgressive reading and transgressive sexuality in the story is not merely the visibility of the perverse, but its *re-cognition*—that is, its repeated and repeatable knowledge—and its *ac-knowledgment* or iterated concession of something already known, or known elsewhere. Regulation itself impedes the ability to "see" and "know" across a generic and institutional divide, as the parable of curricular and extracurricular reading in the story demonstrates. Father Butler fails to see that the *Commentarii de Bello Gallico* and *The Apache Chief* share an imperialistic historical theme with considerable contemporary ideological relevance for the pre-Republican Ireland of his day. Indeed, *The Apache Chief* with its presumable perspective of the embattled and the vanquished, might have served the historical education of Irish boys better than did Caesar's conquest of Gaul. But regulation favors the canon in ways that block the transfer of historical understanding across the generic divide into the popular adventure story. The queer old josser, on the other hand, uses the authority of the canonical to lure the boy into a false *acknowledgment*: "I pretended that I had read every book he mentioned so that in the end he said:—Ah, I can see you are a bookworm like myself' " (25). The old man then inserts regulation ("there were some of Lord Lytton's works which boys couldn't read" [25]) in order to create a transgressive difference to implicate the boy. Curiously, a common historical theme connects the presumably guilty book—

Kershner identifies it as Bulwer-Lytton's *The Last Days of Pompeii*—to the Roman History Father Butler teaches the boys at school. The old man splits the
canon in two, into moral and immoral versions across whose divide knowledge
may be carried only at the risk of culpability.

The bibliophilic seduction of the boy offers an exemplary model for the
function of what Eve Sedgwick calls "ignorance effects" (23), and the role they
play in the positioning of the reader of "An Encounter." The boy's investment in
cultural literacy shifts with his homosocial context, requiring an on-going
strategic deployment of ignorance and knowledge. The fear of appearing too
bookish ("the reluctant Indians who were afraid to seem studious" [20])[4]
among his peers oscillates with the fear of appearing insufficiently bookish with
learned superiors like Father Butler and the seemingly cultivated old man. The
possession or dispossession of learning thus becomes a locus of ethical manipulation, including feigning, disguise, and lying. This psychic regulation of degrees
of acknowledgment signals possible displacements and cathexes between bibliophilic and libidinal desires, in which the reader as much as the narrator may
be implicated. In other words, the reader, like the narrator, may be ethically manipulating the degree of literary and sexual knowledge that is brought to (or ac-
knowledged as brought to) the reading of "An Encounter." On the one hand,
mastery is threatened by queer knowledge. "In fact, everyone feels uncomfortable in speaking to others about this subject, afraid that his listener may know
more about it than he does," Joyce wrote of the Wilde scandal (*CW* 204). At the
same time, the reader of "An Encounter" is challenged to defend the privileged
ignorance of sexually transgressive knowledge. When the queer old josser challenges the boys with the canon ("He asked us whether we had read the poetry of
Thomas Moore or the works of Sir Walter Scott and Lord Lytton" [25]), he manipulates not only their ignorance of the library. It is, on the contrary, a desirous
and reckless bibliophilia that leads the boy narrator to claim unknown and forbidden knowledge in the seeming interest of cultural mastery.

But the boy's reaction to the old man's interrogation about the library is
curious and troubling in its deviousness. Mahony's question in response to the
old man's provocative "Of course . . . there were some of Lord Lytton's works
which boys couldn't read" (25) would seem perfectly sensible.[5] It is the narrator's embarrassment and discomfort we should find suspect: "Mahony asked
why couldn't boys read them—a question which agitated and pained me because I was afraid the man would think I was as stupid as Mahony" (25). The
boy's desire to project himself as a bibliophile in identification with the old man
overrides the protection of "innocence" that ignorance would confer. Does the
boy wish to censor the question because he is agitated and pained for another
reason: because he desires a reply whose forbidden content he knows might

excite him? The old man appears to interpret his agitation in this way, because he answers Mahony's question with a substitution that doubles his original question about literary experience with a question about sexual experience—"Then he asked us which of us had the most sweethearts" (25). Is the narrator's remembered embarrassment at Mahony's question a disguise of snobbery to mask prurience, an alias like the one he assumes in the face of the old man's masturbation ("In case he asks us for our names . . . let you be Murphy and I'll be Smith" [26])? If so, then his "ignorance effect" (Sedgwick 5) is clearly produced for the benefit of the reader. Kershner describes a similar doubling as the "radical instability" of the reader of Victorian flagellation pornography—"He is addressed both as one of an elite of sensibility and as a man who shares the unadmitted desires of all men" (45). On the narrational level of "An Encounter," the reader is constructed in a similarly doubled way as a devious and self-disguising figure: like Mahony we too would like to know the censored matter, and like the narrator we too know that it is simultaneously demeaning and dangerous to ask. Like the schoolboys watching Leo Dillon get caught with contraband reading in school—"Everyone's heart palpitated as Leo Dillon handed up the paper and everyone assumed an innocent face" (20)—the reader too assumes an innocent face to disguise a palpitating heart when approaching the end of the story.

The beating heart with which the narrative ends—"my heart was beating quickly. . . . How my heart beat" (28)—becomes both a somatic and verbal symptom, and betrayal, of the ambiguous response to the fantasy of beating. As such, it betrays the narrator's ignorance effects whose 'paltry stratagem' includes a variety of ocular maneuvers that together parse a virtual grammar of the gaze: looking *into* eyes, looking *for* eyes, looking *at* eyes, looking *without* eyes.[6] The narrator veils the implication of the eyes in pleasure and desire by indirection and confusion. The two boys enjoy a truant communion on the Dublin quays—eating their picnic lunch in silence while "We pleased ourselves with the spectacle of Dublin's commerce" (23). This happy togetherness later culminates in a moment of protoromance on the ferryboat ride that exhibits the magic of a homosocial elopement, "We were serious to the point of solemnity, but once during the short voyage our eyes met and we laughed" (23). This intimate moment of boys looking into each other's eyes in a communion of shared pleasure is followed by the curious double ocular frustration of the narrator's failure to read a Norwegian ship's name or discover a sailor with green eyes. The narration makes the green eyes as indecipherable to the reader as the ship's legend—"I came back and examined the foreign sailors to see had any of them green eyes for I had some confused notion . . ." (23). The narrator's search for male green eyes appears to have been produced so spontaneously under the influence of the shared boyhood idyll that the narration breaks off in confusion and embarrassment before revealing its meaning. Does the *boy* censor his confused notion of the meaning of green eyes, or does the *adult narrator* censor what he knew as a boy? If the ellipsis is the narrator's, and not the boy's, then the meaning of the green eyes is censored for the benefit of the reader—or rather for the benefit of the narrator who needs to avert a self-betrayal that would, simultaneously, damage the reader's innocence. The narrator recovers from the bungled revelation by diluting its narrative consequence ("The only sailor whose eyes could have been called green" [23]) in the pointless anecdote of the "tall man who amused the crowd on the quay by calling out cheerfully every time the planks fell:—All right! All right!" (23). The green eyes are, of course, only provisionally all right, for they will return in the story—like the return of the repressed—with hallucinatory force.

The ellipsis has an effect on the reader not unlike that of the unspecified "sin" in *Dorian Gray*: the reader is pressured to supply a meaning at the risk of self-incrimination. Critics of the story have traditionally acted out a tenacious refusal to surrender the "privilege of unknowing" in their confrontation with this narrative trap. The likeliest possibility—that the boy believes sailors with green eyes are homosexual—tends to be suppressed and displaced onto a contiguous substitute, legitimated by the inevitable overdetermination of censored blanks. Tindall writes, "the boy centers his notions of escape and adventure in 'green eyes,' a private symbol of his romantic ideal" (9). Kershner seconds this general interpretation, attributing the ellipsis to "a realization best left unconscious, because to put it in words would be to denude it of the mystery upon which the image feeds." He then goes on to supply it with a specific literary figure—"specifically, he is looking for the young, red-haired, green-eyed sailor who is the hero of picaresque adventures in the diluted tradition of Marryat" (37). Both Tindall and Kershner attribute the ellipsis to the boy, rather than to the retrospective adult narration. This forecloses the layered possibility that the boy's "innocent" romantic symbol has, by the time of the retrospective telling, become infected with the adult narrator's awareness of, and discomfort with, the homosexual significance of green. Both in the aesthetics of Oscar Wilde, and the sexology of Havelock Ellis ("inverts exhibit a preference for green garments,"[7]), green was associated with homosexuality. If the narrator censors the meaning of "green eyes" to avert a betrayal of either juvenile homosexual desire or adult homosexual panic, the censoring maneuver nonetheless alerts us to a more pointed peculiarity of the narration. Why does the highly literate adult narrator, whose reading references specifically situate his boyhood adventure in the 1890s, make no retrospective comment on Oscar Wilde's trial and imprisonment in 1895–97—a topic surely of relevance to his memory of a juvenile encounter with a pederast at about the same time?

If the boy's encounter with the foreign sailors is marked by expectant attraction, his encounter with the old man is marked by expectant repulsion. He initially conspicuously avoids looking at the eyes that he had "examined" so pointedly as a symptom in the sailors. Nonetheless, his attention to the old man's body—if less focused—is keen, and his procedure is as clinical, if less shrewd, in detecting and reading bodily symptoms. In avoiding the old man's eyes, he concentrates his ocular focus on the mouth, which he reads for signs of decay and decadence. He notes the ashen-gray moustache ("He seemed to be fairly old" [24]) and the missing and stained teeth ("I saw that he had great gaps in his mouth between his yellow teeth" [25]). He situates the man's unpalatable speech in the oral interior behind these gaping apertures ("I disliked the words in his mouth" [25]). The boy's reading of the old man's physiognomy is constructed of expectations learned from paranoid literary encounters with foreigners and strangers—Little Red Riding Hood's dim penetration of the wolf's disguise ("Grandma, what large teeth you have") or the maw of the one-eyed Cyclops. The boy likewise registers symptoms of somatic agitation, which he interprets naïvely ("I wondered why he shivered once or twice as if he feared something or felt a sudden chill" [25]). Little Stephen Dedalus maps the associative etiology of the shiver in *Portrait* much more precisely in his meditation on caning: "A long thin cane would have a high whistling sound and he wondered what was that pain like. It made him shivery to think of it and cold. . . . It made him shivery: but that was because you always felt like a shiver when you let down your trousers" (45).

The scrupulous anatomy of juvenile homosexual panic that Joseph Valente traces in Stephen's schoolboy experiences of real and fantasized punishment in *Portrait*[8] is suppressed and displaced in "An Encounter." Like the boy, the reader is obliged to read symptomatically a set of inconsistent responses in the boy that curiously mirror the old man's own inconsistent and illogical sentiments toward sexuality. The boy is as surprised by the old man's liberality as by his illiberality—a set of surprises interrupted and punctuated by a surprising failure to be surprised. When the old man excuses himself ("saying that he had to leave us for a minute or so, a few minutes" [26]), the boy, apparently shaken by the man's fetishistic fascination with girls' hands and hair, appears unsurprised that the man elaborates the quotidian urination with a further sexual display:

—I say! Look what he's doing!
As I neither answered nor raised my eyes Mahony exclaimed again:

—I say . . . He's a queer old josser!

—In case he asks us for our names, I said, let you be Murphy and I'll be Smith. (26)

The boy's averted eyes and lack of surprise symptomatize a knowledge that the narrative elsewhere shields, and the quickly contrived disguise signals the boy's understanding that the old man's irregular and provocative behavior—presumably masturbation—is intended for his and Mahony's benefit.

The inconsistency in the boy's shrewdness and naïveté is striking, and, I believe, intended to be suspect. Having carefully mounted his guard after the masturbation, the boy produces a patently literal response to the man's provocative question about whipping. "I was going to reply indignantly that we were not National School boys to be *whipped*, as he called it" (27 emphasis original), the narrator reports. This seems as studiously ignorant as his surprise at the old man's insistence on the subject. Indeed, it is a peculiar slippage of an idiom, wrapped in a slippage of a figure, that snaps the boy's rigorous ocular control. Having identified Mahony with the generic victim of punishment in his sadistic fantasy, the old man's locution—"what he wanted was to get a nice warm whipping" (27)—uncomfortably collapses (through the double meaning of "wanted") sadistic and masochistic desire into a single, overdetermined, sentiment. Could it be recognition, identification, and fear evoked by this charged sentiment that prompts the boy to perform the deferred gesture of looking up to seek the green eyes?—"I was surprised at this sentiment and involuntarily glanced up at his face. As I did so I met the gaze of a pair of bottle-green eyes peering at me from under a twitching forehead. I turned my eyes away again" (27).

The most dramatic change Joyce makes in revising his holograph version of "An Encounter" for the 1910 edition of the story is the color of the old man's eyes. The "sage-green" eyes of the hand-written manuscript become the "bottle green" of the 1910 proofs, and the "bottle-green" of the 1914 proofs (*JJA* 4, 5, 6). The change from a natural to a manufactured analogue for the color produces some specific and significant effects. Not only do the "bottle-green" eyes convey greater hardness and translucence than the "sage-green" eyes, but they conjure up a pair of internalized spectacles (thick and green like the bottoms of bottle glass) that intensify the old man's vision. At the same time, the adjective renders his eyes armored and impenetrable. For the boy, the impact of encountering the man's gaze as "bottle-green" would be to encounter a set of doubled, or fortified, eyes that see and glare without being themselves perfectly visible, and whose thickness and dark tint project an alien desire impossible to reciprocate.

The boy's search for green eyes leads to a nightmare version of green eyes; his quest for adventure leads to misadventure, but also of a peculiarly parallel, if twisted, relation to his desire. One could dilate the ellipsis of the boy's unnamed quest as the pastoral version of homosexuality that Joyce found inscribed in the auto-aestheticism of Oscar Wilde. Joyce cites this in his essay—"a vague idea of delicate pastels, of life beautified with flowers" (*CW* 202); " 'I love to see you wandering through violet-filled valleys, with your honey-coloured hair gleaming' " (*CW* 204). The boy's miching (playing truant) with his friend on the Dublin waterfront may be more robust and quotidian, but it conjures an urban homosocial idyll that lacks only a dreamy male figure, a sailor with green eyes, to create a romantic plenum. The boy's walk on the wild side may have inadvertently followed an unconscious historical plot, a walk on the Wilde side. We could construe that at some point during or after the experience the boy recognized this, and like the Victorian public during Wilde's trial, affrighted itself sufficiently to twist desire into a sinister distortion—"their author was denounced as a degenerate obsessed by exotic perversions" (*CW* 204). Wilde's "famous white ivory walking stick glittering with turquoise stones" (*CW* 202) becomes transformed in "An Encounter" into the tapping stick of an old man ("always tapping the ground with his stick, so slowly that I thought he was looking for something" [24]). And his discourse then turns it into a vicious cane for lasciviously whipping young boys. The moral of the social cautionary tale of "An Encounter"—that truant boys may meet sinister sexual predators abroad—has a psychological double: that the vague homosexual desires of young boys may be twisted, by fear of censure and punishment, into self-punishing phantoms of terror and panic.

The operation of homosexual panic in the narrator, and in the narration, becomes more readily visible when "An Encounter" is juxtaposed with its thematic counterpart: the story "Counterparts" in *Dubliners*. Both stories end with the image of a boy being beaten, a parallel that produces the contrapuntal sociological moral that child abuse—the beating of innocent boys—need not be sought abroad and need not be eroticized or attributed to demonized strangers. Children, both boys and girls, are in greater danger of violence and injury from their fathers at home ("The boy uttered a squeal of pain as the stick cut his thigh. He clasped his hands together in the air and his voice shook with fright. —O pa! he cried. Don't beat me, pa!" [98]) than from pederasts abroad, both in fiction and in the life of Joyce's day. Joyce's source for the end of "Counterparts" was Stanislaus's diary entry reporting their Uncle William terrorizing the six- or seven-year-old Bertie (*The Complete Dublin Diary* 37). Nor was familial violence warranted as free of sexual coloration or motivation. Nora Barnacle's brutal beating from her uncle Tom Healy ("Tom beat Nora with his thorn stick until she fell to the floor, clutching his knees and begging him to stop") may have been provoked by Nora's sexual maturation ("She may also have sensed an incestuous longing behind Tom Healy's rage" [Maddox 22]). But if Joyce's

*Dubliners* stories "An Encounter" and "Counterparts" are semantically echoic, their hermeneutical echo resonates with a striking difference, a psychic disturbance that readings tend to repress by coding it as ethical. By sociologically overlapping the theme of abused childhood, the doubled stories suppress or obscure the exaggerated affective power that tabooed erotic elements can bring to a story. The ending of "Counterparts" graphically describes the beating of a boy, yet evokes none of the hysteria of outrage, anxiety, disgust, and excitement that homosexual pederasty and sadomasochism can arouse in a reading public. By letting the stories echo against each other, the irony of this affective and ethical discrepancy—that a speculative erotic discourse has a profoundly more disturbing effect than the representation of an actual violence and cruelty—subjects the reader response to ethical scrutiny. The reader is thus positioned or "gendered" (in Teresa De Lauretis's sense) by a response whose dissociative reflexes align it with the symbolic power and coercive force of patriarchy.

It is important to remember, as Kershner reminds us, that the old man's pornographic discourse is translated through a double prism of perception. He writes, "it emerges as an amalgam of the boy's and the old man's language—or, more precisely, of the old man's language and the two languages of experience and retrospection embodied in the boy's narration" (44). The obsessive, mesmerizing quality of the old man's speech has, therefore, an uncertain locus. Is its hypnotic effect a property of the old man's speaking or of the young boy's hearing? The possibility that the boy internalizes the magnet that attaches to the old man's erotic field may account for the markedly different responses that the boy narrator and Mahony have to the old josser. Both hear the same monotonous voice unveiling its erotic mysteries, but they respond differently to this Siren's song. The narrator's rigid ocular control contrasts with Mahony "who was regarding us with open eyes" (25), and who openly looks at what the old man is doing while the narrator refuses to change his gaze or raise his eyes. While the narrator is "still considering whether I would go away or not" (26), Mahony escapes from the hypnotic orbit. He first uses the pretext of chasing a cat, and when that pretext is lost, he simply stays away—"he began to wander about the far end of the field, aimlessly" (27). Mahony's greater innocence may translate, in the presence of knowledge, into freedom from implication that allows him to escape not only the old man's physical clutches ("my heart was beating quickly with fear that he would seize me by the ankles" [28]), but also his psychological clutches. He escapes implication, too, in the romantic role into which the narrator has cast him—of the dashing boy with the dark complexion and the jaunty cricket club badge on his cap—who comes to the rescue of an innocent in distress. At the end of their adventure, the boys at last have the three you must have to arrange a siege, but the plot has changed from cowboys and Indians into villain, damsel, and hero: "How my heart beat as he came running across the field to me! He ran as if to bring me aid" (28). The famous last line of the story—"And I was penitent; for in my heart I had always despised him a little" (28)—confesses a change of heart, and ends the boy's adventure with a confessed blossoming of refigured homosocial affection that has survived its brutal disruption by homosexual panic.[9]

My opening suggestion that "An Encounter" may have been written to function as a homosexual text simultaneously in and out of the closet, may account for the widely divergent readings the story produces. The narrator's shrewd feints of innocence, ignorance, and unease with sexual feeling and arousal in the story provoke a variety of guarded, disavowing, dissociative responses from the reader or critic. William York Tindall's is illustrative of the most effective form of this evasion, the informed sidestep of the issue of perversity—"The news that perverts are around is no news at all." This is followed by its sublation into the theme of paralyzed idealism—"Case history is there to reveal something else, something at once theological, ecclesiastical, and moral" (19). In reading the story as an elaborate allegory of coded religious questing, the story's sexual agitations are focalized in the old man, and firmly set aside as an irrelevancy. Thirty years later, Kershner's brilliant ideological elucidation of the story's popular intertexts shapes much of the key to the closet without fully acknowledging the narratorial attempts to secure its door. Kershner's key resides in his unraveling of the doubled and deceptively ambiguous nature of the popular texts the story's boys read, which shape them into readers uncertain and anxious about managing their response. The narration of "An Encounter," I would suggest, becomes such a doubled text, generically ambiguous enough to have its pornographic climax subordinated to theological parable, rhetorically provocative enough to lull, worry, subdue, excite the reader into responding, like the boys, with palpitating hearts and assumed innocent faces. No reading can truly domesticate this cunning and troubled textual performance. But in the light of queer theory it becomes possible, at least, to go beyond the word plays, symbols, and paradoxes with which we evade the homosexuality of Wilde—what Stephen in *Ulysses* calls "Tame essence of Wilde" (9: 532). Queer theory lets us recognize in the boys' walk on the wild side, their walk on the Wilde side.

## Chapter 3
# Blind Streets and Seeing Houses: "Araby"

Joyce's "Araby" not only draws attention to its conspicuous poetic language; it offers the beauty of its art as compensation to the frustrations that are thematized in the story. The little boy whose heart is broken by a city "hostile to romance" transmutes his grief into a romance of language. Joyce, whose *Dubliners* stories tend to bear rhetorical titles, makes of "Araby" a rhetorical bazaar that outstrips in poetic exoticism the extravagant promise of the empty and sterile commercial confection that so disappoints the child. In an early essay on *Dubliners*, Frank O'Connor writes of "Araby," "This is using words as they had not been used before in English, except by Pater—not to describe an experience, but so far as possible to duplicate it. Not even perhaps to duplicate it so much as to replace it by a combination of images—a rhetorician's dream, if you like, but Joyce was a student of rhetoric" (20). I construe this gesture of stylistic virtuosity less as an exercise in aestheticism than as a self-critical performance. The story's narrative performance, of offering art as balm to heal the anguish of a modern city's paralysis, enacts the quintessential Modernistic practice repeated in Eliot's "Waste Land," of turning to poetry for modern spiritual redemption. But by evoking literary traditions that the chivalric preoccupations and temper of the story prompt, "Araby" allies itself with diverse nineteenth century medievalisms[1] whose archaic and mannered aestheticism Modernism generally abjures. The paradox of "Araby" 's incongruent Romantic appeal poses a problem that *Portrait* criticism also confronts and resolves as stylistic imitation, parody, or ironic pastiche. But I find it more useful to treat "Araby" 's peculiar language as a textual performance with several conflicting layers: a self-incriminating narration whose rhetorical aims the text encapsulates and subjects to an immanent critique. This critique anticipates the later social criticism of aestheticism by Herbert Marcuse, and particularly his concept of "affirmative culture"—a notion more recently used by Peter Buerger to criticize the self-contradiction in which Modernism implicates art—"art thus stabilizes the very social conditions against which it protests" (7). But I will argue that "Araby" tacitly criticizes affirmative culture rather than abets it, and it does so by destabilizing its own compensatory gesture. It takes its own beautiful rhetorical language and makes it empty and ineffective. This gesture in turn translates "rhetoric" it-self back into its idiomatic *marketplace* sense of elaborate but insubstantial speech. "Araby" the story, the ornate but empty narration, doubles "Araby," the ornate but empty bazaar. "If I go . . . I will bring you something" (32), the boy promises Mangan's sister.[2] But he returns empty-handed—except for the story of their double, encapsulated, frustration. "Araby," the story, offers to readers a similar rhetorical empty-handedness.

I plan to track the story's compensatory strategy—its production of artful language to supplement unsatisfied desire—through a set of ontological opera-tions by which the narrative consciousness attempts to constitute itself as a sub-ject. "Gazing up into the darkness, I saw myself as a creature driven and derided by vanity" (35). The story's closing moral turns on itself by concluding with a parabolic maneuver, by having the narrative consciousness turn itself into an al-legorical figure, "a symbol of" something, as Gabriel Conroy might put it. The boy has been transformed by his own narrative voice into a figure of fable or parable, of the mirrored emptiness that is Vanitas. "Araby" therefore doubles its thematic preoccupation with the chivalric quest implicit in its famous trope of the imperiled Grail ("I bore my chalice safely through a throng of foes" [31]) by further formally cloaking itself in the allegorical and parabolic rhetoric of chivalric literature.[3] The question is whether the closing self-allegorization in-deed constitutes an epiphany[4]—a moment of illuminated enlightenment or the transcendent self-recognition we call *anagnorisis*. Or does the parabolic gesture in the story enfold other philosophical maneuvers that offer knowledge and in-sight as reversible or retractable: an ocular voyeurism that turns upon itself as a "gaze" and recognizes its own quest for self-knowledge as merely another species of narcissism? The 1981 Miami University Research Group Experiment analysis of "Araby" argues an interesting version of this point. "It is not enough to presuppose only that the boy understood that he had been vain," they write. "Rather we have to presuppose that he understood not simply that he had been vain, but also that he couldn't help being unreflectively naïve, and therefore, that he couldn't help being mocked by another side of himself" (245). Do mythification and demythification oscillate hopelessly in this story? The reader confronts a variety of interpretive options at the end of the story that include a "straight" acceptance of the boy's self-estimation as a vain figure who finally recognizes his vanity. We may also respond with sympathy for the idealist's vic-timization by vulgar philistinism, or—as I am suggesting—with criticism of the adult-narrator's exploitation of his juvenile experience by turning it into an aes-theticized social and moral parable.

The curious figure of the reflective darkness ("Gazing up into the darkness I saw myself") of an extinguished dream ("the light was out"), suggests that this

story will be illuminated by blindness. The boy who finds emptiness in "Araby,"
the figure of romance, is in turn found empty, a personification rather than a
person, by the story. The strange locution at the story's end, that has the dark-
ened gallery of "Araby" appear to "see" the boy in a way that lets him see himself, turns an empty space into a dark mirror that catches him in its eye. This
figure in turn recapitulates the strange topopoeia of the story's opening, where
streets are personified as "blind" and houses as "seeing." This topographia
frames the narration in a way that sets it up for a chiasmus: the story that opens
with the "real" estate of North Richmond Street closes with its antipode of the
"unreal" estate of "Araby"—but only after the two places have, as it were, traded
places.[5] What makes the crossing over possible is that "Araby," the name of a
longing for romance displaced onto a mythologized Oriental geography, suppresses the mediation of commerce. It thereby conceals the operations by which
the fantasy of an exoticized and seductive East becomes a commercial fabrica-
tion produced by that realm the boy finds "most hostile to romance"—the marketplace. Commerce produces not only the trinkets and commodities the boy
does not want, the vases and tea sets he spurns, and the parcels he bears like an
irksome cross while shopping with his aunt every Saturday night. Commerce
also produces fantasy and magic through language: "The syllables of the word
*Araby* were called to me through the silence in which my soul luxuriated and
cast an Eastern enchantment over me" (32). The narration of "Araby" is presumably neither a commodity, nor a charity, like the ambiguously configured bazaar
in the story.[6] But it resorts to the same power of language, the power to aestheti-
cize and glamorize what is common and mean ("the magical name"), that the
operation of advertising borrows from poetry. The narrative voice of "Araby,"
with its gift for personification, could easily be that of Little Chandler, or rather
"T. Malone Chandler," as he Celticizes himself—

As he crossed Grattan Bridge he looked down the river towards the lower quays and
pitied the poor stunted houses. They seemed to him a band of tramps, huddled together
along the river-banks, their old coats covered with dust and soot, stupefied by the
panorama of sunset and waiting for the first chill of night to bid them arise, shake themselves and begone. He wondered whether he could write a poem to express his idea. (73)

The "Celtic note" of wistful sadness to which Chandler calculates to aspire can
also be heard in the poetic language of "Araby" when it lapses into pathetic fallacy ("the lamps of the street lifted their feeble lanterns" [30]).

But the personifications of place in "Araby" transcend Little Chandler's
affectations because of the complex temperamental and moral intersubjectivi-
ties the narration establishes between the boy and the places of his habitation

and imagination. North Richmond Street is introduced as blind, mute ("a quiet street"), with emptiness inside ("An uninhabited house stood at the blind end" [29])—a prophetic figure of the boy himself at the end of the story. Much like the story with its confession of solipsistic interiority, the houses on North Richmond Street engage in both sober introspection ("conscious of decent lives within them") and discreet censoriousness ("gazed at one another with brown imperturbable faces"). The story's solipsism and insularity is figured by the opening topography of North Richmond Street as "blind," as a cul de sac and dead end from which escape is baffled. The slippage of meaning that leads the figure of the "blind" from spatial to ocular closure, links the street, and its houses with their virtual hermetic seals, to the larger thematics of closed economies in which exchange and communication are doomed to recirculation. The boy's house—while not clearly identical with the uninhabited house at the end of the blind street—is figured as an enclosure of negativity, of death, waste rooms, waste papers, waste people, and waste lives. The sealed rooms—"musty from having been long enclosed"—circulate as little air as the rusty bicycle pump abandoned in the garden (29). They in turn mirror that figure of closed economy: Mrs. Mercer, the pawnbroker's widow, who extends her late husband's business of recycling used goods to her philanthropy ("collected used stamps for some pious purpose" [33]), and to her communication ("I had to endure the gossip"). Herself constructed like a closed system, Mrs. Mercer, not surprisingly, feels herself endangered by fresh air ("the night air was bad for her"). The story's allusions to baffled pneumatic circulation itself circulates verbal bafflements, like an impaired pentecostal pneuma or wind, from other *Dubliners* stories ("one of them new-fangled carriages . . . them with the rheumatic wheels" [17]).

The slippage of the meanings of "blind" continues to recirculate through the narration's tropological system. The narration describes the boy's voyeurism of Mangan's sister by slipping further meaning off the protective screen that is called a "blind," onto its meaning as an ocular shelter used by hunters to conceal or camouflage them from their prey. "The blind was pulled down . . . so that I could not be seen" (30), we are told. This figurative transformation of the boy's house into a version of a duck or deer "blind" is quite congruent with the boy's subsequent activity of essentially "stalking" the girl, who is described as a "brown figure" like a deer (or dear):

Every morning I lay on the floor in the front parlour watching her door. The blind was pulled down to within an inch of the sash so that I could not be seen. When she came out on the doorstep my heart leaped. I ran to the hall, seized my books and followed her.

I kept her brown figure always in my eye and, when we came near the point at which our ways diverged, I quickened my pace and passed her. (30)

Visually, the boy's voyeurism enacts a curious visual encapsulation that we might miss were it not for the introductory image of the "seeing" houses. The nearly closed blind, with its slit for peeping, functions like an eyelid closed but for a slit—transforming the front parlor into an eye that harbors the peeping boy. The boy's own ocular gesture—"I kept her brown figure always in my eye"—is thus doubled, as the 'seeing' house keeps the boy in its eye.[7] This strange figuration has complex ontological implications since an eye cannot see itself (except as mirrored or reflected, that is, as some other eye would see it). The boy in his hunter's "blind" thus looks out from a blind spot, what Jacques Lacan has termed a "scotoma." The implication of the boy doing his seeing from the site of his blind spot is that he cannot see himself, cannot see himself as a voyeur or a stalker, for example, since he sees himself only as a worshipper or a lover. Unlike Stephen, whose peeping at girls or women may have earned him the threat of ocular extinction—"the eagles will come and pull out his eyes" (*P* 8)—this boy's eyes merely burn in anguish and anger at seeing his own solipsism.

My evocation of the predatory image of the hunter emerging from a "blind" to stalk his prey is not intended to impugn the boy for malignancy—since he clearly intends the girl no harm. But I do mean to conjure up the unwitting or blind psychological oppression that obsessives, particularly obsessive lovers, may inflict on their objects of desire. My aim is to complicate idealistic readings of "Araby" as a love story. Warren Beck writes, "Palpably and poignantly a story of adolescent love, 'Araby' rises to this still larger representation, of subjective division under the clash between the idealist's ardor and adverse insuperable circumstances" (106). Such a reading shares the boy's solipsism, and fails to see the maimed discourse produced by the boy's scotoma, his inability to see himself as the girl, for instance, might see him. The first name of Mangan's sister, so familiar and seductive to the boy—"yet her name was like a summons to all my foolish blood" (30)—is never voiced by the adult narrator. Instead, her name is displaced onto the rowdy boy who is her brother, and the rowdy poet, James Clarence Mangan, described by Joyce as "between the drunkard and the opium-eater" (*CW* 76). Mangan's sister has difficulty in the story extricating herself as a person or a subject from the boy's image or imago of her because the narrative voice, like the boy, imagines itself as safe in its blind. Like the boy himself, the adult narrative voice is able to peep and catch fleeting and fragmentary glimpses of her without having to imagine her as peeping back, and catching the voyeuristic boy, and the voyeuristic narration, in her own "gaze." Indeed, the girl's world of peers organizes itself into such a *peerage*, of boys peering at the girl from the shadows, as she peers for them in vain. The narrator describes the reciprocal peering, in which the girl's is "blind"—"if Mangan's sister came out on the doorstep to call her brother in to his tea we watched her from our shadow peer up and down the street" (30).

As much an imagined "symbol of" something as Gretta Conroy on the stair, Mangan's sister is to the boy (and to the narrator in memory) mute, blind, and empty.[8] She appears to him as a cut-up fetish apprehended chiefly in metonymic parts as a rope of hair, a silver bracelet, a white curve of neck, an illuminated hand, a white border of petticoat. Indeed, critics have used just this metonymic description to indict the girl for being "earthly and material," and to read cruel religious significances into her "noose of hair and her silver bracelet."[9] Her brown figure, like the somber brown houses on her street, is never interiorized or furnished with the thought and feeling that would make her come to life. The narration (like the boy) never stops to wonder whether the girl knows that she is followed every morning, or to contemplate how her knowledge—ensured by the boy's passing her to let her know he has been walking behind her—makes her feel. Does she suspect she is being watched through the slit in the blind? Does she recognize herself as an object of obsession—like Reggy Wylie, who may have stopped riding his bicycle in front of Gerty MacDowell's garden to escape her infatuation? Or does the boy's strange behavior play music on her body, as hers does on his? These questions—which might have encompassed the function of her "gaze," her looking back and keeping the boy, and his narration, in her own eye—are never raised by a narration whose blind spots and solipsisms mirror the closed psychic system of the boy.

The subjectivity of the girl can be imagined at all, even if only extratextually, because she speaks.[10] When Mangan's sister speaks, her speech is like a startling irruption in the boy's fantasy, and in the narration. He had dreamed of how it might be if *he* spoke to her—"I did not know whether I would ever speak to her or not or, if I spoke to her, how I could tell her of my confused adoration" (31). But he did not dream that she would speak to him. Her subjectivity, her feelings, never enter into his fevered imaginings. Thus it is startling when she does speak directly to him, the more so because in her inaugural speech, she announces to him *her* desire. Indeed, she gives her desire a name—"*Araby*. . . . It would be a splendid bazaar, she said; she would love to go" (31). In naming Araby as her desire, Mangan's sister appears to be speaking the extratextual fulness of her own name, as though she explicated and amplified her own magical name by endowing it with the interiority of her own desire. Joyce described James Clarence Mangan as a fabulist of Araby—"The lore of many lands goes with him always, eastern tales and the memory of curiously printed medieval books which have rapt him out of his time" (*CW* 77)—with spiritual kinship to the fictional girl who bears his name. Mangan's sister, then, may be as much a romantic as the boy, although her desire is so thoroughly ingested and internalized by him that it becomes utterly expropriated from her. His gesture in embracing her desire and its name exoticizes her image—"The syllables of the word *Araby* were called to me through the silence in which my soul luxuriated and cast an Eastern enchantment over me" (32). But they fail to lead him to confront the possibility of *her* interiority, or to curiosity about her feelings and intentions in calling to him the magical name. When Joyce does open his texts to the interiority of women in his later fictions—the memories of Gretta Conroy, the fantasies of Gerty MacDowell, and the wondrous inner world of Molly Bloom—his works achieve a poetic dimensionality central to their distinction.

Neither the boy, nor the narrative voice, wonders about her overture, which, unexplained, nonetheless issues a series of interpretive prods to the reader's speculation. Is the girl's convent retreat—like Stephen's in *Portrait*—scheduled to preempt and suppress sexual feeling in pubescent girls? Heyward Ehrlich suggests even more pointedly that "the notoriety of the Dublin Donnybrook fair was perhaps on the minds of the parents of Mangan's sister when they sent her on a retreat during the very week of the Araby bazaar" (320). Does the girl, whose silver bracelet betokens small vanities, resent ("It's well for you, she said" [32]) the Church displacing her dreams and scenes of romantic opulence and exotic splendor with impending puritanical strictures and punitive threats? Knowing that one of the neighborhood boys has been watching and following her, does she determine to initiate a conversation that she knows will serve as a romantic provocation? And what happens when the story ends? Does the boy return without a gift, without a romantic story to tell her, without a reciprocal speech of desire—or any speech? Will she neurotically attach herself to the memory of his unrenewed childish devotion, as Gerty MacDowell does to Reggy Wylie ("He called her little one in a strangely husky voice and snatched a half kiss (the first!)" [13.203]), or as Gretta Conroy does to Michael Furey? This speculative retrieval of the girl's subjectivity and interiority could rip the narration open, and let fresh and stirring hermeneutical air circulate through our reading of the story's suffocating idealism if the text would let us escape its solipsistic enclosures. But the interiority of Mangan's sister is consigned to the fate of the brown houses on her street—destined to be furnished, perhaps during her convent retreats, with the leavings of dead priests. "He had been a very charitable priest; in his will he had left all his money to institutions and the furniture of his house to his sister," the narrator tells us of the former tenant of his house, a stifling enclosure in which stale air "hung in all the rooms" (29). Judging from what we know of this house—that some of the "waste rooms . . . littered with old useless papers" were no more than giant wastepaper baskets—the priest's bequest of his leftover furnishings seem a depressing and moribund legacy for any sister.

Yet the story does contain some apertures that would allow circulation along "flaring" routes ("We walked through the flaring streets" [31]). Children's play and the marketplace are two such open social systems that could allow bodies, activities, communication, and culture to circulate. The streets come alive with the noise in the street that is Stephen's Blakean god, when the Christian Brothers' School sets the boys free, or when the drunken men, bargaining women, cursing laborers, and nasal street singers teem over the shopping district on Saturday night. But the boy's temperament and ideology repeatedly repudiate these active social spaces. His repulsion by the quotidian, by the mass or crowd activities of the teeming marketplace figured as a "throng of foes" (31), assimilates the boy's values to High Modernist ideology. The boy's Arnoldian recoil from mass culture makes him a proto-Modernist, already displaying the cultural elitism of the later Eliot and Pound.[11] The boy, attracted to the Orientalism of "Araby," fails to recognize in the Dublin street life the colorful gestures and music of an indigenous bazaar. Its spontaneous and diverse cultural productions ("the nasal chanting of the street-singers, who sang a *come-all-you* about O'Donovan Rossa, or a ballad about the troubles in our native land" [31]) have an indigenous political significance, as Heyward Ehrlich points out. "In the smaller Irish county fair, safely removed from the watchful eye of Dublin authorities, a strong undercurrent of Irish nationalism could be found in the only entertainment available, the ballad singer whose song contained covert political messages," he writes (316). It is therefore in the streets of Dublin rather than at the Araby bazaar that the boy can hear of the Fenian leader Jeremy O'Donovan, also known as "Dynamite Rossa" (Gifford 45). And the *come-all-you* about O'Donovan Rossa might figure another breath of fresh air, a topical and improvised art designed for spontaneous and mass circulation, to stand in contrast to archaic chivalric books of the sort that shape the boy's imagination and the narrator's rhetoric. The images and lore associated with O'Donovan, including the dynamite and the circulation of exile (he was imprisoned, exiled to the United States, but returned to Ireland in 1891) also make him a foil to the entrapped figures of the story. The street singing in the midst of Dublin's urban vitality also serves as a foil to the francophonic affectations of Araby's staged commercial simulacrum, the *Café Chantant*. The *Café*—all historical evidence to the contrary[12]—is represented as closed in "Araby," its only music the mercenary fall of coins. But the boy is clearly attuned to a different music, perhaps the lure of the uncited but silently glossed *Magic Flute* of Mozart which is, unquestionably, "some Freemason affair" ("I asked for leave to go to the bazaar Saturday night. My aunt was surprised and hoped it was not some Freemason affair" [32]).[13] The opera, with its Eastern occultism, its romantic quest, and trial by a gauntlet of spirits, could serve as chivalric analogue for the boy's imagination. We are left to imagine what songs were sounded, as the boy "went from room to room singing" (33) through the "cold empty gloomy rooms" of his house, on the afternoon of the bazaar.

The boy and narrator display far greater ambivalence toward the liberative potential of children's play, although the boy eventually repudiates that too, once he falls under the spell of Eastern enchantment.[14] The theme of romance is introduced circuitously, along the detour of old books and old gardens. A slip along the verbal gloss of leaves, from yellow book leaves to green plant leaves, makes possible the transition from the musty, hermetically sealed house to the verdant garden and its mysteriously alive environs in back. Poetically, the yellow leaves of the dead priest's chivalric books leave their pages to drink in rain that lets them come to life again as "the dark dripping gardens" behind the houses. The boy's garden seems to have received chiefly allegorical attention as the Garden of Eden, the site of the fall whose Serpent is symbolized by the priest's rusty bicycle pump (Collins 95). But stripped of allegory, the story's gardens are redolent with living odors and resonant with the living music of live creatures—"the dark odorous stables where a coachman smoothed and combed the horse or shook music from the buckled harness" (30). The narrator replaces, in the suppler and more scrupulous prose of this lovely description, the florid and histrionic sentiment elided when the narration cuts short the uncle's impending recitation of Caroline Norton's *The Arab's Farewell to His Steed* ("The stranger hath thy bridle-rein, thy master hath his gold;—Fleet-limbed and beautiful, farewell!—thou'rt sold, my steed, thou'rt sold!" [Gifford 47]). The children's play in the winter evenings is explicitly described as an exposure to fresh air, as a stimulus to circulation—"The cold air stung us and we played till our bodies glowed" (30). Their play breaks through the boundaries that tend to demarcate spaces in the story, ranging across middle-class and lower-class neighborhoods along an undifferentiated set of muddy lanes and wet garden alleys. Conflict contributes to the stimulation—"we ran the gantlet of the rough tribes from the cottages" (30)—both in neighborhood play and in the marketplace, where the boy and his aunt run a gauntlet again—"I bore my chalice through a throng of foes" (31). But for the boy this "mimic warfare," as it is called in "An Encounter," takes on the medievalistic colorations of the Crusades, with the gauntlet of "rough tribes" of (presumably) low-bred children from the working-class cottages representing some sort of infidels. The boy's chivalric fascination with Mangan's sister strips the meaning of gauntlet back to gantlet, to its archaic armorial form as a mail or metal glove, a rigid but protective barrier to touch or human contact. Thus the boy's adoration is figured in the solipsism implicit in the prayerful gesture—"I pressed the palms of my hands together until they trembled, murmuring: *O love! O love!* many times" (31)—that has him touch and speak to himself rather than to his beloved. Invoking the Grail legend a number of years before Eliot in "The Waste Land," the boy's romantic pilgrimage ends in a dark and silent hall likened to "a church after the service"—not unlike Eliot's ruined Chapel Perilous, "There is the empty chapel, only the wind's home" (l. 389).[15]

Is the story or narration of "Araby" the very thing the boy was actually seeking: not a gift for the girl but a gift of idealism and spiritual healing for himself. Is the gift of "Araby" a Modernist poetry as Grail to redeem the paralytic philistinism and commercialism of a moribund European capital, or what Ranjana Khanna calls "a metropolitan colony . . . a buffer zone between England and its other colonies"? (100). Does the narrator compensate the boy that is his disenchanted self, for having found the dream of romance empty, by rebuilding it in the form of a quest narrative in which he is re-aestheticized and re-idealized as a poetic knight errant? Where does such a project leave Mangan's sister, except as a set of synecdochic and metonymic images, a disposable prop? Or does her irreducible *otherness* point the boy to possibilities for breaking out of his solipsism? Ranjana Khanna notes, "What the narrator experiences here is the journey into the other, into Araby and woman, only to realize that the other is not his" (100). What did the boy become, or what other identities implicitly cohabit his function as a poetic storyteller? Is he a slightly snobbish academic like Gabriel Conroy, or an intellectual celibate like Mr. Duffy, or a poet manqué like Little Chandler, or a priest? Has "Araby" become another version of the dead priest's chivalric books with their yellow leaves, an archaic and decadent aestheticism that will inspire other idealistic young boys—our own students, perhaps—to indulge their nostalgia for the solipsistic self-absorptions of first love? If so, has the story itself become a sort of dead priest's leavings? Each of these functions replicates the closed circuit of communication and exchange that thematizes the spiritual paralysis in this story not as a figure of motor cessation but as a pneuma of stale and trapped air, a suffocation by art's dead spirit.[16] The boy's closing confession of vanity, which the narrative urges us to disbelieve, becomes the final rhetorical gesture of empty doubling: the creation of a moral fable with a specious moral.

## Chapter 4

# *The Perils of "Eveline"*

With a small aside tucked into his brilliant 1972 essay called "Molly's Masterstroke," Hugh Kenner turned the *Dubliners* story "Eveline" upside down by listening to a couple of commas. Kenner quotes the narration—" 'He had fallen on his feet in Buenos Ayres [comma] he said [comma] and had come over to the old country just for a holiday' " (20). Kenner goes on to say, "Great issues may be said to hang on those commas, which stipulate not only that Eveline is quoting Frank, but that Frank has been quoting also: quoting from the kind of fiction Eveline will believe, the fiction in which ready lads 'fall on their feet' " (20). The upshot of listening carefully for the literary in these repeated and reported conversational snatches is that Kenner is able to speculate a different end to Eveline's adventure than the one she had fantasized. It is a different ending, too, from what the reader is likely to imagine: "The hidden story of 'Eveline' is the story of Frank, a bounder with a glib line, who tried to pick himself up a piece of skirt. She will spend her life regretting the great refusal. But what she refused was just what her father would have said it was, the patter of an experienced seducer" (21). Kenner's reading turned the story away from its more conventional and superficial reading as an exemplar of Dublin paralysis, and brought it into the more sophisticated tradition of Continental "logocentric" writing. In this spieces of intertextual fiction (of which Flaubert's *Madame Bovary* is an excellent example) both the sentimental and melodramatic novel are refigured by showing impressionable young women seduced and abandoned first by the romance novels they take as models for their own choices. R. B. Kershner agrees with Hugh Kenner, when he writes that "As Kenner recognizes, she really has no choice but to fictionalize her choices" (62). In a more recent essay published in *Semicolonial Joyce*, Katherine Mullin further argues that in addition to romance novels, Eveline would also have been vulnerable to a different sort of textual influence: the competing and conflicting emigration propaganda current in Ireland at the turn of the century.[1]

The elegance of Kenner's reading has survived even the convincing challenges posed to it by Sidney Feshbach, and although Feshbach makes a strong case that Frank's conviction as a bounder can be disputed with historical and other evidence, he cannot rule it out altogether. I hope to take up this challenge in a different vein, by asking the question that Kenner doesn't ask until later, in *Joyce's Voices*. Why does the story of Eveline's close shave with disgrace and ruin remain "a hidden story," as Kenner calls it, and why doesn't the third person narrator simply tell us what is going on? My own readings of the *Dubliners* stories repeatedly produce many such "hidden stories" concealed by the narrative voice, including another hidden seduction and swindle in the story that immediately follows "Eveline": "After the Race." This narrative complicity with seduction and betrayal intrigues me. What is at stake in keeping the reader in the dark about what is going on, and obliging the reader to draw inferences, to speculate, to take risks in creating scenarios from uncertain and partial information? Hugh Kenner seems to suggest that Joyce delights in seducing and betraying the reader in order to expose reader fatuousness—"Penny romances are the liturgy of the innocent. The reader believes such stuff" (81). But I will suggest that the narrative stance may have a different and more benign purpose in "Eveline." The reader obliged to make dubious inferences, to be suspicious, to speculate with fragmented and incomplete information, to create scenarios that are unverified and unverifiable occupies a position very similar to Eveline's own. By withholding knowledge about Frank and his motives in courting Eveline, the narration obliges the reader to participate emotionally in Eveline's dilemma in making an agonizing and difficult life decision whose outcome risks disaster for her whatever and however she chooses. The story may therefore have a large and serious objective when it forces readers into Eveline's own interpretive crisis. Its aim may be to recreate in the reading experience the epistemological anguish faced by immense numbers of Irish persons in the course of that country's history when confronting the decision of whether or not to emigrate. Written before Ireland's great economic recovery in the late 1990s, Brenda Maddox writes on the first page of her 1988 biography *Nora:*—"In every young Irish mind, the question of emigration is as inescapable as it has been since the Great Famine of the 1840s" (3). Katherine Mullin has further explored how prospective emigrants from Ireland were historically belabored with varieties of propaganda both to stimulate and allure migrants to New Worlds, or to serve nationalist efforts to stem the tide of emigration with frightening warnings and exposés.

The story itself makes only a few references to emigration, but they are sufficient to indicate that Eveline has at least a subliminal awareness of the social mobility and population movement that is going on around her—"Everything changes" (37), she thinks. The childhood friends with whom she played in the field built over by the Belfast developer have dispersed—"Tizzie Dunn was dead, too and the Waters had gone back to England" (37). Her father, she learns, also saw schoolmates emigrate to such faraway places as Australia. "He is in Melbourne now" (37), Mr. Hill tells of the priest in the yellowed photograph on the wall. Indeed, Eveline's father has an insular sense of Irish emigration and southern European immigration—" 'Damned Italians! coming over here!' " (40) he complains—while Don Gifford maintains that "There is no evidence of a significant Italian immigration to Ireland during this period" (51). Rather, Gifford suggests, the Italians in Ireland at that time might have been failed immigrants—like Frank McCourt's luckless family in *Angela's Ashes*—on their way back to the old country after unsuccessful efforts to get established in America. "Frank" himself—whatever his real name—would have been one of thousands who left the Ireland of his day to seek a better life elsewhere. Brenda Maddox reports that in 1904, 37,413 Irishmen and women left Ireland for better lives elsewhere, including, of course, James Joyce and Nora Barnacle (46). Whatever the temptation to join Eveline's father and Hugh Kenner in stereotyping sailors as "experienced seducer[s]" (Kenner 21), "Frank" deserves to be counted as an émigré in the larger social context of the story. Indeed, Sidney Feshbach historically supports Frank's story by citing the huge immigration that made turn-of-the-century Buenos Aires a city whose adult population were three-quarters European-born, including not only Italians and French immigrants, but also Irish, Welsh, and Scotch (224). However, Katherine Mullin's statistical table of Irelish emigration to Argentina shows zero movement for 1902 and 1903—and she argues that at the time the story was written, the "stereotype" of the successful Irish pioneer in Argentina "had become obsolete" (176). Nonetheless, Eveline, in contemplating her escape, explicitly counts herself as part of an Irish diaspora—"Now she was going to go away like the others, to leave her home" (37).

Inserted into this context of Irish emigration in the story is the focus on the erosion of Eveline's decision by indecision. The brooding of this young store clerk and involuntary homemaker and surrogate mother takes form as an attempt to sift and evaluate her alternatives through a series of memories,[2] fantasies, images, echoes, and fictions. Together these constitute a welter of what Jean-François Lyotard would call "phrases in dispute"—conflicting and competing discourses that are difficult to adjudicate because they convey different criteria and because their genres and objects are incommensurate. The discourses rioting through Eveline's mind are highly heterogeneous, a cacophony of voices in a jumble of emotional registers—fear, anxiety, desire, longing. Some are unpleasant and threatening: little Keogh warning of the approach of her father and his blackthorn stick, Miss Gavan's reproving "Miss Hill, don't you see these ladies are waiting. . . . Look lively, Miss Hill, please" (37), and her father's sarcasm ("had she any intention of buying Sunday's dinner" [38]) and threats ("what he would do to her only for her dead mother's sake" [38]). Comfort, stimulation, and hope come to Eveline through fiction and art, as both Kenner and Kershner have argued. She fondly remembers the ghost story her father tells her when she is ill,[3] and enjoys the Freudian family romance of abduction and restoration to noble estate in Balfe's opera *The Bohemian Girl.* And she listens to the "tales of distant countries" and "stories of the terrible Patagonians" (39) with which Frank, like a modern Othello, seduces her.[4] And finally, of course, there is the siren song Frank sings to her, and tacitly prompts her to emulate, about "the lass that loves a sailor" (39).

Eveline's indecision arises from her inability to adjudicate between the unpleasant realities of a "Home!" (39) that she knows, and an abroad ("Escape!") that is unknowable and that presents itself to her as patently fabulous. But dichotomizing the safe if dreary knowability of Eveline's "home" with the dangerous but exciting unknowability of "abroad" reductively polarizes and simplifies choices that are far more inscrutable and complex. Nineteen-year-old Eveline counts at least two deaths among her contemporaries—those of her favorite brother Ernest and her playmate Tizzie Dunn. The Ireland of home, the narrative implies, may not necessarily be safer than emigration abroad—the moral of Frank McCourt's memoir of a disastrous Irish repatriation.[5] The ultimate moment of terror that convinces Eveline that she must leave is her recognition that if physical escape from the horrors of home is impossible, if—like Eveline's mother—one can't run away or emigrate, then the foreign and the fabulous will "invade" and colonize the domestic, the home, the mind, until one speaks a terrible, untranslatable language ("Derevaun Seraun! Derevaun Seraun!" [40]) to the tune of an Italian organ grinder. Eveline's mother had transmogrified before her daughter's stricken eyes into an alien, a foreign creature, a domestic Patagonian, and Eveline's choice is therefore much more complex and desperate than choosing between level-headed reality and a flight into fantasy. The betrayal Eveline risks in running away with Frank is not necessarily more egregious than the broken promises Eveline's mother suffered. These promises, literally sacred, had been codified under the aegis of the Sacred Heart of Jesus and Blessed Margaret Mary Alacoque, and displayed on the parlor wall. "I will establish peace in their homes," they promised Mrs. Hill, "I will comfort them in all their afflictions," "I will be their secure refuge during life, and above all in death" (Gifford 49). Eveline's mother clearly found neither peace, nor comfort, nor security in her Irish home—either in life or in dying. And Garry Leonard intriguingly suggests that in her discordant linguistic registers, Eveline's mother gives her daughter contradictory and impossible mandates: to hold the home together *and* to save herself from a "life of commonplace sacrifices closing in final craziness" (40).

The difficulty with Kenner's melodramatic scenario of a seduced and abandoned Eveline, is that it offers a glib and easy answer to her dilemma. His reading reduces the story to a single tragic irony: that Eveline would spend the rest of her life regretting a choice that was unwittingly the right one. But was it the correct choice? While Katherine Mullin concurs with Kenner when she characterizes Frank's enticements as "misleading and exploitative emigration propaganda" (177), she also exposes the seduction and betrayal narratives of "social purity campaigners" as a "white slave trade scare" (183).[6] Garry Leonard convincingly challenges the easy assumption that remaining home was the safe choice when he refers to Eveline's twilight meditation as "this frightening lull in her life, a lull that almost certainly precedes the occasion of being beaten for the first time by her father" (96). Both Garry Leonard and Suzette Henke see the menacing and abusive father as a potentially greater threat to Eveline's safety and welfare[7] than the risk of possible seduction and abandonment by a lying sailor. But the point of the story may be less the adjudication of the correct choice than to have the reader experience the interpretive difficulty and desperate uncertainty of making such a life-altering choice. The Kenner theory sets aside as irrelevant the most interesting movement in the story, which is the difficulty of adjudicating alternatives with incommensurate risks—what Suzette Henke, in a psychoanalytic and religious gloss, calls a "trial of the soul" (22). "Eveline serves both as prosecutor and defendant, analyst and spiritual analysand" in weighing "emotion and romantic fantasy against the judgmental voice of conscience," Henke writes. Robert Scholes's theoretically groundbreaking "Semiotic Approaches to a Fictional Text: Joyce's 'Eveline'," adumbrates the internal complexity of Eveline's "brooding" most precisely—especially with respect to her necessary negotiations of past and future. Scholes places stress on what he calls "focus"—"aspects of the events in any story may be clarified by the narrative focus, while others may be hidden or obscured, temporarily or permanently" (74). The story's "focus" prods him into scrutinizing not only the narrative rhetoric, as Kenner does, but also the temporal rhythms (duration and frequency) of Eveline's deliberative process. "She had consented to go away, to leave her home. Was that wise? She tried to weigh each side of the question" (37), the narrator tells us. Like any momentous decision, Eveline's decision to emigrate appears incapable of escaping provisionality and iterability even after it has ostensibly been "made." She seems to have conveyed her decision to Frank for implementation before she has made her peace with it, and in the hours before departure she again rehearses the pros and cons while passage is being booked and arrangements are being made. "The white of two letters in her lap grew indistinct. One was to Harry; the other was to her father" (39). The letters defer the announcement of her decision to her family in a maneuver that simultaneously prevents obstruction of her escape and allows her to defer burning her bridges until the last possible moment. The *time* at issue in her realization that "Her time was running out" (39) is not only her time in her Dublin home, but also her time for continued deliberation.[8] Eveline's panic attack at the dock may reflect less her cowardice or passivity than her distress that her endless, judicious weighing of pros and cons has come to an end before it has produced a reliable resolution to her dilemma.

Is Eveline as fatuous as Kenner supposes her to be? Is she what Robert Scholes calls "a central intelligence who is not very intelligent" (75)? Or is Eveline Hill far more realistic and circumspect in her considerations than, say, a Gerty MacDowell, dreaming of Reggy Wylie and a dark stranger with burning eyes on Sandymount Strand? Curiously, what follows after the narrative tells us that "She consented to go away, to leave her home" (37) is not a rush of romantic thoughts of Frank, the anticipated sea voyage, the upcoming marriage, and fantasies of a home in exotic South America. Instead, her first thought is an absolutely prosaic acknowledgment that in her present circumstance she is assured the fundamentals for survival ("In her home anyway she had shelter and food" [37])—an admission that implies her awareness that these necessities cannot be taken for granted once she leaves home. We quickly learn what that Dublin shelter and food costs her. Not only does she work at the Stores under an edgy and deprecating supervisor all day. She then returns to the house of her menacing and deprecating father ("she sometimes felt herself in danger of her father's violence" [38]) who makes her beg for her own wages back so she can feed his younger children and clean his dusty house. Nor does she imagine that news of her elopement will incite jealousy in her female coworkers, speculating rather that they will "Say she was a fool perhaps" (37). If anything is remarkable in these early passages, it is how resolutely Eveline refuses to cast herself as a romantic heroine. Eveline's description of her anticipated life with Frank may lack naturalistic specificity—"She was to go away with him by the night-boat to be his wife and to live with him in Buenos Ayres where he had a home waiting for her" (38). But neither does it indulge in the sort of aesthetic domestic fantasy we find in Gerty MacDowell's dreams of "a beautifully appointed drawingroom with pictures and engravings . . . and chintz covers for the chairs and that silver toastrack in Clery's summer jumble sales" (13.231). Perhaps it is Hugh Kenner who may be embroidering the simple description we get of Eveline's plan. He describes Frank's improbable success—"a Dublin sailor-boy has grown affluent in South America, and bought a house and sailed all the way back to Ireland to find him a bride to fill it" ("Molly's Masterstroke" 20). *Joyce's Voices* repeats this characterization, of Frank as "a sailor who has 'fallen on his feet in Buenos Ayres,'" who "has bought a house there and is spending a holiday in a rented room in Ireland." Frank's proposal is again described as a willingness to "take her back as his bride to that South American house, though for some reason not gone into they can't get married till they've gotten there" (81). But the text says nothing of Frank's buying a house in Buenos Aires—only that "he had a home waiting for her" (38).[9] And Sidney Feshbach may be on to something when he writes, "As for the question about why Eveline doesn't think about the house she is going to, the answer may be that she is avoiding thinking about still another house to dust" (224). In other words, Eveline's allusion to the home Frank has waiting for her may be no more than a reassurance to herself that in Buenos Aires she will still have "shelter and food" (37), as she does in her father's house. Perhaps knowing what she does about houses and their care, Eveline simply cannot imagine domestic settings as sites of marital bliss. As for Kenner's question about why Frank won't marry Eveline until they get to Buenos Aires, there are several possibilities. The most cogent is that the Catholic Church's requirement of published banns announcing upcoming marriages would have made a secret marriage impossible in Dublin. And Eveline's father, having forbidden her to see Frank, could be expected to interfere with any publicized plan for the marriage of his nineteen year-old daughter. Brenda Maddox reminds us that, when Nora Barnacle eloped with Joyce at the age of twenty, "she was still a minor" (4).

Frank lends himself to easy typology as the predatory and faithless sailor because of the extent to which he appears deracinated both within and by the narrative: given no clear origin, no "people" identified by class, geography, or business. The business that seems to have finally grounded him in Buenos Aires, allowing him to leave off sailing and to settle in one place, does indeed lack the specificity of Harry Hill's work in "the church decorating business" (38). But Hugh Kenner's famous commas ("He had fallen on his feet in Buenos Ayres, he said, and had come over to the old country just for a holiday" [39]) offer a different interpretation as well. Eveline may realize full well that she has only Frank's word for his South American condition, and she may therefore recognize how perilous it is to trust a visiting stranger in the face of her father's ominous warning, "I know those sailor chaps" (39). Perhaps it is precisely to disrupt that stereotype that Frank gives Eveline an extremely specific employment history—"He had started as a deck boy at a pound a month on a ship of the Allen Line going out to Canada. He told her the names of the ships he had been on and the names of the different services" (39)—one that a suspicious father would be capable of checking out if he was concerned about his daughter's welfare. Sidney Feshbach does what Eveline's father does not: he checks up on Frank's story. He determines that the Allen line did indeed conduct travelers between England and North America, and that (according to James Skobie's

*Revolution on the Pampas*) Irish manual laborers in South America earned excellent wages. A rural migrant worker living in Argentina in the 1890s could apparently pay for a round trip passage between the U.S. and Europe with two
weeks worth of wages (224), and therefore afford to return home on holiday.
"On point after point, Frank's story checks out," Feshbach writes (225). Tales
and yarns constitute the time-honored social and cultural capital of sailors, as
Joseph Conrad demonstrates in his fictions. But telling stories of "the terrible
Patagonians" to Eveline does not, in and of itself, turn Frank into a D. B. Murphy.

Part of the difficulty in forming a just assessment of Frank's character may
be attributed to the uncertain sequence through which the narrative gives us
certain information about him. One particularly illogical sequence has the information that Eveline's "father had found out the affair and had forbidden her
to have anything to say to him," followed by the information that "One day he
had quarrelled with Frank and after that she had to meet her lover secretly" (39).
The first statement suggests that Hill learns that his daughter is seeing a sailor,
and forbids her to see him again, without ever having laid eyes on the young
man. The second statement suggests that father and suitor have met on more
than one occasion, and that the father's ban of his daughter's trysts was the result of a specific disagreement with Frank. If so, what did they quarrel about?
Did Hill try to pry into Frank's financial condition and meet a rebuff? Did he
insult Frank by calling him a bounder? Did the quarrel ensue on a Saturday
night when Frank watched Eveline try to wrest some of her wages back from her
father in order to shop for Sunday's dinner? Did Frank remonstrate with Hill
about his drunkenness, or defend Eveline against her father's abuse in some
other way? Was the quarrel about something inconsequential that merely symptomatized Hill's jealousy of his daughter's sexual maturation and independence? Eveline, after all, appeared to have had no expectations of ever leaving
the parental home—"Perhaps she would never see again those familiar objects
from which she had never dreamed of being divided" (37). Besides the ellipsis
marking Eveline's standing up in terror in her room and her paralysis on the
dock, there are other ellipses in this story whose content informs her decision-
making process without our ability to adjudicate it.

If Eveline is remarkably restrained in imagining the *material* details of her
future life with Frank in South America, she is also relatively restrained in the
rhetoric imputed to her imaginings of her *emotional* life with him. For a girl ostensibly bedazzled by a handsome sailor, her feelings for him are repeatedly expressed in language that points to her concerns for safety and security, rather
than to infatuation. Before we receive any description of Frank, he is mediated
as the invisible vehicle for bestowing respectful treatment on her, giving her the
kind of Hegelian recognition that would constitute her as a person, a subject in

her own eyes: "Then she would be married—she, Eveline. People would treat her with respect then. She would not be treated as her mother had been" (37). Garry Leonard points out the fallacy of this line of reasoning, that it was precisely marriage that visited poor treatment on Eveline's mother (102). And he astutely suggests that Eveline's desire throughout the story is consistently pointed toward an indefinable "elsewhere" that may be equated with unrepresentable female desire, or *jouissance.* Clearly, the notion of *difference* between her present known life and her future unknown life, is what Eveline's ruminations attempt to dilate—expressed by the narrative in the open-ended trope of exploration, "She was about to *explore* another life with Frank " (38, my emphasis). The narrative description given of Frank is indeed flattering. Eveline thinks him "very kind, manly, open-hearted," handsome ("his hair tumbled forward over a face of bronze"), and solicitous ("He used to meet her outside the stores every evening and see her home"). The evidence of his actions does nothing to undermine this judgment. He generously takes her to good seats at the opera, sings for her, gives her playful nicknames ("Poppens," "Evie"), and, of course, tells her about both himself and his tales of distant countries (38–39). Eveline's responses to this highly conventional but flawless courtship is surprisingly measured and cautious, "First of all it had been an excitement for her to have a fellow and then she had begun to like him" (39). Rather than fatuity, the most consistent note that runs throughout Eveline's meditation appears one of thoughtful calculation and consideration. She proceeds as though the explicit warnings of her father, and the tacit proleptic denunciations of her coworkers who would think her a fool for running away with a sailor, were not without effect on her deliberations. After all, Eveline knows from her father that occasional charm and kindness can coexist with relentless oppression and exploitation in the same masculine personality. And although she has no grounds for expecting ill from Frank, neither does she have guarantees that his courtship generosity and affection will perdure. When her final image of her demented mother seems to snap her decision into place—"Escape! She must escape! Frank would save her. He would give her life, perhaps love, too. But she wanted to live. Why should she be unhappy? She had a right to happiness. Frank would take her in his arms, fold her in his arms. He would save her" (40)—the tropes all point to safety, security, and freedom from abuse and abasement, rather than toward romantic or sexual fulfillment. "He would give her life, perhaps love, too" is a curiously qualified locution for the thoughts of a bedazzled girl—and, indeed, nowhere does the story tell us that Eveline is in love with Frank, or loves Frank, or that he has told her he loves her. Eveline's fantasy of Frank enfolding her in his arms has an emotional cast that differs markedly from Gerty Mac-Dowell's dream of a "manly man," who would "take her in his sheltering arms, strain her to him in all the strength of his deep passionate nature and comfort her with a long long kiss. It would be like heaven" (13.210).

The hidden story of "Eveline" has many possibilities, including one that corresponds to the overt narrative. Frank could have been a seducer transformed into a savior:[10] moved by the plight of a girl he began by playfully seducing, he determines to take her away from a stultifying and dangerous home, for example. The nature of the promises that have passed between the couple are left sketchy and undetailed. Eveline has "consented" to go away with Frank to Buenos Aires; he has promised to marry her and give her a home there. The registers of emotional intimacy and commitment that may or may not inform such pledges are highly variable and incalculable in any union, and they remind us that marriage is itself an act of emotional emigration, a commitment to traverse to a different emotional, domestic, and social sphere. The vow that seems to count most in Eveline's deliberations is that Frank has promised to take care of her. Having made and fulfilled such a promise herself—to her dying mother— Eveline can both understand it and believe in the possibility that it can be honored. She can even understand its costs and rewards: "It was hard work—a hard life—but now that she was about to leave it she did not find it a wholly undesirable life" (38). Hugh Kenner concedes Eveline's concession, that in some ways her Dublin home life "is not a bad life." "But," he goes on, "it does not compare in glamour with the life Frank seems to be offering her" (20). Yet there is so little evocation of exotic glamour in Eveline's musings that some critics have imagined a gender role reversal in which it is Eveline who is the betrayer, and Frank who is betrayed. Sondra Melzer asks, "Is the innocent Eveline capable of using Frank as a passport from her present life, even with the implication that their mutual love (or at least hers) was uncertain?" (482). This suggestion opens the possibility of speculating an utterly prosaic basis to the elopement of the lass and her sailor: that of a bargained arrangement between the pair. Its fulcrum, for both the man and the woman, may have been a measure of emotional containment within security rather than romance, passion, or adventure—"He would give her life, perhaps love, too" (40). Such arrangements entail risks for both partners, and although the reader's sense of Eveline's physical and emotional perils is much greater, she clearly feels that Frank has also made a material and emotional investment in their elopement. Her most painful regret on the dock is not the loss of the love of her life but a crippling sense of her own ingratitude: "Could she still draw back after all he had done for her? Her distress awoke a nausea in her body and she kept moving her lips in silent fervent prayer" (41).

The "hidden story" that Hugh Kenner imputes to "Eveline" is produced by holes and ellipses in the story. Robert Scholes names these "paralipse," a discursive strategy identified by Gérard Genette. Scholes writes, "He points to the tendency of fictions to employ strategies he calls 'paralipse' or 'paralepse': that is, the withholding from the reader of information which he 'ought'—according to the prevailing focus—to receive; and the presenting to the reader of information which the prevailing level of focalization 'ought' to render inaccessible. Joyce, it seems to me, is a highly paraleptic writer, in 'Eveline' and in other works as well" (75). The most significant ellipsis in the story is, of course, what happens in Eveline's mind between her two extreme and opposite terrors: her memory of her mother's dementia spurring her to escape and her paralysis on the dock when she cannot go. The interval is blank: we learn neither how she gets from her home to the North Wall, nor what, if any thoughts, have shaken her shaky resolve to go through with their plan.[11] The scene Eveline encounters at the dock reminds us of the first sentence of Brenda Maddox's 1988 biography of *Nora*: "To this day departures by sea from Ireland are noisy, anxious affairs" (3). Maddox is merely describing the modern overnight ferry crossing from Holyhead to Euston Station in London. But her evocation of chaos, fatigue, and worry can be multiplied to imagine Eveline's confusion and distress on the dock, full of soldiers and brown baggage, with the whistles and bells of the steamer announcing its imminent departure. After the stillness and solitude of her twilight reverie, the sense of congested motion and human engulfment Eveline experiences on her way toward the ship conjures up in powerful figurative tropes the phenomenology of emigration. Joyce's description particularly evokes the disorientation and estrangement of joining a large aggregation of strangers in a simultaneous yet noncollective movement away from their homelands. And in another ellipsis, neither Eveline nor the reader hears what Frank is telling her "over and over again" about the passage. Is it something to do with where the ship is going, to Buenos Aires or Liverpool, as Hugh Kenner surmises (*The Pound Era* 37)? Or is he telling her that instead of steaming toward Buenos Aires in one of the staterooms with their "illumined portholes," they will be in steerage with the other immigrants? Not yet on board, is Eveline already experiencing the sensations of the seaborne immigrant—not dancing merrily like the lively crowd below deck in the film *Titanic*—but uncomfortable, ill, and frightened? Eveline's last-minute sensation of nausea and fear of drowning—"All the seas of the world tumbled about her heart. He was drawing her into them: he would drown her" (41)—scarcely seems an unrealistic prolepsis of the immigration voyage.

This negative scenario of a failure to emigrate, of fear of emigration, throws into positive relief the courage required to do so, by the thousands of Irish poor who over the years made their escapes to difficult but different lives abroad.[12] By recovering the biographical moment in which this story was written, one can speculatively give Eveline's moment of panic and fear of peril an informative context and illuminating range. As we all know, James Joyce met Nora Barnacle on June 10, 1904 and eloped with the unmarried twenty-year-old on the night of October 8, 1904—not quite four months later. During this interval Joyce wrote the first two *Dubliners* stories for the *Irish Homestead*—"The Sisters" and "Eveline," which was published on September 10, 1904 (Werner 35). The coincidence between Nora's situation during this interval and the donnée of "Eveline" is, as has often been noted, no coincidence at all. Joyce imported dozens of narrative similarities between his own and Nora's domestic situations into the story, to give its dispiriting home scenes their plausible textures. Eveline's fear of her father's blackthorn stick reflects the violence of Nora's uncle Tom Healy, who beat her with a stick for going out with Willie Mulvagh, according to Brenda Maddox (22). Like Eveline, Nora was then forced to date her young man secretly. Like Eveline, Joyce experienced the death of a beloved brother, George, and, of course, the death of an overworked, exhausted, and abused mother. After the death of their mother, Joyce's sisters were left with the care of the younger children with virtually no provision from a drunken father— a plight dramatized both in Stanislaus Joyce's diary and in "Wandering Rocks" in *Ulysses*. Although Joyce was not a sailor like Frank, Richard Ellmann reported that he looked like one to Nora—"She took him, with his yachting cap, for a sailor" (*JJII* 156). And Hugh Kenner points to the Constantine P. Curran photo of Joyce to note that "Frank" is Joyce's first "Portrait of the Artist" (*The Pound Era* 35). Joyce himself was more improvident than any sailor, making Nora's elopement at least as great a risk as Eveline's. "Nora appreciated the enormity of her decision, even though Joyce feared she did not," Brenda Maddox wrote. "By running away unmarried, she too was breaking with the social order and committing an open act of rebellion. She was burning her bridges and she had no way of supporting herself abroad if Joyce left her. In a non-English speaking country she was unlikely to find work even as a domestic servant" (45). Furthermore, Joyce's friends expected the worst from him—"George Russell said he pitied the poor girl, whom Joyce would certainly abandon" (45).

"Eveline" was written as Joyce was preparing to elope with a twenty-year-old woman who barely knew him, and to whom he had little to offer, except— like Frank—a love of music and a promise to enfold her in his arms. It is intriguing to remember that when the story was published in the *Irish Homestead* on September 10, 1904, Joyce did not yet know the outcome of his and Nora's own plan. What, then, did it mean for Joyce to write a predictive ending to his own elopement scenario in which the beloved refuses to go through with it? Sondra Melzer speculates that the story enacts Joyce's ambivalences about taking Nora Barnacle into his artist's exile with him. She writes, "It must have occurred to Joyce that his own simple country girl, Nora, might see him as a means of escape from the conventionality of her life, just as Eveline saw in Frank an opportunity to escape. On the other hand, did Joyce fear that Nora, upon whom he had come to depend, in some way had cheated or would cheat him of the freedom and independence he sought as artist and rebel?" (482). Melzer's point reminds us of a dramatic gender difference in portraying male and female emigration decisions in Joyce's fiction. Stephen Dedalus's diary entries at the end of *Portrait* mythologize the emigration decision as heroic—"I go to encounter for the millionth time the reality of experience and to forge in the smithy of my soul the uncreated conscience of my race" (276). This rhetoric stands in marked contrast to Eveline's "She had consented to go away, to leave her home. Was that wise?" (37). My own alternative to Sondra Melzer's biographical reading of Eveline's decision is to see the story as a dramatized projection of the perilous emotional and rational process entailed by a decision like Nora's to emigrate by way of an elopement. By making Eveline's South American destination much more foreign and remote than Nora's expatriation to the Continent, the risks she faces are intensified, and the perils of her decision are vastly multiplied. Katherine Mullin's account of the pressures of Irish anti-emigration propaganda in 1904, and particularly the scary warnings to single women to beware of white slave trade predators, would have further increased the trauma of a decision like Eveline's. By displacing the proposed elopement to Argentina, Joyce's story usefully reflects the more common emigration scenario that did not land poor Irish women and men in Paris, Zurich, or even Trieste, but rather on the uncertain shores of the Americas or Australia. Joyce writing of "Eveline" in the interval when his own young woman was making her decision could therefore be construed as either a proleptic exoneration or a proleptic homage to Nora. The story functions both as a gesture of understanding the feeling of peril that might make a young woman unable to go through with an elopement or, conversely, a reversed tribute to the courage required by one who did. The twenty-two-year-old Joyce, having already failed once as an émigré, had no illusions about the lives Irishmen lived abroad, nor about the adventure upon which he embarked his young woman. Brenda Maddox extends homage to both of them—"As they turned their backs on Ireland, at twenty-two and twenty, Joyce and Nora had enormous courage" (46).

## Chapter 5

# Masculinity Games in "After the Race"

Joyce's story "After the Race" exhibits a curious paradox. As the *Dubliners* story representing the most powerful figures—economically and socially—the story itself has emerged as perhaps the weakest in the collection, and the one most vulnerable to critical disparagement. Emboldened by Joyce's own judgment—"The two worst stories are *After the Race* and *A Painful Case*" (*SL* 123)[1]—Warren Beck virtually dismisses the story for being "labored" and "awkward" in narrative technique. In comparison to the other stories in the collection, he finds it "less penetrating," "sketchier," and "the least realized" (123). Whether or not one concurs with these judgments, the story's vulnerability deserves to be explored through a somewhat less formalistic prism than Beck's. Like Beck, I am inclined to find the story's weakness linked to the class and status of its figures. But I am less convinced that the story's vulnerability is a symptom of Joyce's social inexperience with the upper middle class, as Beck supposes. "Possibly Joyce, in weighing such a segment of Dublin life, knew too little of it at first hand, and also shared, if anything, some of its naïveté" (124), Beck suggests. I will argue that the story's lack of penetration and sketchiness may be seen as a strategy for staging the paradoxes of masculinity and masculinism.

R. B. Kershner puts his finger on one aspect of the story's vulnerability when he calls Jimmy Doyle a "helpful" animal (in contrast to Eveline's "helpless animal") "who assists in his own embarrassment" (72). Jimmy's embarrassment, of which the narrator is an agent and the reader an uncomfortable spectator, is dilated within a social space defined by the intersection of an *arriviste* class dimension and a homosocial gender dimension. The social insecurities of the Doyles are inscribed in the Victorian resonances of disparaged "trade" in Mr. Doyle's epithet of "merchant prince" (43). And the narrator is quick to remind us that the species of trade was of a particularly vulgar kind ("He had made his money as a butcher" [43]) with possible overtones of graft and betrayal shadowing its success. "He had also been fortunate enough to secure some of the police contracts" (43),[2] we are told of Jimmy's father. But I believe that Joyce's maneuver in depicting the social world of "After the Race" as exclu-

sively homosocial has the effect of generalizing the Doyles' specific social insecurities by complicating their symbolic order with the perils of gender.

More specifically, I believe that Joyce has the volatile commercial economy
in the story—the thrill of fortunes rapidly gained and lost by Doyle *père* and
*fils*—function to trope the Doyles' equally labile symbolic economy of social regard and prestige. The thrill and anxiety that attends uncontrollable gain and
loss—figured also in the various forms of masculine sport and gaming in the
story—can be psychoanalytically grounded in the constitutive effects produced
by the castration complex in the assumption of gender. This may seem an extreme theoretical reach for explaining the Doyles' emotional stakes in the story,
but I find it useful. Jacques Lacan argues that the knot-like structure of the unconscious castration complex produces a paradox. The psychic terror of loss
that produces pathological symptoms in the male is nonetheless necessary for
the achievement of gender identity. Lacan writes, "There is an antimony, here,
that is internal to the assumption by man (*Mensch*) of his sex: why must he assume the attributes of that sex only through a threat—the threat, indeed, of
their privation" (*Écrits* 281). Both male and female children unconsciously "experience" the perceptual error that elaborates the presence or absence of the
male organ into a narrative of violence and loss whose redemption is accomplished by the compensations and appeasements of the gender identification
process. The condition of apparent absence in the female creates a secondary
misunderstanding with a *temporal* significance. The little girl mistakenly construes her imagined "lack" as meaning that castration has already occurred and
is behind her. For the male child, however, it remains proleptic and in the future, a psychic sword of Damocles that constitutes masculinity as only provisionally unmutilated and perpetually threatened and imperiled. I invoke this
speculative elaboration of the Lacanian theory of gender formation in order to
suggest an etiology or cause of primal anxiety for the febrile temper of the action in "After the Race," and behind the provisionality of the narrative rhetoric. The ontological perils of masculinity are both represented and performed in
the text.

Temporality is, of course, the donnée of the story's title—taken from an interview with one of the French contenders for the 1903 James Gordon Bennett
cup race that Joyce published in the *Irish Times* in April 1903. "Will you remain
any time in Ireland?" Joyce asked the racing champion and automotive tycoon
Henri Fournier. Fournier replied with a question—"After the race?" (*CW* 108)—
and answered that he would not. The temporal order of the interview and the
story are reversed—Joyce interviews Fournier *before* the race, but sets the story
*after* the race. Joyce then goes on to invert the causality of Fournier's success. In
the story, the French firm's fabulous prosperity is still merely anticipated, with

"money to be made in the motor business, pots of money" (45). Indeed, the story sketches a fictional genesis of how an enterprise like "Paris Automobile" might have gotten started with the unscrupulous exploitation of a naïve rich young Irishman *after* the July 1903 Gordon Bennett Cup Race. Judging from Joyce's preface to the interview we could speculate that the young Joyce might have wished to take revenge on the highly successful Fournier ("on great shelves extending from the floor to the roof are ranged motor-cars of all sizes, shapes, and colours" [*CW* 106]). The wealthy young man kept him waiting for hours on several occasions before granting a terse and unresponsive interview, "it is almost impossible to see M. Fournier unless one is prepared to wait two or three hours for one's turn. . . . The morning, however, is more favourable, and yesterday morning, after two failures, I succeeded in seeing M. Fournier" (*CW* 107). In "After the Race" Joyce inverts the psychological temper of the scenario—if not its deep structure. He makes the blasé young Frenchman, who yielded only the dull and meager calculations of speed to Joyce in the interview, now eager to impress the young Irishman with his automotive knowledge: "Rivière, not wholly ingenuously, undertook to explain to Jimmy the triumph of the French mechanicians" (46). Joyce sets the story at a liminal moment when the young Frenchman's fortune hangs in the balance of a fictional transaction whose tender is purely symbolic. He will manipulate the metaphysical desire of Jimmy Doyle, his thirst for prestige and recognition, for social status, that Garry Leonard formulates in Hegelian terms as "Jimmy Doyle's slavish dependence on the Other to authenticate the myth of himself" (116). This Hegelian genealogy informs Lacan's coincidence of the genesis of desire with the genesis of gender, by identifying masculinity as the ongoing negotiation with the Other in the quest for significance, and defense against its loss. One can speculate that the young Joyce—stung by the young Frenchman's *hauteur* and disregard—went on to undergird the founding of the modern French automotive industry with a fable of French masculinism's exploitation of Irish social and cultural insecurity.[3]

Like many other *Dubliners* stories, "After the Race" hints at an embedded hidden narrative that can be inferred and interpretively constructed from the narrative account of the narrative events, but not verified. The liminality of the story's moment—the poising of the events on the evening after the race as a threshold for changing fortunes—holds the key to a specific scenario of a young Irishman's exploitation by a group of sophisticated foreigners whose actions have the ethical significance of a seduction and rape. More specifically, I will argue that the story's hidden action could be characterized figurally as a kind of homosocial date-rape or gang-rape. To construct this scenario, the issue of temporality needs to be clarified with respect to the timing of Jimmy Doyle's investment in Ségouin's company. The ambiguity of the language—"Ségouin, perhaps, would not think it a great sum" and "he was about to stake the greater part of his substance" (44)—leaves the matter somewhat unclear. Garry Leonard assumes that the investment has already taken place ("Doyle has invested a good deal of his father's money in Ségouin's new motor establishment" [115]). But I will suggest that we can account for the Continentals' blandishments of Jimmy and the Doyles better by reading the temporal tense of the investment as proleptic, as anticipated. We can then impute the extravagance of the evening's arrangements and excitements to the grooming of a business deal that has been pledged but not yet consummated. One can speculate even further that the evening's events could be the outcome of a venture to secure Jimmy's promised investment without the legal and commercial encumbrance of the Doyles. By carefully devising a glamorous evening leading to a drunken game of cards, the dazzled and overstimulated young Irishman can be simply stripped of the money he is known to possess ("he really had a great sum under his control" [44]). The cunning and unscrupulous ploy even leaves Jimmy feeling responsible for his own defrauding—"Jimmy did not know who was winning, but he knew that he was losing. But it was his own fault for he frequently mistook his cards and the other men had to calculate his I.O.U.'s for him" (48).

Although my scenario is difficult to prove, there is nothing in the story that precludes it, and it therefore remains available to our reading of the plot.[4] The notion of a conspiracy on the part of a group of young non-Irishman to defraud the rich young Dubliner of his fortune, requires that we assume a deep level of hidden preparation. This would make their plot a variant analogue to the common eighteenth- and nineteenth-century novelistic marriage swindle in which a young cad, feigning greater wealth and rank than he possesses, courts a plain young woman of great fortune with the intent to deflower and defraud her. This plot, which can readily be read into gaps between the lines of the narrator's curious locutions, melds quite seamlessly with many small allusions to masquerade, including gender masquerade, throughout the story. Jimmy's mounting debts, we realize, may have begun not at Dublin University, but at Cambridge, where "he had met Ségouin" (43). Jimmy does not know Ségouin very well ("They were not much more than acquaintances" [43]), and neither does the narrator, who repeats—but does not verify—the rumour of Ségouin's fortune, that "he was reputed to own some of the biggest hotels in France" (43). Jimmy's father's approval of this friendship, and his urging of an investment of Jimmy's fortune in Ségouin's proposed automotive venture, take on the colorations of paternal support for an advantageous "match" for his son. Although it is careful to qualify it as an appearance, the narrative voice nonetheless reports that "Ségouin had the unmistakable air of wealth" (45). Ségouin himself further primes the Doyles by heightening the aura of his commercial eligibility—

"Ségouin had managed to give the impression that it was by a favour of friend-ship the mite of Irish money was to be included in the capital of the concern" (45). The young French motor mavens, aware of Jimmy's twin interests of music and cars ("he divided his time curiously between musical and motoring circles" [43]), take care to satisfy both. Their racing interests and motor enterprise satisfies the latter, and they import a musical Hungarian ("Villona was entertaining also—a brilliant pianist" [44]) to appeal to the former. Jimmy's twin passions can be seen as indulged simultaneously during the triumphal ride back to Dublin after the race, when Jimmy gets to ride in their "lordly car," (45) while being sere-naded by Villona's "deep bass hum of melody for miles of the road" (44).

The title of "After the Race" might reflect, like Joyce's interview with Fournier, a moment in a discourse, perhaps the answer to the query "When?" if the discourse is construed as a conspiracy against Jimmy's money. The narrator himself supplies the "why" of this timing, when he explains that "Rapid motion through space elates one; so does notoriety; so does the possession of money. These were three good reasons for Jimmy's excitement" (44). The liminality of the story's moment *after* the race exploits the ambient effects of elation and celebration after the successful race as atmospheric contributors to the bedaz-zlement and seduction of Jimmy Doyle, who is configured as the ingenue among his "friends." His vanity puffed up with the ride in a gorgeous car and the glow of reflected celebrity, Jimmy is introduced to a French racing cham-pion who dazzles him with a brilliant smile ("the swarthy face of the driver had disclosed a line of shining white teeth" [44]). The event is staged amid a crowd of onlookers transformed into an admiring audience—"It was pleasant after that honour to return to the profane world of spectators amid nudges and sig-nificant looks" (44). An intimate, but gala, dinner is planned for that evening at Ségouin's hotel—an event that even bedazzles Jimmy's family, who have pro-nounced it "an occasion" (45). The strange narrative interlude that depicts the family's pride as they stand in the hallway, approving their son's formal attire and ingratiating themselves with his companion, has the character of the launching of a debutante, or the parental blessing of a young couple on prom night.[5] "Jimmy, too, looked very well when he was dressed and, as he stood in the hall giving a last equation to the bows of his dress tie, his father may have felt even commercially satisfied at having secured for his son qualities often un-purchasable. His father, therefore, was unusually friendly with Villona" (45). But like parents watching their child go out on the town with a young foreigner who is, finally, a stranger—credentialed only associatively by the good name of Cambridge—a "certain pride mingled with his parents' trepidation" (45) as Jimmy goes off with Villona.

The aura of romance that imbues the evening incorporates other figures who are unexpectedly interpolated into the scene. The dinner party is enlarged by the addition of an Englishman named Routh, "whom Jimmy had seen with Ségouin at Cambridge" (46) and therefore does not appear to know. But although it remains undecidable whether the late addition of Routh, and the accidental meeting of the party with the American Farley, are prearranged and part of a plot, the narrator seems to suggest that virtually nothing about the dinner party is casual or spontaneous. Even Jimmy detects Ségouin's deliberate orchestration of the social interactions—"He admired the dexterity with which their host directed the conversation" (46)—and the reader can readily divine Ségouin's intentions. Rivière, who, "not wholly ingenuously, undertook to explain to Jimmy the triumph of the French mechanicians" (46), and Villona, who holds forth on the English madrigal, are set up to appeal to Jimmy's twin passions for motor racing and music, respectively. The narrator's betrayal of Rivière's disingenuousness suggests that other aspects of the heady talk are contrived for Jimmy's benefit. Villona's disquisition on the madrigal sets up both the theme and the mood of the romance of the pastoral. Its conventions eventually infect the narrator's own rhetoric—"The resonant voice of the Hungarian was about to prevail in ridicule of the spurious lutes of the romantic painters when Ségouin shepherded his party into politics" (46). Villona's specific inveighing against inauthentic music and contrived painting might have served as a self-reflexive warning to Jimmy to listen for the spurious in the lute of Villona's discursive music and to question the authenticity of the tableau in which he takes part. Instead, Jimmy's ill-trained imagination is 'kindled' at the outset to represent his friends with an artificial and decadent image. Kershner identifies the "grotesqueries" of this trope as "parasitism and suppressed homoeroticism" (73). "Jimmy, whose imagination was kindling, conceived the lively youth of the Frenchmen twined elegantly upon the firm framework of the Englishman's manner. A graceful image of his, he thought, and a just one" (46), we are told. Jimmy, an incompetent judge of his own words as we see in his later inability to assess the merits, or demerits, of his drunken speech, fails to recognize the potential truth his strange fantasy may embed, of entwined and colluding snakes replacing the ivy of the imagined pastoral scene.

Ségouin is a sinister shepherd in this pastoral under electric lights. As the young Frenchman leads an Irishman and an Englishman "into politics," the narrator's comment—"Here was congenial ground for all" (46)—is either stupid or sarcastic. But the prevailing happy mood is such that Jimmy and Routh are difficult to egg into open political conflict, with "the torpid Routh" slow to react to the Irishman's slow retrieval of the "advanced Nationalist" sentiments his father's prosperity had buried. One could construe that Ségouin's intention was precisely to provoke the "danger of personal spite" (46) in order to give the planned card game, toward which all the various arrangements are tending, a personally and nationally rancorous edge. This ensures that the betting will run very high (48) and require the exchange of paper in the form of I.O.U.s that can be readily manipulated ("the other men had to calculate his I.O.U.'s for him" [48]). Cosmopolitan toasts are repeatedly required to tamp down the incipient national animosities. "The alert host at an opportune moment lifted his glass to Humanity," (46) we are told, and "They drank Ireland, England, France, Hungary, the United States of America" (47).[6] When all animus is past, they toast "the health of the Queen of Hearts and the Queen of Diamonds" (48). These repeated toasts further ensure that by the time the game is in progress Jimmy will have been thoroughly incapacitated with emotional overstimulation and the narcotic effects of excessive drinking.

As the young men stroll through Dublin after their glamorous dinner, their meeting with the American, Farley, appears—or is staged to appear—accidental. The narrator even narrates the exact exchange of surprised greeting, as if to underline that the meeting is unexpected: "—André./—It's Farley!" (47). Farley's role in the swindle plot is crucial to configuring the impending assault on Jimmy's money in para-erotic terms at the same time that he provides the historical context to give Jimmy's robbery a gendered social meaning. On the level of narrative plot, Farley's yacht provides the remote and secluded venue for the swindle's consummation that will make Jimmy's escape impossible. However, the yacht's name—*The Belle of Newport*—sets Jimmy's misadventure in a specific historical moment, the dizzyingly rapid industrial expansions of turn-of-the-century America with their ethically altered acquisition of wealth memorialized in the epithet "robber baron." Further, the yacht's feminized name conjures the double gender track that furrows the *arriviste* universe of new money with parallel perils for the male world of business and investment and the female world of the marriage market. Joyce could not have read Edith Wharton's *The House of Mirth*, which was published in 1905, the year after the publication of "After the Race" in *The Irish Homestead*. But Wharton had begun publishing her stories in *Scribner's Magazine* in the 1890's. Joyce, who is known to have read and liked some of the short fiction of Henry James (*JJII* 193) may have been exposed to an American brand of social criticism that might have complicated the genre of the "gentleman's magazine" story critics believe may have been parodied in "After the Race" (Kershner 72). Wharton's *House of Mirth* retrospectively glosses Farley's world of American Newport society by depicting not only the predations of the marriage market for the "belle of Newport" but also the ravages of ruinous gambling debts Lily Bart incurs by playing bridge beyond her financial resources. *The Belle of Newport*, I would suggest, lays a curiously heterosexual configuration over the ideological homosocial chivalry of

Dumas's *Three Musketeers*—which Kershner sees as the plot enacted by Jimmy Doyle the night after the race (75).

Aboard *The Belle of Newport* the boys' night out mimics a scene of heterosexual play fueled by mirth, liquor, and abandon ("They drank, however: it was Bohemian" [47]) that devolves into the dissipations of orgy. "Villona played a waltz for Farley and Rivière, Farley acting as cavalier and Rivière as lady. There was an impromptu square dance, the men devising original figures. What merriment! Jimmy took his part with a will; this was seeing life, at least" (47). As the group plunges into the card game, Villona plays "voluntaries" (48)—an ironic musical accompaniment to the hidden coercions that force Jimmy to remain in frenzied rounds of games whose pleasure gives way increasingly to unpleasure as Jimmy's losses begin to mount. The chaotic and confusing scene harks back to the merry car ride at the story's opening, whose hilarity is only imperfectly accessible to Jimmy, thanks to the noises of wind, car, and humming that make conversation difficult. "This was not altogether pleasant for him, as he had nearly always to make a deft guess at the meaning and shout back a suitable answer in the teeth of a high wind. Besides, Villona's humming would confuse anybody" (44), the narration concedes. On board the yacht, Villona's music now accompanies the gambling with improvised "voluntaries" that underline the hidden misery of Jimmy's predicament.[7] A coercive situation in which he has lost all control will nonetheless present itself to him as "voluntary"—"it was his own fault for he frequently mistook his cards and the other men had to calculate his I.O.U.'s for him" (48). By the time the narrator utters Jimmy's wish, "They were devils of fellows but he wished they would stop" (48), his protest sounds as anguished and helpless as that of a date-rape or gang-rape victim. The card game, whose ludic surface conceals the rigid code of "honor" that will ensure brutal enforcement of its financial consequences, affects Jimmy like an amorous adventure gone awry and become abusive. By the last game, nothing is left to chance, Jimmy is scarcely in the running ("he would lose, of course. How much had he written away?" [48]), and after a last throb of excitement, the game is over. Jimmy is left abjectly slumped over the table in a stupor of incipient pain. Routh, not Ségouin, has won the climactic game, an outcome that makes it necessary to assume a collusion between the traditional national enemies, the Englishman and the Frenchmen, as well as their American and Hungarian accomplices, to achieve the coup of legally robbing Jimmy of the planned investment.

But the depth of the conspiracy, as well as the extent of Jimmy's loss, affects chiefly the degree rather than the nature of his ruin. Both Jimmy's losses and the scope of his anagnorisis—the altered self-perception produced by recognition of "his folly"—remain indeterminate. Are his losses, though clearly beyond "the limits of reasonable recklessness" (44), still recuperable with the aid of a forgiving father? Or has he squandered his birthright, the "great sum under his control" (44) that represents his entire capital, the familial portion the twenty-six-year-old assumed upon attaining his majority? What illuminations will his anticipated regret bring him with the sobering daybreak? Will his epiphany embrace his layers of degradation—the pain of his father's disgust; self-loathing for his fatuousness as "a creature driven and derided by vanity," like that of the boy in "Araby"; anger at the betrayal by bogus friendship and abused trust? Will it extend to the more intimate recesses of self-recognition—to seeing that his friends' exploitation of him was merely a form of counter-exploitation, and that they exploited his wealth and immaturity as he had exploited their prestige and worldliness? Will he finally recognize that the worth he has lost was always already lost, that he had commanded a spurious regard only on the basis of his detachable appurtenances—his money, Cambridge, smart clothes, and familial indulgence?

The depth of Jimmy Doyle's mourning in the morning is largely incalculable—although we are led to imagine it will exceed mere detumescence, the aftermath and denouement of pleasure, the hollowness associated with the morning after, after the ball, when the party's over. We are supplied with at least one measure of Jimmy's ability to calculate his loss: the "solid instinct" that lets him "translate into days' work that lordly car in which he sat"(45). Jimmy's planned investment was "a serious thing for him" not only because he was staking "the greater part of his substance" on Segouin's motor enterprise, but because he knew precisely "with what difficulty it had been got together" (44). For all his bedazzlement by wealth and glamour, he understands its material base in the substance of the body's labor. We are virtually assured that he will be able to quantify his lordly losses in squandered years'—rather than days'—work. But his ability to admit the psychic brutalization to which he has been subjected remains unknowable. There is every possibility that he could remain in the oblivion into which he tries to sink himself on the morning after the race. He blocks out the morning light with his hands and suspends himself in a "dark stupor" that admits no images of loss, betrayal, or self-reproach, by counting only the raw life that remains, "the beats of his temples" (48). Such an outcome would insert the dark specters of trauma and repression into the fatuousness and blindness that had once been his innocence.

But the reader who has performed a critical analysis of the fate of Jimmy Doyle must confront the lesson of gender that is inscribed in the specific politics of Jimmy's overdetermined violation in this story. Eve Kosofsky Sedgwick's parable of social power requires only minor skewing to effectively map her gender dynamism onto the scene in "After the Race." Pointing out that male entitlement "required certain intense male bonds that were not readily distinguishable from the most reprobate bonds," the condition of male entitlement incorporates the threat of social and psychological foreclosure that inspires "homosexual panic" (185). The plot of "After the Race" is precisely the pursuit of male entitlement through intense male bonding, and although what Jimmy experiences is homosocial betrayal rather than homosexual panic, its outcome produces a similar lesson about the arbitrary and manipulable symbolic ground on which masculinity is constituted as a vulnerability. What Jimmy construes as male bonding in the service of consolidating entitlement turns out to have been a charade that concealed his feminization by the Continentals. His "friends" not only refuse to reciprocate his regard, but they translate his regard for them into the instrument by which they are able to prey on him, and to mutilate his ability to recover the psychic ground from which he could reclaim privilege. His friends strip Jimmy not only of money, but of the membership in homosociality needed to secure the position in the symbolic order that is designated as masculine. Kershner says bluntly, "In terms of all the traditional popular signifiers of virility, Jimmy is unmanned" (77).

The Continentals have "queered" or feminized Jimmy Doyle. They have deployed his naïvete on the one hand, and used his aesthetic sensibilities, his appreciation of style, refinement, glamour, to mark the domain in which his "complicity" was manipulated. That complicity is, of course, spurious since Jimmy is an aspirant to an acculturated masculinism—and the point of masculinity's vulnerability to annihilation that issues from the illusion of its arbitrary and provisional grounding is thereby drawn all the more painfully. Jimmy's extrusion from male privilege demonstrates Teresa de Lauretis's argument that "The term *gender* is, actually, the representation of a relation, that of belonging to a class, a group, a category" (4). Insofar as this positionality of gender is determined by cultural technologies, masculinity in "After the Race" is constructed through such homosocial texts and subtexts as those discussed by Kershner. Dumas's *Three Musketeers*, drinking songs, the choruses of *Cadet Roussel* ("with linked arms, singing *Cadet Roussel* in chorus, stamping their feet at every:—*Ho! Ho! Hohé, vraiment!*" [47])—these fictions guarantee camaraderie and homosocial inclusion without advertising the concomitant requirement of oppressive or exploitive exclusions. The masculinism that inheres in the camaraderie of men requires the exclusion of the feminine and the effeminate in order to define its privilege. Interestingly, Joyce may have achieved an insight into the calculus of masculinity from a curious rejoinder made by Henri Fournier, the prototype of Ségouin, during his 1903 interview. Asked to size up his racing competitors, including a certain Mr. Edge, Fournier demurred by silence. Joyce pressed him by asking, "He won the prize the last time, did he not?"

(*CW* 108) to which Fournier replied, "O yes. . . . But, you see, Mr. Edge won, of course, but . . . a man who was last of all, and had no chance of winning might win if the other machines broke" (*CW* 108). Gender, like being a contender, is a matter of positionality.

But the story does not simply present us with an enlightened insight into the end of gender, because the metaphysical masculinity game that hides beneath the social masculinity games in "After the Race" is, after all, only dimly transparent, if not opaque, to the uncritical, or precritical, reader. We have as much trouble "hearing" or comprehending what is going on, as does Jimmy—whose difficulties with communication (Leonard 114) might serve as a caution to the reader. Like Villona's humming, the narrator's elegant and wry prose distracts us from the holes and silences in his story. Why doesn't the narrative voice that knows enough to ironize the Irish spectators of the Gordon Bennett Cup Race as "the gratefully oppressed" (42) simply tell us of Ségouin's designs on Jimmy's money? Why not describe to us the means and motives of the swindle of the card game that divests Jimmy of money he would gladly have invested? Perhaps I should be obliged to concede that there may be no plot, that the story's donnée may be simply "Jimmy Doyle's Bad Night After the Race." But my question draws attention to the narrative refusal to tell us very much about the Continentals and their orchestrations of this particular evening ending in the debauch, if not complete ruin, of their Irish friend. The narrative reticence illuminates the strangely liminal—and, I would argue, sinister—position of the narrator as one of "them," as a Continental, or a crypto-Continental. Surely the narrator who "knows" so much about Jimmy and his family and their values also "knows" something about the Continentals and their friends and their values? Why would he not "know" the motives and maneuvers of Jimmy's "friends"? Why could he not tell us whether or not there is a conspiracy, a callousness, a carelessness, or some other attitude that contributes to the evening's outcome? By refusing to betray what he knows, the narrator can legitimately be construed as a discursive accomplice to a plot to defraud and humiliate Jimmy Doyle without betraying the conspirators or incriminating himself (a narrator gendered not only as male, but as masculinist). The narrator's part in the game of masculinity is to expose Jimmy's foolishness, his vulnerability and fatuousness and its cost, but without, simultaneously, exposing his friends' villainy. The narrator takes care not to compromise Ségeouin and his friends as "gentlemen," even though the last word of the story is as ironic as the title opening the next story, "Two Gallants." The effect of this maneuver is troublesome for us, as readers, because it allies us with Jimmy Doyle and positions us, epistemologically in the same place. The narrator's collusion with the Continentals also constructs us, the readers, as "helpful animals" assisting in our embarrassment, as Kershner puts it. We confusedly apprehend Jimmy's appalling state at story's end, perhaps blame him for it in some inchoate way, yield some empathy for his pain,[8] and yet fail to discern fully or clearly the mechanism by which it was achieved. The narrative control of information and interpretation appears designed to obstruct and frustrate our *political* understanding of the story. In terms of gender politics, the narrator has contributed to our own proleptic "queering." By giving us the illusion that he confides in us, that we are sharing in the male bonding necessary for entitlement as "knowing" or comprehending readers, we are given the illusion—like Jimmy—that we belong to the circle of masculine privilege. But these very gestures and maneuvers simultaneously extrude us from the conspiracy by making us helpless to penetrate it and thereby to assert our claim as cognoscenti and manipulators of the gender system.[9] By having its narrative "perform" the dynamic of masculinism that it thematizes in "After the Race"—the exercise of privilege and male bonding dependent on the marginalization and extrusion of the arbitrarily feminized—the story's text teaches us masculinity's paradoxical constructions through the experience of our own troubled, inconclusive, and imperfect reading.

## Chapter 6

# Gambling with Gambles in "Two Gallants"

Like a number of other *Dubliners* stories, "Two Gallants" is uncertain on the level of significance because it is fundamentally uncertain on the level of narrative and plot. Some crucial information is strategically withheld from the reader that obliges us to construct a crude scenario of what we think is going on in this story. This scenario—that a repellent young man doubly despoils a young servant girl of "virtue" and money—is readily supported by the story's central trope of a Celtic harp and its mournful song ("*Silent, O'Moyle!* . . . Lir's loneliest daughter / Tells to the night-star her tale of woe" [Gifford 59]) to produce an equally crude allegory of Ireland's colonial degradation figured as a complicitous surrender to sexual predation:

With this image of the harp as fulcrum, the chiasmic structure of the simple, deeply significant action of the story achieves its balance. As Corley moves up to the money paid him by the slavey, he moves down at the same time to the ultimate degradation of a gallant, the absolute denial of the romantic ideal. And in both aspects of this act, he is the "base betrayer," not only of his own potentially gallant manhood, but of Ireland as represented in him. (Boyle 101)

Extratextual scholarship readily supports this allegory, whether it proceeds by explicating the quotidian geography of street names and places (Torchiana) or by poring over Joyce's letters. In his letter to Stansilaus, for example, Joyce refers to the elder Dumas, and to the theories of gallantry inscribed in Guglielmo Ferrero's *The Young Europe* and *Militarism.*[1] Elaborated with this textual information and with theoretical formulations, the ethical restatement of the story's central scenario takes on political complexity. R. B. Kershner puts it this way— "Gallantry, in short, is a variety of objectification and depersonalization that is especially pernicious because it mimics and parodies romantic devotion while replacing the interpersonal element with impersonal economic exchange" (86).

But to complicate the allegorical reading or its scholarly elaborations, I think it worth returning to the story's strategically controlling narrator and the occlusions, silences, and mysteries with which he (a provisional "he," since the gendering of that voice is itself an issue) hermeneutically hobbles and torments us. The chief gap, I will argue, resides in the cleaving (in both senses of the word) of that "two" in the story's title. The narration's principle task is to interrogate the identity implied by that "two," to explore the tensions in the reciprocities, collusions, and dependencies of the two "paired" "young" "gallants." My difficulty in speaking of the two men without consigning their every characteristic to the qualification of the "so-called," is mirrored in the awkward wrestling of critics to find a rhetoric adequate to the way the story seems to mediate their relationship through a sexual project. Suzette Henke strains for a language of ethical outrage when she writes, "Lenehan, for his part, derives voyeuristic satisfaction from Corley's adventures and, while downing a plate of peas, fantasizes about his friend's triumphant sexploitation of this gullible country lass" (26). E. L. Epstein, on the other hand, replicates their obscenity—"It has been suggested that the 'oil' and 'pivot' of the description make Corley out to be mechanical, a mere copulation-machine. I believe he resembles something more physical, something which corresponds to his role in the story—an erect phallus. (And Lenehan is his 'hanger-on.')."[2] Epstein's brief note doesn't support the untenable metaphoric notion of the servile Lenehan as Corley's balls, but his impulse to translate the story into pornographic allegory has some justification.

I will argue something similarly outrageous, if not entirely outraged, in this essay, and that is that I believe "Two Gallants" is designed to enact, and thereby unmask, some fundamental premises of *pornography* taken in its Greek etymological sense, as a writing about harlots or prostitutes (*porne*). "Two Gallants" is porno-graphy insofar as it is a tale of the production of prostitutes—an illustrated etiology of their social construction from economic need and cultural disesteem—that resembles modern pornography (and prostitution) in its foregrounding of the obscene and prurient to peripheralize and occlude economic motives, forces, and transactions. Under "prostitutes" I include not only the exploited slavey of the story, and the girlfriend Corley cites as her predecessor, but the "two gallants"[3] themselves and, beyond them, the story's readers. In broadening the meaning of "prostitution" in this way, I intend it to encompass fiscal and symbolic economies in which labor is unproductive and can only circulate minimal resources throughout a bankrupt system. Such a reading extends Joyce's social critique beyond the Irish allegories ("a slack and indifferent nineteenth-century Irishry that stands by as the nation is defrauded" [Torchiana 91]) produced by the story's traditional criticism. Indeed, I am inclined to read the narration's literal display of pathetic fallacy in the Celtic harp of the story—"His harp too, heedless that her coverings had fallen about her knees, seemed weary alike of the eyes of strangers and her master's hands" (54)—as a "blind." Lenehan uses this term for a diversion to throw someone off the track when he tells the Citizen and his cronies in "Cyclops" that the "courthouse is a blind" and that Bloom "had a few bob on *Throwaway* and he's gone to gather in the shekels" (12:1550). The narrator's rhetorical act in exhibiting Ireland metaphorically as a sad, degraded whore employs a blunt and obvious pathos that distracts the reader's attention from the more trenchant and unsentimentalized degradations in the story to which both narrator and reader may remain "blind." The more modern, Ibsenite[4] critique of bourgeois mores and bourgeois storytelling emerges intertextually rather than in crude tropes. It emerges through the story's placement between a gambling story ("After the Race") and a shotgun wedding story ("The Boarding House"), and by reading "Two Gallants" through its *sequellae* in *Ulysses*, where we again meet Lenehan and Corely.

Before attempting this intertextual suture of two fictions, it is important to begin with the story's beginning, in order to establish with precision the nature of the troublesome gaps. The conspicuous lyricism of the opening paragraph sounds the melody of a verbal harp arranging its phrases in lovely musical variations—"The grey warm evening . . . a mild warm air. . . . the warm grey evening air" (49) that creates not only an aesthetics of urban recreation, but also an aesthetics of poetical prose. Frank O'Connor finds in this "beautiful paragraph . . . a remarkable development of the prose style in the earlier stories" (21). "Like illumined pearls the lamps shone from the summits of their tall poles upon the living texture below" (49) not only exhibits poetic language, it proffers it with an air of exhibitionism, displaying prose as a beautiful woman might be displayed to a cultured customer. The opening passage also announces and enacts a misleading theme of "circulation"—the passage and exchange of warm air, milling people, and lambent words. But it suppresses its coming enactment as unproductive pedestrian, physiological, and economic movement and exchange. Corley and Lenehan will walk and talk ceaselessly—both in this story and in *Ulysses*—and get nowhere, and their figurative circulation of young blood will be checked as sexually sterile ("I was afraid, man, she'd get in the family way. But she's up to the dodge" [51]) and medically and economically dry, leeches sucking fiscally anemic organisms and squeezing blood out of turnips. When the two men appear, they are introduced as anonymous strangers—"Two young men came down the hill of Rutland Square" (49)—who are initially seen but not heard. "One of them was just bringing a long monologue to a close," we are told, but the narration tells us neither what was said nor names its discursive nature and effect. We infer that one of them told a joke producing laughter in the other from a totally externalized description ("the narrative to which he listened made constant waves of expression break forth over his face from the corners of his nose and eyes and mouth" [49]). The narrative objectivity—betrayed by the fluency of expression and rhetoric—nonetheless serves to establish Lenehan's behavior, grimaces, and laughter as a mask that belongs to the masquerade of his "sporting" costume. The yachting cap, white rubber shoes, and light waterproof "expressed youth" (50), we are told, although their prudent function to keep him dry betrays his thirty years as much as does his paunch and his thinning and graying hair.

The narrative action of the opening could also be described, in content and form, as a pantomime. We are shown two figures *miming* a conversation, in narrative language that *mimes* ("made constant waves of expression break forth over his face from the corners of his nose and eyes and mouth") what narrative language would normally say, that Corley's joke made Lenehan laugh. The pantomimic quality of the story's opening may be construed as a paradigm announcing the strange sign-system of the story as a whole. For this story of the "two gallants" and the slavey will continue to function as a pantomime even when speech is restored to the figures, and will continue to require that the readers actively interpret a series of ambiguous and unexplained gestures. When Lenehan is finally properly introduced by name and reputation ("Most people considered Lenehan a leech" [50]), this aspersion is quickly qualified to mean that he sings for his supper, as it were, or performs for his drinks. Lenehan uses the devices of an amateur vaudeville comic in the way of making a living— "He was a sporting vagrant armed with a vast stock of stories, limericks, and riddles" (50). Thus we may relate Lenehan's *modus vivendi* to that of the street musician with the harp—an ad hoc performer working for provisional donations. In this respect Lenehan fits Joyce's construction of "the tradition of the Irish writers of comedy that runs from the days of Sheridan and Goldsmith to Bernard Shaw" (*CW* 202). The bitter edge of this characterization comes through when he describes the luckless Oscar Wilde as "court jester to the English." The story's opening signals that we will receive such a performance, a bit of melodrama ("Lenehan made a tragic gesture. —Base betrayer! he said" [53]), a bit of pornography, a bit of caddish impudence to which we too might say "Of all the good ones ever I heard . . . that emphatically takes the biscuit" (51).[5]

The narrative voice completes its cinematic approach by moving from scanning the colorful Sunday street crowd to the silent focus on the two figures. Now close enough to hear their conversation, we are given to understand that we break in upon it *in medias res*—"And where did you pick her up, Corley? he asked" (50). The remaining action of the story will be the enactment and test of this conversation, in which a man boasts of his sexual and romantic prowess. The tension experienced by Lenehan, and presumably the reader as well, will hang on whether or not Corley can make good his boast. Thus the action of "Two Gallants" is already inscribed in the two-part narration delivered by Corley, and becomes in a sense a pantomimic superfluity, acting out in silent gestures what has been first delivered in words of discourse. The mimetic function of narrative is reversed as narrative predicts rather than reports an action, or rather repeats an action that, Corley boasts, is infinitely repeatable. Indeed, the portent of Corley's story (and of "Two Gallants") seems to reside in the peril of *repetition*, particularly in reference to the relation between word and deed. But I hope to show that it is *reversal* that finally takes the biscuit.

Corley tells his story in two episodes reversed in time—a present case followed by a past case—whose relation is symptom and cause as well as statement and implication. The story of how Corley met the unnamed slavey—whom we will *see* (or "squint" at, like Lenehan) but not *meet*—achieves its effect by a reversal of convention, particularly gender convention. Corley has effected a *reverse* courtship, a *reverse* gallantry, and a *reverse* prostitution. Instead of giving his young lover ("I spotted a fine tart") the generosity and honor of gallantry, he calculates to deceive her ("I told her I was in Pim's") and defraud her. "Cigarettes every night she'd bring me and paying the tram out and back" (51), Corley boasts to Lenehan, without remorse at having her steal from her master and defray their expenses from her meager salary. By passing himself off as middle-class (the fictional "lost" job at Pim's gives him respectability: "The Pims were Quakers and were widely regarded in Dublin as models of sober commercial reliability" [Gifford 57]), he clearly plays to her middle-class aspirations ("she thinks I'm a bit of class, you know"). Corley's second story of how he began treating women this way will reflect on the first, and illuminate the young woman's peril. Conventional courtship ("I used to take them out . . . pay the tram or take them to a band or a play at the theatre or buy them chocolate and sweets") was quickly recognized as an unprofitable "mug's game" (52)—"damn the thing I ever got out of it" (52). The one young woman whom he did get something "off of" ended up a prostitute "on the turf." The reader readily apprehends this peril for the present slavey, particularly if her petty thieving to get Corley her master's cigars costs her her job and references.

When the gold coin glistens in Corley's hand at the end of the story, no narrative explanation is necessary because the reader has been equipped to supply both action and moral—though not totally without ambiguity. We construct either of two scenarios from our inferences. The young woman has been importuned for money on a trip to the Donnybrook field where Corley took her on the first tryst. She has either given him the equivalent of nearly two months' salary (Gifford 62), and thus bankrupted herself—possibly for a ruinous investment in a hope for middle-class marriage. Or she has stolen the money from her master, in which case she has utterly delivered herself into the power of a policeman's son and police informer. In either case, the brink of "the turf" looms closer for her at the end of the story than it did at the beginning. The narration thus becomes a peculiar "pornography," a writing about prostitutes, or at any rate *reverse prostitutes*, young women who perversely ruin themselves by paying rather than earning from sex.

This solution to the riddle of the coin by no means settles the much more central and troublesome riddle of the story, namely, why two young men would make the gratuitous ruination of a woman a *joint* project—particularly since it appears to profit only one of them.[6] This mystery—which I believe is the real crux of the story—has two parts. First, why is Lenehan involved in the project of Corley's seduction, and second, why does the narrator not tell us why Lenehan is involved in Corley's project? With this question posed, we are reminded that the narration, in fact, splits when the two men separate in the middle of the story. The narrator, curiously, stays with Lenehan (who does nothing but eat peas and drink ginger beer) instead of following Corley and the slavey to the Donnybrook field to report *their* conversation and *their* doings. The story, it turns out, quite deliberately eschews a pornographic turn, and chastely foregoes an opportunity to narrate the operation and activity of seduction (what does Corley tell or promise the slavey to get her to produce the money?). Instead, we merely receive Lenehan's fantasy of it—reported, as so much in this story, in the form of pantomime. "In his imagination he beheld the pair of lovers walking along some dark road; he heard Corley's voice in deep energetic gallantries and saw again the leer of the young woman's mouth" [57]). But although the way Suzette Henke reads this fantasy—as prurient voyeurism—seems nearly inescapable, the psychological context that generates it is far more lugubrious than salacious.

In the interlude of Lenehan's walking, eating, and anxious waiting a generic shift occurs that transforms the narrative from locker-room escapade to naturalistic pathos. When performing for Corley, Lenehan "wore an amused listening face" [49]), which is described as an assumed mask. "Now that he was alone his face looked older," we are told, and the solitary Lenehan is described as unmasked, his performer's backstage life revealed as lonely, empty, and squalid. The narrator's description of the pathos of the weary harp has now been transferred to the pathos of another weary instrument of entertainment. "He knew that he would have to speak a great deal, to invent and to amuse, and his brain and throat were too dry for such a task" (56), we are told, reminded that Lenehan can barely afford a meager plate of peas and a soft drink. We are prodded to understand that Lenehan's behavior with Corley—his avid voyeuristic interest in Corley's romantic conquests and flattery of his profitable sexual exploits—was such a performance. But a performance is by definition not identical with its motive. If Lenehan was "playing" at being a cad's audience and toady—"You're what I call a gay Lothario, said Lenehan" (52)—then his calculated and performed gestures must be set off against some other motive, attitude, or intention with respect to Corley's treatment of the slavey. But it is precisely this authentic state of Lenehan's affairs, feelings, and labor, that the narrator veils. Several clues prod us to make inferences, and we are thus obliged to engage in an activity of speculation that itself replicates Lenehan's ruinous occupation: gambling. "No one knew how he achieved the stern task of living, but his name was vaguely associated with racing tissues" (50).

I will now speculate wildly—though not groundlessly—on the nature of Lenehan's performance with Corley, and on the conditions that motivate it, by reading "Two Gallants" backwards in time through its seeming *sequellae* in *Ulysses*. Although *Ulysses* was, of course, written later than *Dubliners*, the time of many of the stories is coterminous with the general time frame of *Ulysses*.[7] The year of "Two Gallants" is indeterminate in the story, although the month is specified very precisely as August. The age and condition of Lenehan and Corley appear similar to their appearance in *Ulysses*. But I find no necessity for assuming, as Torchiana does, that the events of *Ulysses* occur *after* those in the story ("As for Corley, Joyce saw to it that he would fall upon even more evil days by early morning, 17 June 1904" [106]). Since "Two Gallants" transpires in August, the events of *Ulysses* would need to follow almost a year later if Torchiana is correct. But there is no reason why the events of "Two Gallants" can't be thought to occur in August 1904—six or more weeks *after* Bloomsday. By supposing this, I can create a heuristic fiction that, while not verifiable, usefully employs the added information about Lenehan and Corley that Joyce provides in *Ulysses*.

According to this scenario, June 16, 1904 is a disastrous day for Lenehan. We first see him emerging from the office of the editor of *Freeman's Journal* carrying the "*Sport*'s tissues." His first words are "Who wants a dead cert for the Gold cup? . . . Sceptre with O. Madden up" (7:387). All day Lenehan functions as a tout—although it is not clear whether he is paid by *Sport* (Boylan's secretary, Miss Dunne, calls him "that gentleman from *Sport*" [10:394]) or whether he disburses his tip for a certain Ascot winner so prodigally in order to lubricate future good will. He is in excellent form all day, playing word games, telling his *Rose of Castille* riddle, his limerick about Professor MacHugh, and his own story of feeling up Molly Bloom on the carriage ride after the Glencree reformatory dinner. He mooches cigarettes by courteously lighting them for his smoking friends, who then feel obliged to offer him one. In "Wandering Rocks" he stops in at the bookmaker's to place his bet on Sceptre—which appears to be quite large ("Madden had lost five drachmas on Sceptre . . . Lenehan as much more" [14:1125])—and dissuades Bantam Lyons from betting on the twenty-to-one long shot *Throwaway*. He meets Boylan at the Ormond Hotel bar and assures him that "Sceptre will win in a canter" [11:374]) and flirts with a barmaid while waiting for the wire to announce the results of the race. The loss is devastating. When we see Lenehan in Barney Kiernan's, he's described a having "a face on him as long as a late breakfast" (12:1179) and he's told "You look like a fellow that had lost a bob and found a tanner" (12:1215). Having promoted the losing horse all day, Lenehan has lost not only what appears to be a considerable amount of money, but his credibility as a racing tout and possibly whatever sort of income it brought him. Later, in the early hours of the morning, Stephen runs into Lenehan's friend Corley on his way to the cabman's shelter. Corley complains that "His friends had all deserted him." Specifically, he says that "he had a row with Lenehan and called him to Stephen a mean bloody swab with a sprinkling of a number of other uncalledfor expressions" (16:146).

We don't learn what the row between Corley and Lenehan was about, but I will hazard a guess. If the row occurred that evening, it may be that after realizing his gambling losses, Lenehan tried to collect money from Corley. We know from "Eumaeus" that Corley borrows from the brokest of the broke, and even manages to squeeze a halfcrown out of the homeless, jobless Stephen. He may in past have borrowed from Lenehan, who now faces debts of his own, possibly including some to urban "gombeen men"—the moneylenders who lend "small sums of money to workmen at usurious interest" (159)—as we learn elsewhere in *Dubliners*. According to the narrator of "Grace," their clients from time to time "smarted in person or by proxy" under the "exactions" of their enforcers (159).[8] On June 17, 1904, Corley, with "Not as much as a farthing to purchase a night's lodgings" (16:145), may well have angrily rebuffed Lenehan as a "mean bloody swab" for trying to collect his loan at such a moment. This background would do much to explain the situation of "Two Gallants." We can readily imagine that after the colossal mistake of touting the wrong horse in the June 1904 Gold Cup, Lenehan's formal or informal business would be hurting, and he might not yet have recovered by August. He therefore approaches Corley again for repayment of his loan, but this time far more carefully. Corley is, as usual, "on the rocks" (16: 156), but he thinks he might be able to get some money out of his current slavey. This, I speculate, is what Lenehan and Corley are discussing when the narrator spots them coming down the hill of Rutland Square. Lenehan is properly nervous and skeptical, but can't afford to show his anxiety. It's impossible to know what is at stake for him, but if he must produce money to repay his own debts by a certain time, he may be risking life and limb on Corley's gamble.

Lenehan therefore encourages Corley's boasting not only to flatter and encourage him, but in order to mollify him after their previous falling out. He also wishes to assay his possible success. His questions—"Well . . . tell me, Corley, I suppose you'll be able to pull it off all right, eh?" (52)—may express more anxiety than prurience if Lenehan has something personal and serious at stake in the outcome. "But tell me, said Lenehan, are you sure you can bring it off all right? You know it's a ticklish job. They're damn close on that point. Eh? . . . What?" (53). This insistence also explains Corley's irritation and Lenehan's nervous desistance—since Corley's alternatives for raising Lenehan's money may be far more unpalatable and uncertain. "Lenehan said no more. He did not wish to ruffle his friend's temper, to be sent to the devil and told that his advice was not wanted. A little tact was necessary" (54). Lenehan's curious insistence on looking over the slavey ("Let's have a squint at her, Corley" [54]) now takes on a meaning that even Corley can't divine ("Are you trying to get inside me?" [54]). Of course Lenehan doesn't need or want an introduction. As a racing tout, he is accustomed to inspecting horseflesh to estimate a horse's potential for winning. He simply carries this practice over into his current gamble.

By transforming Corley's exploit with the slavey into a gamble, the narrative events of "Two Gallants" assume the figurations of the Gold Cup in *Ulysses*. Lenehan's success is always in the hands of other sportsmen—O. Madden, the rider of Sceptre, or Corley, the seducer—with Lenehan doomed to wait out the results. But there the similarity ends. During the Gold Cup, Lenehan was buoyant with confidence and the free drinks and cigarettes earned by his popularity. On this occasion he's pessimistic and broke. He has had to bribe Corley with his own precious cigarettes, stay out of the pubs, frequent working-men's temperance eateries, where he looks out of place ("To appear natural he pushed his cap back on his head and planted his elbows on the table" [57]). He has had to cadge free biscuits from grudging curates—a bit of gall that mimics his own favorite idiom for gall ("That takes the biscuit!" [50]). During the last half-hour of his wait, Lenehan's nerves become so taut that the narrative begins to betray the excess stake that is elsewhere concealed. The psychic agitations of Lenehan as he waits on Merrion Street are far too violent if Lenehan's role in Corley's project is merely voyeuristic. Lenehan also strikes me as too nervous and edgy for stakes that are merely gratuitously profitable, as Garry Leonard suggests—"Lenehan would shove off with little or no excuse if he did not like Corley's prospects of buying a few rounds later in the evening" (122). One moment Lenehan is sure it will work ("he was sure Corley would pull it off all right" [59]); the next he is sure it will not ("He knew Corley would fail; he was sure it was no go" [59]). His anxiety is described in overwrought language—"He suffered all the pangs and thrills of his friend's situation as well as those of his own" (59)—accompanied by overwrought gestures:

All at once the idea struck him that perhaps Corley had seen her home by another way and given him the slip. His eyes searched the street: there was no sign of them. Yet it was surely half-an-hour since he had seen the clock of the College of Surgeons. Would Corley do a thing like that? He lit his last cigarette and began to smoke it nervously. He strained his eyes as each tram stopped at the far corner of the square. They must have gone home by another way. The paper of his cigarette broke and he flung it into the road with a curse. (59)

Why would Corley give Lenehan the slip, if the whole project is a game contrived for their joint amusement with the aim of a night's drinking as its profit? Yet Corley might well wish to give Lenehan the slip if he were returning empty-handed and had still to face the reckoning for the loan. Or, even more basely, Corley might have gotten the money but decided not to let Lenehan have it after all. Even when Corley does turn up, Lenehan's fear of Corley's failure is translated into a visceral trope of physical violence and pain—"An intimation of the result pricked him like the point of a sharp instrument. He knew Corley would fail; he knew it was no go" (59). And as Corley walks swiftly toward Stephen's Green, Lenehan does indeed pursue him ("Anxiety and his swift run made him pant" [60]) as though Corley were giving him the slip. By the end of the story Lenehan, "breathing uneasily," confronts Corley with barely contained violence—"He was baffled and a note of menace pierced through his voice.—Can't you tell us? he said. Did you try her?" (60). When the gold coin is produced, Lenehan is provisionally saved.

Let me now theorize the implications of my speculative insertion of a financial transaction between Corley and Lenehan as the motive for Corley's sexual project on this particular evening. This situation recodes the story's title in a highly gender-significant way. The title is emptied of its irony and reinfused with new meaning, because gallantry was indeed affirmed by its events. Only the meaning of the terms has shifted gender—from a man's honorable relation to a woman to a man's honorable relations to other men. The hidden superior moral code of the story is the homosocial one—the set of rules that defines honor between men. In turn-of-the-century Ireland these rules regulate the informal exchanges of money that keep men liquid in a system of minimal resources.[9] Honor requires men to grant small loans, pay up on bets, stand drinks, and settle debts in cases of necessity. This male code of honor is strained when the informal transactions press against commercial and legal obligations that might be met with force, such as evictions for unpaid rent, the threat of furniture repossession, loan sharks' enforcement of unpaid debts, and the like.

"Two Gallants," I argue, presents not one hidden financial transaction but two—one semi-visible, the other nearly invisible—that are related as implying contrasting codes of male honor. The ironic significance of the double code can be read in the resonant meaning of Lenehan's panicked fear: "Would Corley do a thing like that?" (59). The point of outrage within the story is not that Corley would seduce, deceive, exploit, and defraud a young slavey (in danger of being "brought to police court through doting on a Corley" [Beck 145]). Outrage bristles at the prospect that Corley might welsh on repaying a badly needed debt when he had the means to do so. That Corley honors the bargain confirms his gallantry where it matters. In this homosocial world still infused with the ideology of Dumas's *Three Musketeers* (as Kershner argues for both "After the Race" and "Two Gallants" [74–77, 81–86]), the "two gallants" maintain the code of "all for one, one for all." Their seeming identity—momentarily sundered by the narration and threatened by its events—is restored in the end. The ironic twist to this ironic tale of displaced honor does not occur until *Ulysses*, when Corley's shadowy occupation ("He was often to be seen walking with policemen in plain clothes, talking earnestly" [51]) is unmasked as police snitch. Corley commodifies his gallantry toward men as surely as he commodifies his gallantry toward women: selling them out when the occasion and the need arises. He repays Stephen's loan of the halfcrown with gratuitous gossip about another Dubliner—"he informed Stephen about a fellow by the name of Bags Comisky that he said Stephen knew well out of Fullam's. . . . Anyhow he was lagged the night before last and fined ten bob for a drunk and disorderly and refusing to go with the constable" (16:205).[10] Corley is indeed a "base betrayer"—only the term is melodramatic and comic if the victim is a woman, and ethical and serious if the victim is a man.

With this twist the story's philosophical point may be enlarged to conclude that morality in Dublin—even morality of the most serious kind as in honor among men—is unmoored by arbitrariness and randomness. Honor between cads is provisional at best, and in all probability no one is safe from Corley's informing: neither the thieving slavey who does not know his real name and therefore cannot implicate him, nor Lenehan, if Corley were to get the goods on him, nor Stephen, for that matter. The two senses of "the turf" operative in this story—horse racing and prostitution—depend on a structural homology of the interchangeable and arbitrary roles of horses and women, and the infinite repeatability of the activity. This is why my reading finally does not depend on the 1904 Bloomsday Gold Cup for credibility—because Lenehan's bankruptcy could have been caused by any Gold Cup, or any race, or any gamble gone bad—just as Corley's luck in gambling on a woman's affection could have worked with any slavey. The larger economy behind this bankrupt morality is something akin to the collapse of all symbolic economy—all honor or value. Corley may be a corrupt cad, but we see him in *Ulysses* virtually begging for a job carrying sandwich boards. In a bankrupt financial economy in which there is no productive labor, human beings are forced to squeeze money out of the self, their bodies, their discourse, their wits, their luck. People in Dublin, and perhaps by implication in the Ireland of the early twentieth century, are shown to be running on empty in *Dubliners*.[11] We see empty or "stony" people obliged to squeeze each other for resources they don't have—dry leeches sucking other dry leeches, eating dry biscuits like Lenehan, or sucking the empty air of cigarettes. Lenehan squeezes Corley who squeezes Stephen who squeezes AE for small loans—though on this August day they squeeze a slavey who perhaps squeezes her master.

The same principle of empty circulation may also govern discourse in "Two Gallants." The story remains a pantomime, an empty or mutilated language, even when discourse is offered. The narrator frequently gives us words without their meanings and we realize only afterwards that we have been told nothing. What do we learn when the narrator tells us of Lenehan, "He suffered all the pangs and thrills of his friend's situation as well as those of his own" (59)? What *is* Corley's "situation," and what *is* "his own"? If we contrast the narrators of the *Dubliners* stories with the narrators of *Ulysses*, we note the amazing amplitude and prodigality of information we receive in the novel. The narratives of *Ulysses* tell us much more than we have a right to know, than we need to know, and, in some cases, than we want to know. In contrast, the "style of scrupulous meanness" that governs the writing of *Dubliners* exceeds the aesthetic economy of a taut and muscular Modernism. It also performs an ethical retention and control, a penurious stinginess about releasing excessive or satisfying information, motivated by bourgeois protection of privacies and regulation of social truths. Thus the narrator of "Eumaeus" is an informer who informs on the informer and thinks nothing of betraying Corley's moral indecencies. In contrast, the narrator of "Two Gallants" is the Third Musketeer who upholds the male code of honor and doesn't embarrass his friends by revealing that Lenehan is in desperate trouble and that Corley is pressed to pay up, and feared, by Lenehan, to be unreliable. By concealing the economic transactions behind the sexual schemes of "Two Gallants," the narrator also conceals that the prostitute of his porno-graphy is not the slavey but Corley himself. If Corley is the first "gallant" for paying his debt to Lenehan, the narrator is the second gallant of the "Two Gallants," for concealing the plight of a Corley obliged, by his desperate poverty, to sell his sex to the slavey for a gold coin.

The narrative plays along with the moral fiction of melodramatic base betrayal, the indulgence of the seduction and exploitation of women tolerated by Romantic fiction, as Kershner has shown (83–84), but refuses to discuss the precarious moral codes of honor among gentlemen. The reader is put in the position of a d'Artagnan—perhaps a more naïve version of an aspiring musketeer—scandalized or titillated by the amoral boldness of the gay Lothario, but inducted into the code of male honor by the example of narrative discretion rather than by participatory initiation. Put differently, the reader is obliged to play the bourgeois response to prostitution—scandalized and titillated by its transgressions of social mores, but shielded from acknowledging its own role in the moral bankruptcies that underlie its hypocrisies in confronting the vulgar economic truths of the modern world. This is the sense in which I argue that "Two Gallants" acts out, but unmasks, pornography—a dishonest and manipulative writing about harlots. Ada Ciniglio sees the "two gallants" of the title as part of a different trio: the "three Gallants" on their way to a wedding banquet, who meet Coleridge's "Ancient Mariner." Her scheme is intriguing because it would make the reader the Gallant detained, the epiphanic "sadder and wiser" listener instructed by the tale of transgression.

But I maintain that the reader of "Two Gallants" is split—like the reader of many *Dubliners* stories—into a gullible narratee or a prescient critic, depending on whether we trust the narration or the text (the narration with gaps filled in and missing information supplied), the teller or the examined tale. Put differently, the narration is Ibsen (a dramatization of bourgeois hypocrisy and blindness) while the text is Zola (a story with disagreeable particulars and squalors detailed). "The worst thing that will happen, I suppose, is that some critic will allude to me as the 'Irish Zola'!" (*SL* 86), Joyce promised his publisher Grant Richards. Joyce was right in specifying that it would take a critic to identify the story as Zola. The common reader constructed by the story is more likely to respond to the entertainment provided by the pantomime climaxing in the cheap thrills of a trick ending, like that of an O. Henry or a Maupassant (Kershner 88). Like the harpist on Kildare Street, the narration gilds the vulgar economies of the Dublin streets with the melancholy of the Celtic note, the imagined Romanticism of a Little Chandler, throwing more than a little moonshine into our eyes. Like the young slavey, we are vulnerable to being taken in by the poetry of the narrative palaver—"He too gazed at the pale disc of the moon, now nearly veiled, and seemed to meditate" (53)—thinking we've come upon "a bit of class." But in the end we experience the dynamic tension of all its parts and effects: narrative bedazzlement and moonshine, melodrama and swashbuckling adventure, costumes and finery, scandal and shock, poetry and slang, discretion and gesturing, veils and secrets, layered transactions and layered betrayals. All these effects work together to explain why Joyce considered "Two Gallants" one of the best stories of *Dubliners.* "To omit the story from the book would really be disastrous," he wrote Grant Richards on May 20, 1906. "It is one of the most important stories in the book. I would rather sacrifice *five* of the other stories (which I could name) than this one. It is the story (after 'Ivy Day in the Committee-Room') which pleases me most" (*SL* 88).

## Chapter 7

# Narrative Bread Pudding: "The Boarding House"

"She made Mary collect the crusts and pieces of broken bread to help to make Tuesday's bread-pudding" (64), we learn of Mrs. Mooney, the butcher's daughter, in "The Boarding House." The passage goes on to enact the servant's gesture of boarding house thrift by serving us the twice-baked crusts, as it were, of the previous evening's events. The form this narrative bread pudding takes is the redaction of a trimmed and hard account of Mrs. Mooney's and Polly's confrontation the night before, from which the interesting substance or "meat"—the juicy sexual and transgressive content—has already been extracted and consumed in advance. Why would Joyce, at the advent of his career in 1905, leave the opulent novelistic and dramatic possibilities of nineteenth-century literature behind, and feed us this bland and tasteless bread pudding of a story? The austerity of the narration makes it clear that Joyce is here "modernising himself," as William Johnsen puts it (6). But the story of this story is not over, as we are surprised to discover that in *Ulysses* the ongoing scandal of the Mooneys and the Dorans is served up again, in "Cyclops," this time in an unsavory glut of succulent detail. The stylistic disparity between the two accounts—one cold and spare, the other hot and excessive—draws attention to the story's rhetoric and makes it clear why Joyce declared himself "uncommonly well pleased" (*SL* 63) with it. He clearly knew exactly what he was doing with this experiment in styles of narration.[1] His retrospective revisitation of this family in *Ulysses* does more than sate our narrative hunger by giving us the story's ending and moral: that young people united in shotgun weddings tend not to live happily ever after. By supplementing with prurient gossip the insubstantial bread pudding of the *Dubliners* story, a point about the function of narrative language and composition seems added as well. Joyce uses *Ulysses*, I would suggest, to critique the modernistic prose of "The Boarding House" as a replication of and collusion with the hypocritical moralism that is the story's donnée.

In offering an anatomy of a shotgun wedding, Joyce has "The Boarding House" implicitly critique Christian morality's vulnerability to serve immoral purposes, following a modern philosophical tradition inaugurated by Nietzsche's *Genealogy of Morals*. This double transgression of sexual despoliation "remedied" by union enforced with threats of social, economic, and physical violence exposes the hypocrisies of a bourgeois morality that is sanctioned and buttressed by the institution of the Church. Bob Doran is made vulnerable to Mrs. Mooney's coercions by his sacramental confession prior to their confrontation—"the priest had drawn out every ridiculous detail of the affair and in the end had so magnified his sin that he was almost thankful at being afforded a loophole of reparation" (65). The weight of force in the story resides in institutions, and although they are never represented as such in the story, this force is tacitly vested in forms of language and communication: the confession, the legal case, the threat, blackmail, the negotiation, the bargain, the marriage proposal. Joyce anticipates in "The Boarding House" Michel Foucault's elucidation of the role of institutional discourse in the service of social domination.[2] This point is quite overt and accessible in the story. What is less accessible to the reader is the prospect that art or fiction might itself represent one of these institutional discourses bent on social domination, and that the narration of "The Boarding House" is itself suspect and must be interrogated for misdirection[3] and provocation to misprision.

What initially exempts the art of "The Boarding House" from skepticism by a readership accustomed (since the eighteenth century, at least) to unreliable narration, is precisely the Flaubertian purity of its modernistic style. The story's narrator has the impersonality and objectivity promoted in Stephen Dedalus's aesthetic theory, and therefore invites no resistance to judgments that appear to emerge from facts that seem to be speaking for themselves. Yet there are two possible explanations why the composition of this story (as well as the others in the collection) was so significant to Joyce that he fought for it with great urgency. In defending the integrity of the stories' language to Grant Richards in 1906, Joyce pleaded that the "points on which I have not yielded are the points which rivet the book together. . . . I fight to retain them because I believe that in composing my chapter of moral history in exactly the way I have composed it I have taken the first step toward the spiritual liberation of my country" (*SL* 88). In the absence of narrational commentary and opinion, the "composition" of the story would bear the burden of providing the informational wherewithal for interpretation and readerly judgment. But beyond that, the "composition"— presumably encompassing the selection and arrangement of scenes as well as the rhetoric and epistemology of the narration—would make it possible to see the extent to which the seemingly formalistic and disinterested narration nonetheless manipulates the material in ways that create opportunities for misguided interpretation. Modernistic prose, with its spare and lean language and the seemingly narcissistic self-reflection that appears to give it purely formalistic and aesthetic self-interest, is revealed, in Joyce's stories, to be by no means innocent.

The exposure of the ideological complicity of the narration in the very hypocrisies and coercions it purports to critique depends precisely on those elements of composition that make the text behave performatively. The narrative voice that begins by telling us of Mrs. Mooney—"She was a woman who was quite able to keep things to herself" (61)—quickly demonstrates that it too, no less than Mrs. Mooney, Bob Doran, or Polly Mooney, knows how to keep things to itself. The narration frequently gives us only redactions—synopses or summaries—of characters' thoughts and memories that are themselves already redacted, already edited and trimmed for a leaner and harder presentation. These redactions can aptly be troped as narrative crusts or rinds because they are rational and literary forms for thoughts whose content is omitted. The story is structured according to virtually classical unities.[4] A double set of confessions on Saturday night (Polly confessing to Mrs. Mooney and Bob Doran confessing to the priest) is followed by a double meditation (Mrs. Mooney's calculation of her strategy and Bob Doran's terrified anticipation of its consequences) on Sunday morning precisely between 11:17 and 11:30. The story's climax is an implicit pairing of double sacrificial rites: the "short twelve" Mrs. Mooney will attend at the pro-cathedral on Marlborough Street after the off-stage slaughter of Bob Doran as her sacrificial lamb ("She dealt with moral problems as a cleaver deals with meat" [63]). But the confessions, the actual affair of Bob and Polly, the painful confrontation between Mrs. Mooney and Bob Doran, and the farcical marriage proposal it produces, are all *unrepresented*[5] except through the cold redactions Joyce referred to, in a letter to Stanislaus, as "the frigidities of 'The Boarding-House' " [*SL* 69]. Joyce—whose titles in *Dubliners* often serve as rhetorical euphemisms for the text—deliberately makes of the story a textual boarding house in which the reader is served narrative bread pudding.[6]

As a story composed of the rhetorical crusts of redactions, "The Boarding House" raises the issue of authority that the impersonality of modernistic writing simultaneously affirms and subverts. The narrative redaction gives us fragments of information that imply that the narrative voice knows more than it tells. This allows the narration to project or adumbrate a totalized understanding of the whole affair, of which it tells us little and shows us less. At the same time, the fragmentariness of the redactions renders the narrative account incomplete and singular enough to admit the possibility of other versions and other accounts. The product of this double-sided hermeneutical effect is not only the misprision of the story's moral issues, but also the misjudgment of the moral neutrality of modernism's style of "scrupulous meanness." The most troublesome of the narration's hermeneutically misleading fragments occur at the end of the story, when Polly Mooney's thoughts are indicated but not represented—"She rested the nape of her neck against the cool iron bed-rail and fell into a revery. There was no longer any perturbation visible on her face" (68). We are told the occurrence and the effect of the reverie—that is, its form or crust—but not its content or substance.[7] While producing a stylistic effect of simplicity and an affect of peace and calm, the narrator has promoted an interpretation of Polly Mooney's role in her lover's institutional predation without having ventured an opinion or made a statement. But the implicit interpretation produced by the narrative—that Polly is a cool player in her mother's game—preempts alternative and different interpretations that could make this story far more heteroglossic and complex than it seems. Once we factor in the silent discourses with which the story is fraught, its interpretation begins to dissolve into a series of "phrases in dispute" that are extremely difficult to adjudicate. Eventually the story obliges us to take sides in a moral case, and to choose between the prosecution arguments of Mrs. Mooney ("He had simply taken advantage of Polly's youth and inexperience: that was evident. The question was: What reparation would he make?" [64]) and Bob Doran's statement of defense ("He had a notion that he was being had" [66]; "It was not altogether his fault that it had happened" [67]). The narration leads or misleads the reader into positions from which an objective adjudication becomes virtually impossible. The text of "The Boarding House" produces the undecidability of phrases in dispute that Jean-François Lyotard names the *differend* (Valente, *James Joyce and the Problem of Justice* 8–9).

This *differend* relates not only to meaning but to problems of aesthetic form and class as well, for by the end of the story (and its sequel in *Ulysses*) the reader is obliged to adjudicate forms of art and their moral and social responsibilities as well. Joyce's language, in his defense of his stories to Grant Richards, points resolutely toward their ideological, if not directly didactic, aims. Calling *Dubliners* "my chapter of moral history," and promising with it to make progress toward "the spiritual liberation of my country" (*SL* 88), Joyce claims for his fiction extra-aesthetic functions motivated by his need to defend "The Boarding House," among others, against charges of vulgarity. We see in this maneuver the ironic tensions of a Modernism driven by anxiety about its own Arnoldian elitism to embed idiomatic slang and obscenity in its formal discourse in order to target it for critique, only to be indicted for the impropriety of these very citations. The narration of "The Boarding House" works overtime to ally itself with the proper diction of a Bob Doran against the "soldiers' obscenities" (62) of a Jack Mooney, only to have the word "bloody" nearly cost Joyce its publication. But Joyce held firm, and defended the fidelity of Jack

Mooney's violent speech ("Jack kept shouting at him that if any fellow tried that sort of a game on with *his* sister he'd bloody well put his teeth down his throat, so he would" (68). He told Grant Richards, "I shall delete the word 'bloody' wherever it occurs except in one passage in 'The Boarding House.'" (*SL* 89). The 'bloody' does not itself belong to the "style of scrupulous meanness" (*SL* 83) that makes the story's narration the rhetorical antonym of the cultural texts cited within the story itself: the music hall song ("*I'm a . . . naughty girl*") Polly Mooney sings and *Reynolds's Newspaper*, Bob Doran's favorite tabloid. Indeed, the irony of Joyce's publishing problems is that the narration of "The Boarding House"—like that of many *Dubliners* stories—makes a strenuous effort to maintain itself as high art. The narrator of "A Boarding House," unlike his counterpart in *Ulysses*, produces a disciplined and formal discourse of moral seriousness in resistance to the low art that he fears pressing against it from within the story.

The narration of "The Boarding House" can be construed as attempting to resist, more successfully than Bob Doran, both the moral and cultural degradations of the boarding house's denizens. The narrative rhetoric clearly aims to set itself in sober and credible opposition to alternative versions of the affair of which it is aware—for example, the scandal-mongering of the boarders. Through Mrs. Mooney's free indirect discourse, it tells us discreetly, "All the lodgers in the house knew something of the affair; details had been invented by some" (65).[8] But the narrative version ultimately fails as badly as Bob Doran does in holding malicious defamations harmless and at bay. Later, in "Cyclops," the scandals crowded out in "The Boarding House" triumph as the sole surviving account of the Mooney-Doran marriage. In *Ulysses* the calumnies of Bantam Lyons and Paddy Leonard and the unnamed narrator are permitted to flourish unchallenged. We detect at least one discrepancy: the implied threat Bob Doran senses in Jack Mooney's truculent glance on the boarding house stair is literalized in "Cyclops" into a verbal threat—"Gob, Jack made him toe the line. Told him if he didn't patch up the pot, Jesus, he'd kick the shite out of him" (12: 815). It is impossible for the reader to adjudicate the reliability of the competing versions, or to elude the embarrassment of enjoying *Ulysses*'s vulgar, scandal-mongering account—with its juicy substance—more than the frigid redactions of the "Boarding House" narrator. The two versions put high art and low art, Modernism and the tabloid mentality of *Reynolds's Newspaper*, into conflict as Lyotardian "phrases in dispute." Our choice between them, as readers, also becomes a moral choice with a twist, because it mirrors the hypocrisies of a Bob Doran who speaks like a monk and acts like a libertine.

Against secret enjoyment, the reader of "The Boarding House" is prodded to side with the high art of the story's narration against the rhetoric of slander in "Cyclops." By treating "The Boarding House" as the morally correct version of the Mooney-Doran affair, the reader sanctions a mode of narration and discourse that, in its modernistic disinterest and probity, sets itself against "Cyclops" 's discourse of aggression. Indeed, the commitment to form over content in "The Boarding House" expresses itself as an attitude toward violence that itself becomes part of the moral stance of this narration about violence. Joyce lets the narration of "The Boarding House" draw attention to the metaphorical uses of its content. When the text tells us that Mrs. Mooney "dealt with moral problems as a cleaver deals with meat" (63), the reader is invited to interpret the text through a tropology of social practices that—like the butcher's trade—provide a civilized concealment to hidden violence and brutality. The figure of the butcher's trade thus sets up the problem of the story's rhetoric as one of maintaining a concept of violence with a separable outside and inside—a clean, sanitary public shop on the outside and a hidden bloody *abattoir* where animals are slaughtered on the inside. But the violence in this story refuses to let neither narrative nor rhetoric demarcate it into clean and dirty, external and internal, language and meaning. Mrs. Mooney's metaphorical meat cleaver[9] is also her husband's literal weapon of choice for domestic violence—"One night he went for his wife with the cleaver" (61)—and "The Boarding House" cannot contain its thematic violence with its trimmed, swabbed, and packaged narrative redactions. "Why do you not object to the theme of 'The Boarding-House'?" Joyce asked Grant Richards, baffled at the objection to the expletive "bloody" in the text. Joyce asks why violent language is more troubling than the story's violent content. It is an excellent question, given that the common intensifier ("Is it not ridiculous that my book cannot be published because it contains this one word which is neither indecent nor blasphemous?" [*SL* 85]) is literalized by its context because Jack Mooney is capable of making his rhetorical threat to "bloody well put his teeth down his throat" come true for the young English *artiste*. In Mooney's mouth, "bloody" signifies bloodthirstiness. Yet Jack Mooney's vulgarism and violence is twice removed in the narration—embedded as a citation in the redaction of Bob Doran's memory. Through such multiple indirections *Dubliners* attempts to hold at bay the violence that "Cyclops"—that most violent of *Ulysses* chapters—happily releases. The flat, hard, dry crustiness of the narration of "The Boarding House" attempts to conceal and contain a violent tale of threatened murder, assault, tacit prostitution, blackmail, culminating in the social and sexual coercions of the shotgun wedding. The story is bread pudding with a nasty center of blood pudding.

The narrator's opening account of the Mooney marriage is riddled with gaps and contradictions that foreground the incomplete and impoverished information produced by the exercise of redaction:

She had married her father's foreman and opened a butcher's shop near Spring Gardens. But as soon as his father-in-law was dead Mr Mooney began to go to the devil. He drank, plundered the till, ran headlong into debt. It was no use making him take the pledge: he was sure to break out again a few days after. By fighting his wife in the presence of customers and by buying bad meat he ruined his business. One night he went for his wife with the cleaver and she had to sleep in a neighbour's house. (61)


Ostensibly, this is an explanatory preface to the events about to be narrated, an illuminating prehistory that will (retrospectively) help us understand Mrs. Mooney's behavior in the moral travesty that will transpire in her boarding house. But the redacted form makes the information ambiguous, if not deliberately misleading. The substance that is missing from the account is causal explanation. Is Mrs. Mooney the victim of a bad marriage and a bad husband, as the trimmed and clean account implies, or is there another version implicit in the timing and the events of the plot? Did Mooney go to the devil after his father-in-law's death because some constraint or coercion—governing both his work as foreman in his trade and as husband to the butcher's daughter—was lifted by that event? What constraint? Was it a physical threat by the butcher whose physiognomy can be reconstructed genetically from that of daughter and grandson, the "big imposing woman" (62) and her son with a thick bulldog face and short thick arms ("He was also handy with the mits" [62])? Or was it the moral force of a "reparation" and a forced wedding? If so, then the shotgun wedding about to transpire in the story belongs to a family genealogy that gives it an even more significant and disturbing historical dimension. Is "The Boarding House" the story of an isolated scandal, a social anomaly and a moral transgression? Or does it imply that entrapment was a conventionalized and regularized way for parents "who could not get their daughters off their hands" (65) to arrange marriages in the social climate of an Irish historical period in which celibacy and delayed families were crucial forms of population control. Florence Walzl writes, "for over a century following 1841, Ireland had the lowest marriage and birth rates in the civilized world. As a natural concomitant, it also had the highest rate of unmarried men and women in the world" ("Women in Irish Society" 33). The skepticism and cynicism that is invited by making the reader speculate on what the redaction leaves out inevitably turns on the redaction itself, and on its seeming collusion in concealing a wider moral and historical problem. Like Mr. Mooney, the narration may have packaged bad meat as good meat, as it were, and thereby produced a story that itself becomes a ruined (fictional) business.

The synoptic, incomplete, and edited family history lacks the explanatory "meat" it implicitly promises because it gives no precise etiology for the failure

of the Mooney marriage. What did Mooney fight his wife about in front of their
shop customers? Why did he go after her with the cleaver one day? What enraged and perturbed this shabby little man (who is himself described as looking
like bad pork [McLean 520–21] with his "pink-veined and raw" little eyes) into
assaulting the large, imposing, determined woman he had married? The question is undecidable, although it seems to have to do with one or the other side of
the issue of providence. Either Mooney—unlike Bob Doran—was simply improvident, in which case his double retention by the butcher is curious. Or he
fought Mrs. Mooney because his labor earned him the right to none of the
family resources, and he was forced to pilfer his own business—or rather her
business, since he seems to have had no claim on the shop—for his needs. Once
separated from his wife, he appears to have absolutely nothing, and the reader is
informed that she "would give him neither money nor food nor house-room;
and so he was obliged to enlist himself as a sheriff's man" (61). The marriage
compact, whatever its initial terms, clearly failed Mooney sufficiently that he ruined both aspects of his business, the butcher shop and the marriage itself. Both
the marriage and the narration seem to have reduced Mr. Mooney to a cipher
or a signifier of lack—that is, a human crust or rind. The narration—giving
us Mooney's violent and worthless outside without giving us his inside, his
motives or subjective feelings—formally replicates his thematic emptying and
negation. The marital separation extrudes Mr. Mooney from the family as well
as from the narration. The only subsequent reference to him treats him as a
mock-stranger—"a disreputable sheriff's man" (63)—whose last access to his
daughter is severed by Mrs. Mooney's extreme measure of withdrawing her
from the workforce and keeping her home. Mr. Mooney is cut off from the
family and from the story as though by a rhetorical cleaver.

The story's narration changes with the marital separation of the Mooneys
and assumes forms that disturbingly replicate the management of the boarding
house. Once the narrator begins telling us about Mrs. Mooney's new business,
the rigid, synoptic redaction of the prehistory is replaced by a kind of narrative
license—a far more relaxed and liberal story-telling whose gratuitous details
and needless indulgences are a welcome relief from the earlier informational
dearth. The narrator gives us enough innuendo about the rowdy clientele from
Liverpool and the Isle of Man (Gifford 63), and the music hall *artistes* who lodge
there, to corroborate Bob Doran's concern about the "certain fame" (66) Mrs.
Mooney's boarding house is acquiring. Further, the narrative voice is as voluble
and indiscreet about the second generation of Mooneys as it was terse and but-
toned about the first. We learn the specific vices (swearing, gambling, womaniz-
ing, and lewd gossip) that make Jack Mooney a "hard case" (62), and are given
an unconvincing description of Polly's putative combination of a naughty out-

side and an innocent inside. The narrator's chatty gossip with the reader in this section seems to betray the determined reserve of the opening. This contradiction raises the possibility that the narrator manages us as Mrs. Mooney manages her lodgers—"She governed her house cunningly and firmly, knew when to give credit, when to be stern and when to let things pass" (62). The narrator, having begun sternly, gives us a few passages of readerly "credit" or indulgence, for which (like Bob Doran) we shall have to pay later. The textual boarding house of the story subjects us to certain moral economies and discursive disciplines that—like Mrs. Mooney's practice with her lodgers—are calculated to make us unwilling victims of the story's thematic and narrative hypocrisies. By subjecting us at story's end to the laconic deprivation of narrative crusts— telling us little and showing us less—the text seems to take revenge on the reader for having desired (like Bob Doran) a sweeter, tastier, more entertaining fictional or poetic fare than that offered us by Modernism's scrupulous meanness. Readerly desire—for the moral liberties and discursive delights of, say, the adultery novel—are punished in "The Boarding House" by the thematic and narrative hypocrisies of story crusts: tales of 'reparation,' justice, and the outside of stern action, masking the sinister calculations and cynical subornings of pleasure on the inside.

Mrs. Mooney's nickname *The Madam* makes explicit the continuities of her various businesses. The boarding house is analogous to the bordello and the butcher shop because in each a profit is made out of the body and its necessities: the home is turned into a business, the sexual body is turned into a business, the animal body is turned into a business, and shelter, sex, and food are transformed from natural necessities into commodities. But Mrs. Mooney clearly carries on more than one business at a time, and if her boarding house is a prix fixe affair ("fifteen shillings a week for board and lodgings [beer or stout at dinner excluded]" [62]), she carries on, like her son, a little gambling on the side. The narration explicitly tropes her endgame on Sunday morning as a game of chance: "She counted all her cards before sending Mary up to Mr Doran's room" (65). But even before this, Mrs. Mooney has been moving Polly around like a pawn in a game of chess. Polly is clearly her ante, her stake or investment, in a venture with a possible jackpot. Her son acts as her enforcer or muscle, the narrator of "Cyclops" seems to imply—"Gob, Jack made him toe the line. Told him if he didn't patch up the pot, Jesus, he'd kick the shite out of him" (12: 815). Mrs. Mooney's ambiguous intentions with her daughter are betrayed around the nice pivot of the word "business." When the narrator tells us, "Polly, of course, flirted with the young men but Mrs Mooney, who was a shrewd judge, knew that the young men were only passing the time away: none of them meant business" (63), we are led to think that Mrs. Mooney is reassured and relieved.

But the very next sentence betrays her disappointment—"Things went on so for a long time and Mrs. Mooney began to think of sending Polly back to typewriting when she noticed that something was going on between Polly and one of the young men" (63). Clearly Mrs. Mooney wanted a young man to mean "business." Polly as ante conflates with the more lurid function of bait for prey.[10]

But the overt allusions to prostitution made by the narrator of "Cyclops" ("And the old prostitute of a mother procuring rooms to street couples" [12: 814]) fail to register the complex and bogus role respectability and morality play in Mrs. Mooney's game. As the narrator shows us Mrs. Mooney rehearsing her case on Sunday morning, it becomes clear that her transaction with Mr. Doran will suppress all reference to money except as a disavowal. Mrs. Mooney tries out a rhetoric of self-righteousness in her mind by claiming a disinterest in money—"Some mothers would be content to patch up such an affair for a sum of money; she had known cases of it. But she would not do so" (65). She further elides the commercial character of her boarding house in order to be able to pose as a despoiled hostess when she thinks, "She had allowed him to live beneath her roof, assuming that he was a man of honour, and he had simply abused her hospitality" (64). Doran's fifteen shillings per week are simply suppressed. Her open refusal to patch up the affair for a sum of money lets her disavow her secret fiscal calculations, whose vulgarity the normally circumspect narrator cannot disavow. Mrs. Mooney's financial predation is figured in extremely coarse commercial slang—"She knew he had a good screw for one thing and she suspected he had a bit of stuff put by" (65)—an uncommon descent into low idiom that makes the respectable front of the narrative language conspicuously visible. Mrs. Mooney may be a metaphoric type of "Circe" who turns men into swine, as Barbara McLean suggests in her clever note in the Winter 1991 issue of *James Joyce Quarterly* (520–22), but she is, simultaneously, a butcher's daughter for whom (unlike Circe) swine are a source of profit. But her cleaver, it must be remembered, is respectability and its power of blackmail—the very same sword Bloom raises against Bella Cohen when he intimates that a scandal could hurt her son at Oxford.

When the narration of "The Boarding House" switches to Bob Doran upstairs, the narrative voice returns to a prim and formal diction ("Mr Doran was very anxious indeed this Sunday morning" [65]). It seems to corroborate Mrs. Mooney's own judgment that she would *win* because "He was a serious young man, not rakish or loud-voiced like the others" [65]). The substance of his thought further seems to confirm the shrewdness of her strategy in exploiting the young man's bourgeois respectability by cloaking her own vulgarity in it. "But his family would look down on her. . . . She *was* a little vulgar" (66), he worries. But there are troublesome inconsistencies and gaps in the narration whose significance become clear only retroactively as the jokers in Mrs. Mooney's deck: the mistakes in her calculations. The first symptom is the curious discrepancy between the putative control and rationality of Bob Doran's thoughts and the extraordinary physical agitation exhibited by his body. His hand trembles too much for him to shave, and the continual misting and fogging of his glasses suggest that he is either in a hot sweat or weeping. There are clearly two Bob Dorans here—the sober and respectable bachelor clerk and the highly unstable weakling, prone, we later learn, to periodic collapses. The two are recognized and reconciled neither in Mrs. Mooney's nor in the narrator's conceptualization of him. The joke on Mrs. Mooney is that Bob Doran, too, knows how to keep things to himself. And what he has kept to himself is that he is neither as good a catch as he appears to be, nor immune to moral hypocrisy. Mrs. Mooney has been fooled by the separation of outer and inner, which shapes an extreme contradiction in Bob Doran's case. He sustains the contradictions in his character by means of a temporal compartmentalization that confines his periods of drunkenness, lewdness, and blasphemy to a monthly bender: "for nine-tenths of the year he lived a regular life" (66). Mrs. Mooney wins only *because of* Doran's weakness and instability. His public character, so embarrassingly in evidence in "Cyclops," will rob her daughter both of the respectability and of the money the forced marriage was meant to provide. By the time of *Ulysses*, the "Cyclops" narrator retells Paddy Leonard's story of saving Bob Doran from arrest for "fornicating with two shawls and a bully on guard, drinking porter out of teacups" (12: 803) in an after-hours "shebeen." Leonard, and the narrator who repeats it, clearly find the spectacle of Doran's humiliation hilarious—"And the two shawls killed with the laughing, picking his pockets, the bloody fool and he spilling porter all over the bed and the two shawls screeching laughing at one another" (12:807). Since Doran is frankly described as being "rolled" by two prostitutes, the "Boarding House" is clearly not the only time he is "had" by unscrupulous women.

This *Ulysses* story about Bob Doran and the two "shawls" in bed—which may or may not be true—nonetheless fills a discursive gap in Bob Doran's self-justification in "The Boarding House." We are told that "As a young man he had sown his wild oats, of course; he had boasted of his free-thinking and denied the existence of God to his companions in public-houses. But that was all passed and done with . . . nearly" (66). The ellipsis amends and qualifies the rehabilitation, and the later story of the two shawls contradicts the narrative syntax that tries to make the "wild oats" chiefly heretical rather than sexual. Clearly the narrator presenting to us Bob Doran's thoughts in free indirect discourse is giving him the sort of "credit" denied him by Mrs. Mooney, when she rehearses her case. She is in no mood to cut him any slack: "He was thirty-four or thirty-five

years of age, so that youth could not be pleaded as his excuse; nor could ignorance be his excuse since he was a man who had seen something of the
world" (64). Doran's indirect "nearly," which corrects a near lie and retracts the
total rehabilitation of the wild oats, is never elaborated by the narrator. Instead,
the narrative voice goes to some pains to reinforce the monkish image of Bob
Doran by referring to him twice as a "celibate." The narrative "credit" takes the
form of giving Doran credibility in spite of the qualifications, gaps, and discrepancies in his account. As a result we are vulnerable to being moved by Doran's
rather synecdochic memory of his romantic seduction. The memory is produced for the explicit purpose of exoneration: "It was not altogether his fault
that it had happened" (66). The evidence conjured for this purpose gives a domestic and *light* version of a delicate and metonymic eroticism. He remembers
Polly's appeal in fragments ("the first casual caresses her dress, her breath, her
fingers had given him" [67]) and in displacements ("From her hands and wrists
too as she lit and steadied her candle a faint perfume arose" [67]). His memory
highlights details whose fetishistic features as foot and fur ("Her white instep
shone in the opening of her furry slippers" [67]) are not immediately apparent.
The boarding house of Doran's romantic memory is one of stillness and warmth
("He scarcely knew what he was eating, feeling her beside him alone, at night, in
the sleeping house" [67]). How do we reconcile this sweet, domestic place with
the site of the raucous "reunions" at which Polly sang naughty songs and flirted
with the men, and the men made free allusions to her? Bob Doran's memory totally extracts Polly from the marginally respectable boarding house and its
rather rough clientele, and gives her a tender wifely role ("And her thoughtful-
ness! If the night was anyway cold or wet or windy there was sure to be a little
tumbler of punch ready for him" [67]). This account implies that Bob Doran
was seduced by the domestic solace sorely missed in his bachelor living, rather
than by the free and racy gaiety of Polly's entertainment and coquetry in the
house. What was Bob Doran's participation in the noisy reunions? And where
did Polly fit into one of his monthly benders? Without the later correction of
the story of Bob Doran and the two shawls in bed—which reminds us of the
putatively abandoned wild oats—the decent narrative account of Bob's sweet
romantic memory might well seduce us into exonerating him altogether.

Once it begins to represent Bob Doran's thoughts, the narrative voice of
"The Boarding House" shifts sympathy and takes sides with him against the
Mooneys. It thereby implicates itself in the moral hypocrisies of the story. The
narrational sympathy with Doran seems to take as its moral premise that
the Mooney entrapment and implied violence is more transgressive than Doran's lust.[11] But a stronger interpretive inference is that the narrative prejudice
in abandoning Mrs. Mooney and shifting to Doran's side is motivated by class,

and specifically by language. Bob Doran's general superiority is grounded in philology. Against the discursive transgressions of the Mooneys—Jack's obscenities, Mrs. Mooney's low slang, and Polly's solecisms—Bob Doran upholds critical standards of proper usage and grammar, "sometimes she said *I seen* and *If I had've known*" (66). His rhetorical question—"But what would grammar matter if he really loved her?"—answers itself in the posing with an imbricated set of functions. The question establishes Doran's superiority twice over: confirming taste and distinction precisely by having grammar matter, and heart and sentiment by offering that it may not. But the credit Doran accrues through his defense of linguistic correctness—a credit both extended and retracted by its extension to matters of biblical philology in the "shawls" anecdote in *Ulysses*—must be qualified and questioned, like his putative romanticism, for self-serving disingenuity. "The Boarding House" tells us only that his rehabilitation notwithstanding, he "still bought a copy of *Reynolds's Newspaper* every week but attended to his religious duties and for nine-tenths of the year lived a regular life" (66). *Reynolds's Weekly Newspaper*, Gifford tells us, was a "fourpenny record of social and political scandals" (66), a forerunner of modern tabloid journalism. Doran's skepticism toward religion—"he had boasted of his free-thinking and denied the existence of God" (66)—does not seem to extend to the tabloid press, suggesting that his own prurient curiosities and credulities give him good reason to fear scandal. Doran's heresies take a specifically philological form in "Cyclops," when he questions biblical authority on the ground of historical authorship. He is reported as "talking against the Catholic religion, and he serving mass in Adam and Eve's when he was young with his eyes shut, who wrote the new testament, and the old testament, and hugging and smugging" (12:805). Doran's scholarly interests are discredited by his forum, the two prostitutes who transform his question into a dirty joke, "*How is your testament Have you got an old testament?* (12:810), that, Gifford and Seidman suggest, puns on "fundament" (340). The curious narrative concatenation of wild oats and heresy in the moral account of Doran is dramatized in this scenario. The "Cyclops" version of Bob Doran's transgressions is the *Reynolds's Newspaper* reportage of his doings—that is, the version that would most interest himself if he were reading about someone else. The *Dubliners* version, on the other hand, is the sober, self-justifying account that would be cloaked in his own genteel idiom and shaped by the gaps and omissions of his own hypocrisies.

The story ends by describing Polly Mooney sitting on the bed in Bob Doran's room, waiting for a marriage proposal. Yet curiously, this closure to the story's donnée—namely the intricate history of this proposal—takes the form of a virtual blank, or—to return to my earlier metaphor—the thinnest of crusts. Not only is the dramatic meat of the upcoming proposal with its ghastly pretenses

and ironies withheld from us, but the tight-lipped narrative style tells us nothing of Polly's version of the affair, and very little of what she is feeling. Either
Polly resists narrative penetration, giving her simile of "a little perverse
madonna" new meaning, or the narrator, like Bob Doran, is not interested in
Polly's subjectivity and makes no attempt to see or represent what goes on in
her mind or in her heart. The narrator tells us that the sight of the pillows
"awakened in her mind secret amiable memories" (68), but doesn't tell us what
they are. We are told that her memories give place to hopes and visions of the
future—"Her hopes and visions were so intricate that she no longer saw the
white pillows" (68)—but they are not shared with us. The narrator makes it
clear that Polly Mooney has not only an inner life of the body ("the blood
glowed warmly behind her perfumed skin" [67]) but also an inner emotional
and mental life. But either the narrator has no access to it, or chooses not to give
the reader access to it. The third possibility is that the narrator sees Polly
Mooney precisely as Bob Doran does, entirely as configured by a surrounding
texture of metonymies (flannel, fur, perfume, candle, punch, pillows, and, later,
in the "Cyclops" narrator's account, patent leather boots and violets) that please
the senses. Bob Doran's account, in retrospect, gives indication only of the comfort Polly provided for him, without evidence that he "knows" her at all.

Furthermore, all of the narrative information about Polly—and particularly her own words, leave open the question whether she is always acting and
performing, as in the little song she sings when she is introduced into the
story—"*I'm a . . . naughty girl. / You needn't sham: You know I am*" (62). Do her
signs or gestures—such as "the agitation of her bosom" Bob Doran feels
through his shirt—represent "her" own feelings or nature, or do they belong to
a calculated performance? Polly's shift from aching distress with Bob Doran to
solitary composure in the bedroom after he leaves is particularly suspect.
Suzette Henke says she "doffs her mask of distress" (28) and even Garry Leonard, who treats her performance sympathetically as an unconsciously internalized feminine role, sees her "moving unconsciously from the role of imperiled
maiden to that of the offstage actress preparing herself for a new role" (141).
Polly's words, when they are strung together—"I'm a naughty girl . . ."; "What
am I to do?"; "O my God!"; "Yes, mamma?"—constitute a little melodrama whose
most dramatic moment—"She would put an end to herself, she said" (66)—
sounds patently false.[12] Her actions, too, are inconclusive. She weeps a little,
alone, after Bob leaves, but her restorative gestures, "refreshing" her eyes and ad-
justing her hairpin in profile, appear to have all the calculation that would make
her her mother's daughter. The relationship of her outer and inner self that
the question of performance raises, remains undecidable—although not to the
scandal-mongering Dubliners. The "Cyclops" narrator firmly resolves the in-

consistencies of Polly's public appearances against her—citing as evidence her self-display when she attends church with her husband. "Then see him of a Sunday with his little concubine of a wife, and she wagging her tail up the aisle of the chapel with her patent boots on her, no less, and her violets, nice as pie, doing the little lady" (12: 811), he reports. If Polly looks proper, she is "doing the little lady," whereas if she looks improper, she is thought to be genuine. "Bantam Lyons told me that was stopping there at two in the morning without a stitch on her, exposing her person, open to all comers, fair field and no favour" (12: 400), the narrator reports.

Polly is more absolutely bared and publicly exposed than any other Joycean female, but without being narratively "penetrated," as though, indeed like a little perverse Madonna, she remains inviolate. But the resolute exteriorization of Polly Mooney raises disturbing possibilities of misprision. By being an enigma, a mystery, Polly continues to invite narrative penetration at the same time that clues persist that there may be something *wrong* with this young girl who has "a habit of glancing upwards when she spoke with anyone" (62). The "Cyclops" narrator's description of her as a "little sleepwalking bitch" (12: 398) gives us pause to consider if Polly might be mentally or emotionally impaired in some way. Could her putative promiscuity be less a vice than the pathology of a disturbed young woman or the abused innocence of a mentally deficient girl? Then, again, perhaps she is a young Molly Bloom, taking charge of her sexual life as she pleases even in the face of scandal. These possibilities, too, are undecidable, but they remind us that all interpretations of this enigmatic figure will function as narrative violations, and put us as speculative readers on the side of the more unsavory clients of the boarding house and Barney Kiernan's pub. We are left with the possibility that Polly Mooney's exteriorization makes her a narrative crust or rind with an inviolable center that may be an absent or missing center, no center at all, an unlocatable—a "sleepwalking"—subject. That may be too why her subjectivity remains irretrievable in the later texts[13]—unlike such other mysterious Joycean women as the bird girl of *Portrait,* who may be given an imaginable interior in the thoughts of Gerty MacDowell. Any attempt at exonerating Polly Mooney, however, crosses sharply with the narrative agenda of "The Boarding House" teller. The narrative agenda presses the point that unlike the weak and scrupulous Bob Doran, the Mooneys have "crust," that is, a bold and vulgar audacity in the way they play their games and in the way they use bourgeois morality for their own purposes and designs.

Among *Dubliners* stories, "The Boarding House" arouses relatively little critical interest, perhaps for two reasons. The "case" we are asked to decide seems pretty open-and-shut, and the mode of narration is dull and uninteresting. The result, I have tried to suggest, is narration as bread pudding—that is, a story in which there is little for readers or critics to get their teeth into, by way of interpretation. Unlike "The Sisters," "Araby," and "The Dead," where the narrative language draws a great deal of attention to itself, the "Boarding House" narration is unobtrusive and impartial. It needs the contrasting wedge of the "Cyclops" sequel to dilate its seemingly homogeneous mass and restore a sense of multiple meanings and internal contradiction to its bland discursive texture. But once considered as tacitly self-interrogating and self-incriminating, "The Boarding House" can be restored to its historical moment in modern literature as an example of modernistic writing problematizing itself in its genesis. The story complicates the overturn of Victorian pieties blind to the violence of social control by betraying misogynistic and class biases in its seemingly progressive agenda. The predations of the lower-class Mooneys may not, after all, exonerate the less blatant predations of bourgeois self-righteousness and cultural superiority. And the formalistic control of language may silence less disciplined discourses that could complicate the truth, and thereby have Joyce's style of "scrupulous meanness" contribute its own measure of violence to its censure of violence. "The Boarding House" may indict its own frigidities as clearly as "A Painful Case" indicts celibacy when it turns the adultery novel on its head by making abstention from adultery the equivalent of murder. Narrative bread pudding—as spare and thrifty as modernism itself—may (Joyce seems to have been telling us all along) not be blameless.

## Chapter 8

# *Men Under a Cloud in "A Little Cloud"*

If we imagine a first-time reading of "A Little Cloud"—rereading the story as though we had never read it before—we realize that for the first third of the story the narrator leaves us entirely adrift (like a 'little cloud'?) as to certain significant issues of time and place. The opening paragraph strongly suggests that the protagonist has recently been reunited with an old friend he has not seen for eight years—"Eight years before he had seen his friend off at the North Wall and wished him godspeed. Gallaher had got on. You could tell that at once by his travelled air, his well-cut tweed suit and fearless accent" (70). We virtually "see" the protagonist sizing up the first impression the returned old friend has made on him—scrutinizing his air, suit, and accent. It isn't until many pages later, when Gallaher greets Chandler at Corless's ("Well, and how have you been pulling along since I saw you last? Dear God, how old we're getting" [74]) that we realize the reunion is taking place only then, and that Chandler's prior estimations and encomia of Gallaher had been entirely proleptic, future projections of the status of fantasy. That "well-cut tweed suit" the narration had let us "see" by rhetorically inviting us to watch Chandler lay eyes on it ("You could tell that at once by his travelled air, his well-cut tweed suit . . ." [70])—never materializes in fact and effectively doesn't exist. Whatever suit Gallaher wears at Corless's is entirely eclipsed by its sartorial opposite, a gaudy and politically incorrect "vivid orange tie" (75).

This tale of homosocial jousting for prestige and metaphysical mastery figures its sense of the insubstantiality of judgment and estimation as a "little cloud"[1]—a sign or omen or signifier that is nothing in itself and yet can determine our sense of prospects, our moods, our emotional atmosphere. In this respect, we see two men "under a cloud," in ironic and illogical ways in "A Little Cloud." While it is Gallaher who left Dublin under a "cloud" of suspicion ("he had got mixed up in some shady affair" [72]), Gallaher manages to depress and dispirit his old "friend" during a single, very brief reunion eight years later. Why does this happen, we may ask, when Chandler's anticipated and revised estimate of his friend's success is so clearly largely phantasmal?[2] The Gallaher he meets at Corless's is "well-travelled" chiefly by having visited what Garry Leonard calls "the more lurid tourist-traps" of such cities as London, Paris, and Berlin (154). The "fearless accent" Chandler expected to hear turns out to be crass and offensive—"Gallaher's accent and way of expressing himself did not please him. There was something vulgar in his friend which he had not observed before" (77). And, in his heart, Chandler characterizes Gallaher's "vagrant and triumphant life" as produced by a career of "mere tawdry journalism" (80) and the cultivation of cynically exploitive attitudes toward marriage and respectability ("I mean to marry money. She'll have a good fat account at the bank or she won't do for me" [81]). Sexually, Gallaher shamelessly presents himself as a species of male whore. Why then is Chandler defeated by Gallaher, and why do readers and critics, generally validate this defeat—in spite of Gallaher's obvious vulgarity, dissolution, and sexual venality?

I believe that the answer resides in a highly perverse narrative manipulation that brings the problematic criteria of Dublin's homosocial bonhomie into the story, and thereby tries to configure the reader (male or female) as a masculinist chauvinist. Gallaher appears to have spunk in the way Chandler does not—a judgment that Gallaher, Chandler, and the narrator accept in a tacit collusion that is extended to the reader. Yet our ability to discern that the norms of masculinity in this story are constructed in a strange, contradictory, and repulsive way should make us uneasy with both Gallaher's and Chandler's gender and sexual estimations of each other. That we both experience and ignore this unease, and follow the narrative prompts to think Gallaher more manly than Chandler, proceeds from a performative collusion of narration and readerly judgment. By looking critically at internalized values that translate into gender norms for the three major figures of the story—narrator, Gallaher, and Chandler—we can see how the reader is pressed both into complicity and into resistance by their construction. That construction is itself revealed as existentially unmoored and phantasmal—that is, being a "man" is produced not by a male's actions or behavior but by largely negative subjective states—desires, fears, and envies—that produce masculinity (as Jacques Lacan has argued) under the sign of the threat.[3] The complexity of the contradictory gender ideologies in the story is further complicated by the strange way sexual and social values are linked to estimations attached to various genres of writing and art. In one sense, the story might be read as a contest of the masculinity of not only the school-friends, Chandler and Gallaher, but of poetry and journalism as their respective arts of choice. If so, how does the story's narrative language fare in this metaphysical contest of gender, genre, and prestige?

The narrator's introduction of Thomas Chandler (who is never called that by the narrator even though he consistently refers to Gallagher by his byline, Ignatius Gallaher) predisposes the reader to patronize Chandler socially and in gendered terms before he even becomes a dramatized figure in the story. As the anonymous pronominal "he" of the first paragraph, Chandler is first glimpsed purely relationally, as a Hegelian metaphysical slave, conferring respect, recognition, and homage on a phantasmal masterful Gallaher.[4] In the next paragraph he is introduced as "Little Chandler" with the explanation that "he was called that" because although "but slightly under the average stature, he gave one the idea of being a little man" (70). By narrative admission, Chandler is not physically a small man, yet as evidence for this "idea" of him as "a small man," an inventory of physical traits is marshalled. While these are not in themselves effeminate (quiet voice, refined manners, fair silken hair and moustache, etc.), they are shaded with vaguely effeminate implications (fastidious grooming including a "discreetly" perfumed handkerchief, manicured nails, teeth characterized as "childish white teeth," etc.). This pre-judgmental, or prejudiced, diminution and infantilization of Chandler[5] by the narrator is virtually impossible to dislodge or revise even when challenged by ensuing information and subsequent narrative events. The "little cloud" that shadows Thomas Chandler in the text is, among other things, the cloud of "littleness."

Thomas Chandler remains "Little Chandler" in the narrative discourse, even though Ignatius Gallaher calls him "Tommy," and we soon realize that in all probability he is called "Little Chandler" only behind his back and without his assent. In this way, narrator and reader become complicit in a patronizing form of unkind gossip about this man, and the "story" of "A Little Cloud" becomes an exercise in masculinist belittlement and sexual diminution. The ultimate power of that narrational epithet, which has no other corroboration within the story, is the extent to which it has infected critical discourse. Warren Beck, who produces one of the most complex and nuanced readings of the end of the story, nonetheless adopts the narrator's diminution of Chandler, and refers to him as "this little fellow" (163), a "little actor" (165), and likens him to "many a wavering little man" (175). Beck also echoes the implication of effeminacy that clings to the diminution, calling him "childish, effeminate Little Chandler" (176), and relegating him to a type of "femininely intensive fellow" (167). When Earl Ingersoll does the same, he nonetheless puts "feminized" in quotation marks, to signal the constructed sense of the designation (123).

To fully dilate the ironies of this story, we must explore the question of *why* the narrator would offer us a less flattering picture of Thomas Chandler than of Ignatius Gallaher. I find it useful to begin by looking at the narration of three situations in the story: Thomas Chandler alone in the city, Thomas Chandler with Ignatius Gallaher at Corless's, and Thomas Chandler in his own home. Thomas Chandler alone—at his desk in King's Inn on the afternoon of his meeting with Gallaher, or walking through Dublin on his way to Corless's—is represented as a man beclouded with poetic desire. Poetry is both the end and means of Chandler's desire: he would like to see himself represented as harboring poetic sensibility, as a poetic figure, a man who transcends quotidian life by losing himself in the perception of beauty and of loss as transmogrified by aestheticized language. "He tried to weigh his soul to see if it was a poet's soul" (73), and judging that it might be, he gives himself a poetic name ("T. Malone Chandler" [74]) and mentally pens favorable reviews for the poetry he has yet to write ("*Mr Chandler has the gift of easy and graceful verse. . . . The Celtic note*" [74]). Clearly Thomas Chandler is here satirized as a poetaster, a *poet manqué*, an effete and solipsistic romanticist—perhaps enfolded in Joyce's greater critique of the Celtic revival's futile aesthetic escapism ("That they may dream their dreamy dreams / I carry off their filthy streams" [*CW* 151]). The reader is prompted to patronize Chandler's poetic desires and to view them as fatuous and jejune ("He was not sure what idea he wished to express but the thought that a poetic moment had touched him took life within him like an infant hope" [73]). Vincent Cheng gives us a nuanced political anatomy of Chandler's desires, noting, "What we have here is a culturally constructed desire for 'culture'— high culture in its Eurocentric cosmopolitan essence" (118). But even if Chandler looks to poetry chiefly for symbolic self-aggrandizement, his poetic fantasies could be construed as first symptoms of an anti-Philistinism, an inchoate resistance to bourgeois complacency with ambitions more internal and transcendent than crassly commercial or purely social.

The narrator goes to some pains to juxtapose Chandler's philosophical posturings ("Melancholy was the dominant note of his temperament, he thought, but it was a melancholy tempered by recurrences of faith and resignation and simple joy" [73]) with their patently unsuccessful poetic expressions. But this narrative maneuver is itself problematic. We are given a putative "sample" of Chandler's production of figuration that almost literally names his poetic experiment a *pathetic fallacy*: "he looked down the river towards the lower quays and pitied the poor stunted houses" [73]). The narrative discourse goes on to elaborate Chandler's pathos for the houses in richly detailed personification. "They seemed to him a band of tramps, huddled together along the riverbanks, their old coats covered with dust and soot, stupefied by the panorama of sunset and waiting for the first chill of night to bid them arise, shake themselves and begone" (73). One might almost be seduced by the arresting elegance of this image—pathetic fallacy or no—had the narrator not already undercut it by showing Chandler completely oblivious to the hordes of grimy children who actually live in such tenements—"He picked his way deftly through all that minute vermin-like life" (71). But the class-inflected denigration produced by the naturalism is here the narrator's—not Chandler's—since we know that "Little Chandler gave them [the children] no thought" (71). Yet is Chandler's aes-thetic tramp trope for the houses (faithfully reproduced by the narrator, we trust) necessarily inferior to this naturalism that transforms the children into squatting mice? At times, indeed, the poetic language of the story is indetermi-nate with respect to attribution[6] and we can't be certain whether a metaphor is the narrator's or, by the operation of a kind of Uncle Charles Principle,[7] a stylis-tic projection of Chandler's inauthentic desire to imitate a "Celtic note." Is it the narrator who rhetorically enacts the casting of an aesthetic spell, the production of "glamour" in its archaic sense, in the release of a shower of poetic fairy dust? The fairy dust is here poetic language that magically transforms a quotidian Dublin park into a pastoral scene—"The glow of a late autumn sunset covered the grass plots and walks. It cast a shower of kindly golden dust on the untidy nurses and decrepit old men who drowsed on the benches" (71)? Or is this lan-guage the poetic analogue of Chandler's spiritual ethos, his desire to cast poetic magic dust over his "sober, inartistic life" (73)?

When Chandler is described as approaching Corless's, the narrative lan-guage remains suspended between Chandler's fantasy and its own (possibly parodic) exhibitionism. In Chandler's imagination of the glamour promised by "the value of the name" of "Corless," he conjures up rumors and memories of elegant entertaining, dining, dress, and conveyance—oysters and liqueurs served by Continental waiters to gowned ladies in "noisy dresses and many wraps" alighting from cabs "escorted by cavaliers" (72). Is it the narrative voice or Chandler himself who produces the classical allusion in their description—"Their faces were powdered and they caught up their dresses, when they touched earth, like alarmed Atalantas" (72)? This prose is not bad, and the sim-ile is provocative, if not clearly apt.[8] The scene is scarcely the product of obser-vation since Chandler passes it quickly and doesn't turn his head to look. It is therefore either Chandler's language of fantasy or its transliteration by the nar-rator that we hear. Are we, as readers, to be impressed by its erudition or irked by its pretension? The question is important because the treatment of Chan-dler's poetic desires implicates the narrative's poetic language. If we are meant to deride Chandler's poesy, does the story's own style become indicted for using aesthetics in the interest of social pretension and snobbery?

Curiously, Chandler's fantasies of Corless's are not substantiated by the narrative. Chandler's reverie of achieving poetic success so distracts him that he passes Corless's by and has to retrace his steps, and at the entrance, we catch no glimpse of cabs, ladies, cavaliers, or other indices of glamour. The Corless of his imagination is shown to be as phantasmal as the Gallaher of his imagina-tion. Once inside Chandler suffers a curious hallucination of the critical gaze—imagining that everyone stops to begin "observing him curiously" (74), a mistake he corrects "when his sight cleared a little" and he realizes that "nobody had turned to look at him" (74). The exposure of this moment of acute self-consciousness heightens our sense of Chandler's insecurity and lack of confidence—and yet the narration's unkind and belittling scrutiny of him enacts the very gaze he fears and fantasizes. Neither Corless nor Gallaher live up to Chandler's glamorous expectations. He will end up having a few drinks at a bright and noisy bar with an overbearing and seedy braggart he comes to disrespect sufficiently that all envy should reasonably have been allayed. Afterwards, Chandler should have gone home disillusioned and thankful for his bourgeois life. The reader's estimation should have mirrored this correction in response to a revised narrative estimate that Chandler is worth more as a man and as a human being than Gallaher. Given what we see of their exchange, the encounter of the two men at Corless's should have produced a narrative and readerly education in sexual and gender values that should have transformed the narrative into a didactic feminist exemplum.[9]

When Chandler at last catches sight of Gallaher in actuality, the narrative immediately abets his disillusionment by drawing attention not to a look of prosperity of the kind Chandler had fantasized earlier in the day, but to his thinning hair and the "unhealthy pallor" (75) of his face. The "vivid orange tie" eclipses the suit that Chandler had imagined as a "well-cut tweed" (70). And—importantly—Gallaher says nothing about his journalistic triumphs and instead deflates any glamour in his profession: "It pulls you down. . . . Press life. Always hurry and scurry, looking for copy and sometimes not finding it: and then always to have something new in your stuff. Damn proofs and printers, I say, for a few days" (75). Gallaher says nothing to fuel Chandler's fantasies of the romance of writing, and Chandler is given no encouragement to pursue the conversation about the possibilities of a writing career. As a result, Chandler never brings up his scheme of adopting a poetic name ("He would speak to Gallaher about it" [74]), or asking Gallaher if he "might be able to get it [his poetry] into some London paper for him" (73). Instead, their reminiscences about the successes and failures of various school chums quickly snag on the topic of sexual knowledge and experience, and remain hooked there for the duration of their encounter. The recrudescence of this adolescent preoccupation produces a psychological and discursive regression in both figures toward which the narrative voice remains noncommittal in a way that ultimately works to Chandler's disadvantage.

How this disadvantage is produced becomes clear only in retrospect, when toward the latter part of the story we realize that there are things about both Gallaher and Chandler that the narrator has deliberately withheld from us. Their conversation at Corless's veers off in the direction of the sexual and the immoral when Chandler hints that their friend O'Hara has "gone to the dogs" not only on account of "boose," as Gallaher proposes, but as Chandler hints, on account of "[o]ther things, too" (76). Gallaher immediately uses this hint of illicit knowledge to twit Chandler about his probity ("You're the very same serious person that used to lecture me on Sunday mornings when I had a sore head and a fur on my tongue" [76]) and thereby reinforces the narrator's prior infantilization of Chandler. Yet Chandler knows more, and has more sexual curiosity and experience than Gallaher suspects or the narrator has been willing to reveal. We now recall the earlier narrative disclosure that "whenever he found himself in the city late at night," Chandler courts "the causes of his fear" by walking in the darkest, narrowest lanes animated by "wandering, silent figures" and "low furtive laughter" (72). Retrospectively it becomes clear that the narrator had declined to explore this passage, to explain why a man who "punctiliously" leaves his job every day "when his hour had struck" (71) finds himself walking in the city late at night. Nothing precludes the possibility that those dark and narrow streets may be, as Garry Leonard reasonably surmises, "those frequented by prostitutes" (150). Leonard supposes that Chandler would not respond to their solicitations. However, I would suggest that this confidence is produced by the narrator's and Gallaher's deliberate efforts to shape Chandler into an innocent and virginal figure.

During Chandler's and Gallaher's conversation at Corless's we might expect the anticipated gender structure that figures Gallaher as a sexually experienced and worldly roué and Chandler as an innocent and provincial naïf to become reversed. One should be able to hear in Gallaher's boastings and exaggerations the marks of their gender opposite—masculinity as a masquerade of certain fictions and clichés drawn from low and disreputable cultural genres, offered as a simulacrum that betrays the paucity of the real thing. What confounds this readerly perception, however, is the narrator's interference in the gender dialectic by working resolutely on the side of Gallaher. While the narrative voice undermines Chandler, only Gallaher's theatrical performance—unaided by the narrator—gives him away. Gallaher betrays in his own boastful dialogue the superficial and probably spurious nature of his experience and knowledge. For example, he is obliged to produce a telling correction, "Talk of immorality! I've heard of cases—what am I saying?—I've known them: cases of . . . immorality" (78), and the concession that he reports second hand gossip— "Some things he could not vouch for (his friends had told him), but of others he had personal experience" (78). It is difficult to see just how Gallaher would have personal knowledge "with details" of the scandal of the English duchess ("which he knew to be true") or the secrets of the religious houses on the Continent. In *Ulysses* a clever Gallaher is identified as working for Alfred C.

Harmsworth, a publisher of two London papers but also a purveyor of sensational popular literature.[10] Gallaher is therefore likely to have been no stranger to contemporary tabloid journalism or Victorian pornography, likely sources for the kind of scabrous fare he dishes up for an "astonished" Chandler.

Almost immediately after this recital, which has Chandler's astonishment cast him again as a sexual novice, Gallaher himself produces a biographical fact that the narrator barely glanced earlier, and then only as a negative: that Chandler is married and has a child. By having Chandler blush before each confirmation of wife and child ("Little Chandler blushed again. 'We have one child,' he said" [79]), the narrative continues to intensify his virginal image at the very moment it produces evidence to the contrary. The narrator further colludes with Gallaher's insulting tribute—" 'Bravo,' he said, 'I wouldn't doubt you, Tommy' " (79) by showing Chandler looking "confusedly at his glass" and biting "his lower lip with three childishly white front teeth" (79). At the very moment both the narrator and Gallaher must concede Chandler's adulthood, his consummated marriage and paternity, both specifically demean his masculinity by expressing surprise through denial ("I wouldn't doubt you") and representing him as infantilized as an embarrassed child. The reader is, of course, prompted to accept Gallaher's implicit estimation of Chandler as an improbable man. But it is important to remember that the semiology of the blush is finally indeterminate. Chandler could have blushed for any number of reasons ("A trifle made him blush at any time" [80]) besides being embarrassed by mention of his marital and parental status. His blush might as easily signify pride or satisfaction. This entire exchange between Gallaher and Chandler is externalized, and reflects nothing of Chandler's thoughts or feelings.

What does follow this exchange is a reversal of roles to which, I believe, the narrator scarcely does justice. Chandler for the first time puts forth a self-representation to his friend of his own civilized, settled, socially established life as a paterfamilias with a home: " 'I hope you'll spend an evening with us,' he said, 'before you go back. My wife will be delighted to meet you. We can have a little music, and—' " (79). Gallaher rebuffs this polite invitation even before it is completely uttered—and even when Chandler is willing to accommodate his friend's pressed schedule by moving it forward to that very evening. The interpretation prompted by both narrator and Chandler of this refusal is the one that Chandler later articulates to himself—"He saw behind Gallaher's refusal of his invitation. Gallaher was only patronising him by his friendliness just as he was patronising Ireland by his visit" (80). But Gallaher's sudden desire to break away and hurry off to his card game has other possible explanations that neither Chandler nor the narrator consider. The reunited friends never discuss the shady affair that forced Gallaher to depart Ireland under a cloud sufficiently threatening to prevent him from returning for eight years even though he was just across the channel. The question of Gallaher's expatriation, with its hints of scandal and possible criminality, could too easily come up in an evening's reminiscences with the wife at the Chandler home. Alternatively, Gallaher might fear an uncomfortable turning of the tables, that the sight of Chandler's young family in their tidy home amid domestic comfort could highlight his own "vagrant" and sordid existence, his own permanent entrapment in a morally pimply and aimless adolescence.

Yet Chandler effectively takes control during the remainder of the scene at Corless's, insisting on a last round of drinks, acknowledging to himself that he is better bred and better educated than Gallaher, and insisting that Gallaher too will settle down to domestic life before too long. Garry Leonard is one of the few critics who have appreciated Chandler's cleverness in this scene ("I might add, the quality of his conversational strategy with Gallaher is underappreciated—perhaps because his later collapse at home is so abject" [157]), which flushes out a possibly defensive and increasingly repulsive Gallaher. Warren Beck too feels that at the end of their meeting, Chandler "positively takes his own position" (177). The whole discussion of marriage should have vindicated Chandler—in the reader's eyes as well as his own—were it not for a narrative undercutting of his initiatives. The narrator refocuses our attention on his blush, points out that small whiskeys and cigar have fuddled Chandler because "he was a delicate and abstinent person," and lets us know that the effect of "sharing Gallaher's vagrant and triumphant life, upset the equipoise of his delicate nature" (80). At the very moment Chandler asserts himself against Gallaher by displaying his own signifiers of manliness and holding his ground, the narrator resolutely reinfantalizes him by showing him blushing, delicate, and sensitive, and by using the code of the "abstinent" to desexualize him once again. Gallaher's defense against Chandler's bold toast to a proleptic marriage for "Mr and Mrs Ignatius Gallaher" (81) is to first demean the institution as putting one's "head in the sack," and then to strip it of both romance and respectability by treating it as a species of prostitution ("There are hundreds—what am I saying?—thousands of rich Germans and Jews, rotten with money, that'd be only too glad" [81]). Gallaher's final thrust, aimed directly at Chandler's connubial sexuality, is to treat marital sex as an unpleasant taste in the mouth. With an utterly coarse and insulting oral gesture, he strips any final value or charm from Chandler's young married estate. "He imitated with his mouth the act of tasting and made a wry face. —Must get a bit stale, I should think, he said" (82).

The resistant reader longs to have this break in the evening, and in the narrative, followed by Chandler's angry revision of his earlier flattering expectations of his old friend's success, and by his repudiation of what has become a patently worthless friendship. Yet the shocking denouement of the story is Gallaher's inexplicable victory. For Chandler returns to his home with Gallaher's despicable values now internalized ("he does swallow Gallaher's line," Kershner says [99]) and trains them upon his family and his domestic life. That these values have also been narrational values with a significant impact on the reader, can be seen in an analysis like Suzette Henke's, which more than most extends the diminution and unsexing of Thomas Chandler into his familial role. Henke's reading of the Chandler marriage transforms his "childlike and helpless" nature into the cause of "a pathological relationship of Oedipal dependency" with his wife (31). Annie, in turn, is seen as "reducing her immature consort to infantile status" and then displacing this "impotent father" with her infant son (31). Henke's reading is perfectly reasonable and consistent with the narrative prompts. With the help of a complicit narrator, Gallaher has indeed managed to proliferate his castrative innuendos about his old friend into the readerly and critical realm. But I find in Garry Leonard's resistance to the narrative promptings of this final scene in the story a significant alternative for exploring the instability of the story's narrative outcome. Leonard doesn't believe that Annie Chandler would not have listened to her husband's poetry, nor that the glances of hatred exchanged by the couple are permanent (168–69). Reading against the narrative cues makes some resistance to the reader's narrative complicity possible.

The curious tension in the narration of the final scene is raised by the discrepancy between the realistic representations of an attractive, well-run home and family life, and the cynical and disaffected shadow or *cloud* cast on it by Chandler's eyes as they are newly infected by Gallaher's libertine filter. Remembering the distortions the specter of Gallaher has earlier wrought on Chandler's perception of his surroundings—"For the first time his soul revolted against the dull inelegance of Capel Street" (73)—we now see this demeaning perspective imported into his home. Chandler's home is a place of thrift and mortgages,[11] to be sure, but with pretty furniture and extended family support, the young couple appears to have made successful adjustments to the emotional and domestic exigencies of marriage. The only ominous signals are Chandler's nocturnal wanderings, and his putative lack of thought of wife and child on this reported afternoon and evening—although this could be a temporary amnesia readily explained by his distraction by Gallaher on this particular day. Is the Gallaher filter that turns his wife's pretty eyes and his pretty furniture "mean" a temporary and provisional cloud—a *little* cloud—over the marriage? The passion and rapture he finds missing in Annie's eyes is so patently Gallaher's orientalizing overlay ("He thought of what Gallaher had said about rich Jewesses" [83]). Or are we to take it as having produced an epiphany, a revelation of Chandler's true spiritual state of affairs, as the narrator prods us to believe? Chandler's jaundiced reaction to the photo is certainly colored by Annie's snit at his late and empty-handed return from the office. And his cold "Hm! . . ." (83) shows him refusing to soften at the memory of the gift of the pale blue summer blouse she wears in the picture. Yet this memory nonetheless opens the narrative into a rare glimpse at the complex romantic and domestic negotiations of newly-weds. The recollection produces a small short story: Chandler's thrilled and nervous purchase of the blouse, Annie's delight at the surprise followed by angry dismay at the price, her inadvertently hurtful words and gestures, her attempts to make up with kisses and thanks. In the end, her affection for the blouse—now embedded with a complex marital history—is memorialized by her wearing it in the photograph. The entire little drama of the blouse reveals degrees of romance, delight, intimacy, difficulty, and accommodation in the Chandler marriage that are undreamt in Gallaher's swinish philosophy.

Chandler's contemplation of his home and his wife's picture could have been presented in myriad moods at many alternate moments, and it is clear that Chandler's story could have been told on a sunnier day than this particular one, without Gallaher's cloudy shadow oppressively leaching its color and warmth. As Leonard points out, "in reviling his wife's expression because he finds it insufficiently supportive of himself, he is simply doing to her what Gallaher has just finished doing to him" (165). Warren Beck concurs that Chandler robs himself of his earned domestic joy by letting himself be "foolishly unsettled by Gallaher's transit of his horizon" (179). Gallaher's transit further upsets the couple's routine on this particular day, when Annie's sister Monica is no longer on hand to run an errand to the corner store or hold a sleeping child who might wake up if he were put down. Chandler is consequently physically entrained in domestic confinements on the evening he is least conditioned to tolerate them.[12] The contretemps that results from his efforts to escape them intellectually—by reading the opening poem of Byron's 1807 *Hours of Idleness*—creates an ironic juxtaposition between life and poetry that tries to indict the fatuousness of Chandler's poetic melancholy even more cruelly than had the earlier narration. We do briefly note a curious narrative discrepancy, when we are told, "A volume of Byron's poems lay before him on the table" (83). The opening narration had quite definitely told us that Chandler never took the books on his shelves down to read them. "He had bought them in his bachelor days and many an evening, as he sat in the little room off the hall, he had been tempted to take one down from the bookshelf and read out something to his wife. But shyness had always held him back; and so the books had remained on their shelves" (71). How did the book get off the shelf? There is no mention that he takes it down between the opening of the section—"Little Chandler sat in the room off the hall, holding a child in his arms" (82)—and the moment when he finds that "A volume of Byron's poems lay before him on the table" (83). Either Chandler's memory, or the narrator's, has exaggerated his shyness, for the books seem to circulate more than they have let on. The contretemps occurs when Chandler's reading of the poet's elegy for the dead girl is interrupted by a brush with real infant mortality. The crying of Chandler's infant is escalated into near convulsions by his shouting in the child's face to "Stop!" (84). Joyce produces here a violent clash of literary genres, as the Romantic elegy is irrupted and mimicked by naturalism.

In their resistances to the narrative prompts to read "A Little Cloud" as "one more story of a Dubliner circumstantially restrained from escape into a larger life" (Beck 179), Leonard and Beck remind us that smug complacencies and foolish escapisms form the dialectical dilemma of every Dubliner. Indeed, the pressure to decide between resignation and resistance to one's lot in life may be the dialectical dilemma that defines the bourgeois condition. The famous problem of Dublin *paralysis* may therefore be a model for a much more universal problem of making life choices in a nonutopian state. What "A Little Cloud" dramatizes both thematically and performatively is the role that projection, fantasy, and ideology can play in shaping the perception applied to these choices— and particularly the role played by gender ideology, as I have tried to show. The narrator of the story, I have been suggesting, is in one respect a double of Gallaher, a voice of belittlement and disparagement that colors our reading and interpretation of a story about a man's internalization of the belittlement and disparagement to which he is subjected on one evening. The curious twist, however, is that of style. In replicating the dirty work of Gallaher in aggrandizing itself at Chandler's expense, the narrative voice resorts not to the naturalism of Gallaher's literary medium, journalism, but chiefly to the aesthetic and poetic diction of Chandler's desire. Is the narration of "A Little Cloud" a projection of Chandler as Gallaher sees him or as Chandler sees himself through Gallaher's eyes? Or is the narration of "A Little Cloud" a melancholy Celtic version of Chandler's little (that is, insignificant) life clouded by a little (that is, insignificant) sadness on one particular day? Could Chandler's "It's nothing, Annie . . . it's nothing. . . . He began to cry" (85) apply as well to Chandler's "tears of remorse" at the end of the story? Has it all been just "a little cloud" that momentarily shadows people who are otherwise all right. "But wherefore weep?" as Byron's poem would say (Gifford 72).

Where does all this leave the reader? The problems created by the power of pre-judgment, by prejudice, by projection, by the warping of perception by desire—these are all dangers to which the reader of "A Little Cloud" is made vulnerable by the narrative voice and its various inflections. I earlier suggested that the narrator *tries* to construct the reader as a masculinist chauvinist. I

would now propose that it is his *style* of narration that prevents him from suc-
ceeding entirely. By telling the story in the poetic language of Chandler's desire,
the narrative shapes the reader by story's end more into a Chandler who has internalized Gallaher's values, than a Gallaher who disdains a Chandler. We are
induced to give Gallaher more ambivalent respect than we do Chandler, even as
we are seduced by the poetic prose of Chandler's own cultural fantasies. Perhaps
we have been led into this arena of insubstantial judgment and estimation of
manhood and art by a narrative voice that could itself be characterized as "shy"
or embarrassed about the "effeminacies" of its own aesthetic impulses. Perhaps
it is this problematic imbrication or intermeshing of a theme, by which we are
led to respect brash and robust journalists more than sensitive daydreamers,
with its conveyance by an aesthetic poetic form that undermines just this judgment, that produces the reader's uneasiness and vacillations. In the end, the
reader too is under "a little cloud," as we emerge from our experience of uncertain judgments and evaluations of manhood and art by recognizing that values
and norms—particularly those of gender—are constructed phantasmally out of
words.

## Chapter 9
## *Farrington, the Scrivener, Revisited: "Counterparts"*

When Joyce's brother Stanislaus read his story "Counterparts," he wrote to Joyce that the story showed "a Russian ability in taking the reader for an intracranial journey" (*SL* 73). In response to this critique Joyce asked himself precisely what is meant when people say that something is "Russian," and he came up with two answers. He surmised that most people probably meant "a certain scrupulous brute force in writing," and he himself found the predominant Russian characteristic to be "a scrupulous instinct for caste" (*SL* 73). It is curious that the word "scrupulous" occurs in both descriptions, and it is significant that a scant month later, Joyce applied the word to his own writing in *Dubliners* when he claimed for it "a style of scrupulous meanness" (*SL* 83). This use of "scrupulous"—with its clear connotations of a deliberate and purposeful moral probity and a precise and punctilious care over a matter—both fit oddly with the lack of purpose and control implied in "brute force" and in "instinct." Joyce was reading a great deal of Russian literature while writing a number of the *Dubliners* stories, and he mentions Lermontoff, Turgenieff, Gorky, and Tolstoy in his September 18, 1905 letter to Stanislaus. Yet although he does not mention Nicolai Gogol, Gogol's tales surely exhibit most exquisitely that "instinct for caste" to which Joyce alludes.

The scrupulous "instinct for caste" in "Counterparts" makes it tempting to think that Joyce might have put his story of a copyist into dialogue with two other famous nineteenth-century short stories about scriveners. One of these—Melville's famous "Bartleby, the Scrivener" about a scribe in a New York law office—has already been remarked as an analogue for "Counterparts." And I would suggest consideration also of Gogol's story "The Overcoat," about a scrivener crazed by the theft of his new coat. There is, alas, no evidence that Joyce read either story, and Morris Beja, whose essay "Farrington, the Scrivener" is the eponym of my title, states, "I am confident that Joyce would not have known what was at that time an obscure tale by a largely neglected writer, when he wrote his own story in 1905" (111). Yet although I too find that Mr. Alleyne's line to Farrington, "I may as well be talking to the wall as talking to you" (87) uncannily evokes Melville's tale of the walls of Wall Street in "Bartleby," I follow Beja in eschewing the question of influence. Instead, I think it worth exploring why Joyce, like writers of the nineteenth century, was captivated and troubled by the figure of the literal writer who reproduces words that are not his own: the manual scribe, or human copying or Xerox machine, as Suzette Henke calls him (32). Gogol's and Melville's scriveners, with their mechanical and inhuman production of writing, reflect in disparate techniques Joyce's donnée that there is something particularly soul-killing about the profession of writing when that writing is the literal and manually mechanical reproduction of another's language and another's thought. The production of writing as a pure materiality seemed to represent to "creative" writers a kind of living death. Melville troped it by metaphorizing scrivening as the production of dead letters, and Gogol lampoons this perversion of art when he gives his Akaky Akakyevich—his very name a patronymic copy—an unaccountable passion for copying letters. Melville and Gogol met the challenge of creating sympathy for oppressed clerks by imbuing them with various kinds of pathos, ending their empty and isolated lives with sad deaths, while checking sentimentality with varieties of fantasy and humor. Joyce opted for a later model of naturalism by creating his scrivening protagonist resolutely against type, and by giving his narrative voice access to the physical and psychological effects of a man's unbearable subjugation. But in its attention to copying and repetition as forms of discursive entrapment, Joyce also gives "Counterparts" a metatextual function. The way the story of "Counterparts" unfolds demonstrates to us why the scrivener's story cannot be told by the scrivener.

"Counterparts" has been most compellingly interpreted by those critics who have paid the most scrupulous attention to the implications of the repetitive nature of the scrivener's work as a trope and model for an environment in which repetition creates an ethos that turns men into machines. Numerous critics have explored the implications of the repetitive and mechanical nature of Farrington's work for symptomatizing his dehumanization and powerlessness.[1] My own analysis will revisit these variants of the relation of repetition to mechanization in the story, but will press this focus more fully into the realm of the body, the realm of the social, and finally the realm of the narrative and the metatextual. By keeping an eye, at the same time, on Joyce's keen departures from the conventions of nineteenth-century scrivener narratives, I hope also to elucidate the highly uncomfortable position into which the story's style of "scrupulous meanness" puts the reader. Specifically, I believe the narration places the reader in a position of ethical scrupulosity in having to adjudicate the painfully paradoxical moral situation in which victimization turns a human being into a victimizer. Joyce himself alerts us to this problem when he tells

Stanislaus, "I am no friend of tyranny, as you know, but if many husbands are brutal the atmosphere in which they live (vide Counterparts) is brutal and few wives and homes can satisfy the desire for happiness" (*SL* 130).

One of the first things that is striking about the story's setting is the extent to which "scrupulosity" is a protocol of the law office of Crosbie & Alleyne in which Farrington is employed. Don Gifford explains that although typewriters were in use at the time of the story's setting, scriveners or copy clerks were still needed for "copying legal documents in handwriting because typewritten copies were not accepted as legally valid copies of legal documents in the early twentieth century" (72).[2] In the offices of Crosbie & Alleyne, Miss Parker, the typist, and Farrington, the manual scribe, work side by side. Since the copied texts had legal consequences, a legible hand, accuracy, speed, and the ability to meet deadlines were clearly paramount requirements for the job ("The chief clerk began to hurry Miss Parker, saying she would never have the letters typed in time for the post" [90]). This exigency produces the highly regimented environment that gives the Dublin law firm of Crosbie & Alleyne the industrial ethos of a factory[3] rather than the civilized climate of a professional place of business. Clerks are oppressively monitored, their work presumably checked for accuracy and their attendance clocked for diligence.[4] In this environment the human body is instrumentalized as a mere mechanical tool, with its needs, feelings, and urges completely peripheralized as extraneous to the workplace. Joyce's note that Russian writers have a "scrupulous instinct for caste" assumes even greater relevance for this story if we reflect that the overlap of working-class and white-collar environments evokes a biological sense of the word "caste." Specifically, *caste* is an entomological term, defined as "one of the distinct forms among polymorphous social insects, performing a specialized function in the colony, as a queen, worker, soldier, etc." (*Random House Dictionary* 230). To think of Farrington as a drone who has been impressed to function as a worker bee (rather than as the soldier more befitting his aggressive temperament) fits well with his own choice of metaphor for the office after his impertinence to Mr. Alleyne. Ruefully, he reflects that "he knew what a hornet's nest the office would be for him" (94).

But if Joyce is indeed working within a tradition of clerk and scrivener narratives—a tradition that more peripherally includes Charles Dickens's Bob Cratchit as well—then one of the conventions he violates is that of depicting clerks and copyists as thin and pallid men. Unlike the delicate and insubstantial starvelings of the nineteenth-century fictions, Joyce makes his scribe Farrington a robust physical presence—"tall and of great bulk" (86) with a volatile body and a psyche structured like a human volcano. The blood and viscera of Farrington's body press outward to his exterior, his dilated blood vessels making his face inflamed, its flesh exteriorized in "the colour of dark wine or dark meat" (88), and making the whites of his bulging eyes "dirty" (86). His "great bulk" makes his movements heavy and taxes his lungs—"he halted, puffing with labour and vexation" (86), and his alcoholic needs for drink press upon him as a series of sharp thirsts and dull aches. Further, Farrington is keenly assailed by smells, detecting the "moist pungent odour of perfumes" (89) before he sees Miss Delacour, and anticipating the smell of liquor as much as its taste—"his nose already sniffed the curling fumes of punch" (93). Farrington's body is the antithesis of a machine: a massive, unregulated, dynamic, and highly sensate organism whose hydraulics of blood, thirst, passion, and anger are calibrated throughout the story as on the verge of eruption or implosion. In gauging Farrington's feelings, the narrative prose resorts to the trope of an instrument that can predict but not control the unregulated natural phenomenon of the storm: "The barometer of his emotional nature was set for a spell of riot" (91).

Against the roiling exigencies of this exaggerated clerical body, the imposed controls and regulations of the office regimen function like those of a miniature penal system. The "general reprehensibility" and "inexcusable" behavior of Farrington (as Warren Beck calls them [187]) work so forcibly to justify the oppressive workplace regime as to mask its own inexcusable suppression of worker autonomy and dignity.[5] But Joyce takes pains, I believe, to rupture the assumptions of a just ethical economy in the office operation by foregrounding the demeaning nature of the managerial controls. Farrington may abuse his skimpy half-hour lunch "hour" by taking longer to eat. But in this office the welfare of the working body is clearly subordinated to productivity, and its needs for food and alimentary relief are treated by the management as exploitations of the working day that require rigid enforcement and control. "How many courses do you want, I'd like to know" (87) Alleyne sarcastically asks Farrington, without reckoning that Farrington's large frame may indeed require more food and more time for eating than Alleyne's puny one. Farrington may behave like a truant schoolboy when he sneaks off to his snug, but his need to secure permission from the chief clerk to use the toilet exposes a degrading control of the adult working body in that office. Nor does the chief clerk hesitate to embarrass Farrington before the firm's clients by alluding to the urinary incontinence with which alcoholic incontinence is masked: "I know that game, he said. Five times in one day is a little bit . . ." (89). The effect of this humiliating "address in the presence of the public" contributes to the lack of concentration that impairs Farrington's ability to copy, as it contributes to his generally enraged condition ("All the indignities of his life enraged him" ([90]). This is no mere rhetorical lament, for the indignities are real. By having the narrator report the chief clerk's indelicacy, the reader—along with the office workers and the firm's clients—learns how many times Farrington has peed that day. The narrator has other intimate access to Farrington's body that allows him to express his state of mind in violent tropes of somatic assault and deprivation—"A spasm of rage gripped his throat for a few moments and then passed, leaving after it a sharp sensation of thirst" (87). Farrington's "intercranial journey," as Stanislaus Joyce aptly named it—drawing attention to physical brain and skull rather than to thought or ideas—includes diagnosis of his body's exigencies brought on by thirst and rage. "The man recognised the sensation and felt that he must have a good night's drinking" (87), we are told.

Given the white-collar setting of "Counterparts," the prominence of Farrington's body and its pressures has tended to obscure its subjugation by the workplace in favor of indicting the grossly physical Farrington himself. Donald Torchiana calls him "a hog of a man" and his story "an extended 'swine song' " (141). The nineteenth-century scrivener narratives arouse great reader pity for both the physical privations of the starving Bartleby and the freezing Akaky and their long-suffering mildness. But Joyce constructs Farrington's gross physicality and violent temperament in ways that make it very difficult to read against the narrative prompts that lead critics like Warren Beck to treat him in many respects like an animal, with "almost animal lurkings and chargings of an amoral creature" (186).[6] The narrator reinforces such assumptions when he tells us that Farrington "longed to execrate alound, to bring his fist down on something violently. . . . His body ached to do something, to rush out and revel in violence" (90). The passivity that is the hallmark of Gogol and Melville's scriveners, and that rises to no more than Akaky's pathetic search for justice and Bartleby's passive-aggressive "I prefer not to," is dramatically inverted in "Counterparts" into a viscerally produced and dangerously thwarted aggression. Farrington's fantasy of crashing his fist into the bald egg-shaped head of Alleyne (91) looks forward to the contemporary phenomenon of mild post office workers shockingly running amok one day—going "postal," we now call it. Only Farrington is not a mild-mannered clerk. The shock of the ending, when Farrington viciously beats his small boy with a stick, recognizes that Farrington's aggressive fantasies are not, in fact, socially containable and will be acted out in spaces where privacy, control, and impunity give him sway. In a city of terrible fathers, Farrington is depicted as the most monstrous.[7] Farrington is thereby specifically rendered as a type of *anti-scrivener* (Beja calls him an "anti-Bartleby" [113]) by having the narrator violently wrench him *out of* the scrivener tale tradition. By re-embodying, re-tempering, and de-isolating the scrivener, Joyce deliberately forfeits the easier earlier pathos in the interest of creating a far more challenging sociological dynamic that presents a far more intractable moral problematic for readers to adjudicate. Given contemporary sociological awareness of the dangers of a provocative workplace and the genealogical nature of abusive behavior, Joyce's insights in "Counterparts" are very modern. He effectively anticipates the moral and legal complications the sociology of snapped workers and domestic abusers continues to pose in the late twentieth and early twenty-first centuries. Warren Beck notes that "Sociologically this short and simple annal is one of Joyce's most widely implicative stories" (187).

Scriveners derive their privileged appeal as figures of oppressed workers in the fictions of creative writers because it is the production of language and writing that is centrally implicated in their oppression. Even in a relatively humane workplace like that of Bartleby's Wall Street office, the actual labor of the copyist is conceded to be sufficiently uncomfortable, irksome, and exhausting as to produce the various pathologies and eccentricities Melville attributes to its denizens. Of the task of proofreading multiple hand-written copies, Melville's narrator admits, "It is a very dull, wearisome, and lethargic affair. I can readily imagine that to some sanguine temperaments it would be altogether intolerable. For example, I cannot credit that the mettlesome poet Byron would have contentedly sat down with Bartleby to examine a law document of, say five hundred pages, closely written in a crimpy hand" (119).[8] Joyce, as has often been noted, transfers the mimeticism of the copyist's writing to the working-place discourse, and thereby makes the conversations through which office work must be conducted a brutal vehicle of abuse effected through verbal mimicry and repetition. If copying, or written mimicry, is dehumanizing because it forces a speaking subject to endlessly produce the words of another, verbal mimicry in the story becomes a contrapuntal form of social violence that cruelly uses a person's own spontaneous words to mock them. Alleyne's violent dislike and abuse of Farrington is putatively set off by an act of mimicry, as Farrington concedes when he remembers "the day Mr. Alleyne had overheard him mimicking his North of Ireland accent to amuse Higgins and Miss Parker: that had been the beginning of it" (92). But was Farrington merely mimicking Alleyne's own penchant for mimicry? Even before learning of Farrington's original transgression, we hear Alleyne mimicking the delivery of Farrington's half-uttered explanations and excuses—"*Mr. Shelley says, sir* . . . Kindly attend to what I say and not to what *Mr. Shelley said, sir*" (87).[9] That mimicry has become for Farrington a rhetoric of violence becomes clear when he taunts his terrified and apologetic little son with it—"He began to mimic his son's flat accent, saying half to himself: '*At the chapel. At the chapel, if you please!*'" (98). The poor child himself can only counter by imitating another borrowed language of intercession, "I'll say a *Hail Mary* for you, pa, if you don't beat me . . ." (98).

Farrington works in a place whose product is binding and consequential language, and yet this same place deprives him not only of any meaningful forms of writing and speaking for himself, but of any effective defense or response against his employer's discursive totalitarianism. Farrington's words, before they have even fully left his mouth, are used as a cudgel against him. Tanja Vesala-Varttala fully dilates this intolerable condition, pointing out that Alleyne's aim is "to overmaster Farrington and to violate and threaten his 'face' as much as possible" (237).[10] Although he concedes Alleyne's "privileged bullying," Warren Beck consistently describes Alleyne as "justifiably incensed" and as giving "just rebukes abusively uttered" to "the shirker and escapist" Farrington (189–90). But is Alleyne justifiably incensed? It would seem so, given that Farrington has undeniably failed to complete the copying of the Bodley and Kirwan contract and the Delacour correspondence.[11] Faced by the violently bitter tirade heaped upon Farrington in the presence of Miss Delacour, is Farrington provoked to lie about the two missing letters for which he will be excoriated? Perhaps not, but it is instructive that his lie is treated no differently than what may earlier have been the truth. When he tried to explain to Alleyne that the chief clerk, Mr. Shelley, had given him different priorities, his "But Mr. Shelley said, sir——" is promptly mimicked by Alleyne as a lying excuse—"*Mr. Shelley says, sir*"(87). When he claims untruthfully that "I know nothing about any other two letters," Alleyne responds with a mimicry that now contains a cruel literal twist—"*You—know—nothing. Of course, you know nothing*" (91). It is as though Alleyne had taken up the narrator's "he said stupidly" (92) and licensed himself with it to call Farrington stupid in front of Miss Delacour and the whole office.

But what if Farrington's lying is, arguably, justified, or at least understandable? What if the narrator is complicit with the oppressive atmosphere of the office by reinforcing its sense of Farrington as a shirker, by suppressing or otherwise attenuating evidence that might offer a somewhat different perspective? A speculative and unverifiable counter-narrative could be constructed of what transpires in Crosbie & Alleyne that afternoon. What if we consider that Farrington is working on two specific projects on this particular day: the Delacour correspondence and the Bodley and Kirwan contract. Mr. Shelley learns that Miss Delacour will be visiting the office in the afternoon, and so instructs Farrington to put aside the Bodley and Kirwan contract, which must be ready by four o'clock, and tells him to first finish the Delacour correspondence. While Farrington is working on the Delacour letters, Alleyne furiously rings the bell and demands to see Farrington in his office, where he upbraids him for not having finished the Bodley and Kirwan contract. Farrington tries to explain that Mr. Shelley told him to hurry and finish the Delacour file, which still has two letters missing. But Alleyne cuts him short before he can give this explanation, abuses him for taking too long for lunch, and—while Farrington is leaving—

threatens "that if the contract was not copied by evening Mr. Crosbie would hear of the matter" (88). Farrington goes back to his desk, counts the sheets of the contract left to be copied, tries to write, can't, needs a drink, and sneaks out to the snug on the pretense that he is going to the toilet. When he returns, Miss Delacour is already there, and he learns that Mr. Alleyne is calling for him. He is told to bring the Delacour correspondence to Mr. Alleyne's office, and does so, hoping that "Mr. Alleyne would not discover that the last two letters were missing" (89). He "put the correspondence on the desk and bowed respectfully but neither Mr. Alleyne nor Miss Delacour took any notice of his bow" (90). Farrington now returns to his desk to resume work on the Bodley and Kirwan contract. He hears Mr. Shelley hurrying Miss Parker to finish the letters in time for the post, and remembers that he too must finish the contract in time for the post. He has trouble concentrating with his mind muzzied by the porter, and realizes in despair that he can never finish the fourteen pages in time. He gets so upset that he makes an error and has to start the page over again. He can think only of escape to the pubs with his friends, and therefore fails to hear his name called, presumably either by Mr. Shelley, or by Mr. Alleyne, himself, who has come downstairs and is standing with Miss Delacour outside the counter. When he looks up, the office has become a theatrical space readied for a spectacle of punishment—"all the clerks had turned around in anticipation of something" (91). Farrington now receives a "tirade of abuse" about the two missing letters in front of the entire office. What can Farrington say in a situation like this? That Mr. Alleyne countermanded Mr. Shelley's instructions and that the letters were unfinished because he was forced, on peril of losing his job, to finish the Bodley and Kirwan contract instead? Could he really have afforded to place the blame on the contradictory orders of his superiors, by way of explanation, in front of all their subordinates? Would he have been allowed to get an explanation out at all, or have been cut off as he was cut off earlier by Alleyne, with a mocking mimicry? What Farrington does is probably the only generally face-saving thing he can do: to lie that he knows nothing about them, and that "he had made a faithful copy" (91).

The above scenario is unverifiable for an interesting reason: Alleyne's interruption and interdiction of Farrington's explanation of what Mr. Shelley said also deprives the reader of the explanation. This, of course, raises several other questions. Why did Farrington not explain to Mr. Shelley that Mr. Alleyne has changed the priorities? We only know that Mr. Shelley is a critical and hard taskmaster who speaks to Farrington "severely" (89) and hectors Miss Parker to hurry, "saying she would never have the letters typed in time for the post" (90) rather than offering her help or encouragement. And Shelley is sufficiently ungenerous, in the eyes of his employees, that Farrington foregoes asking the

cashier for an advance when he sees him emerge from the office with Mr. Shelley—
"It was no use trying to say a word to him when he was with the chief
clerk" (92). We simply don't know the risks Farrington would incur in reporting
to Mr. Shelley, Mr. Alleyne's words—"Kindly attend to what I say and not to
what *Mr. Shelley says, sir*" (87). But the larger question remains why the narrator
fails to give us a better explanation for why Farrington may be unable to finish
the work, and leaves us with the impression that Farrington is simply an idler or
a shirker? Why does the narrator not report Farrington's interdicted thoughts—
for example, what he planned to report to Alleyne about what Mr. Shelley
said—in favor of reporting his murderous glare at the fragile egg-head of Alleyne, and the sharp thirst that gripped his throat? In tacitly blaming Farrington
for all the awkward situations of his workday, the narrator almost seems to imitate Alleyne, who lets Farrington stand there for some minutes without dismissing him, and then accuses him of idling for not having departed—"—Eh? Are
you going to stand there all day? Upon, my word, Farrington, you take things
easy!" (88). Is the narrator, in some sense, Alleyne's *counterpart*? Once we look
for them, there may be other narrative omissions of information that might
have meliorated the impression of shirking, and have shed more light on Farrington's difficulties in doing his job. For example, upon his return from Alleyne's office, we learn that "He took up his pen and dipped it in the ink but
continued to stare stupidly at the last words he had written: *In no case shall the
said Bernard Bodley be. . . .* The evening was falling and in a few minutes they
would be lighting the gas: then he could write. He felt that he must slake the
thirst in his throat" (88). We have been prepared by the earlier narrative mention and interpretation of Farrington's alcoholic thirst to privilege this exigency
over asking what the statement "then he could write" might mean. An answer
readily suggests itself when we learn that the evening is dark and foggy, and that
the gas lamps outside have already been turned on. Perhaps between the time
the light fades and before the gas lights are turned on in the office, it is difficult
for Farrington to *see*. His staring "stupidly" at the page might bespeak an ocular
difficulty rather than a dim wit. What could Farrington do at his desk at all,
during this interval of dim twilight in the office before the lamps are lit, when
the poor light makes him vulnerable to the errors that might spoil a page and
require its rewriting? His nipping out to the snug might take on a slightly less
refractory air, if we were given such narrative explanations.

The only satisfaction Farrington receives in the course of this work day is
also the one that will cost him so dearly as to further ruin his evening and perhaps his life, if he ends up being "hounded" out of the office, like "little Peake"
(93).[12] For the abuse heaped on him, "one brief climactic instant of Farrington's
story is singled out as though in compensation," Fritz Senn points out (28). To

Alleyne's hectoring "do you take me for a fool?" Farrington responds with unconcious wit, "I don't think that that's a fair question to put to me" (91). Senn notes, "His final impertinence takes the form of a literal answer to a kind of question that is obviously rhetorical and, as such, the exclusive privilege of superiors" (29). It is telling that in this only moment of spontaneous self-expression, Farrington speaks not his own language or his own idiom, but merely mimics Alleyne's own previous sarcastic habit of literalizing the other's words and throwing them back in his face. Yet ironically, in spite of its witty and counter-aggressive effect, Farrington's retort is literally the only truthful response that could be made to Alleyne's locution. Alleyne is correct in asserting that Farrington has lied, but the demotic "Do you take me for a fool?" is nonetheless a rhetorically "unfair" question designed less to elicit the truth than to coerce an insincere and fraudulent self-abasement. Since the mock-question is unanswerable in this punitive public context, Farrington does the only thing he can do: he converts it into a verbal boomerang whose wit lies in the comment's direction rather than in any overt words. Crosbie & Alleyne is a workplace of textual production in which all speech acts are marked by violence, and no truths seem capable of being uttered.

Alleyne's furious demand for an apology ends the office episode of the story with an ellipsis in place of the elided abject apology Farrington must offer, and thereby spares the reader yet another scene of Farrington's protracted and intensified humiliation. Outside the office, wondering how to find money for a night's drinking, Farrington appears to have achieved a nadir of despair and self-recrimination: "Mr. Alleyne would never give him an hour's rest; his life would be a hell to him. He had made a proper fool of himself this time. Could he not keep his tongue in his cheek?" (92). We are curiously prompted to accept this harsh self-judgment, and even to applaud Farrington's ability to acknowledge that he has made a mistake, without recognizing how thoroughly this implies Farrington's—and the reader's—internalization of the office's oppressive practices and abusive treatments. There has been a total suppression—in Farrington and in the narrative account—of the possible counter-interpretation, that Farrington may have been virtually goaded into his outburst by the cumulative effects of the day's abuses and humiliations. His working life is already a hell to him—yet one he has created for himself by his sloth and his impertinence, we are now prodded to believe. And the continuation of the plot, with its depiction of Farrington's dissolute and unproductive evening's drinking, will continue to intensify the narrative impression of Farrington as a shirker, an escapist, and now a wastrel.

Why does the story spend almost as much time expounding Farrington's evening pub crawl, as his afternoon in the office—and what is the relationship between the two?[13] The pub narrative of "Counterpart" marks another significant aberration from the Melville and Gogol scrivener narratives, whose protagonists are depicted as abstemious, celibate, and reclusive—emptied of virtually all physical, sexual, and social desire. Joyce restores to his scrivener physical, social, and sexual hungers whose satisfaction turns out to be as frustrating and difficult to achieve outside the workplace as in it. This may be so because not only do the oppressions and humiliations of the workday leach into the larger social world of the evening, but because the narrator ultimately maintains a stance complicit with thwarting Farrington's attempt to rise to dignity. At first, there is hope that the homosocial world of the Dublin pubs will offer a potentially therapeutic space in which Farrington's spiritual wounds can be healed and his social status can be restored. As Robert Scholes points out, "in the pub, he is given by the narrator for the first time the dignity of being referred to as 'Farrington' " (384). And indeed, Farrington makes a heroic attempt to salvage something of his pride and his dignity—and, not insignificantly, his manhood— by appropriating the story of his smart retort to Alleyne and tranforming it into a repeatable and circulating pub anecdote that will feature him as a kind of workplace hero. The soul-killing structure of discursive *repetition* could thereby be rehabilitated to serve a socially meliorative and rehumanizing function. However, the failure of Farrington's recuperative efforts in the pubs speaks to the ineluctable interpenetrabilities of the spheres of work, social space, and home, and the inability to compartmentalize their economies of violence.

Before beginning his pub crawl, Farrington compounds the day's mistakes by pawning his watch for the six shillings that Gifford reckons to be "worth between $30 and $35 in modern pub exchange," an amount that "would probably represent one-fifth to one-fourth of his weekly wage" (75). The narrator gives us no way of knowing what sort of necessity a watch represents to a man who must work against deadlines in his office all day. But the "little cylinder of coins" he rubs between his thumb and fingers momentarily transforms Farrington into the kind of man he could be, and would like to be. It is also the kind of man he never *will be* (an echo of the script of "*In no case shall the said Bernard Bodley be*" [90]): a joyful man who overlooks Dublin's noisy and mean streets with "proud satisfaction" and who stares "masterfully at the office-girls" (91). For a few moments, Farrington turns into an *anti-scrivener* or, more ominously, into a potential Alleyne. However, he uses this assured moment to rehearse his anecdote of the "smart answer," as Joe Donnelly calls it in "Clay," for presentation to his friends in Davy Byrne's: "—So, I just looked at him—coolly, you know, and looked at her. Then I looked back at him again—taking my time, you know. *I don't think that that's a fair question to put to me,* says I" (93). His murderous rage is transformed into an unruffled "coolly, you know" and the spontaneous blurt is transformed into a calm deliberation, "taking my time, you know." Garry Leonard points out that Farrington's imaginary editing of the scene also significantly deletes the respectful "sir" from the original retort, and notes: "Equally significant, however, is what he retains: the arbitrating presence of Miss Delacour's gaze" (178). Farrington's inclusion of the ocular gesture of looking to Miss Delacour for approval does more than mimic Alleyne's own gesture. It also draws our attention to an aspect of Farrington's perception that the narrative obscures with its allusion to his "dirty eyes": namely, that Farrington is a keen observer and interpreter of gestural semiotics and body language. If we return, for a moment, to what he may have observed in this regard in the office, further dimensions of the inconsistent protocols of the workplace become visible.

For a man who mercilessly hounds his workers to greater diligence, and for an office in which there is constant frantic pressure to meet deadlines, Alleyne's comportment with his client Miss Delacour, is curious. The narrative explanation is given as though it had some relevance for Farrington: "Mr. Alleyne was said to be sweet on her or on her money. She came to the office often and stayed a long time when she came" (90). The scene the narrator reports, presumably witnessed by Farrington, is one utterly atypical for this office: a professional encounter in which gestures are languorously slowed down ("smoothing the handle of her umbrella and nodding the black feather in her hat") and body postures are relaxed. "Mr Alleyne had swivelled his chair round to face her and thrown his right foot jauntily upon his left knee" (90), we are told. Clearly the office protocols are reconfigured for the benefit of favored clients to represent a civilized, relaxed, and congenial atmosphere that is rigorously denied the workers at any time. In this scenario of Miss Delacour's visit to Alleyne's office, Farrington becomes an invisible factotem. He is dismissed with a tap on the file and a wordless "flicking" gesture of dismissal that the narrator nonetheless translates into a polite order of a kind Alleyne is shown incapable of uttering in reality: *"That's all right: you can go"* (90). The urbane Alleyne in Miss Delacour's presence is an imposter violently exposed by his tirade upon discovery of the missing letters. The spectators' response to Farrington's smart retort to this tirade is also conveyed by body language—"There was a pause in the very breathing of the clerks," and "Miss Delacour, who was a stout amiable person, began to smile broadly" (91). This silent response is clearly a balm to the battered Farrington, who may even have mustered the unconscious courage to stand up to Alleyne as defense against the indignity of being used as his boss's prop for impressing Miss Delacour. We might speculatively wish to complete this plot with the hope that Mr. Alleyne "had done for himself in the office" (97) too, at least as far as Miss Delacour is concerned, and that she realizes she can do better than having a repellent, ranting little martinet as her attorney.

Garry Leonard calls the exotic and colorful English *artiste* that Farrington encounters in the back parlor of Mulligan's later in the evening "the counterpart of Miss Delacour," thereby drawing attention to the continuities and repetitions between the working day and the social evening.[14] These begin with Farrington first offering his rehearsed repetition of the smart answer to Nosey Flynn. Nosey Flynn, reported in *Ulysses* as also occupying a special nook in Davy Byrne's, rewards him with both approbation ("saying it was as smart a thing as ever he heard") and "a half-one" (93). The story is repeated to O'Halloran and Paddy Leonard, and this time elicits tailors of malt and O'Halloran's own smart retort story. Finally, Farrington's co-worker Higgins, the "man with two establishments to keep up" (who got Joyce into endless trouble with Grant Richards) repeats the story with vivid gestures ("Everyone roared laughing when he showed the way Mr Alleyne shook his fist in Farrington's face. Then he imitated Farrington, saying, *And here was my nabs, as cool as you please*" [94]). After having been forced, like Miss Delacour, to witness Farrington's discursive humiliation, the reader with any sympathy may be so pleased with these hard-earned discursive satisfactions as to forget how utterly bogus they are, and how completely the pub-story falsifies what transpired at Crosbie & Alleyne's that afternoon. "Of course, the calm and masterful 'Farrington' that Higgins is imitating *was not present* during the scene with Mr. Alleyne," Garry Leonard writes (179), and suggests that Farrington is watching an ideal mirror image of himself in the imitations of others.[15]

Had Farrington quit drinking after leaving Davy Byrne's, he could presumably have returned home with some money remaining in his pocket, some satisfaction in the successful delivery of his story, some pride restored, and some physical discomfort alleviated by the various malts and drinks consumed. Why does Joyce protract his evening, into more and more socially remote venues, and into encounters with the more socially removed characters of the artistes? What is the point of having Farrington continue to two more pubs, and to subject him to the new humiliations of being brushed off by the beautiful Englishwoman and beaten at arm-wrestling by the English acrobat? On the level of pub customs, logistics, and alcoholic urgency, drinking is interrupted or terminated only when funds dry up or the bar closes. Thus the party at Davy Byrne's breaks up when Nosey Flynn and Higgins run out of funds. Farrington, Leonard, and O'Halloran move on to the Scotch House, and then on to Mulligan's after it closes. Joyce seems to use this improvisational geography to have Farrington descend into a kind of defamiliarized underworld peopled by strangers and foreigners who create a different cultural caste system that will also defeat him. The second phase of pub-crawling is necessary, I believe, to disrupt an easy dichotomy between an oppressive working life and a liberating social life. Joyce seems to want to make the point that "caste" operates oppressively in both. In addition, the unflattering narrative voice is implicated in the disparagements both worlds visit upon the scrivener.

Once Paddy Leonard introduces Weathers into the group at the Scotch House, the cultural tenor of the party changes to Farrington's disadvantage. Whiskey is drunk with expensive Appolinaris, the rules of reciprocity are protested, the "talk became theatrical"(94) with, presumably, little interest in having Farrington repeat his smart answer story yet again. The topic of sex is introduced when Weathers promises to take the men backstage and introduce them "to some nice girls" (94). We now learn for the first time that Farrington is married. The narrative rhetoric now extends the earlier intimation of Farrington's roving eye "staring masterfully at the office-girls" (93) to suggest that he is capable of philandering. "O'Halloran said that he and Leonard would go but that Farrington wouldn't go because he was a married man; and Farrington's heavy dirty eyes leered at the company in token that he understood he was being chaffed" (94). In a story in which fairness is throughout at issue, one might complain that the narrator is not being entirely fair at this moment. The physical effect of Farrington's eyes, "his eyes bulged forward slightly and the whites of them were dirty" is here troped, by association with "leered," into lewd ogling— even though there is at that moment no woman on the scene. The intimation, however, seems confirmed at Mulligan's, when "Farrington's eyes wandered at every moment" in the direction of the striking young Englishwoman with the peacock-blue scarf tying her hat, and the bright yellow gloves reaching to her elbow. Once again we see Farrington's acute observation of gestures, "the plump arm which she moved very often and with much grace," and the "oblique staring expression" of "her large dark eyes" (95), and his interpretation, or misinterpretation, of them as seductive signals. Joyce here resexualizes the scrivener and even endows him with some aesthetic discernment; yet the narrative prompt will lead us to find his proclivities, ones we will be quite willing to forgive in a Leopold Bloom, swinish when they appear in a Farrington.[16]

Farrington's disappointed anger at the woman's imagined brush-off recreates the condition earlier in the office, when his "imagination had so abstracted him" (91) that he lost all sense of his surroundings and failed to register the ominous appearance of Mr. Alleyne and Miss Delacour at the counter. At Mulligan's, the dangerous new situation is created by the discussion of feats of strength that Farrington's abstraction had blocked out. Farrington neither seeks, nor can escape, the predicament of being put forward as a strong man, since it is cloaked in patriotic banter—"the other two had called on Farrington to uphold the national honour" (95). The arm-wrestling contest is a set-up for Farrington's humiliation. If he wins, it redounds little to his credit, since he is so clearly the much larger man of the two. If he loses—and he loses—his humiliation is intensified by the advantage his great size should have given him, and made especially embarrassing by the symbolic stakes of the "national honor." By reporting Farrington's imagined violence all day—"He felt strong enough to clear out the whole office single-handed" (90)—the narrator has also set the reader up to expect that Farrington will easily win, and we too are therefore surprised by his defeat "by such a stripling" (96). Once again, the narrator could have ameliorated Farrington's humiliation by pointing out that as an acrobat, the young and slight Weathers has a body trained for upper-body strength and stamina. Its contest with Farrrington's easily winded and unwholesome bulk was *not*, in fact, entirely "fair," as Farrington (pronounced *Fair*-ington?) claims. But by putting the blame on Weathers's putting his weight behind his arm, Farrington misses the point of the unfairness, and further reveals himself to be a sore loser and a lousy sport. His character continues to be repeatedly impugned by the narrative voice, even while the lesson implicit in his experiences—that Farrington's great size and violent temper count for nothing in the face of small men who are invested with power and other advantages pursuant to their "caste"—goes narratively unregistered. By having Farrington fare (pun intended) as badly in the pubs as in the office, Joyce makes the point that physical power does not readily translate into social power. This point redresses the very different symbolic management of size and respect deployed in the story that precedes "Counterparts": "A Little Cloud."

By the start of the third section of "Counterparts," his return to his home, the final rout of Farrington's dignity has been accomplished. In addition to his earlier losses—"He had done for himself in the office, pawned his watch, spent all his money; and he had not even got drunk" (97)—his remaining assets as a man have also been despoiled. The lost arm-wrestling match and brush-off by the artiste have negated his great size and whatever imagined sexual attractiveness it might have conferred. "His heart swelled with fury . . . his fury nearly choked him" (97) as he heads reluctantly for home. "He loathed returning to his home" (97), the narrator tells us, and its site near the Beggar's Bush Barracks, where Donald Torchiana locates it, does not make it sound enticing. Finding a cold, dark, empty kitchen from which the wife is absent, where the fire has gone out and there is no dinner waiting for him, is clearly no justification for beating a small and defenseless child. But neither is this a home condition designed to soothe or quiet a man in a dark and violent mood. Warren Beck's calling his home a "lair" implies that Farrington's brutish presence makes it one, and that the domestic shell he encounters that evening is no more than he deserves. He has, after all, drunk the proceeds of the pawned watch, and this leads us to presume that he generally drinks his family's sustenance. Nonetheless, to a man coming home after the kind of day Farrington has had, a home with no fire, no heat, no light, no dinner, no wife, may present itself as the last straw. Farrington comes home in a dangerous mood, and O'Halloran already saw the danger signs in the last pub, when he shushed and hurried Farrington out before his social constraints could give way altogether—"Sh,sh! said O'Halloran, observing the violent expression of Farrington's face" (96). But the "little boy" charged with lighting a lamp, hastily building a fire, and cooking a dinner for a defeated, hungry, drunken man, has no such shield. No child should bear such a burden, and we find ourselves wishing that Ada Farrington had anticipated the danger of exposing her child to the temper of a man coming home late from the office, tired, hungry, and most likely drunk, on a cold, dark, and foggy February night.

The allusion to the bullying reciprocities of the couple—Ada "bullied her husband when he was sober and was bullied by him when he was drunk" (97)—raises other interesting questions, such as whose bullying came first. We are led to believe by the narrated day that Farrington's drinking has produced Ada's justifiable reaction over the course of the marriage. But why could it not have been the other way around? Why could Farrington's alcoholism not be construed as his defense against an intolerable shrew? The narrator tells us that "He loathed returning to his home" (97) without explaining why. Is it because he fears he is not yet drunk enough to stand up to the tirade of an angry and reproachful wife and that a third bout of failure and humiliation is in store for him? Is the Ada he encounters when he is sober the *counterpart* of Alleyne, yet another small person with the power to harangue and humiliate him? We are led to believe that only in his home, shared with the sharp-faced little woman and the five children, does Farrington's physical size, strength, and aggressive temper translate into authority and literal power. But is this true only when he is drunk enough to overpower them without scruple, and not at other times? I realize that I am pushing my argument to the unacceptable extreme here of seeming to shift blame away from Farrington and onto the innocent Ada and her luckless home, and I wish, finally, not to really believe in the justification of my own argument. But I feel provoked to this exercise, as an exercise, because the narrative deck has been stacked so decisively against Farrington. A reader's resistance to the story's impregnable ethical conclusion has virtually no chance of credence or sympathy. It is much easier to conjure up a different counter-narrative, of Ada Farrington as belonging to the victimized sisterhood that includes Mrs. Kernan, Mrs. Dignam, Mrs. MacDowell, Mrs. Hill, and even May Dedalus. When their stories are told by a narrator with the husband's interests as the agenda—as in the later story "Grace"—then it is the wife's counternarrative that must be read against the narrative grain.

But by giving this story its brutal ending—of a drunken, enraged man viciously beating a small child trying to serve and placate him—the narration destroys all sympathy for Farrington. The scene is unthinkable in the scrivener tale convention. Imagine a frustrated and brutalized Bob Cratchit coming home and beating a terrified Tiny Tim with a stick. Why does Joyce commit such an act of intertextual violence—effectively annihilating a tradition of clerking reform fiction—by making his protagonist so shamelessly savage as to make him irredeemable? For one thing, because it is true, as we learn from Stanislaus Joyce's diary. Stanislaus tells of his uncle, William Murray, beating his son "Bertie, then an infant of six or seven," who "begged Uncle William not to beat him and promised to say a 'Hail Mary' for him if he didn't" (37). But Warren Beck is insistent that Joyce is also intent on desentimentalizing the naturalistic stereotype of the oppressed clerk with an appeal to the responsibilities of individualism. "But in contrast to some naturalistic treatments of such a concept, with Farrington it does not falsify a total social reality by sentimentalizing and thus denaturing the underdog; it still implies his primary responsibility" (188), he writes. Has Joyce indeed shifted the ethical valence of the scrivener genre from Marxism to existentialism? Not necessarily, I think. Given the contemporary sociology of genealogical abuse—that abusers produce abusers—the ending of "Counterparts" could be reckoned as the fulfillment of a parable of the unstoppable violence engendered by the oppressive workplace.

But for an alternative consideration, I would go back to the trope of the scrivener and the theme of frustrated, imprisoned, and doomed expression that governs the spoken discourse in the story. I would argue that an important factor in the unstoppability of the discursive workplace violence is the failure of discourse—like that of tiny Tom's "Hail Mary"—to function as a direct and effective instrument of defense or redress. This is true within the story, where Farrington's abusive conditions cannot be narrated or told without compounding Farrington's humiliation. He cannot confront Mr. Alleyne with them, nor his chief clerk, nor even Higgins, except—if he is to salvage his pride and "face"—as a counter-aggression, a mimicry and mockery of Alleyne. And in the pub he cannot repeat his smart retort to his boss with its context of humiliation and abuse intact—as a story of self-vindication in the face of public violence—without erasing from the mythologized version all traces of his pain. To whom could Farrington tell the story of his violated existence? To his office workers? To his friends in the pubs? Certainly not to the wife who is herself victimized by his undisciplined work habits, squandered wages, and threatened livelihood. Imagine Ada Farrington, had she been home, sympathizing with the smart retort her husband made to Mr. Alleyne in the office once she learns that his watch is pawned and his job threatened. Garry Leonard insightfully recognizes Farrington's copying mistake of the sentence "*In no case shall the said Bernard Bodley be . . .*" (90) as Farrington's own ontological life sentence: "This clerical breakdown nearly results in a nervous breakdown and underlines, in concentrated and stark terms, that in no case shall Farrington be" (180). Farrington can tell his story, with his pain and humiliation intact, to no one. Instead of a scrivener story that might inform an agenda of reform, Joyce produced a scrivener story about the impossibility of telling a scrivener story.

## Chapter 10

# Narration Under the Blindfold in "Clay"

"Clay" is a *deceptively* simple little story by design: its narrative self-deception attempts, and fails, to mislead the reader. But as a special case of the blind leading the blind, "Clay" also offers the multiple revelations that come with the restoration of sight: it allows us to see the blind spots in Maria's story and, in them, to see ourselves as their cause, if not their instrument. Joyce displays a surprising philosophical and technical maturity in this very early work, whose object is, I believe, to dramatize the powerful workings of desire in human discourse and human lives. In "Clay" this desire, whatever its etiology or source, must contend with the symbolic values that attach to socially constructed categories of inclusion and exclusion: class, gender, age, and normative figurations of the body. The perfect protagonist for this purpose is indeed the *old maid*: a figure who seems to lack everything and therefore embodies total desire. Her desire is that of all human beings: a desire for recognition and prestige. And it is the task of "Clay's narration to let a poor old woman without family, wealth, or social standing maintain her human status in paralytic Dublin, by telling her story in a way that will be credited by those who hear it. In pursuit of this goal, "Clay" will attempt to mislead the reader. It fails, curiously, when we become deaf to its telling, as it were, and start *seeing* its events without the interference of the narrative voice. Only then can we recognize that the text has functioned like a bandaged wound. The narration, in this metaphor, functions as a *patch,* an emblem as well of genteel poverty, an attempt to bridge the gap between class circumstance and class desire, a discursive attempt to claim possession of the virtues and values (in the absence of the resources) of the middle class.

In addition to its textual functions, the narrational manipulations of "Clay" produce extra-textual effects as well. Let me demonstrate. In developing an allegory of Maria as "the Poor Old Woman or Ireland herself," William York Tindall writes, "Shopkeepers condescend to her; and when a British colonel is polite to her on the tram, she loses her cake" (30). A British colonel? The narration tells us only that "Maria thought he was a colonel-looking gentleman and she reflected how much more polite he was than the young men who simply stared straight before them" (102). Tindall has risen to the narrative bait and has swallowed Maria's efforts to inflate the bumptious attentions of a garrulous old drunk into the courtly devoirs of a gentleman of rank from the ruling class. He never questions, for example, what a British colonel in pre-republican Ireland would be doing on the Drumcondra tram in mufti. This small mistake is quite unimportant in itself,[1] but it is symptomatic of a larger impulse in the critical history of the story that, curiously, precisely mirrors Maria's own quest. Readers and critics of the story frequently can no more accept the possibility of Maria's insignificance than can Maria herself. The impulse behind the critical tradition of "Clay," with its heavy emphasis on allegorizing Maria in some form—as either Witch or Blessed Virgin, for example—is therefore a curiously collusive response to the story's rhetorical aim of aggrandizing Maria. This allegorizing tendency extends beyond the boundaries of the story to a strain in Joyce criticism as a whole that Derek Attridge and Daniel Ferrer call the "transcendentalist" approach to Joyce's fiction (5), and that they trace back to T. S. Eliot's influence as a critic of Joyce. The motives impelling its allegorizing strategies include the need to save modern fiction from charges of triviality, vulgarity, and nihilism by assimilating it to larger symbolic orders and traditionally sanctioned systems of value. But behind its quasi-religious motivation, Eliot's transcendental aesthetics are impelled by a class ideology that equates the spiritual torpor of modernity with the material squalor of its masses. Joyce, however, explores in "Clay" the psycho-politics of one of the least significant members of such an urban mass.

The critical need to create significance out of pointlessness also shapes the reading that many of my students have been taught before they come to my classes: specifically, that the meaning of the story depends on interpreting the "clay" as "death." This symbolic equation is generally delivered as though it constituted some sort of punch line, some sort of illumination that makes sense of an otherwise meaningless joke. "Death" is, of course, a privileged figure in medieval allegory, and, in this interpretation, Maria's failure to perceive its prophetic beckoning through the symbols of the game makes her—all evidence of her sincere Catholic piety to the contrary—a kind of vain and foolish *Jedermann*. But the reading of "clay" as "death" is anomalous within the context of the story, for even if All Hallow Eve is the night the dead walk abroad in folk tradition,[2] thought of death is conspicuously absent both from the narration and from its representation of Maria's thoughts. When Joyce does want a story read through a tropology of "death" (as in "The Dead" or in "Hades"), he weaves a complex texture of incident and allusion to guide us to his meaning.

I will suggest a different way of reading "Clay" that takes its cue from the interpretive backfire that reveals at the heart of the desire for significance the operation of its lack. The critics' need to capitalize Maria, to transform her negative attributes into positive symbols—from poor old woman into Poor Old Woman, from witch-like into Witch, from virginal into Blessed Virgin—betray how little esteem the social construct of the ungarnished old maid is able to muster. It is not Joyce, I will argue, who promotes the old maid to metaphoric status as much as he explores her need, and her strategies, for promoting herself. These strategies are narrational and rhetorical, as "Clay" becomes her defense against her interiorization of all the derision and contempt that has been her traditional portion. As an older or aging spinster, she has status as a superfluous or useless excess in a country that in the century following the Great Famine "had the highest rate of unmarried men and women in the world" (Walzl, "Women in Irish Society" 33). To the extent that these strategies fail, the reader is implicated and functions as a critical actor in the story. Joyce dramatizes the social consequences and psychological costs of feeling oneself designated as insignificant as a repressive force that splits all the discursive elements of the story in two: the story's subject, its narrative mode, and its reader. Maria divides into two versions of herself (into admirable and pathetic, bourgeois and proletarian, Lady Bountiful and victim). The narration is split in two, into testimonial and exposé, prattle and pantomime, empty language and expressive silence. And the reader is split in two—into gullible narratee and cynical critic, flattered ear and penetrating gaze, consumer of realism and dupe of naturalism. This fractured discourse of "Clay" is produced by the interplay between the two senses of *significance* working through the text: *significance* as an experience of psychological importance or ontological prestige, and *significance* as the linguistic or semiological meaning produced by language. It is the exigencies of the first (Maria's need to be significant) that brings about the manipulations of the second, as though the text were trying to control its own meaning because its interpretation *mattered* to Maria.[3]

At this point it is necessary to emphasize two theoretical points about the nature of desire that help to account for the curious *social* function of the narration of "Clay" and for the phantasmal nature of the narrative voice. In metaphysical terms, desire is always born out of an *imaginary* lack, and desire is therefore always desire for recognition from others.[4] Maria's lacks are imaginary because, like everyone, as an organism she is a plenum. She has everything sufficient for life, and the things she lacks (marriage, wealth, class, beauty) exist only symbolically, in the significance they have for her. Their significance is itself grounded in the way these attributes of identity and being are considered desirable by "others." Maria is victimized by class and gender ideology as a result of the way class and gender attributes become socially codified and significant. Such differences as those between male and female, between being married and single, being sexually active and celibate, being fertile and barren, for example, become ontologically as well as semiotically significant within the symbolic order of Maria's society. As an old maid, Maria is made especially to suffer from her assorted *lacks*. Of course, being an unmarried, childless, and virginal woman doesn't make Maria intrinsically less valuable. But it does endow her, in her social world, with a negation of prestige whose consequences are encoded even in something as trivial as a card game called Old Maids. This game overtly plays on the old spinster as the nightmare image of undesirability, whose visitation is greeted with dread and disgust as though she could spread her own negativity, her status as loser, to all she touches. It is, in fact, a different children's game that Maria plays in "Clay": a game of divination that foretells the future life of young virgins (*JJII* 158), a future whose state-of-life symbols (ring and prayer book, for example) express the signs of sexually marked and unmarked states. Maria's inappropriate inclusion in the game—she is, after all, an adult and already has a life—betrays the way a sexually unmarked life, a life negatively marked as virginal, is treated by her society as a life perpetually deferred.[5]

The symptoms the old maid's lacks produce are therefore not solitary brooding and depression, but social strategies designed to capture significance by winning the approval of the "other." This theoretical background helps to shape a more precise explanation for the sense we have that, although "Clay" is narrated in the third person, it is *really* Maria speaking.[6] I would formulate it this way: narrative speech in "Clay" is, for the most part, uttered in the language of Maria's desire; it is Maria's desire speaking. And because it is the function of the narration to restore significance to Maria, it preserves the triangular structure of an eavesdropped conversation: the narrative voice of "Clay" describes Maria as she would like to catch someone speaking about her to someone else. Expressed differently, the narration is putatively directed toward us, to tell us about Maria, but its true beneficiary is Maria herself, whose prestige is certified by being "recognized" by objective and anonymous "others." This imaginary social function of the narration is demonstrated with an explicit and literate double in the flattering reviews Thomas Chandler in "A Little Cloud" would like to imagine as bestowed on the verses he has yet to write. "Clay"'s narration has its analogue in Chandler's invention of flattering "English critics" for his hypothetical writing. The personification of "Clay"'s narrative voice, if we were to construct a "narrator" from these functions, would produce an impossible social hybrid. This narrator would be a creature that is simultaneously Maria's social superior (like the authoritative and eloquent Protestant matron) and her metaphysical inferior (as loyally committed to her admiration and protection as the "vassals and serfs" of her song). This is why the narration is ultimately so counterproductive on its errand of desire. It is as though Maria sends us an inadequate signifier to extol her merits: a servant in the penetrable disguise of master. It is not the narrator, but the flawed stratagem of devising a narrative voice that will speak flatteringly of her, that betrays Maria's ontological plight.

Some of the distinctive features of "Clay" 's narration can now be explained in terms of its function of gratifying Maria's desire for recognition. Its rhetoric is shaped to restore to Maria, discursively, everything that might seem to constitute a social "lack" for her: beauty, husband, children, home, wealth, status—albeit with the qualifications and feints of psychological realism. Restored, these things remain as imaginary as when they were "lacks," but they allow Maria to feel *as though* she possessed them. The narrational rhetoric presents her *as though* she enjoyed the security of wealth ("how much better it was to be independent and to have your own money in your pocket" [102]). Maria is presented *as though* she had the affection of a family ("he had wanted her to go and live with them" [100]). The narration treats her *as though* she had emotional, if not biological, children ("but Maria is my proper mother" [100]) and enough attractiveness for her purposes ("she found it a nice tidy little body" [101]). The effect of these restorations is to create a version of Maria's condition that she presumably would like to believe, although the narration does not ultimately succeed in making it tenable. According to this, Maria is a well-bred, middle-class, maiden lady living on a small but independent income from a job that earns her the respect of coworkers and superiors. Though unmarried and, of course, childless, she enjoys the affection of a surrogate family that had once employed her more as a governess than as a domestic and that still cherishes her as a favorite sort of godmother who visits them on holidays laden with gifts. This version of Maria's life is contradicted by a second, repressed version that is never articulated in the narrative speech, but must be read in the narrative silences, ruptures, and evasions that lie between the lines, or in the margins of the text. These silences constitute the smudged and effaced portions of the "Clay" palimpsest. According to this second, unconscious version which she *knows* but does not *recognize*, Maria works long hours for meager pay as a scullion in a laundry for reformed prostitutes who make her the butt of their jokes. She is ignored and patronized by everyone, including the family whose slavey she once was and from whom she succeeds in extorting only a minimal and ritualized tolerance by manipulating their guilt and pity. These two versions are intrinsically related, and it is important to remember that they are both psychically *authored* (but not *authorized*) by Maria. The first, positive version functions to replace and abolish the second, whose *truth* about her insignificance Maria finds intolerable. It fails in spite of the inestimable advantage of being articulated in speech. Maria's fears can utter the negative version of her life, her paranoid *truth*, only in silent semiologies: a wince, a blush, a lost object, a moment of forgetfulness, a mistake. "Clay" 's narration becomes a psychological mise en scène in which desire is attacked from within.

The drama that transpires within the narrative speech of "Clay" inevitably triggers a hermeneutical drama that fragments and conflicts the reader. Although I will reify this reader as "we" in my discussion of the story, I intend the plural to encompass not only the collectivity of actual readers, but also the multiplicity of roles that the "reader" as a fictional construct of the story embodies. This reified *we* encompasses such readerly roles as the gullible narratee, the skeptical critic, the self-reflexive meta-reader. "Clay" also utilizes, I believe, the extent to which the reader has been historically constructed by novelistic convention. "Clay" 's narratee, for example, the putative listener who believes that Maria's life is simple, but good and admirable, embodies the ideology of a docile consumer of nineteenth-century narrative conventions. This interpretation reflects the *fiction* of Victorian fiction: that mousy governesses and plain dependents, the Jane Eyres and Esther Summersons, can become the heroes of their lives and stories by their everyday acts and virtues—a fiction cruelly subverted by Flaubert in "Un coeur simple." But as discrepancies mount between what is said and what is shown, the reader is transformed into a critical gaze, hostile to Maria's desire in its determination to see her not as she wishes to be seen, but as *she wishes not to be seen.* This vision corresponds to the aims and methods of naturalism, as it exposes beneath bourgeois desire and delusion the occluded squalor and humiliation in the lives of the poor. Where the reader as narratee hears the testimonials of Maria's admiring coworkers, for example, the reader as critic sees old prostitutes amuse themselves at her expense. But Joyce ultimately subjects even this naturalistic *truth* to a final interrogative twist that causes the text to reflect the reader's smug superiority like a mirror. In the end, the reader of "Clay" is read by the text.

The reader's collusions and defections from the narrative agenda are partly conditioned by the authority (and its erosion) of the narrative voice. "Clay" could not be narrated in the first person, by Maria herself, because if Maria is really as insignificant as she (unconsciously) believes, we would undoubtedly dismiss her flattering version of herself as empty boasting or wishful thinking. Furthermore, the narration engenders doubt as to whether Maria *could* speak for herself. She is, after all, quoted directly only in her reactive speech, as affirming or disclaiming the statements of others, "*Yes, my dear*" and "*No, my dear*" (99).[7] We don't know if her elided "actual" speech would possess the refinement of accent and diction required to convey the favorable impression that is its object. It makes sense, therefore, to imagine Maria implicitly inventing, or wishing she could invent, a spokesperson who will speak *for* her (while pretending to speak *of* her) in the ways she cannot speak for herself. This narrator (the fictitious embodiment of this invented or wished-for narrative voice) must therefore be rendered respectable, and to this end an important strategy in the arsenal of desire is produced: imitation. The narrative voice probably does not speak in the language of Maria's actual class—whose diction can't be verified from the text—but in the idiom of someone mimicking the accents of respectable bourgeois folks, like the matron of the *Dublin by Lamplight* laundry— "so genteel" (100). In this, the narration of "Clay" operates precisely on Hugh Kenner's "Uncle Charles Principle" insofar as " 'The Uncle Charles Principle' entails writing about someone much as that someone would choose to be written about" (*Joyce's Voices* 21). The gentility of Maria's attitudes and opinions is characterized by her imputed accentuation of the positive ("she found it a nice tidy little body" [101]) and polite circumlocutions ("how easy it was to know a gentleman even when he has a drop taken" [103]. In speaking of her, the narrative voice represents, if not the language of the bourgeoisie, then Maria's notion of both the sentiment and the phrasing of proper middle-class speech. R. B. Kershner writes of this language, "If 'Counterparts' is a paradigm of linguistic aggression, 'Clay' is the model of affirmative appeasement" (105).

The narrative voice further buttresses its credibility by producing documentation of Maria's prestige in the form of testimonials from witnesses in all strata of her world. Strategically clustered at the beginning of the narration, in order to create a favorable first impression, these testimonials are curiously self-canceling because each tribute to Maria appears to depend on pushing aside an unpleasant reality in her world. One of the laundry women, for example, will certify Maria's influence and moral persuasion in language that inflates Maria's diplomatic skill by setting it in an implied climate of bullying and violence. "And Ginger Mooney was always saying what she wouldn't do to the dummy who had charge of the irons if it wasn't for Maria" (99), we are told. The cook illustrates Maria's domestic skill by replacing with an aesthetic image ("the cook said you could see yourself in the big copper boilers" [99]) the grimmer visage of Maria's drudgery as she scours and scrubs the pots to make them shiny. But the most prestigious testimonial comes from a witness in authority whose commendation is quoted verbatim—"One day the matron had said to her:—Maria, you are a veritable peace-maker!" (99). Maria's peace-making, the estimation of the matron, and the matron's fine vocabulary—"veritable"—are all paraded here, and any remaining skeptics are offered additional corroboration—"And the sub-matron and two of the Board ladies had heard the compliment" (99). But not only does this lavish praise for Maria's intervention paradoxically draw attention to the chronic quarreling and dissension that seem to necessitate it: later narrative events sharply dispute these claims for its success by dramatizing just the opposite. Maria's meddling into the Donnelly brothers' quarrel[8] nearly kindles a marital fight. We may hear of her peacemaking, but we see these efforts prolong and multiply discord.

This complimentary prattle becomes exposed as empty words about the self that fill the space of Maria's insecurities as soon as we confront the censored blanks in the narrative discourse. The first of these occurs when a string of pleasantries about the *Dublin by Lamplight* laundry is punctured by a curious complaint. We are told that "There was one thing she didn't like and that was the tracts on the walls; but the matron was such a nice person to deal with, so genteel" (100). The text creates a series of related enigmas about the laundry: that it has a puzzling religious and institutional character rather than a more logical commercial nature, and that pious Maria is inexplicably offended by a religious text on its walls. This informational gap clearly defines the story's narratee as a naïf who will be impressed by the elegant Ballsbridge address, but whose ignorance about the precise nature of *Dublin by Lamplight* can be exploited to Maria's good account. Groping for an explanation, the puzzle about Maria's complaint diverts the narratee's attention from the nature of the laundry and draws it to the only difference that seems to signify: the sectarian difference between Catholic and Protestant. The complaint is interpreted as another of Maria's virtues, a theological virtue, no less, in the form of her Catholic orthodoxy affronted by Protestant bible-thumping. Only the reader armed with the knowledge that *Dublin by Lamplight* was a charitable institution for reformed prostitutes (Beck 204) can foil this narrative stratagem and discover what it conceals. It tells us that Maria knows the kind of place that is her home, and that the tracts on the walls are a constant reminder of that fact. Even if she could overlook the vulgarity and the violence of the women, anyone who visits her at the laundry finds its status advertised on its walls.[9] It is worth noting the skill of the narrative voice in keeping the true nature of the laundry a secret, and its cunning in remarking, but disguising, Maria's discomfort with it.

If we explore the sermiotics of Maria's complaint just a little further, however, its structure as a censored blank comes into even clearer focus. The laundry's scandal—the sexual promiscuity whose abolition is its premise—is communicated to us through a series of displaced negations or effacements. The narrator transforms us, in a sense, into a myopic or blind person, confronted by a wall we cannot see that contains writing we cannot read, even though we are given to understand that it is there. The blindfold motif is thus introduced as a structure of reading before it becomes thematized in the children's game later in the story, the children's game set in Drumcondra, famous (as Torchiana tells us [160]) for housing St. Joseph's Asylum for the Blind. If readers *could* read the tract on the wall of the laundry, they would find in the text only the erasure of the vice, the bleaching of the stain, as it were, in the exhortation to reform that is its message. But as it stands, we as readers are given to read all of this only through the disapproval in Maria's eye as she gazes at walls we do not see.

The transitional passages that relate Maria's journey from Ballsbridge to Drumcondra reflect an apparent narrational shift to accommodate a changing ontological perspective of Maria. The laundry and the Donnelly home represent sheltered interior spaces in which Maria appears to be socially encoded in flattering and affectionate terms as valued coworker and dear family friend. But her journey thrusts Maria—anonymously and without credentials—into an outer world of crowded trams and frenetic shoppers in which she must make her way existentially, without the help of flattering testimonials. The narrative voice is obliged to adopt a seemingly existential mode in this section, relying on description as much as on interpretation, and reporting action as much as attitude. This makes the manipulation of the reader's favorable response more difficult—a problem that produces a set of self-correcting narrative maneuvers. The narration really only *seems* more objective in this section, and while this lends it a particularly credible sound, it exerts itself no less in Maria's service. Whenever the narration cannot quite prevent us from catching glimpses of unflattering external perceptions of Maria, our attention is quickly diverted from the potentially critical eyes of strangers to Maria's laudable mental apparatus. For example, the determined objectivity of the report "The tram was full and she had to sit on the little stool at the end of the car, facing all the people, with her toes barely touching the floor" (102) risks implying that the passengers might have found her pathetic. There she is, "facing all the people" like a child on a dunce stool, with her conspicuous shortness ("her toes barely touching the floor") uncomfortably exposed. But the eyes of the strangers are occluded by a deft narrative move into Maria's mind. There we find no painful self-consciousness whatsoever as she busily tends her affairs ("She arranged in her mind all she was going to do"), cheers herself with happy anticipation, and weaves her concern over the Donnelly boys' fraternal quarrel into home-spun philosophy: "but such was life" (102).

It is not until we see Maria hopelessly dithering about between the two cake shops that we begin to suspect flaws and distractions in her putative mental composure. If she already "arranged in her mind all she was going to do" on the tram, why does she only begin to tackle her major decision of the evening, what treat to buy the Donnelly parents, when she has already finished her shopping in Downes's cake-shop? Standing outside the shop she begins her deliberations from scratch, "Then she thought what else would she buy: she wanted to buy something really nice. They would be sure to have plenty of apples and nuts. It was hard to know what to buy and all she could think of was cake" (102). Of course all she could think of was cake—having just come out of a cake-shop after a protracted wait! A series of revisionist questions suggest themselves at this point. Was Maria distracted in her planning on the tram by the critical stare of the other passengers? Was it really the scanty icing on the Downes's plum-cakes that prompts her to visit another shop or is it her embarrassment and an-noyance at having to re-enter a shop that had served her rather tardily only moments before? Once she decides on plumcake, why does she vacillate so much in the Henry Street store that she earns a smart prod from the clerk? The narrative voice mentions only the stylish saleslady and Maria in the shop, but it does not actually say that they are alone. Is the shop crowded with people who look on testily while Maria takes forever making her decision? I ask these ques-tions to draw attention to the incompleteness and illogicality of what is nar-rated. The narrator's assertion of Maria's composure is often at odds with depictions of her nervous and disorganized behavior, obliging the reader to trust either the narrative speech or the narrated gestures. However, notwith-standing the gaps that invite the investigation of the increasingly skeptical reader, the narrative voice still ably protects Maria from exposure at this point by covering even her self-betraying blush at the clerk's sarcastic wedding refer-ence with an elaborate courtship anecdote as the narration continues on the Drumcondra tram.

If the revisionist reading of the shopping incidents are initiated entirely by the critical reader, the narration itself offers an initial version of what happened on the Drumcondra tram that is subsequently revised in a way that exposes the first account—so flattering to Maria—to have functioned as a "lie." We are given an anecdote of gallantry that mitigates the sense we may have received earlier—through Maria's defensiveness ("she didn't want any ring or man either" [101]) and the revealing blush at the clerk's offer of wedding cake—that she may suffer from a painful and humiliating sense of unmarriagability. But the small vignette on the tram portrays Maria as not only pleasing enough to still attract the atten-tions of a distinguished ("colonel-looking") gentleman, but as capable of enter-taining his courtesies with perfectly well-bred ease and aplomb, "favoured him with demure nods and hems thanked him and bowed" (103). His tipsy-ness is mentioned only as a trivial afterthought embedded in an exoneration-"she thought how easy it was to know a gentleman even when he has a drop taken" (103). But later, when the forgotten plumcake is missed, we receive a different version of Maria's reaction, one that the narrative voice had, in fact, concealed from us—"Maria, remembering how confused the gentleman with the grey-ish moustache had made her, coloured with shame and vexation" (103). This "confusion," and the blush of remembrance it evokes, bears witness to a riot of hopeful, painful, uncontrollable feeling that erupts in Maria at every mention of the subject of marriage—a subject one had assumed was long ago serenely settled as outside her realm of plausible possibilities. We are now invited to recognize that the narrative prose, with its genteel accents, had been giving us the romantic distortions of Maria's desire. It has conveyed the wish to see in a fat, flushed old drunk a courtly gentleman whose military bearing is a metonymic expansion of a grey moustache, and whose social imbibing ("when he has a drop taken") is a synecdochic contraction of intemperate swilling. It is important to ask why the narrative voice would tell us the "truth" about Maria's encounter with the colonel-looking gentleman—namely, that he aroused "confused" feelings in Maria—after having troubled to conceal or censor just that fact in the first place. The answer is that the narration does not technically "lie" in the sense of deliberately concealing a known fact. Rather, it exhibits the "blind spot" that is the epistemological consequence of desire: that as we look for a glorified image of ourselves in the admiring eye of the other, we fail to see ourselves as we are at that moment, as seekers of glorified self-reflections in others' eyes. As the language of her desire, Maria's narration is doomed to fail in its attempt to direct and control how others see her precisely because it has such a "blind spot" and cannot, therefore, entirely manipulate the truth about her—or about itself. Her narration cannot see itself as a language of desire, as it were: it cannot see the insecurities and fears that are its source. The forgotten plumcake catches both Maria and her narrative voice off guard. It causes the narrative voice, shaken by Maria's discomposure, to blurt out a series of damaging revelations, beginning with Maria's hidden excitement on the tram. It also blurts out her urgent need to trade scant resources for good will ("At the thought of the failure of her little surprise and of the two and fourpence she had thrown away for nothing she nearly cried outright" [104]). And it reveals her bad manners in moments of stress ("Then she asked all the children had any of them eaten it— by mistake, of course" [103]). Preoccupied as it is with soothing Maria's distress, the narrative voice that earlier said too little now says, perhaps inadvertently, too much—"the children all said no and looked as if they did not like to eat cakes if they were to be accused of stealing" [103]). This is an important and prescient observation because it supplies the children's motive for their subsequent trick-or-treat-like reprisal against Maria. But the narration obscures its significance by immediately shifting attention away from the injured feelings of the children (who receive no apology from Maria and no sympathy from the narrative voice) and onto the attention lavished on Maria. She is plied with stout, nuts, and entertaining anecdotes—ostensibly to distract her from her loss. The narrative agenda here is clearly to establish Maria's privileged status in the Donnelly household, as it previously established Maria's privileged status in the laundry. The shadowy children, whose unspecified number, gender, and names indicate both Maria's and the narrator's lack of interest in them, are repressed like unpleasant thoughts and behave accordingly. They erupt in unexpected places and in devious ways, and although we never clearly see them there, their grievance is behind the disturbance in the game that causes the narration to falter and nearly fragment. The narration must move quickly and deftly to recover without exposing Maria: "Maria understood that it was wrong that time and so she had to do it over again: and this time she got the prayerbook" (105).

There are such sizable gaps in the narration of the game that the reader is obliged to reconstruct through elaborate inference both a scenario of what happens on the level of plot and an interpretation of what it means. Yet critics who plunge into this task without interrogating the reason for the gaps, and questioning the function they serve in supplementing the narrative, risk being manipulated into narrative collusion. For example, Warren Beck, whose excellent reading of "Clay" I much admire, nonetheless perfectly duplicates the narrator's function of protecting Maria when he construes the game's disturbance as an elaborate protection of Maria (212–14). His reconstruction—that Mrs. Donnelly protects Maria from the shock of receiving the ill omen of "death within the coming year"—begs many questions. If "clay" is a traditional symbolic object in the game, then surely it has been chosen, and survived, by players in previous years and is neither taken seriously nor feared? Why must Maria, who is neither ill nor seemingly concerned with her mortality, be protected from the omen on this particular occasion? If the "clay" is a traditional figure in the game, why doesn't Maria recognize it in the "soft wet substance" she touches and note, with satisfaction, Mrs. Donnelly's kindness in sparing her its meaning? There is nothing in Beck's explanation that the narrative voice, at least, could not report to us explicitly.

I would argue that the narrative fracture of this episode makes sense only if there is something to hide, from Maria, and from us, if we are to be maintained as appreciative narratees. I believe that the narration suppresses the causal link between the lost plumcake and the sabotaged game. The maligned children's reprisal takes the form of a trick that is itself an eruption of the "truth" of the children's true feelings; had it worked, it would have forced further, involuntary, self-betrayals from Maria. The children are coerced into providing involuntary testimonials to Maria's generosity ("Mrs Donnelly said it was too good of her to bring such a big bag of cakes and made all the children say:—Thanks, Maria" [103]) and are prevented from expressing their obvious dislike of her except through the veil of ambiguity. While the narrator nudges us to interpret "O, *here's Maria!"* as a joyful welcome, we can, in retrospect, hear in it the inaudible expletives and qualifications of resigned hostility and displeased surprise, as in *"O god, here's Maria already."* The prank with the garden dirt serves to express and gratify the Donnelly children's aggression toward Maria with minimal risk to themselves. It is perpetrated by the older next-door girls (presumably immune to punishment from the Donnelly parents),[10] and it is a trick that cunningly mitigates the pranksters' blame by manipulating the victim's own imagination to inflict the shock and repulsion that are its harm. For it strikes me as curious, if the "clay" is a symbolic object in the game, that Maria guesses neither its meaning *nor the nature of its substance.* It seems clear to me that Maria is subjected to a much more primitive, conventional, universal childish trick. This is a trick that depends on making the victim mistake a neutral and benign substance (spaghetti, mushroom soup, Baby Ruth bars, in its American versions) for a repulsive, usually excretory material (worms, vomit, feces, etc.). The point of the children's joke, I believe, is to make prim, "genteel" Maria recoil in shock and disgust at the mistaken sensation of touching "excrement"—only to reveal to her, upon removal of the blindfold, the harmless garden dirt. The embarrassment would be self-inflicted: the victim would be betrayed by her own "dirty" mind. Joyce could readily have gotten the idea for such a trick as a version of traditional Hallow Eve games and charms from Nora, who played them as a girl in Galway. Mary O'Holleran, Nora's girlhood pal, describes a somewhat similar game and trick:

We had a party one Holly eve night My father used to make games for us such as cross sticks hanging from the ceiling there would be an apple on one stick soap on the other and a lighted candle on the other stick our eyes would be covered so we could not see and my father would spin the sticks around and we would bite at the apple my father would put the soap in Noras mouth the house would be in roars of laughter while Nora would be getting the soap out of her mouth. (*JJII* 158)

The remarkable thing about this trick in "Clay," of course, is not only that it fails—that Maria doesn't get it—but that a trick, as such, is never mentioned in the story at all, meaning that the narrative voice doesn't "get it" either:

They led her up to the table amid laughing and joking and she put her hand out in the air as she was told to do. She moved her hand about here and there in the air and descended on one of the saucers. She felt a soft wet substance with her fingers and was surprised that nobody spoke or took off her bandage. There was a pause for a few seconds; and then a great deal of scuffling and whispering. Somebody said something about the garden, and at last Mrs Donnelly said something very cross to one of the next-door girls and told her to throw it out at once: that was no play. Maria understood that it was wrong that time and so she had to do it over again: and this time she got the prayer-book. (105)

This is narration under a blindfold.[11] Like Maria's literal blindfold or "bandage," the gap in the narration—the narrative voice's failure to explain to us what really happened—represents, metaphorically, the "blind spot" that marks the site of Maria's psychic wound, her imaginary lacks and fears. For at issue here is more than the simple repression in Maria's failure to make the connection between garden dirt and excrement. She dare not recognize the trick itself, that a trick has been played on her: that she is an object of ridicule, the butt of jokes, a person without sufficient authority to restrain the pranks of malicious youngsters. What is censored by the narration is the significance of what happens, and that significance is the demonstration (once more) of Maria's fear of utter insignificance. What Maria fears is not the touch of excrement on her fingers, but the recognition that her only "family"—like the rest of the world—treats her "like shit." This explains as well why the word "clay" never appears in the story except as its title. The "soft wet substance" in the narrative is never named because the very ambiguity of its identity is fraught with such cruel danger to Maria's ego.[12] The naming of the story poses a similar crux, a similar danger; the chosen title, "Clay," therefore promises an interpretation of Maria's life that preserves complex registers of truth-telling and lying. For the narration of "Clay" is "clay"—in the sense that it is a polite circumlocution that eradicates the dirt and squalor of Maria's life, and thereby replicates her own efforts as a slavey. "Clay" names and exhibits the work of a rhetorical scullion.

Maria's song, her third task in the triadic fairy tale structure of the story, marks—like her earlier efforts of the gift and the game—an unsuccessful social ritual, a failed attempt to govern her symbolic relationships with others to her better advantage. Once again, there is ambiguity in the request that she sing. Perhaps the family asks Maria to sing less because it gives them pleasure ("Mrs Donnelly bade the children be quiet and listen to Maria's song" [105]) than because it is an effective way to get rid of her, to hint that she has overstayed her welcome. "At last the children grew tired and sleepy and Joe asked Maria would she not sing some little song before she went" (105). Maria responds on two levels to the double meanings of this request. Consciously, she fulfills the conventions of parlor performance by acting like a demure girl, feigning reluctance to extort coaxing ("Do, please, Maria!" [105]) and by delivering her song with blushing modesty. Unconsciously, she answers this extrusion from the Donnelly "family" with a song of exile: a song written in language of desire even more explicit than the narration of "Clay." Maria chooses a song from an opera, *The*

*Bohemian Girl,*[13] that presents a nearly perfect example of the infantile wish fantasy Freud called the "family romance": the child's fantasy that its parents are really imposters, and that its "true" parents are royalty or aristocrats to whom it will one day be restored. The prescience of Bunn's princess, abducted in infancy by gypsies but still able to divine her true estate (*"I dreamt that I dwelt in marble halls / With vassals and serfs at my side"* [106]) nicely mirrors Maria's own implied sense of class displacement. She too feels trapped in a class below that compatible with her breeding and sensibility ("she knew that Mooney meant well though, of course, she had the notions of a common woman" [101]). The song—another version of Maria's desire expressed in the borrowed language of the superior class—is such a perfect analogue to the narration of "Clay" that Maria's lapsus, her omission of the verse depicting courtship and a marriage proposal, seems almost superfluous. But Joyce uses the specifically romantic content of Maria's repression (suitors, husband, love) to carefully focus the sexual etiology of her inferiority complex. It is not poverty alone, but the negative symbolic value of being an old maid and being unloved, that makes her feel robbed of significance. Because the performance of the song operates on several semiological levels, it requires a complex act of decoding. It is therefore not clear, from the text, whether Joe listens to the song or to the singer. Does he hear the pathos of her own plight in Maria's song and weep for her, or, made maudlin by an excess of stout, is he moved to tears by the pain of the Bohemian Girl ("What's Hecuba to him, or he to Hecuba, / That he should weep for her?" [*Hamlet* 11:21]) while he remains deaf to Maria's song of exile and longing?

When "Clay" ends—fittingly, with blindness and lost objects—what has been accomplished? "Clay" remains a hypothetical speech act, Maria's story as no one will ever tell it, as she could not tell it herself, but as it might be imagined being told. For Maria, the story, far from remedying her lacks, has multiplied them, but not until they have passed through the detour of a flattering lie. But is the story, in its residual meaning, merely an exhibition of a pointless life, or is it the exhibition of the failure of Maria's denial of its pointlessness? It may seem to come to the same thing: but in the difference between a judgment (that Maria's life is pointless) and her failed resistance to that judgment is lodged that attitudinal half-turn away from Maria and toward the critic who does the judging. By producing Maria's interpretation, we are implicated in her estimation (offering it as narratee, withdrawing it as critic) and, consequently, implicated in her victimization. The naturalistic "truth" of her poverty and isolation, that we uncover by seeing "through" the narrative agenda, makes her life hard enough. But what disturbs her contentment with her lot and ruins the efficacy of a kind of Ibsenite "life lie" are the insecurities produced by her fears of the estimation and interpretation of the "other." In her insecurities, in her fears, we should see our own "evil eye" as readers, encoded as we are within the story as the washerwomen, the shopkeepers, the young men on the tram, the children, and Society ("with a big ess," as Gerty MacDowell would say). It is we, as critical and perceptive readers, who create the pressures that necessitate Maria's defensive maneuvers in inventing her story.

I was myself prodded to make a self-reflexive turn beyond my naturalistic reading of "Clay" by students who stubbornly refused to let me get away with an elision necessary to sustain my reading of the story. They asked insistently: what about the narrator describing Maria (a mythical three times, no less) in the unmistakably stereotyped features of a witch, "the tip of her nose nearly met the tip of her chin" (101, 105)? This is indeed a problem, because surely the narrative voice does not flatter Maria here. Yet the voice and context in which the narration delivers these descriptions are very revealing of a kind of necessary concession fronted with the best possible "face," as it were, that one finds elsewhere in the story. Following the initial description of the kitchen, with its flattering signs of Maria's industry in its cleanliness, coziness, and orderliness, we receive a no-nonsense description of Maria's physical appearance: "Maria was a very, very small person indeed but she had a very long nose and a very long chin" (99). The bluntness and plain objectivity of this sentence is as eloquent in what it does *not* say as in what it *does* say. Neither the narrative voice, nor any character in the story, ever says or is described as thinking that Maria is plain or homely, deformed or grotesque-looking, hideous or witch-like. Such interpretations are produced strictly by the inference of the reader and are therefore hermeneutical, not rhetorical, products of the text. Indeed, the rhetoric of the description softens its sense in subtle ways. The description of Maria's stature, while quite emphatic in its "very, very small . . . indeed," nonetheless averts and replaces more evaluative judgments that would interpret her size as an abnormality or deformity and identify Maria as a dwarf or midget. Also by calling attention to her size and body first, as though they were her salient feature, the more damaging information about her facial physiognomy is rendered less conspicuous. The curious syntax, with the "but" serving as a possible qualification ("Maria was a very, very small person indeed but she had a very long nose and a very long chin") could even be read as a compensatory tribute. It may imply that Maria's childish height is effectively countered by distinctive, well-marked adult features. I am suggesting here only that the narrative voice appears to try to put a good face on Maria's face—not that it succeeds in convincing us.

During the tea (101), Maria twice produces the famous laugh in which "the tip of her nose nearly met the tip of her chin"—a laugh repeated a third time at the Donnelly house, just as she is blindfolded for the game. The common feature of these occasions is that they each represent moments of extraordinarily heightened—but uncomfortably ambiguous—attention to Maria: she is told she is sure to get the ring; a toast is drunk to her health with clattering tea mugs; the children insist on blindfolding her for the game. Is Maria being singled out for affectionate tribute, or is she being pressed into service—as dwarves and midgets historically were—as jester and fool? If the latter, does the narrative voice strategically use an uncharacteristically unflattering image of Maria—"the tip of her nose nearly met the tip of her chin"—to divert our attention from much more painful revelations? Does this rhetorical maneuver turn Maria from tormented buffoon into indulgent good sport ("she knew that Mooney meant well, though, of course") and mask as jolly heartiness her grimace of pain? Does Lizzie Fleming twit and goad Maria nearly to tears about the ring, obliging the narrative voice to gallantly mask Maria's face at that painful moment with a most genteel turn of phrase—"when she laughed her grey-green eyes sparkled with disappointed shyness" (101)? The narration has here produced another highly ambiguous scene whose possible interpretations hold the extremes of estimation for Maria. Was the tea a celebratory event, with Maria made much of by people who love her, and did she express her pleasure in a grimace of hilarity? Or was it a frequent ritual of cruel humiliation in which the aging prostitutes mock Maria's unlosable virginity?

Maria never sees that "the tip of her nose nearly met the tip of her chin" because it is, ironically, her most public gesture: her response to uncomfortable moments in the limelight. Perhaps, when terrified by extreme exposure, she loses altogether her ability to compose herself into a controlled form. When she later looks at herself in the mirror, in the privacy of her room, she doesn't see her face at all. She sees only her body, as it looked when it was young and when, perhaps, its size was less conspicuous. And she serenely approves what she sees—"In spite of its years she found it a nice tidy little body." The narration shows us only Maria's contented acceptance of her appearance, and records no negative reaction on its own part, or on the part of any character in the story. If no one notices or reacts to Maria's very long nose and very long chin, then why would a reader infer she is ugly and witch-like? With such a question the story turns itself to the reader like a mirror: a turn announced in the opening paragraph of the story when "the cook said you could see yourself in the big copper boilers" (99). It invites us to inspect our own visage in Maria's efforts to scour away the squalor of her life. Why do readers think Maria is ugly? Because we possess, if our place in the symbolic order of our culture is a safe distance from its margins, a hermeneutical touch as poisonous as that of any witch who ever turned prince into toad. We take minute anatomical deviations—a few inches in height, a few centimeters extra on a nose or a chin, and—pouf!—we construct a witch-like hag that we expel from possibilities of desirability or estimation. "Clay" tricks us with the same trick the children try to play on Maria. It offers us a benign, neutral substance—a woman, just a woman—and we recoil with cries, or at least thoughts, of "witch!" as surely as we would recoil with cries of "shit!" from the harmless garden soil. "Clay" reads the reader when it implicitly asks "Which is the witch?"

*Chapter 11*
# Shocking the Reader in "A Painful Case"

James Joyce's story "A Painful Case" is about a *story* that is painful for a reader: a newspaper article of the same title that gives Mr. Duffy a disturbing shock when he reads of Mrs. Sinico's death. This shocked reading produces a moment of classical anagnorisis when the man recognizes his implication in the woman's fate. But is Joyce's *story*, "A Painful Case," painful for the reader as well? I hope to concur with critics who have thought so,[1] and argue that even though the reader is not implicated in Mrs. Sinico's pain, the narration obliges "us" to vicariously experience the shocks to her heart, the last of which kills her. "Death, in his opinion, had been probably due to shock and sudden failure of the heart's action" (114), the surgeon reports to the *Dublin Evening Mail*. The thematic presentation of James Duffy's painful shock upon reading "A Painful Case" is encased in a performative reenactment of reader shock—potentially *twice*. I will argue that the narrator treats us precisely as Mr. Duffy treats Mrs. Sinico, and suggest on less hermeneutical evidence that it also treats Mr. Duffy as Mrs. Sinico treats him—thereby producing a second after-shock. In the process, the reader is given an opportunity to feel what the woman feels[2]—and, in a more surprising way, to realize that the man's subjectivity might have been as occluded as the woman's, and can be retrieved only at the price of painful readerly implication. There is a method to Joyce's careful contrivance of reader shock and discomfort. I will suggest it is to engage the reader not only in an ethical re-thinking, but an ethical re-feeling of the two great Irish sex scandals of the late nineteenth century: the case of Charles Stewart Parnell, and the case of Oscar Wilde.

Before embarking on this exploration of readerly shock, the status and function of the narrative voice and the narration must be considered. Taking as their cue the narrative description of Mr. Duffy's "odd autobiographical habit" that leads him "to compose in his mind from time to time a short sentence about himself containing a subject in the third person and a predicate in the past tense" (108), many critics of the story have held that the narrative voice is closely reflective of Duffy's own, and may be identified with him. "Indeed, Joyce foregrounds Duffy's dialogic participation in several places, suggesting that

Duffy may be his own narrator," R. B. Kershner writes (111). This identification does not preclude unreliability or irony, and the debates surrounding the sincerity and significance of Duffy's epiphany at the story's end suggest that registers of hypocrisy and fatuity may coexist with despair not only in the character's soul but in the narrational rhetoric as well. However, I hope to demonstrate much more problematic complicities between the narrative voice and Duffy with much more egregious manipulations of the reader's emotional and ethical response. Heuristically this demonstration is best served by retaining, initially at least, loose personifications of narrator and reader as more or less unified subjects and agents that are rendered increasingly fragmented and cognitively disrupted as the reading process offers conflicting interpretive possibilities that cannot be resolved.[3] This demonstration is heuristically abetted also by framing the imagined reading of this story temporally as a first reading, a virgin reading, as it were, followed by immediately troubled rereadings that are set historically in the intellectual milieu of Joyce and his brother Stanislaus. The young Joyce brothers were two turn-of-the-century readers excited both by the great nineteenth-century Continental fiction they encountered in school and disturbed by the sex scandals that had shaken the Irish political and literary landscape during their youth and adolescence. I will therefore proceed by reading "A Painful Case" twice. My aim the first time is to pay special attention to the parallels between Mr. Duffy's treatment of Mrs. Sinico and the narrator's treatment of the reader. But the second time I will draw attention to a kind of black hole in the narration that effectively decenters the story and leaves not only Duffy's moral nature in pieces but also our own.

I begin, then, with a first reading of the woman's story, and with the moment when both Mrs. Sinico and the reader receive a simultaneous shock. In the passage describing the growing attachment between Duffy and the woman, the prose betrays "every sign of unusual excitement" (111)—to cite its own description of Mrs. Sinico—and applies the brakes of Duffy's own techniques of aphorism and "disembodiment," as R. B. Kershner calls it (112):

> The dark discreet room, their isolation, the music that still vibrated in their ears united them. This union exalted him, wore away the rough edges of his character, emotionalised his mental life. Sometimes he caught himself listening to the sound of his own voice. He thought that in her eyes he would ascend to an angelic stature; and, as he attached the fervent nature of his companion more and more closely to him, he heard the strange impersonal voice which he recognised as his own, insisting on the soul's incurable loneliness. We cannot give ourselves, it said: we are our own. The end of these discourses was that one night during which she had shown every sign of unusual excitement, Mrs. Sinico caught up his hand passionately and pressed it to her cheek.

Mr Duffy was very much surprised. Her interpretation of his words disillusioned him. He did not visit her for a week. (111)

The prose here leads us to believe (like Mrs. Sinico herself) that we are caught up in a love story that is racing toward consummation. Like Mrs. Sinico, we are set up to overreach our romantic expectations and suffer a verbal version of a rude *coitus interruptus*. "Mrs Sinico caught up his hand passionately and pressed it to her cheek. Mr Duffy was very much surprised" (111). Indeed, it is we as readers who are very much surprised by Mr. Duffy's surprise. Why on earth would he be surprised by her gesture? This man and woman are reported to have shared the vibrations of exalting music, entangled their thoughts in an emotionalized discourse, and shared an intimacy that had given expression to the woman's fervent nature—"he attached the fervent nature of his companion more and more closely to him" (111). Duffy's cold surprise must have felt to Mrs. Sinico like a figurative slap in the face for having presumed an amorous expectation—an expectation that Duffy treats as a woman might treat a threatened date rape. Is Duffy offended by the sexual overture or scandalized by the adulterous advance? In either case, why? We are never told.

I will return to this complex moment of romantic and ethical misprision and its strange gender reversals again, after generically contextualizing the reader's parallel shock. The entire narrative leading up to this moment has conditioned the reader to expect an *adultery story*. Both the social scene that is set, and the emotional climate that is rhetorically created, point in this direction. For a story that will be about the refusal of intimacy, the opening narrative of "A Painful Case" begins by offering a curious excess of intimate information about James Duffy, so much so that its sharing with the reader becomes itself an invitation or seduction to intimacy. In a carefully arranged sequence of opening revelations, the narrative descriptions penetrate this impenetrable man's environs, his room, his bookshelf, his desk, his private journal, his temperament, his mental habits, his daily routine, his tastes. We are allowed to scrutinize his face as an intelligent and sympathetic woman might scrutinize it, attempting to read his character from his physiognomy. "His cheekbones also gave his face a harsh character; but there was no harshness in the eyes which, looking at the world from under their tawny eyebrows, gave the impression of a man ever alert to greet a redeeming instinct in others but often disappointed" (108). Even before Emily Sinico has appeared on the scene, the reader has been made the solitary and privileged witness, or voyeur, to a self-styled, post-Nietzschean Romantic hero—"sublime, contemptuous, ironic"—as René Girard might describe his *askesis*.[4]

Nothing in this opening description prepares us for the surprising turn the narrative takes when this man who "had neither companions nor friends, church nor creed" and who "lived his spiritual life without any communion with others" (109) meets a woman at a concert who begins a conversation with him. The narrative makes a curious maneuver at this moment—ignoring the conversation, which is not reported—to register Duffy's surprisingly alert curiosity and attention to the woman's character, face, and body. Engaged in the most casual of conversations, he tries to memorize her face ("he tried to fix her permanently in his memory" [109]). He goes on to interpret the emotional meaning of her eyes ("Their gaze began with a defiant note but was confused by what seemed a deliberate swoon of the pupil into the iris, revealing for an instant a temperament of great sensibility" [109]. The narration that earlier looked into Duffy's eyes for signs of his character, now shows Duffy looking into Mrs. Sinico's eyes for signs of hers. The reader feels drawn into the crosshairs of a love story that almost literally begins "at first sight." Although Duffy meets *two* women, he remarks the daughter only as a gauge to the mother's age. The narration further promises a level of frank maturity when it traces Duffy's gaze from the woman's eyes to her breast—"and her astrakhan jacket, moulding a bosom of a certain fulness, struck the note of defiance more definitely" (110).

When Duffy meets the woman again a few weeks later at a concert at Earlsfort Terrace, he takes surprising initiative in awaiting a moment when her daughter is diverted "to become intimate" (110). The context gives "intimate" no sexual connotations. But Duffy's arrangement to speak to the woman privately, learn her name and that of her husband, and make dates to meet her alone, function as gestures that signal to Emily Sinico, and to the reader, that he prepares to court her as a lover. The expectation of adultery is further reinforced by certain semiotic prompts. These include the woman's name, which reminds Mary Lowe-Evans of Emma Bovary (397); the story's locale of Chapelizod, the putative chapel of Tristan and Iseult,[5] and the gloss—in the professional title of Captain Sinico—of the unsympathetic husband in the Parnell affair, Captain O'Shea.[6] Once this last gloss is registered, other tacit similarities to the adulterous romance between Charles Stewart Parnell and Katharine O'Shea come into view. These are mature relationships: Emily Sinico is thirty-nine when she meets the forty-year-old Duffy; Katharine O'Shea was thirty-five when she met the thirty-three-year-old Parnell. Duffy, like Parnell, gains access to the Sinico home as a family friend, and Captain Sinico, like Captain O'Shea, is frequently absent from home and judged by Duffy to be indifferent to his wife. "In Parnell's view the lady in question had been deserted by her husband for several years," biographer Paul Bew wrote of O'Shea (42). And Margery Brady contends that Katharine O'Shea wished to contest her husband's divorce suit on the ground of his infidelities (90)—infidelities insinuated too in reference to Captain Sinico's "gallery of pleasures" (110).

The narration of the couple's romantic adventure—"Neither he nor she had any such adventure before" (110)—contextualizes itself as an adultery story, and as the relationship blossoms into greater intimacy, the narration becomes lyrical with metaphorical intimations of impending sexuality. "Little by little, as their thoughts entangled, they spoke of subjects less remote" (111). We are not told what these "less remote" subjects are, but the trope of entanglement, with its botanical imagery of enfolding vines and branches points toward the sexual imagery of enfolding human limbs.[7] The botanical imagery is further infused with allusions to temperature, nurturance, and gestation—"Her companionship was like a warm soil about an exotic" (111). On the narrative level, the image of Mrs. Sinico's unlit lamps darkening the room, the lingering vibrations of distant music, and the chords of transcendence in the prose describing Duffy's feelings—all set a discursive stage for consummation when Mrs. Sinico passionately catches his hand and presses it to her cheek. "Mr. Duffy was very much surprised. Her interpretation of his words disillusioned him" (111). This moment produces a highly imbricated crisis of interpretation that involves not only the man and the woman, but also the narrative voice and the reader. The narration had clearly interpreted Duffy's words, gestures, and feelings in precisely the same way Emily Sinico interpreted them, and the narrative voice, deeply embedded in Duffy's feelings during this culminating discourse, suggests that Mrs. Sinico had misinterpreted nothing. Duffy's cold and instantaneous withdrawal is therefore as shocking to the reader as to her—following upon the provocative arousal stimulated by both the narrative voice and Duffy.

Duffy's abrupt withdrawal has turned the impending adultery narrative into a frigidity narrative, a mode of story-telling that orchestrates a reader deprivation and frustration that recapitulates Emily Sinico's deprivation and frustration. Or, to put the matter more extremely, the story has turned into an emotionally sadistic narrative. It has ventured on a mode of story-telling that incites in the reader a desire for romance, a wish for a story about the fulfillment of love even if illicit, only to abruptly punish that desire with a brutal refusal and rebuff. And for the reader, as for Emily Sinico, insult is added to injury when not only is passion withdrawn and withheld, but its withdrawal is justified with a tacit, self-righteous indictment of the woman as guilty of vulgar lechery. Not only have the narrative redactions of the trysts deprived the reader of the expected love scenes, but the narrative withdrawal embarrasses the reader as Duffy's withdrawal embarrasses Mrs. Sinico. We expect the narrative voice to come to Emily Sinico's defense, but it does not. Instead, it colludes with Duffy's course of aggressive withdrawal—telling us nothing of what she feels, nothing of what she says during the painful three-hour-long argument as they walk in the Park in the cold. The narrative reports only the outcome of what must have been a painful and emotionally charged break-up, and its justification, in Duffy's terms—"They agreed to break off their intercourse: every bond, he said, is a bond to sorrow" (112). Only Emily Sinico's body is given mute expression in this scene—"she began to tremble so violently that, fearing another collapse on her part, he bade her good-bye quickly and left her" (112).

Four years later, when the *Dublin Evening Mail* reports her death by a slow-moving train, we again learn nothing of what Emily Sinico has felt or suffered in the intervening four years, and nothing of what she felt or suffered as the slow-moving train bore down on her. "The evidence showed that the deceased lady, while attempting to cross the line, was knocked down by the engine of the ten o'clock slow train from Kingstown, thereby sustaining injuries of the head and right side which led to her death" (113). This report nonetheless produces a stunning moment of literary déjà vu as we are transported back to nineteenth-century Moscow, to another railroad track on which another woman in despair confronts an oncoming train, a woman whose polysyllabic name echoes that of Emily Sinico: Anna Karenina. Tolstoy gives us what Joyce withholds—the exquisitely painful body language of the woman supplemented by the riot of the woman's thoughts and feelings:

A feeling such as she had known when about to take the first plunge in bathing came upon her, and she crossed herself. That familiar gesture brought back into her soul a whole series of girlish and childish memories, and suddenly the darkness that had covered everything for her was torn apart, and life rose up before her for an instant with all its bright past joys. But she did not take her eyes from the wheels of the second carriage. And exactly at the moment when the space between the wheels came opposite her, she dropped the red bag, and drawing her head back into her shoulders, fell on her hands under the carriage, and lightly, as though she would rise again at once, dropped on to her knees. And at the same instant she was terror-stricken at what she was doing. "Where am I? What am I doing? What for?" She tried to get up, to drop backwards; but something huge and merciless struck her on the head and rolled her on her back. (894)

There is strong evidence that Joyce had Tolstoy's *Anna Karenina* in mind as he was writing "A Painful Case." On September 24, 1905, Joyce wrote to Stanislaus to ask him to verify certain details in the story. "Are the police at Sydney Parade of the D division? Would the city ambulance be called out to Sydney Parade for an accident? Would an accident at Sydney Parade be treated at Vincent's Hospital?" (*SL* 75). Six days before he wrote this letter, Joyce had written another in which he gratefully responded to Stanislaus for detecting Russian influences in his stories. However, "As for Tolstoy I disagree with you alto-gether," Joyce wrote. "Tolstoy is a magnificent writer. He is never dull, never stu-pid, never tired, never pedantic, never theatrical! He is head and shoulders over the others" (*SL* 73). A little later in the letter, Joyce excoriates the English liberal press for its political criticism of Tolstoy. "Did you ever hear such impudence? Do they think the author of *Resurrection* and *Anna Karenina* a fool?" (*SL* 73).

Bringing Emily Sinico and Anna Karenina into dialogue with each other dramatizes Joyce's inversion and perversion of the adultery narrative. The nineteenth-century Continental adultery novel was ideologically ambivalent about adultery—creating sympathy for the woman who pursues it, yet devising her self-punishment in a maneuver designed to be ethically uncomfortable for the reader. Access to the adulterous woman's motives and feelings gave readers insight into the pain and sublimity of the *Liebestod* that is her fate. Why would Joyce write "A Painful Case" as a story in which there is *no* adultery, in which it is the *failure* of adultery—not its commission—that putatively drives the woman to suicide, and in which her *Liebestod*, if that's what it is,[8] is brutally stripped of all romance and transcendence? At least one plausible possibility may be that fifteen years after the scandalous adultery, divorce, censure, and death of Charles Stewart Parnell, the topic of adultery and its punishments re-mained an unresolved ethical wound in the Irish conscience. Joyce, who would revisit the scandal a decade later in the famous Christmas dinner scene in *A Por-trait of the Artist as a Young Man*, may in 1905 have created a satirical parable about the self-righteous prescriptions of Parnell's censors. "A Painful Case" could be read as an imaginary scenario of a hideously ironic outcome had Par-nell resisted the temptations of adultery, and behaved as Dante Riordan and the priests demanded.

In the censorious version of the Parnell scandal, Kitty O'Shea was thought to have acted the whore—as the story of "a very famous spit" that John Casey retells at the Dedalus family Christmas dinner in *Portrait* makes plain. Casey's story tells of a crowd in Arklow protesting against Parnell shortly before his death, when an enraged old woman "called that lady a name I wouldn't sully this Christian board nor your ears, ma'am, nor my own lips by repeating" (*P* 36). Clearly Joyce did not share this view of the woman Parnell addressed in his let-ters as "My own wifie" and "My own darling Queenie" (Bew 43), who bore him three illegitimate children in her late thirties, and held him as he died, eleven years after they had met. Margery Brady reports that Parnell's last words were, "Kiss me, sweet Wifie, and I will try to sleep a little" (Brady 126). In his 1912 Tri-estine article on "The Shade of Parnell," Joyce characterized Parnell's fall, "like lightning from a clear sky":

He fell hopelessly in love with a married woman, and when her husband, Captain O'Shea, asked for a divorce, the ministers Gladstone and Morley openly refused to legislate in favour of Ireland if the sinner remained as head of the Nationalist Party. . . . The high and low clergy entered the lists to finish him off. The Irish press emptied on him and the woman he loved the vials of their envy. (*CW* 227)

Reading "A Painful Case" as a satirical rendition of a man doing the right thing by the public Irish mores negatively pays unique tribute to Parnell's uxorious adultery as one of the defining features of his greatness. Joyce endowed Duffy with what he called Parnell's "sovereign bearing, mild and proud, silent and disconsolate" (*CW* 226). But he made James Duffy—a man who flirts with politics, literature, philosophy and woman with no willingness to give, commit, or risk—the absolute antithesis of Charles Stewart Parnell, who wholeheartedly gave, committed, and risked everything for both a country and a woman.[9] Parnell refutes in advance Duffy's retroactive social exoneration: "He asked himself what else could he have done. He could not have carried on a comedy of deception with her; he could not have lived with her openly" (116). Why not? Given his complete social indifference, what had Duffy to lose except his adventureless job as a bank cashier? As a popular, powerful, and highly visible politician, Parnell had everything to lose and he risked and lost it all. In 1936, Winston Churchill wrote of Parnell:

He dedicated himself to a single goal, the goal of Ireland as a nation, and he pursued it unswervingly until a rose thrown across his path opened a new world, the world of love. And, as he had previously sacrificed all for Ireland, so, when the moment of choice came, he sacrificed all, even Ireland, for love. A lesser man might have given more sparingly and kept more. (quoted in Brady 133)

If it is the business of the adultery novel to explain to us why there is adultery, "A Painful Case" refuses to explain to us *why there is no adultery* when all the presumptive conditions for its commission are clearly in place. Given Duffy's atheism, indifference to society, and amorality, what possible inner or outer constraints could have prevented him from yielding to Emily Sinico's overture? His reaction to this warm and giving woman made no sense at the time of his rejection of her, and it continues to make no sense after he reads of her death. Duffy's anguished self-examination gives only oblique and suspect explanations for why he rejected the woman. His moral excoriations of her are histrionic and exaggerated ("He saw the squalid tract of her vice, miserable and malodorous. . . . that she could have sunk so low" [115]). And as he generalizes her alcoholism to a wider, and retroactive degeneracy, the troublesome excess of recoil at her gesture is reiterated again, "He remembered her outburst of that night and interpreted it in a harsher sense than he had ever done. He had no difficulty now in approving of the course he had taken" (115). If Duffy's behavior was inexplicable then, his self-justifications after her death are even more so. There is something simply wrong with this whole story whose central question— "Why had he withheld life from her?" (117)—is never answered by either Duffy or the narrator.

And yet we are given a clue to this mystery—a solution in plain sight, like Poe's purloined letter, a solution totally obvious and yet functionally so shocking that critics and readers have overwhelmingly failed or refused to see it.[10] This clue has surprising authority for it is provided not by the narration, but by James Duffy himself, when we are given a glimpse into a journal entry he wrote two months after his break-up with Mrs. Sinico:

One of his sentences, written two months after his last interview with Mrs Sinico, read: Love between man and man is impossible because there must not be sexual intercourse and friendship between man and woman is impossible because there must be sexual intercourse. (112)

The narration has pried into the most private recesses of Duffy's papers in his desk, given us his most secret comment on his break-up with the woman, and yet makes nothing of this aphorism, and gives us no encouragement to ponder its significance for explaining Duffy's action. As a result we are distracted by its clever style that Kershner elegantly summarizes as "enumeration and inventory, classical balance and antithesis, analysis, neat causal connection, and passive-voice construction" (111). But what if this utterly private thought, intended to be shared with no other human being, is taken at face value: as a revelation that James Duffy cannot give himself to this woman because if he could love, he would love a man? The narration has not authorized this interpretation, and told us nothing explicitly that would support it.[11] Consequently, to speculate in explicit ways about James Duffy's sexuality obliges the reader to come to terms with what Joseph Valente has called "the compulsory heterosexuality that has encumbered even the most critically astute, theoretically sophisticated, and politically progressive Joyce scholarship" (1). By opening the gap into a queer interpretation of the story, the reader's shock or surprise becomes an ethical boomerang, exposing the strength of the heterosexual assumptions and their control of the generic conventions of romantic fiction that we have reflexively brought to the story. In treating Duffy as a promising heterosexual lover, the reader had treated him with Emily Sinico's own expectations.

The indeterminacy of the failure of adultery in the story has previously obliged the reader to adjudicate whether its cause was Duffy's morality, prudery, asceticism, asexuality, frigidity, or the simpler possibility that Duffy, while heterosexual and attracted by the woman's personality, was simply not attracted to Mrs. Sinico sexually. Once the possibility of homosexuality is considered, the reader must take ethical responsibility for now imagining the thoughts, feelings, and anxieties of the possibly homosexual man. If we remember that Duffy lives in a social world that punishes homosexuality even more harshly than it punishes adultery, Duffy's isolation, asceticism, aloofness, and misanthropy take on a wholly different character. His abstemiousness could now imply an avoidance of temptation—for example, dining in the dull eatery in George's Street "where he felt himself safe from the society of Dublin's gilded youth" (109). The narrative assurance that opera and concerts "were the only dissipations of his life" (109) now takes on a hint of defensiveness. We can now understand differently why he cannot write his thoughts, why his most intimate emotional expressions take impersonal and general form, and why a woman's romantic overture could have caused him surprised distress. Duffy's dismissive scorn of "the criticisms of an obtuse middle class which entrusted its morality to policemen and its fine arts to impresarios" (111) reminds us that the trial of Oscar Wilde would have been recent history at the time of this conversation.[12] If the concealment of Duffy's sexuality may be imagined not only in a social closet but further internalized in latency, then his autobiographical resort to a "disembodied" voice no longer seems particularly "odd" (108). We now also have a better explanation of why Duffy never registers the looks or charms of Sinico's daughter, and why Duffy might have misconstrued Emily Sinico's open nature and generous feelings.[13]

In this light, Joyce's narrative description of the growing intimacy between James Duffy and Emily Sinico becomes a rhetorical tour de force that enacts the fluidities of emotional need, personal response, and spiritual longing dammed by an erotic threshold:

He thought that in her eyes he would ascend to an angelical stature; and, as he attached the fervent nature of his companion more and more closely to him, he heard the strange impersonal voice which he recognised as his own, insisting on the soul's incurable loneliness. We cannot give ourselves, it said: we are our own. (111)

The rhetorical gestures in this passage strain toward intimacy even as they snap away from confession in a torque of impersonal obliquity and generalized prohibition. We can now better understand Duffy's subsequent transformation of painful personal meaning into a style of equivocal epigrammatic pronouncement. The epigrammatic structure of "Love between man and man is impossible because there must not be sexual intercourse and friendship between man and woman is impossible because there must be sexual intercourse" [112]) now resonates with much greater clarity to the encrypting signature of Oscar Wilde. Garry Leonard's astute observation—"Duffy very much wants to be his own third person so that other people might become entirely extraneous to what would then be the closed circuit of his identity" (215)—also takes on special poignancy if we imagine a homosexual Duffy. As a closeted or latent homosexual, Duffy would be consigned to a life without interlocution or dialogic possibility, with no one to whom he could safely disclose himself and communicate his true thoughts or feelings.

Duffy's rhetorical torsion away from confession infects the narrative voice as well to replace emotional representation with the facticity of externalized reportage. Once we interpret Duffy's rebuff of the woman's romantic overture as homosexual recoil,[14] the reader must revisit with a queer perspective the redacted scenes in the story. We remember that we learned nothing of what transpired during the week of silence ("He did not visit her for a week; then he wrote to her asking her to meet him" [112]). And we learn virtually nothing of the transactions of the break-up ("It was cold autumn weather but in spite of the cold they wandered up and down the roads of the Park for nearly three hours" [112]). In order to speculatively retrieve these narratively censored scenes which conceal from us the drama at the heart of this story, the heterosexual reader experiences a thickening of identity and a doubling of vision as different questions pose themselves in an effort to enter a gay subjectivity. What sensation of panic and responsibility might Duffy have felt upon recognizing that this woman had fallen in love with him? How did his own feelings of recoil present themselves to him? What choices was he able or obliged to ponder?[15] Would he tell her or not tell her his predicament? What psychological vulnerabilities and social risks would the disclosure of such a secret pose to him? What, if anything, did James Duffy tell Emily Sinico of his dilemma during that three hour break-up in the Park? Perhaps he explained why he could not love her. Perhaps he told her nothing. If not, what forms of discursive deception and indirection would have been required to justify the break-up of their relationship? Was her fit of trembling caused by disappointment and embarrassment only, or did Emily Sinico glimpse the larger and more tragic meaning in Duffy's pronouncement that "every bond . . . is a bond to sorrow"? (112).

The narration tells us nothing of this and thereby puts us in a risky interpretive quandary. Why doesn't the narrative voice tell us more and let us hear the break-up dialogue so that we might infer with more security what went on between this couple? If "A Painful Case" is indeed a story about a man in the closet, then it is also a closeted story.[16] Why would Joyce have written it like this?

A plausible answer may lie in the historical conditions that not only linked the scandals of Charles Stewart Parnell and Oscar Wilde to each other in Joyce's mind, but that extended their caution of the punishment that "exceptionalism"[17] visits on gifted Irishmen to himself. Joyce tropes the fates of Wilde and Parnell in similar figures of hunted animals in the essays he published in 1909 and 1912 respectively in the Trieste paper *Il Piccolo della Sera*. Joyce writes of the persecuted Wilde, "He was hunted from house to house as dogs hunt a rabbit" (*CW* 203). He described Parnell, "He went from county to county, from city to city, 'like a hunted deer', a spectral figure with the signs of death on his forehead" (*CW* 228). Given the unrelenting and serious censorship problems Joyce faced in his protracted nine-year struggle to get Maunsel & Company to publish *Dubliners*, could he have hoped to write openly about either adultery or homosexuality? In 1906 Grant Richards objected to mere allusions to "a man with two establishments to keep up" (*SL* 82). As late as 1912, Joyce's solicitor George Lidwell urged Joyce not to run afoul of Dublin's Vigilance Committee. Its object, Lidwell explained, "is to seek out and suppress all writings of immoral tendencies," and he cautioned Joyce that "if the attention of the Authorities be drawn to these paragraphs it is likely they would yield to the pressure of this body and prosecute" (quoted in Ellmann 330). One may gauge the extent to which this climate of censorship was internalized in the circumspection of the oblique allusions with which Joyce and his brother Stanislaus discuss the unnamed homosexual theme of Oscar Wilde's *Dorian Gray* in their private correspondence.[18] Writing a homosexual story in the climate of 1905 and 1906 would have been unthinkable, particularly if we remember the scandal produced as late as 1928 by the obscenity trial and conviction occasioned by Radclyffe Hall's chaste lesbian novel, *The Well of Loneliness*.

My speculative reconstruction of "A Painful Case" remains indeterminate and unverifiable—itself a somewhat scandalous shadow or double of the adultery narrative with which it is entangled in ambiguity and equivocation. But this inability to "prove" the reading can itself be read as a performative effect. The narration enacts the "love that dare not speak its name" by refusing to speak it and refusing to let Duffy speak it except as a prohibition ("Love between man and man is impossible because there must not be sexual intercourse" [112]). These narrational effects make the reader the enforcer of a regime of unknowing that requires the speculative crossing of a cognitive line to turn the narrative closet to glass, as Eve Sedgwick might put it. Sedgwick writes of *The Picture of Dorian Gray*:

Published four years before Wilde's 'exposure' as a sodomite, it is in a sense a perfect rhetorical distillation of the open secret, the glass closet. . . . Reading *Dorian Gray* from our

twentieth-century vantage point where the name Oscar Wilde virtually *means* "homosexuality," it is worth emphasizing how thoroughly the elements of even this novel can
be read doubly or equivocally, can be read either as having a thematically empty "modernist" meaning or as having a thematically full "homosexual" meaning. (165)

Since Joyce did not read *Dorian Gray* until he revised "A Painful Case" in 1906,
James Duffy may be assumed not to have read it—although the narrator's failure to mention Wilde among Duffy's authors does not prove that Duffy had no
Wilde on his shelves. Further, since the history of English usage does not translate "gay" into "homosexual" until the 1930s or later (*New Fowler's Modern English Usage* 324), one cannot read a coded meaning into Duffy's acquisition of
Nietzsche's *The Gay Science* after his break-up with Mrs. Sinico. Yet Eve Sedgwick reads Nietzsche through a Wildean optic.[19] She thereby finds his writings
"full and overfull of what were just in the process of becoming, for people like
Wilde, and their enemies, and for the institutions that regulated and defined
them, the most pointed and contested signifiers of precisely a minoritized, taxo-
nomic male homosexual identity" (133). From the retrospective intertextualiza-
tion of both Wilde and Nietzsche into the homosocial jousting of "Telemachus"
in *Ulysses*, Joyce may have planted *The Gay Science* in Duffy's library as an overdetermined referent.

  "A Painful Case" therefore remains, more than *Dorian Gray*—of which
Joyce wrote "It is not very difficult to read between the lines" (96)—an opaque
closet at best. But nonetheless, once a queer reading is considered, the reader
must contend with ethical incrimination in "the epistemology of the closet." As
Sedgwick explains: " 'Closetedness' itself is a performance initiated by the
speech act of a silence—not a particular silence, but a silence that accrues particularity by fits and starts, in relation to the discourse that surrounds and dif-
ferentially constitutes it" (3). In "A Painful Case" the discourse that constitutes
"the closet" is the one that resolutely interprets Duffy's refusal of heterosexual
love as volitional in specific registers of ethical culpability coded as egotism,
narcissism, solipsism, and coldness. An ethical leap is required to imagine that
Duffy's "hunger-strike against desire" (as Earl Ingersoll suggestively calls it
[126]) could be prompted by a criminalized, prosecutable, and therefore frustrated and perhaps repressed desire for a same-sex object. This possibility does
not readily *occur* to either the narrator or the reader, and it is this *not-occurring*
that is precisely the epistemologically closeting gesture. Once the queer interpretation does occur to the reader, it produces the Tiresian optics that abash the
reader in ethically productive ways. At story's end, Duffy's regret and remorse
may enfold not one but two closeted lives: that of the abandoned wife ("how
lonely her life must have been, sitting night after night alone in that room"

[116])[20] and that of his own monological existence. If Emily Sinico may be imagined as the only person on earth who might have known his secret ("it revolted him to think that he had ever spoken to her of what he held sacred" [115]), then her loss represents the loss of his only witness, his only validation. This insight restores an achieved fullness of pain to the loss of the woman's friendship[21] expressed in the other half of Duffy's private aphorism, "and friendship between man and woman is impossible because there must be sexual intercourse" (112). These reflections bend our attention on the exceptional possibility of absolute closeting that Sedgwick ascribes only to the homosexual. Can Duffy's life be construed as consignment to a life undisclosed to anyone and thereby reduced to a Derridean trace, unregistered on any consciousness? "His life would be lonely too until he, too, died, ceased to exist, became a memory—if anyone remembered him" (116). Duffy's mourning for the dead woman is accompanied by his mourning for himself, as though he were already ontologically dead. Perhaps nowhere in Joyce's work is paralysis invoked more poignantly than in this subject's inability—on literal peril of death, if we recall that Parnell and Wilde were both dead within a few years of their scandals—to be anything other than static, still, and silent.

## Chapter 12
# Genres in Dispute: "Ivy Day in the Committee Room"

Joyce's "Ivy Day in the Committee Room" ends with a stirring poetic performance—Joe Hynes reciting his elegy on the occasion of the death of Parnell. This recitation is followed by an exercise in literary criticism. "What do you think of that, Crofton? cried Mr Henchy. Isn't that fine? What?" (135). Given that Mr. Crofton is an Orangeman, a Conservative, and not a Nationalist, his answer "that it was a very fine piece of writing" (135) must be read as a highly equivocating judgment, one that says one thing but means another. But Crofton's response reminds us that Hynes's poem in praise of a famous politician is both a discourse of art and a discourse of politics. These discourses—reminiscent of Jean-Francois Lyotard's "phrases in dispute"—are superimposed and intermeshed in such a way that an unequivocal, unified response becomes virtually impossible. On the crudest level this might be a problem of admiring the poetic diction while refusing its patriotic sentiment or, conversely, concurring with its political encomium while regretting its archaic and florid form. But all the while a greater question about the commensurability of the discourses of art and politics resonates to us from the corridors of literary and poetic history. Both the poem and the story "Ivy Day in the Committee Room" itself deliberately confront us with the question of what constitutes a just and adequate literary address to, and representation of, that indefinable and elusive phenomenon we call *politics*.

Joyce clearly felt that "Ivy Day" was a remarkably successful piece of writing. In his famous May 20, 1906 letter, defending "Two Gallants" against the objections of the publisher's printer, he indicated by implication that "Ivy Day in the Committee Room" was the story in the volume that up to that point in time pleased him most (*SL* 88).[1] Perhaps every piece of *Dubliners* criticism tries to answer this same question: what would have made a story so successful in Joyce's eyes that, over a period of years, he would passionately defend every word against the challenges of printer, editor, and publisher, and a potentially hostile readership? "A Dubliner would denounce 'Ivy Day in the Committee Room,'" Joyce told Richards on May 5, 1906. Florence Walzl gives a succinct view both of why this might have been Joyce's favorite story, and why he might have expected *Dubliners* to denounce it. She writes: "It emanates from deeply held political views, fervent emotions, and a polemical impulse to expose to the Irish people their consummate folly in rejecting Charles Stewart Parnell, Joyce's great hero. Its thesis is that the body politic in Ireland is corrupt, and the theme of the story is betrayal. In the reversal of the order of theological virtues in the final triad, 'Ivy Day' comes first and presents a picture of malevolence and antagonism that is the reverse of the benevolence and love that charity should represent" (Bowen and Carens 180). But I would like, with benefit of Lyotardian theory, to complicate Walzl's view somewhat. I believe that while *Parnell* is certainly Joyce's "great hero," the problem of depicting Irish feelings about Parnell—his role as a *signifier* in Irish political sentiment and mythology—is for Joyce a highly problematic matter. Representing the complexity of this problem far outstrips any simple polemical impulse on Joyce's part to baldly mirror their betrayal and corruption back to his countrymen. Indeed, we might see Joe Hynes's poem and Joyce's story as precise if generically opposed counterparts: both commemorations of Ivy Day—commemorations of the death of Parnell—but in different genres or phrase regimens that remain in conflict and cannot be translated one into the other or justly adjudicated. By addressing the problem of discursive justice to the case of Parnell—a project with which the nine year old Joyce began his artistic career by writing "Et Tu Healy"—Joyce makes poetry and fiction ethical enterprises, exercises in "doing justice" to history, to persons, and to art itself. But however pleased Joyce was with his story, the problem of "doing justice" to Parnell was not resolved in "Ivy Day" with Joe Hynes's poem. It ultimately required revisitation in a plethora of genres, from the savage Christmas Dinner argument in *Portrait*, to the desultory discussion in the Cabman's shelter in "Eumaeus," to Joyce's journalistic piece in *Il Piccolo della Sera* on "The Shade of Parnell." The outcome of these heterogeneous generic exercises is the demonstration that genres, like phrases, cannot produce justice because they occlude and displace each other and thereby cannot totalize an indisputably equitable discourse.

Jean-François Lyotard assigns to genre a stake, an orientation to procure a success proper to it. The stake of the genre of ethics, Lyotard claims, is justice (129). And although politics is not itself a genre, Lyotard writes of politics that "it bears witness to the nothingness which opens up with each occurring phrase and on the occasion of which the differend between genres of discourse is born" (141). In its most vulgar gloss, one could take this to mean that in the disputing phrases or rhetorics of political discourse, politics bears witness to the kind of hot air that Joyce metaphorizes in the heated, flatulent, apologetic, "Pok" of "Ivy Day" 's stout bottles, and in the more grandiloquent gas that blows from the rhetorical windbags of "Aeolus" in *Ulysses*.[2] But a more serious analogue to this sense of Lyotardian politics and ethics may be found in the image of Stephen Dedalus as a young boy "trying to write a poem about Parnell on the back of one of his father's second moeity notices" (*P* 73). The sheet of paper, like a moebius strip, bears two conflicting phrase regimens back to back, the demand for back taxes or City Rates unwittingly underwriting the juvenile elegy for the dead and betrayed politician who fought against tenant evictions and for agrarian rights. "Ivy Day in the Committee Room" might be read as a performative version of that double-sided sheet of paper. On one side we have the municipal campaign for a candidate who is a major landlord, according to Mr. Henchy— "*He has extensive house property in the city and three places of business and isn't it to his own advantage to keep down the rates*" (131). Back to back, on the other side, we have a poem that completes young Joyce's or young Dedalus's early effort to produce the apotheosis of Parnell—"He dreamed (alas: 'twas but a dream!) / Of Liberty" (134). These heterogeneous discourses fail to communicate because they are phrases "put into play within a conflict between genres of discourse. This conflict is a *differend*, since the success (or validation) proper to one genre is not the one proper to the others" (Lyotard 136).

The genres of the embedded texts that "Ivy Day" puts into conflict—Joe Hynes's heroic elegy to Parnell and the formal municipal campaign card of Richard J. Tierney, Poor Law Guardian—mobilize esteem for politicians by explicitly or tacitly imputing an idealistic transcendence to them. The genre promises the power of discourse to persuade the public of a politician's embodiment of causes and ideals that transcend self-interest—a criterion that renders these genres Romantic rather than postmodern or pagan, in Lyotard's sense. By this criterion the Parnell lyric in its rhetorical amplitude and elevated diction is clearly more generically successful. Its idealism patently defeats Tierney's compact campaign card respectfully requesting the favor of vote and influence, whose implied promise Joe Hynes scornfully dismisses as what James Fairhall calls "jobbery" (299)—"The fellow you're working for only wants to get some job or other" (121). Parnell's mythic power arose from his ability to make his lack of self-interest utterly convincing. Joyce invokes this Romantic criterion explicitly when he contrasts Parnell with a Disraeli who was "a diplomatic opportunist" and a Gladstone who was "a self-seeking politician" (*CW* 226) in his essay "The Shade of Parnell." But if the "Ivy Day" 's canvassers might be expected to absorb themselves into the causes of the politicians they support, the story's naturalism divides them into what Kershner calls "two dialogical centers of power in the story" (120). On the one hand, we have Joe Hynes, who indeed identifies himself as much with the politics of the Labor candidate Colgan as he does with Parnell.[3] R. B. Kershner, on the other hand, describes Mr. Henchy as "the ultimate conversational opportunist" (122) who, Garry Leonard adds, cynically scorns "every living manifestation of power" as "the self-serving scheme of a manipulative scoundrel" (231).

This is the state of affairs that leads Kershner to echo Florence Walzl, by calling "Ivy Day in the Committee Room" "an anatomy of the degraded state of Dublin politics in 1902" (120). In this widely shared reading of the story's donnée as political corruption, the specific political sin is *betrayal*, according to Walzl.[4] This interpretation is fortified by Joyce's letter to Stanislaus, in which his questions about municipal elections and the Royal Exchange Ward are followed by his comic prayer for pen and ink that he may "write tiny sentences about the people who betrayed me" (*SL* 76). Joyce's further hint that Anatole France "suggested *Ivy Day in the Committee Room*" (*SL* 146) to him is elaborated in Ellmann's note as possibly pointing to France's "The Procurator of Judea," in which Pontius Pilate's administrative memoir fails to remember Jesus Christ.[5] Critics further analogize Parnell and Christ by noting the configuration of the Wicklow Street Committee Room as a New Testament cenacle, peopled by what Brandabur calls "Judas figures" (109).[6] These various allusions and clues indeed appear to authorize casting the story's ethical genre into that of a parable of political betrayal. Specifically, the betrayal of ideals by the men in the Wicklow Street Committee Room reprises the betrayal of Parnell in the *other* "Committee Room." "Committee Room No. 15" in the House of Commons in London was the site of the bitter debate that culminated in Parnell losing the leadership of the Irish Parliamentary party in the "aftermath of the disclosure of his affair with Mrs. Kitty O'Shea" (Walzl, Bowen and Carens 182). The unprincipled banter of Joyce's canvassers could thus be construed as both mirror and legacy of the faithlessness that brought Parnell low. Such a reading upholds the Romantic criterion of political apotheosis as the model of civic virtue, designed to inspire the Christian criterion of selfless dedication as the measure by which turn-of-the-century Dubliners are found morally debased. Supporting Florence Walzl's conviction, Warren Beck writes that "Joyce never quite forgot what was perhaps his boyhood's one lasting parental inculcation, an apotheosis of Parnell" (241).

But I would investigate if "Ivy Day" 's own genre as a kind of naturalistic drama does not dispute the criterion of political apotheosis altogether by implying a distinctly different ethical object of success. I would take this to be the achievement of social justice ensuring "that the distribution of what there is to distribute is well carried out" (Lyotard, *Just Gaming* 22). In other words, I want to suggest that "Ivy Day in the Committee Room" not only *critiques* politics but actually *practices* politics. Invoking the story's literary mode as that of *naturalism* is prompted both by the reminder that Joyce considered Gerhard Hauptmann's play about the strike of Silesian textile workers, *The Weavers*, a "master-piece" (117), and was reading Maxim Gorky in September of 1905. Indeed, throughout this period of *Dubliners* composition, Joyce invoked Émile Zola as a literary master or gold standard for the writers of his day. "Who called Moore the English Zola?" Joyce asks Stanislaus in his 7 December 1906 letter (*SL* 140), and two months later, in February 1907, he notes, "One writer speaks of Synge and his master Zola (!) so I suppose that when *Dubliners* appears they will speak of me and my master Synge" (*SL* 147). Some months earlier, in May 1906, Joyce had tried to relieve Grant Richards's fears of prosecution with the mock assurance, "The worst that will happen, I suppose, is that some critic will allude to me as the 'Irish Zola'!" (*SL* 86). But I believe not only the notoriety and celebrity of Zola was on Joyce's mind, but also his literary innovations. In "Ivy Day," it is specifically naturalistic *drama* that seems to me invoked, for the story's construction is very specifically *dramatic*. Jean-Paul Riquelme remarks how little thought process is reflected in the *Dubliners* stories of public life. "Of the three stories, 'Ivy Day' eschews the presentation of consciousness most completely," he writes (120).[7] He goes on to note that these stories tend to lack a central protagonist—an observation that points to naturalistic drama's convention of subverting ideologies of individualism by favoring the presentation of collective protagonists or protagonists *en ensemble*. Warren Beck, too, observes that "Ivy Day" is written "less in the Joycean short story mode than that of the one-act play, but with quite enough description and narrated action to 'produce' it in the mind's eye and ear" (238). He notes, "Like a one-act play, 'Ivy Day' has complete unity of time and place" (239). I identify this structure even more narrowly as a species of *naturalistic* drama in order to recollect that naturalism aspires to the genre of ethics, in Lyotard's sense, by seeking to distribute justice to marginalized classes of persons rather than to individuals. "Ivy Day" seeks to do justice not only to the signifier of Parnell but also to the class of ordinary Dublin men whose lives are the micropolitical landscape that Parnell's marcopolitical policies and strategies sought to address.[8] Put differently, "Ivy Day" performs the "nothingness" of politics that opens up in the spaces between disputing and incommensurate discourses by obliging us to take in the relations of power that keep discourses from translating or communicating with each other and that thereby escape articulation.

Most definitions of "Naturalism" in literary dictionaries point to its inspiration by scientific theories, particularly those of Darwin, that underlie varieties of philosophical determinism. They therefore stress the highly *objective* representational modes that literary Naturalism was consequently obliged to deploy. *The Oxford Companion to English Literature* writes—

The Naturalists shared with the earlier Realists the conviction that the everyday life of the middle and lower classes of their own day provided subjects worthy of serious literary treatment. These were to be rendered so far as possible without artificiality of plot and with scrupulous care for *documentation*, i.e. for the authenticity and accuracy of detail, thus investing the novel with the value of social history. Emphasis was laid on the influence of the material and economic environment on behaviour, and, especially in Zola, on the determining effects of physical and hereditary factors in forming the individual temperament. (688)

The piece goes on to note that naturalistic drama was particularly inspired by Ibsen, "whose interest in heredity was easily explicable in naturalistic terms" (688). It is productive to put this reminder of naturalism's link to Ibsen together with Joyce's intense early interest in drama. By remembering Joyce's early interest in Ibsen's and Hauptmann's plays, we can read the opening *scene* of "Ivy Day"—reporting old Jack's conversation with Mr. O'Connor about raising sons—as infusing the crude and humorous hypocrisies of the old man with a more interesting sociological significance. The old man's complaint about his nineteen-year-old son's "boosing about" and then taking "th'upper hand of me whenever he sees I've a sup taken" brackets the ineffectual method by which he thought to make the boy "someway decent." "Only I'm an old man now I'd change his tune for him. I'd take the stick to his back and beat him while I could stand over him—as I done many a time before," he says (120). The physical and hereditary factors—alcoholism and aggressivity—are here placed in an environment in which brutalizing children with a stick is considered conscientious upbringing. This kind of justification led the National Society for the Prevention of Cruelty to Children to claim that "drunkenness was the main factor in the majority of cases which they handled, " according to James Fairhall (297).[9] Maternal efforts to bolster her son's self-esteem and assertiveness ("The mother, you know, she cocks him up with this and that" [120]) are derided as a ruinous undermining of needed discipline ("That's what ruins children, said Mr O'Connor" [120]). With just a few strokes of dialogue, Joyce opens "Ivy Day in the Committee Room" with a scene of familial and social dysfunction in which both social and genetic heredity plays a part.[10] Fairhall further weaves alcohol, colonialism, tenements, and unemployment together as the environmental background for the election issues that he considers the embedded "subtext" in "Ivy Day in the Committee Room." In Fairhall's view this is "the conflict between Irish bourgeois nationalism and Irish labor, but also the contradictions between Joyce's own Parnellite and socialist allegiances" (290).

The genetic inheritance of his father's own deleterious proclivities is only one of the many obstacles that constitute the sociological legacy of young Dubliners like old Jack's son. The more significant generational problem is one that the story will generalize to every man who passes through the Committee Room, and that will be at issue in their political discussions: the problem of employment. Old Jack reports this conversation with his son: " 'I won't keep you,' I says. 'You must get a job for yourself.' " (120). This languid conversation in front of the Committee Room's dim fire—"Mr. O'Connor shook his head in sympathy, and the old men fell silent, gazing into the fire" (120)—distracts us from the salient condition of the men. Old Jack and Mr. O'Connor are brought to the Committee Room *by their jobs, such as they are,* and "Ivy Day" is in some sense incidental to why they are there. The story is structured and focused in such a way that we are prompted to treat the meeting of the men in the Committee Room as a social event, as though they were there to celebrate Ivy Day rather than to await their wages after a day's—or several days'—work. This structural tension in the story between "politics" as a topic and "politics" as a condition of having and not having, of power and powerlessness, becomes Joyce's strategy for illuminating a different kind of betrayal. This betrayal lies in the way the legacy of Parnell was treated by the Dubliners of his own day. The distribution of what there is to distribute as a thematic and a discursive issue in the story puts versions of John Stewart Parnell's macropolitical platform of tenant's rights into play with the micropolitical issue of the Dublin canvasser's prosaic needs to be paid for their labor. In other words, what the men *do,* their jobs as campaign canvassers, and the question of whether or not they will get paid, are as much a matter of the "politics" in the story as what they say about this or that politician. But the exchange of labor and wages remains indeterminate and difficult to adjudicate in "Ivy Day" partly because political canvassing is itself an ephemeral and seasonal labor whose efficacy is difficult to monitor. Mr. Henchy disparages Crofton's efforts as a canvasser while aggrandizing his own—"he's not worth a damn as a canvasser. He hasn't a word to throw to a dog. He stands and looks at the people while I do the talking" (129). And when the invisible narrator reports of Mr. O'Connor that "as the weather was inclement and his shoes let in the wet, he spent a great part of the day sitting by the fire in the Committee Room" (119), the reader is prompted to judge O'Connor as a slacker. We are prompted to think him undeserving of "the spondulics" (122) he so impatiently awaits, a case of shirked labor earning a shirked wage.[11] But we don't know for how many days the men have been canvassing, and for how many days they are owed wages, and there is little in the narrative focus that encourages us to consider what a critical factor their pay—however little or much they deserve it—plays in their lives. Mr. O'Connor, in spite of being depicted as a shirker for staying indoors on the rainy and cold Ivy Day, is able to report to Henchy that he has indeed "served" Aungier Street. He has also called on Grimes, as he was apparently asked to do, and has dealt with Grimes's indecision and reservations very competently—"He asked me who the nominators were; and I told him. I mentioned Father Burke's name. I think it'll be all right" (123).

The narration almost inadvertently gives us sufficient information to allow us to treat the men's anxiety about getting paid as something other than a joke produced by their seeming shirking. I would even try to reprieve the canvassers from the moral indictment that Vincent Cheng calls "a prostituted shoneen politics that would sell its services to anyone willing to pay for them, regardless of political affiliation or ideology" (124). Given the Ivy Day anniversary, Mr. O'Connor's leaky boots may be specifically glossed as a potentially fatal poverty, recalling the wet shoes that Leopold Bloom cites as one possible cause of Parnell's death[12] on that day eleven years before—"whether it transpired he owed his death to his having neglected to change his boots and clothing after a wetting when a cold resulted" (*U* 16: 1315). The "husky falsetto" in which O'Connor, a young man with the pimples of an adolescent and the grey hair of an old man, asks "Did Mr. Tierney say when he'd be back?" (119) is not interpreted by the narrative voice. We are not told if it may be construed as a symptom—perhaps of the cigarettes he rolls and smokes, but also, perhaps, that he is sick with a cold. Perhaps O'Connor needs to go home and go to bed but cannot afford to leave without collecting wages he may justly have earned by his previous days' canvassing—"I hope to God he'll not leave us in the lurch tonight" (121). The poverty of O'Connor's wet feet is matched by Henchy's worry that "I expect to find the bailiffs waiting in the hall when I get home" (124)—an explanation for why he works to elect a man he disrespects ("I can't help it," [123] he says). James Fairhall has scant sympathy for the complaining men who fail to submerge their private needs into the larger electoral issues in which their canvassing implicates them: "Still, an odor of corruption floats over the story, with personal economic interest being the driving force instead of public spirit" (299).

Yet I would argue that Joyce uses these micropolitical distribution problems—"How does he expect us to work for him if he won't stump up?" (123)—to act as witness to the "nothingness" of politics that lies between the conflicting and competing phrase regimens of the campaign rhetoric and the rhetoric of private anxiety and personal need. Henchy's political logic on behalf of his candidate flies directly in the face of his own economic interests. ("*He's a big ratepayer. . . . He has extensive house property in the city and three places of business and isn't it to his own advantage to keep down the rates?*" [131]). James Fairhall points out that "the phrase '*extensive house property*' can be nothing other than a euphemism for tenements" (300). Yet unless Henchy comes home with the wages he needs to pay his rent or mortgage, he faces eviction or the impounding of his furniture. Besides being causally linked, these disparate

speech acts of Henchy's, the public canvassing rhetoric and the personal explanation of why he must work as a canvasser, are politically linked in a way that
puts them ethically at odds. The decoding of this link requires a historical understanding of the Dublin franchise of the turn of the century, a complex issue
informed with somewhat conflicting perspectives by Don Gifford and James
Fairhall. Gifford writes that the "Franchise in Dublin was confined to male citizens over 21 who were £10 householders, i.e. those whose houses were listed on
the tax rolls as being worth £10 or more in 'annual rent.' In 1901 there were
34,906 eligible voters out of a population of 290,638 in Dublin" (89). Although
Fairhall argues that "The Local Government Act of 1898 first vested a sizable
portion of the working class of Ireland with the right to vote in the city elections" (290), Gifford insists that "Precious few members of the 'labour classes'
were enfranchised to vote in Dublin, 1902" (91). If Tierney's platform is to keep
the rates down, then he patently serves the interests of landlords rather than urban tenants. Indeed, as a Poor Law Guardian, he would have been one of the
elected ratepayers whose job it was "to make the parish the hardest task-master
[of the poor], so as to drive able-bodied men to seek honest work elsewhere and
not hang in laziness on parish relief" (Gifford 89). In other words, it is precisely
the kind of policy that Tierney stands for that forces the men in the Committee
Room to take on canvassing when they have no other paid work available to
them. The "nothingness" of politics inhabiting the difference between the genre
of political rhetoric and the genre of private anxiety may be figured in literary
terms as a circular irony: the Poor Law Guardians, Tierney among them, deliberately make public relief so difficult that unemployed, or underemployed men,
like Henchy are forced to work—even, in need, as canvassers to help elect politicians dedicated to further degrading their material estate. Tierney at least appeared capable of paying them—"It isn't but he has it, anyway. Not like that
other tinker," old Jack says (121)—but his failure to pay them could land them in
the very tenements whose rates Tierney pledges to keep down.[13]

"Ivy Day" 's narration never does announce the arrival of the wages promised the needy men in the Committee Room ("No money, boys" [122]), and
there is an ominous hint that Tierney will pay up only if he wins—"It's no go,
said Mr Henchy, shaking his head. I asked the little shoeboy but he said: *O, now,
Mr Henchy, when I see the work going on properly I won't forget you, you may be
sure. . . .* Blast his soul! Couldn't he pay up like a man instead of: *O, now, Mr
Henchy, I must speak to Mister Fanning. . . . . I've spent a lot of money?*" (123). The
sense of deferral that permeates the story's dramatic action, waiting for the
wages, waiting for Home Rule, waiting for King Eddie to bring capital to the island, proleptically gives "Ivy Day in the Committee Room" the paralyzed existential character of a kind of *Waiting for Godot*. Of what there is to be

distributed only the case of stout is delivered—and, indeed, the only equitable and uniform distribution that appears to supersede the politics of Ireland is the custom of standing drinks. Richard Tierney, the publican, withholds the canvassers' wages but stands drinks, much as Joe Hynes (indicted by Henchy as a sponger in "Ivy Day") withholds repayment of Bloom's three pound loan but stands drinks all around in "Cyclops." But the distribution of the stout, and its melioration of cynicism among the men in the Committee Room ("Ah, well, he's not so bad after all. He's as good as his word anyhow" [128] says Henchy), is itself a problematic event in the story, and one that has received some illuminating critical commentary. The porter indeed seems to function as the opiate of the Irish people,[14] and Joyce slyly glosses the Marxian epigram by linking it to religion when he has Mr. Henchy say of Father Keon, "God forgive me, he added, I thought he was the dozen of stout" (127). But although the arrival of the porter and its consumption is made to seem politically insignificant by the narration, it carries a freight of political resonance. James Fairhall points out that "the influence of drink and drink sellers" in the politics of local Irish elections were a particularly critical target of the labor candidate Connelly (the historical counterpart of Colgan). He adds that drink was also a factor in Connelly's 1902 defeat: "Free booze was scarcely the deciding factor in Connolly's defeat, but it did play a part. On the eve of the 1902 election, more than three hundred pints of porter were quaffed gratis at the public house of the Wood Quay Ward's Nationalist alderman; and on election night itself, one of the Nationalist candidates gave away drinks at his own pub" (296). Since the narrative suggests that the Black Eagle is the pub owned by the candidate Tierney,[15] the free beer he sends the canvassers is at least somewhat implicated in this problematic practice. But both Seamus Deane and David Lloyd give the function of drinking an even wider political significance. Deane argues that it is "the linkage between a political conviction that does not or cannot in these circumstances endure and the consequent and addictive consumerism which these marginalized canvassers crave to indulge, through alcohol, tobacco, political oblivion and 'manly sentiment', that Joyce dwells upon here" (32). And David Lloyd gives Irish drinking in *Dubliners* an even more complex function than symptom and antidote to anomie when he proceeds to "situate Irish drinking as one element in a matrix of such historically shifting cultural differences, differences of practices and social form that prove unincorporable either by colonial or by nationalist modernity and that remain accordingly ungathered by history, as a kind of dross or irregularity of which neither sense nor use can be made" (141).

Perhaps the stout in the story should be read as a metaphor for other ideological opiates that palliate the canvassers. For example, Hynes's poem, like the porter, serves to momentarily unite these men of different temperaments and political proclivities into a warm and muzzy union that Seamus Deane terms "this moist fellowship." He writes, "by the time the poem is over, every class position, every political conviction, every version of 'decency' has been abandoned" (32). The harsh critical judgment largely accorded the men in the Committee Room raises again the question of the stake of the genre of Joyce's "Ivy Day in the Committee Room." Does the story itself merely distribute warm stout to its readers to warm us with the entertaining rhetorical hot air of Irish politics? Does it indeed intend to bring Dubliners up short as they confront their own ideological corruptions and betrayals in the story's mirror, as Florence Walzl suggests? Does the story distribute to the bankrupt canvassers a kind of justice, and, if so, what wages do they deserve—kicks or haypence, as Hynes might put it? The range of politically sophisticated critics that includes Kershner, Fairhall, Cheng, and Deane, among others, has certainly dealt kicks to the men, and to Mr. Henchy in particular, with only occasional haypence for the pro-labor Joe Hynes. The chief sin of the men appears to be what Deane calls "a perverted class consciousness" (30) most visible in Old Jack's "gratefully oppressed" admiration for the moneyed candidates and rebuke for the lack of pretension of his low-born and unpretentious Lord Mayor—"*Wisha!* says I, *what kind of people is going at all now?*" (128).[16] But the others appear guilty of this as well, and Deane particularly takes the "vicious and slithery Mr. Henchy" (28) to task both for his sharp and derisive tongue against resisters to the status quo ("the hillsiders and fenians and socialist-nationalists in particular—have to be renamed as traitors, Castle hacks, spies, spongers, people of low origin" [31]), and for his willingness to reconcile himself to Edwardian imperialism under the guise of male cameraderie ("Male cameraderie is offered here as an alternative to or as something that transcends class" [30]). Fairhall and Deane quite overtly judge the men by specific political criteria—namely their refusal to embrace resistance politics in general, and progressive socialism, in particular—and fault them, in Fairhall's case, for quite simply working for the wrong man rather than for the right one, namely the Labour candidate. Such a criticism constructs the story into the genre of didacticism—the exemplum or moralistic lesson—a formulation that may explain why political critiques of Henchy echo in their language of derision some earlier moralistic critiques of the story, such as Father Boyle's, published in the 1968 *Twentieth Century Interpretations of "Dubliners"*. Boyle goes so far as to call "the vile" [105] Henchy "the true villain of this story, the hypocrite whose lips speak fairly to all and whose heart rots in its self-absorption" (114). He even suggests, "in passing," that Henchy "probably deflected the previous consignments [of empty stout bottles that the delivery boy requests for return] to his own profit" (105). It is difficult to imagine Boyle's narrative basis for translating Henchy's hypocrisy into thievery. Why could not old Jack have diverted the empties as easily?

My aim in pointing to the political and moral criteria at work in these criticisms is less to defend Henchy and the other men, than to highlight that this generic construction of the story as a didactic parable is just that—a critical construction. As such it stands in productive tension with my own construction of the story as a naturalistic drama—a genre that might lay greater blame for their myopic politics on the men's mean and meager economic and social environment, troped by the rainy cold, the weak fire, the withheld wages, and the palliative stout. I remain arrested by Mr. Henchy's "I can't help it. . . . I expect to find the bailiffs in the hall when I go home" (124) in response to O'Connor's rhetorical question, "How does he expect us to work for him if he won't stump up" (123). When Henchy asks what brings the socialist Hynes to the committee room, O'Connor replies, " 'Usha, poor Joe! . . . he's hard up like the rest of us" (124). Joyce does not attempt to make his readers walk a canvassing round in O'Connor's wet shoes. But he nonetheless arrests our sympathetic attention with the telling physical and material details of this raw evening's scene in the dark, denuded room warmed and lit by insufficient coals and candles. We register the toothlessness implied in old Jack's "moist" open mouth "munching once or twice mechanically as it closed" (118) and his weary gestures. We learn about O'Connor's unwholesome pimpled skin, premature grey hair, hoarse voice, and leaking shoes. Henchy with his "snuffling nose and very cold ears" (122) brings the freezing night into the room with him. He rubs his frozen hands over the fire "as if he intended to produce a spark from them" (122), and minutes later is still seen snuffling and rubbing, and spitting copious phlegm into the fire. Perhaps the most pathetic figure is the short, shabbily-clad figure of Father Keon, with only a frock-coat with turned-up collar to keep off the icy rain, and with a face like "damp yellow cheese save where two rosy spots indicated the cheekbones" (125). His errand to consult Fanning on "a little business matter" (126) is generally read as an extension of the group's general corruption and disrepute to the clergy. But this vignette of a priest in dubious standing with no clear institutional home or support also folds him into the general destitution of the men in the Committee Room. I do not wish to imply that these sharply focused details of a sharply reduced physical and material condition should be read as cause, symptom, or exoneration of the men's inability to transcend what Fairhall calls "the dominant ideology" (302). Willfully or not, they certainly appear to maintain their debased status quo by their putatively self-defeating resistance to political resistance and social change. But their own conflicting discourses (of defeated cynicism, irrational hope, suspicion and derision, sentimental nostalgia, and the like) are nonetheless underwritten by the subtextual materiality that does not allow itself to be translated into the recipes for their salvation and redemption implied by one or another "politics." I return to my initial appeal to Lyotardian theory to give greater specificity to the answer of what sort of justice the story itself distributes to its figures. The answer may be construed as a hedge against judgment, but it must nonetheless be risked. Perhaps the story distributes justice to everyone in the equivocal sense of paying them their "due" in doubled and conflicting judgments of indictment and sympathy, ridicule and respect, made even more uncertain by the lack of stable criteria for what politics demands of its citizens. Lyotardian theory may further allow us to see Joyce's "Ivy Day in the Committee Room" less as an anatomy of the bankruptcy of turn-of-the-century Irish politics (in the inefficacy, cynicism, pettiness, and inconstancy of those who ply it) than its deconstruction as "just gaming." Perhaps politics is revealed as a matter of discursive play and jousting in different genres that fail to communicate or translate into one another and therefore fail to produce justice. Like Crofton, we are tacitly asked of the story at its end, "Isn't that fine? What?" (135), and our judgment, that it is indeed fine, does justice to too many perspectives in the story to mean any one thing.

## Chapter 13

# *Critical Judgment and Gender Prejudice in "A Mother"*

Narration inevitably provides readers of fiction with a *lens* or *filter* that manipulates their perception of the virtues and vices, the strengths and weaknesses, the charms and vulgarities of fictional characters. Joyce's story, "A Mother," demonstrates how gender ideology can serve as a particularly powerful narrative filter capable of conditioning an entire critical reception. For many years, the dominant response to "A Mother" was shaped by such strong critics as David Hayman and Warren Beck, who read the story as a satire on the self-defeat of cultural pretensions. In their argument, they took their cue in condemning Mrs. Kearney from the narrative's own condemnation of the *strong* woman. Hayman writes, "Despite its public background, 'A Mother,' as Joyce later thought of it and as he doubtless intended, is the clearest exposition of the theme of the dominant female, a type he despised, feared and might have married" (124). Warren Beck concurs. "The defeat of Mrs. Kearney is to be fully approved of," he writes, "especially for its kind of poetic justice in the ruination, by her own excesses, of the very ambitions she most sought to advance" (276). But more recently a group of sophisticated gender critics has gradually mounted a complex revisionary project to read "A Mother" against the programming of these early narrative assumptions.[1] Jane Miller calls "A Mother" "perhaps the most overlooked and underrated story in James Joyce's *Dubliners*" (407). By using a different *filter* equipped with the *lens* of gender analysis, feminist critics have transformed Mrs. Kearney from virago to victim of a gender ideology that punishes strength and courage in women. This has allowed them, along the way, to reveal the story's symbolic deconstruction of the male establishment that opposes her. Garry Leonard draws this conclusion most pointedly. "Masculine order has been resoundingly reaffirmed by the conclusion of the story, yet Joyce's final image suggests that when a woman such as Mrs. Kearney mounts a successful attack against the existence of the committee, the Law of the Father is left with only one shaky leg and a prosthetic Phallus to balance upon" (271). By further training their focus on the basis of judgment within and outside the story, these gender revisions have brought new problems with the story's textual performativity into sharper focus. I will train my own eye on one of these: the function of the *review* as a product of gender prejudice within the narrative, and within the narration. I am particularly intrigued by the way this story of a musical performance focuses on off-stage or behind-the-scene events, on the backside, as it were, of performance. And I will argue that *reviewing*—the work we all do as critics—also has a backside, and is also vulnerable to off-stage or behind-the-scenes machinations and manipulations. This behind-the-scenes process may be equated with the extra-aesthetic dimension of art and criticism: the social, the political, the ideological. And I will make the point that in the case of "The Mother" the unseemliness of the spectacle of the strong woman, of an unseemly Mrs. Kearney, is produced by behind-the-scenes attitudes and their manipulations that taint judgment by coming before the evidence, by pre-judging, that is, by *prejudice*.

For my point of departure in revisiting "A Mother" I'll begin with one of the most sophisticated readings of the story I could locate, one that explores the irrepressibility of that which every narrative displaces, and which Jean-François Lyotard has named the *differend*. This element of undecidability or locus of ex-emption from adjudication is created by the peculiar nature of narrative as a structure of aporia. I use this term more in the philosophical sense, as a doubt produced by evidence both for and against a proposition. In the case of narra-tion, the structure of aporia is produced because its version of events is obliged to displace other versions of events, to produce a tacit counter-version for every version, a tacit counter-judgment for every judgment that it renders. Joseph Va-lente's brilliant reading of the story in the Winter 1991 *James Joyce Quarterly* as the intersection of two forms of *differend*—the colonial and the sexual or gender—creates a powerful impression of giving us the last word on the story, the reading that encompasses or absorbs all other readings. Valente writes:

> I want to focus here on a narrative wherein this sort of colonial *differend*, toward which Joyce himself bore the status of disenfranchised other, intersects with another, the sexual or gender *differend*, regarding which he occupied a position of relative privilege. In this way, I hope to unchain the multiple contortions of the question of justice at the level of both the action represented and the act of representation. The text to be considered is 'A Mother,' wherein a nationalistic recital is the scene for the airing of a gender grievance which cannot be 'phrased' or sustained. (430)

Without challenging Valente's model of the dynamic discursive intersections in the story, I would nonetheless argue that Mrs. Kearney's gender grievance can indeed be sustained—if not inside the narrative then nonetheless extra-textually or critically.

The burden of Mrs. Kearney's gender grievance is the violation of her daughter's contract when payment may be withheld—a complaint that has it-self been interpreted in contradictory ways by critics. David Hayman notes that payment is an issue in both "Ivy Day in the Committee Room" and in "A Mother" and finds that in both stories the characters "are self-seekers pretend-ing to a moral position they do not hold, in quest of insignificant and half-earned rewards" (123). He essentially finds the concert itself as characteristic of "overstuffed affairs designed to provide quantity without quality" (126), and therefore considers Mrs. Kearney's grievance a "petty cause" (130). Linda Rohrer Paige also dismisses the violated contract as a valid issue of grievance. Treating it as a mere instrument for control, she transforms the mother from Kathleen's defender into Kathleen's oppressor. "The 'contract' seems not only a means for this *Dubliners* mother to guarantee a monetary hold on her daughter's perfor-mance, but also it serves, metaphorically, as a vehicle for retaining other kinds of strangle holds on Kathleen, binding her both physically and emotionally" (331). Martha Black, on the other hand, makes the anthropological gender argu-ment that "Mother-right was traditionally associated with blood ties and father-right with the importance and validity of oaths, pacts, and contracts made by men . . . but when her daughter's contract is broken [Mrs. Kearney] behaves for a moment like an outlaw, a supporter of mother-right and hence a defender of the daughter tied to her by blood" (139). These conflicting interpretations of the gravity of the "contract" in the story reveal the layered set of issues that the story's donnée encompasses. These include such fundamental issues as the commercial status of art, the recompense of artists and their rights in disputes over recompense, and—more specifically—the right of female artists or per-formers to compensation and to redress in securing wages. More significantly, conflicting treatments of these issues focus attention on the way the issue of gender modulates interpretation of the story's stakes. For example, it is Beck's contention that "from Joyce's view there is less at stake" (259) in "A Mother" than in "Ivy Day" or "Grace." Yet following her discussion of "Ivy Day," Mary Power writes, "The problem of money and the public trust deepens in 'A Mother' " (220).

This assessment of the stakes in the story's plot and narrative treatment re-quires a consideration of the political significance that the concept of *the con-tract* had for turn-of-the-century women. Mrs. Kearney voices twin complaints that are clearly linked for her: that "They wouldn't have dared to have treated her like that if she had been a man" (148), and the threat that her contract will be violated. These anxieties point precisely to women's historical necessity to re-sort to the law and to juridical devices to defend against gender prejudice. Mrs. Kearney's efforts to enforce a contract must be set against the powerful politi-cal campaign by Victorian feminists to secure the legislative protection of the

Married Women's Property Acts of 1870 and 1885. In her 1988 edition to John Stuart Mill's *The Subjection of Women*, Susan Moller Okin explains the stakes of this legislation:

In the 1860's, married Englishwomen had virtually no rights under the common law. Upon marriage they entered into a legal condition called "coverture," in which they could not own property (even the wages they earned if employed), make a contract or a will, nor sue or be sued. (vii)

Because it is processed in Mrs. Kearney's parlor, Joseph Valente argues that "From the moment of signing, [Mrs. Kearney's] contract has already been privatized and delegitimated" (433). But the fact that she is able to sign a contract at all—in her home or anywhere—is the result of a hard-won legal milestone in the Western history of women's rights. This fundamental civic right is only several decades old when Mrs. Kearney relies on it, only to find it mysteriously abrogated and ineffectual to protect her interests or those of her daughter.

I will return to the relationship between prejudice and law, and the law's function as a necessary countervailing force to prejudice, later in my discussion, after exploring further the relationship of performance, review, and prejudice. As he does with many of his fictions, Joyce proleptically inscribes into "A Mother" a post-narrative ending that will occur after the story's textual ending, and that in this case is a newspaper review of the Eire Abu Society concert that is the subject of the story. Although the review itself is, of course, withheld, its conditions are elaborately detailed in the story in a way that questions in advance the legitimacy of the reviewer and the partiality of the review. In the story, a man identified as Mr. Hendrick is sent by the *Freeman Journal* to cover the concert. But because he is bored by concerts and *artistes*, he goes to cover a lecture at the Mansion House by an American priest instead, after fobbing Mr. O'Madden Burke off on the Eire Abu Society as his substitute. "—O'Madden Burke will write the notice, he explained to Mr Holohan, and I'll see it in" (145). O'Madden Burke, does indeed stick around for the concert, to review not only the musical performances, but the social and rhetorical performance of Mrs. Kearney as well: "Mr O'Madden Burke said it was the most scandalous exhibition he had ever witnessed. Miss Kathleen Kearney's musical career was ended in Dublin after that, he said" (146). Kathleen Kearney is pronounced artistically dead not for her playing but for her mother's clumsy cultural politics. Given the inscription of the *review* in the story, Richard Ellmann's account of the biographical experience that provided James Joyce with the material for "A Mother" is especially revealing. The August 22, 1904 concert at the Antient Concert Rooms, at which Joyce sang along with J. C. Doyle and the legendary John

McCormack, was glowingly reviewed in the *Freeman's Journal*. Interestingly, the review-styled diary-entry of Joseph Holloway presumed, like Joyce's story, to review the management of the performance as well as the performance:

> The attendance was good but the management of the entertainment could not have been worse. The Irish Revivalists are sadly in need of a capable manager. At present they invariably begin considerably after the time advertised and make the audience impatient; thus they handicap the performers unwarrantably. . . . The substitute appointed as accompanist in place of Miss Eileen Reidy, who left early in the evening, was so incompetent that one of the vocalists, Mr. James A. Joyce, had to sit down at the piano and accompany himself. (*JJII* 168)

Jane Miller, in her comprehensive essay on "A Mother" in the Winter 1991 *James Joyce Quarterly*, notes that Richard Ellmann interviewed the accompanist, Eileen Reidy, for his biography of Joyce in 1953 but "evidently never asked her why she had to leave the concert early" (424). This historical review-judgment of the performance of the management diametrically opposes that of O'Madden Burke at the end of the story. Further, we see that Joyce's story dilates the elision in the review, the mystery of why the accompanist abandoned the concert, with the supplementary story of the stage mother.

If we arrange these two reviews of the Eire Abu Society concert—the historical and fictional—as alternative versions of the same event, the pairing defines our critical dilemma as one of deciding who is to blame for the concert debacle: the weak male management or the strong woman, Mrs. Kearney. The difficulty with adjudicating this question is that the narration prevents the reader from approaching it impartially. A double judgment upon Mrs. Kearney is already inscribed into the narration both on the level of narrative event or plot and on the level of its telling. Indeed, the narrator pronounces judgment on Mrs. Kearney before the events unfold,[2] thereby confronting us with a prejudgment or prejudiced introduction to the case. In order to determine what is at stake for Joyce in foregrounding the discourse of a prejudiced or misogynistic narrator in the story, it may be useful to place "A Mother" into the context of a larger literary history. One could speculate, for example, that Joyce may have called his story "A Mother" in order to pair its title with a notoriously misogynistic work of modern drama: August Strindberg's *The Father*.[3] Simply pairing the strong women in these texts creates a false analogy, however. The vicious scheming by which Strindberg's monstrous wife drives her husband to be judged insane has no parallel in Mrs. Kearney's limited and localized ambitions to further her daughter's career on the musical stage—although both women do fight for their daughters' careers in the context of patriarchal institutions. But I believe Joyce takes a crucial issue from Strindberg's drama and has it play a significant thematic and performative role in the *review* and judgment of Mrs. Kearney: namely the vulnerability of perception to manipulation, and the power of discourse to influence and pervert judgment. Early in Strindberg's play, Laura tells the Doctor who will later put a straightjacket on her husband, "No, you must hear me first—before you see him" (14). The narrator of "A Mother" does essentially the same thing—making us hear *him*[4] first before we see Mrs. Kearney, before giving us the opportunity to see her and judge her for ourselves without his mediation. The narrator's preemptive description of Mrs. Kearney echoes Strindberg's description of the Captain's wife. Mrs. Kearney, like Strindberg's Laura, is deplored for a "romantic education," and for making major familial decisions "out of spite." "Miss Devlin had become Mrs. Kearney out of spite" (136), the narrator of "A Mother" tells us, just as Strindberg's wife is accused of educating her daughter "out of spite." We are told many other unflattering things about Mrs. Kearney before we ever have a chance to *see* her, to meet her, to watch her in action, and to judge her for ourselves. We are told that she "was naturally pale and unbending in manner," and that she has "ivory manners" (whatever that means—a reference to her piano playing or to her aloofness?). And we are told that "she sat amid the chilly circle of her accomplishments, waiting for some suitor to brave it and offer her a brilliant life" (136).

Before the narration of the Eire Abu concert begins and its events unfold, Mrs. Kearney has already been condemned by the narrator not for what she says or does, but simply for what she is. Her existential performance has been preempted by the narrator's rhetorical performance, which has characterized her for us as cold, rigid, selfish, and afflicted with pretensions. But besides being inflected by Strindberg's *The Father*, the narrative judgment also seems infected by the precedent of Gustave Flaubert's *Madame Bovary*. Mrs. Kearney is simultaneously ridiculed for her failure as a Romantic heroine—described as a frigid Sleeping Beauty whom no prince will broach—and for the frustrated romantic notions she displaces onto Turkish Delight, and refuses to relinquish upon marriage. Joyce's oblique allusions to *bovarisme* in the figure of Mr. Kearney are unmistakable: Mr. Kearney, like Flaubert's Charles Bovary, is a figure of petit-bourgeois probity—a sober, thrifty, pious bootmaker devoted to the care of his wife and daughters, whose serious speech the narrator muffles in a "great brown beard" (137). Within the norms of the homosocial world of Dublin, family men are portrayed most commonly as drinking themselves and their families out of jobs, financial security, and social respectability. Simon Dedalus, Tom Kernan, Paddy Dignam, Bob Doran, and Farrington are just the more egregious examples.[5] Conversely, men like Thomas Chandler, Leopold Bloom, and Mr. Kearney, who provide for their families and cater to their wives, are perversely denied esteem according to a Romantic ideology that codes masculinity as temperamentally excessive, self-indulgent, and profligate. To the narrator Mrs. Kearney is insufficiently romantic in temperament and excessively romantic in aspiration; Mr. Kearney is too unromantic altogether to pass the muster of a gender ideology itself riddled by inconsistent and unclear gender norms.

To counteract the narrator's prejudice against Mrs. Kearney at the beginning, the story is best analyzed backwards, by beginning with its ending when the negative narrative judgment of Mrs. Kearney has been universally confirmed and approved. "After that Mrs Kearney's conduct was condemned on all hands: everyone approved of what the Committee had done" (149). But what the Committee had effectively done was to heed the advice of Mr. O'Madden Burke, a man with no official connection to the concert except as an unofficially deputized reviewer: "—I agree with Miss Beirne, said Mr O'Madden Burke. Pay her nothing" (147). By paying her nothing during the intermission, the Committee violates precisely what it promised Mrs. Kearney, albeit under duress, before the opening: "Mr Fitzpatrick held a few banknotes in his hand. He counted out four into Mrs Kearney's hand and said she would get the other half at the interval" (146). What gives Mr. Burke the authority to judge a labor dispute? The narrator's description of him is totally superficial, as Mary Power has pointed out (219), all metaphors and empty signifiers that amount to no more than an imposing size and a pompous name:

One of these gentlemen was Mr O'Madden Burke, who had found out the room by instinct. He was a suave elderly man who balanced his imposing body, when at rest, upon a large silk umbrella. His magniloquent western name was the moral umbrella upon which he balanced the fine problem of his finances. He was widely respected. (145)

Garry Leonard points to a further irony, "that Mr. O'Madden Burke deliberately exploits his Irish name to garner public respect for his masculine gender in the same way that Mrs. Kearney planned to use her daughter's Irish name to garner public approval for her feminine gender" (146). We are given no basis for the bald narrative assertion that "He was widely respected."[6] If the narrator prejudices us against Mrs. Kearney, he prejudices us in favor of Mr. Burke purely on the basis of something very much like that "abstract quality as a male" Mrs. Kearney is ridiculed for respecting in her husband.

If we set aside how the narrator describes Mr. Hendrick and Mr. Burke—the figures of reviewer and moral critic at the end of the story—and look instead at what they *do*, we receive a disturbing insight into the various contaminants of disinterested judgment. Mr. Hendrick, the official *Freeman* reviewer, allows himself to be flattered by a flirtatious Miss Healy possibly intent on using her charms to secure a favorable review of her singing. And one is prompted to wonder if the drinks offered to Mr. Hendrick and Mr. Burke ("who had found out the room by instinct" [145]) are bribes disguised as hospitality. The narrator strongly intimates just that when reporting the same practice by Mrs. Kearney: "She pushed the decanter towards him, saying:—Now, help yourself, Mr Holohan! . . . —Don't be afraid! Don't be afraid of it!" (138).

Mrs. Kearney too is on the side of the impresarios during her initial enthusiasm for the concert, herself willing to supplement a thin house with "paper" or tickets distributed for free. But her partiality is not a professional requirement, as is Mr. Hendrick's and Mr. Burke's, and is therefore not at issue. In the case of Mr. Burke, the drinks proffered to enhance his aesthetic appreciation of the show appear also to lubricate his partisanship with the concert management in its labor dispute with Mrs. Kearney.

But if we disregard the narrator's pre-judgment of the issue and attempt to adjudicate the labor dispute on its merits, a much more problematic case emerges. In the eyes of O'Madden Burke and the concert committee, Mrs. Kearney's crime is an act of cultural terrorism; her ultimatum, "She won't go on without her money" (146) is seen as a threat to ruin a collective cultural enterprise to which she had contractually committed her daughter's service. Mrs. Kearney stands condemned of using a form of social violence to satisfy her own willfulness at the expense of innocent participants. "Mrs. Kearney might have taken the *artistes* into consideration" (147), the baritone complains. And indeed, the narrator describes the damage her disruption inflicts on the performance in excruciating detail. The initial "pleasant noise" that "circulated in the auditorium" rises to "sounds of encouragement, clapping and stamping of feet," and eventually erupts into to a "clamour . . . punctuated by whistling" (143–46) as the start of the program is more and more delayed. The initial bonhomie and good cheer of the performers is rapidly dissipated as they are upset and factionalized by the dispute. The ambitious and nervous opening act, Mr. Bell, has his nerves strained to the point where he was "shaking like an aspen" (147) by the time Kathleen finally accompanies him to the stage. By the intermission the dressing-room is in an uproar. We are invited to assume that all of this upheaval and dispute is quite simply Mrs. Kearney's fault. Only by recalling Joseph Holloway's historical observation, that the concert management was disastrously faulty (*JJII* 168) in the historical event, are we encouraged to probe the larger management issues more fully. Knowing that Mrs. Kearney was worried about the timing of the payment, why does Holohan go off to entertain the *Freemen* reviewers instead of alerting Mr. Fitzpatrick to the problem and producing a satisfactory response for Mrs. Kearney before the start of the program? He presumably does not even return to the stage until the program start has already been delayed, and then wastes further precious time by haggling with Mrs. Kearney before finally limping off to fetch Fitzpatrick.

Why could Mrs. Kearney's action not be treated as a noncollective version of the legitimate labor practice of the "strike"? The narrative tone aligns the reader so clearly with Burke and the concert management in condemning Mrs. Kearney as rigid, willful, and selfish, that we are discouraged from examining the facts of the case, and adjudicating for ourselves the justice of her claims. The story gives us these facts: that "a contract was drawn up by which Kathleen was to receive eight guineas for her services as accompanist at the four grand concerts" (138). Eight guineas is eight pounds eight shillings. Some of the professional performers, like the baritone, were paid in advance. "The baritone was asked what did he think of Mrs Kearney's conduct. He did not like to say anything. He had been paid his money and wished to be at peace with men" (147). When Mrs. Kearney refuses to let Kathleen play at the beginning of the fourth concert, she is apparently paid four pounds ("a few banknotes . . . [h]e counted out four into Mrs Kearney's hand" [146]) and told "she would get the other half at the interval." Correctly, she points out that technically she has not yet received half of the promised eight guineas (eight pounds and eight shillings)— "This is four shillings short" (146). At the interval she is told that "the other four guineas would be paid after the Committee meeting on the following Tuesday and that, in case her daughter did not play for the second part, the Committee would consider her contract broken and pay her nothing" (148). At the interval, Kathleen is presumably still technically owed four guineas and four shillings and the missing four shillings from the first installment. Like the characters backstage in the story, we as readers are called upon to take sides for or against Mrs. Kearney. Do we agree with Martha Black who argues, "Mrs. Kearney's daughter does not get equal pay for equal work, and the committee does not honor her contract" (139)? Or do we side with Suzette Henke in her characterization that "Mrs. Kearney . . . is so obsessively motivated by greed and financial ambition that she compromises her daughter's musical career for the sake of bolstering her own ego and maintaining a self-righteous principle" (41).

This issue is itself critically prejudiced by a gloss on the conventions of theatrical payment that Don Gifford produces in his *Joyce Annotated: Notes for "Dubliners" and "Portrait of the Artist as a Young Man"*. Gifford's reference work is indisputably reliable and indispensable, as every scholar of *Dubliners* can attest. But in this instance Gifford allows an interpretive judgment to creep into his annotation, for he patently takes sides against Mrs. Kearney when giving his explanation:[7]

The payment would not have been exorbitant for four performances had Kathleen Kearney been an experienced performer. As it stands the contract indicates Mrs. Kearney's pretension for her daughter in both the amount of money itself (eight pounds, eight shillings) and the fact that it is expressed as the fashionable "guinea" rather than flatly as eight pounds. In the argument about the payment of the contracted fee later in the story the weight of tradition is against the Kearneys. Theatrical and musical contracts of this quasi-amateur sort were regarded (and are still to a certain extent in England and Ireland) as more promising than binding, provided the person was not an established star. The promise was that the contracted fee would be paid if the concert was a financial success; if not, the performers would share whatever proceeds there were after expenses had been paid. Mrs. Kearney's attitude is in violation of this unstated assumption about the improvisatory nature of economic agreements in the theatrical and concert worlds. (99)

Gifford's key word in this explanation is "unstated" with respect to the provisional nature of the payment in the contract. Neither the narrator, nor anything in the story, states this convention or understanding, even though Mrs. Kearney's exasperated quest throughout the second half of the story is precisely to seek out the rules governing payment. There is then what Joseph Valente calls the "undecidable idiomatic nuance surrounding the term contract" that, in his view, "makes Mrs. Kearney's grievance impossible to 'phrase' or sustain but hides this possibility from her" (433). But I would argue that it is this unstated assumption, convention, or nuance that threatens Mrs. Kearney—not the feared loss of wages. Her anxiety can be seen as driven by fear that the law, and the contract as the apparatus that protects her against prejudice and gender discrimination, may be mysteriously invalidated or set aside without her consent or without any explanation. Mrs. Kearney is justifiably alarmed about the prospect of her daughter's payment when the third concert is canceled. "But, of course, that doesn't alter the contract, she said. The contract was for four concerts. Mr Holohan seemed to be in a hurry; he advised her to speak to Mr Fitzpatrick" (140). Mr. Fitzpatrick tells her he would bring the matter before the Committee.[8] She asks Mr. Holohan again before the fourth concert, and he again tells her to see Mr. Fitzpatrick. When she presses him, "Mr Holohan said it wasn't his business" (144). Joyce has the story portray Mrs. Kearney clearly as not understanding the contingencies and social modifications of the contract, and having her dogged attempts to get this crucial information and explanation repeatedly rebuffed. Put differently, her frustrations spiral as the result of the repeated *run-around* she is given. Mrs. Kearney's final bitter complaints are not about the money—"I'm asking for my rights" (148) she tells the men—but about Holohan's refusal to answer her questions and to admit her, as an equal, into the community whose practices forge the social modifications of conventions and contracts. "And when I ask when my daughter is going to be paid I can't get a civil answer. . . . You must speak to the secretary. It's not my business. I'm a great fellow fol-the-diddle-I-do." (149). Both Mrs. Kearney's complaint against the concert management and Mr. Holohan's final condemnation of Mrs. Kearney are phrased specifically in gender terms. "They wouldn't have dared to have treated her like that if she had been a man," she tells her sympathizers, and he tells her "I thought you were a lady" . . ."That's a nice lady! . . . O, she's a nice lady" (148–49).[9] As Garry Leonard points out, "At no time in his responses to her questions does Mr. Holohan address the issue of whether or not she is right (nor do any of the other men)" (145).

One might say the same thing of the narrated story itself—that the narrator might have treated the labor dispute differently had the complainant been a man, that had a man demanded an explanation of the contingencies of his contract, the narrator might have presented him as neither unreasonable nor willful. The narrator further manipulates the reader's misogyny when he deliberately withholds from us the explanation of the conventional modifications of the contract that would make Mrs. Kearney's bewilderment explicable, and enlist our sympathy for her frustrated search for information and justice. And perhaps had it been a tenor or a baritone demanding to enforce his rights, O'Madden Burke might not have leaned on his moral umbrella with such resounding disapproval. Regarded in this light, we can surmise that at stake in this gendered disapproval of female activism is nothing less than the historical judgment of feminism itself. The story poignantly represents the moral opprobrium heaped on women who forego feminine tactics, like Miss Healy's flattering and flirting for a good review, and who instead risk condemnation when they marshal contracts and laws on behalf of their rights.

But we might give this reading of "A Mother" as a performance of gender prejudice a final twist by returning it to the specificity of Joyce's own history. Why would Joyce have turned his own most triumphant concert appearance into a performative allegory of gender injustice in the artistic and cultural marketplace? This question can be answered only obliquely and speculatively, by considering the way in which art is itself "feminized" in relation to the Symbolic Order, particularly with respect to its rights to compensation and to its status as meaningful labor. In 1905, when he was writing "A Mother," Joyce went to considerable pains to convey to Stanislaus that his opinions were those "of a socialist artist" (*SL* 61) pondering with the utmost seriousness the conundrum of how artists may earn by their labor. Indeed, Joyce must labor, in this May 1905 letter to his brother, to defend his socialism against hypothetical charges of self-interest. "Some people would answer that while professing to be a socialist I am trying to make money: but this is not quite true at least as they mean it. If I made a fortune it is by no means certain I would keep it. What I wish to do is to secure a competence on which I can rely, and why I expect to have this is because I cannot believe that any State requires my energy for the work I am at present engaged in" (*SL* 61). Ellmann's consistent imputation of self-serving motives to Joyce's socialism itself creates a kind of *differend*, an inability to adjudicate whether an artist's argument for a state subsidy is an idealistic or a selfish maneuver. Ellmann likewise imputes a self-serving motive to Joyce's embrace of the literary political activism of Ibsen and Hauptmann. "He thought, too, that a political conscience would give his work distinction, as he thought it had given distinction to the work of Ibsen and Hauptmann" (*JJII* 197). Could Joyce not as easily have found in the feminist conscience of Ibsen and the labor conscience of Hauptmann a moral and a liberative aim that he wished to emulate? Joyce's own difficulties in exempting his argument for artistic support and recompense from imputations of selfishness and greed are mirrored, with an added gender twist, by Mrs. Kearney's difficulties in "A Mother."

Joyce's 1905 anxieties about the condition of artists were prophetic of a future experience when in 1912 Joyce would suffer the indignity and agony of a violated contract at the hands of George Roberts of Maunsel & Company. The incident makes the contract dispute in "A Mother" look like a picnic. Upset by the text of *Dubliners*, the publishing company's solicitors advised "Roberts that Joyce had broken his contract by submitting a book he knew to be libelous, and offered to bring suit to recover Roberts's expenses" (*JJII* 331). Joyce not only had his contract abrogated, but was threatened with a legal suit if he did not recompense the press "towards recovering our loss" (*JJII* 331). Joyce's response was infinitely more overwrought, aggressive, and unseemly than Mrs. Kearney's. He wrote and published the obscene broadside "Gas from a Burner" in revenge— an act that apparently caused Joyce's own father to indict him with virtually the same words Mr. Holohan used to excoriate Mrs. Kearney. " 'Pappie kicked up blue hell when he read it and said, 'He's an out and out ruffian without the spark of a gentleman about him' " (*JJII* 337), Charles Joyce reported to his brother James. In retrospect, Joyce's representation of the universal condemnation of Mrs. Kearney for her unladylike protest against an abrogated contract becomes uncannily proleptic of his own vulnerability to a gender reproof— though Joyce earned his with a hilariously vicious poem. In "A Mother," gender becomes Joyce's own *lens* or *filter* for exploring the confounding of strength and weakness in the arena in which art, justice, and politics intersect.

*Chapter 14*
# Setting Critical Accounts Aright in "Grace"

"Grace," as is well known, was at one time intended to be the last of the *Dubliners* stories, the capstone of the collection. Critics have therefore tended to read it for its plenary function of completing and summing up the significance of the preceding tales. In that tradition, I would like to press the story's significance beyond the book's confines, and argue that "Grace" functions— perhaps less by design than by historical convergence—to dramatize what would become a crucial ethical issue in the politics and aesthetics of Modernism. Although Ezra Pound learned social credit theory only in the 1920s, and articulated his rage at *usura* even later, in the 1930s, thinking of artistic form and production in economic terms informed Modernist ideology from its beginning. Writing "Grace" in 1905, I will argue, Joyce produces an early adumbration of these modernistic concerns, by converting the theme of *usury* into a rhetorical and narrative project without abandoning its social referent. My reading will rely on a speculation that the "silence, circumlocution, and ideological evasions" (136) Kershner finds central to the story are even more profound and significant than we have supposed because they function as a defense against rhetorical usury and at the expense of defrauding the story's creditors. In reading the story in this way, I follow a direction announced by Fritz Senn in 1980, when he wrote of "Grace": "It becomes an obligation for readers and critics who will in fact set right the various accounts presented in the story and, first of all, not be taken in by mere glibness or assurance" (125).

Before decoding these self-reflexive economic tropes, I need to delineate the source and the substance of my speculation that Tom Kernan did not fall down the lavatory steps, as everyone (including Molly Bloom) supposes. Instead, I infer that he was deliberately pushed down by the "muscle" or enforcer of his moneylender, Mr. Harford.[1] Although the narrator of "Grace" tells us that Kernan "lay curled up at the foot of the stairs down which he had fallen" (150), the cause of Kernan's fall nags at various figures throughout the story, and Tom Kernan never gives a straight answer about what happened to him. It is the young man in the cycling suit[2] who answers Mr. Power's question, "How did you get yourself into this mess?" by volunteering "The gentleman fell down the stairs" (152). The pub's manager and the constable inspect the stairs and "agreed that the gentleman must have missed his footing" (153). When Mr. Power a second time "asked him to tell how the accident had happened" Tom Kernan pleads he can't speak—"I 'an't, 'an, he answered, 'y 'ongue is hurt" (153). At Kernan's home, Mr. Power explicitly exonerates himself to Mrs. Kernan—"Mr Power was careful to explain to her that he was not responsible, that he had come on the scene by the merest accident" (155), and when Mrs. Kernan asks "Who was he with to-night, I'd like to know?" (155) Mr. Power shakes his head and says nothing.

Earlier the pub's manager had established that Mr. Kernan was drinking with two men:

> —Was he by himself? asked the manager.
> —No, sir. There was two gentlemen with him.
> —And where are they?
> No one knew. (150)

But Tom Kernan himself brings up "Those other two fellows I was with—" when he later thanks Mr. Power during his friends' bedside visit.

> —Who were you with? asked Mr. Cunningham.
> —A chap. I don't know his name. Damn it now, what's his name? Little chap with sandy hair . . .
> —And who else?
> —Harford.
> —Hm, said Mr Cunningham. (159)

The narrator now decodes the "Hm" that makes the company fall silent by noting that "the monosyllable had a moral intention" (159). Inscribed in the "Hm" is Harford's identity as one who had "begun life as an obscure financier by lending small sums of money to workmen at usurious interest" (159). The narrator goes on to describe how in partnership with Mr. Goldberg of the Liffey Loan Bank, Harford had become an urban "gombeen man" whose victims excoriate him with an associative anti-Semitism only too familiar from the later poetry of Ezra Pound and T. S. Eliot:

Though he had never embraced more than the Jewish ethical code his fellow-Catholics, whenever they had smarted in person or by proxy under his exactions, spoke of him bitterly as an Irish Jew and an illiterate and saw divine disapproval of usury made manifest through the person of his idiot son. At other times they remembered his good points. (159)

Like Kernan's cronies, who now appear to understand what happened but remain silent, the narrator too remains silent and leaves it to inference to complete the enigmatic story. We are cued, I suggest, to believe that Harford and the sandy-haired stranger were responsible for Mr. Kernan's "accident"—a masked discipline of a delinquent borrower.[3] Kernan, of course, may not divulge what happened to him, and he therefore plays innocent:

> —I wonder where did he go to, said Mr Kernan.
> He wished the details of the incident to remain vague. He wished his friends to think there had been some mistake, that Mr Harford and he had missed each other. (160)

What difference does it make whether Tom Kernan fell down the stairs drunk or was worked over by his loan sharks? The second explanation sharpens the historical and social specificity of his *fall from grace*, and complicates the role of agency in the story's parodic or ironic donnée of spiritual fall and redemption. By pointing to Dante's *Divine Comedy* as the story's frame,[4] Stanislaus Joyce inspired a tradition of reading "Grace" as a religious allegory that parodies the spiritual and moral failings of Dubliners. That earlier tradition of allegorical interpretation, which included Boyle, Newman, Niemeyer, and Baker, among others, has more recently been replaced by extremely interesting secular readings of the morality of the story (Herr, Kershner, Leonard, Torchiana, and Klein).[5] Kershner triggers an important insight when he notes that attention to Kernan's alcoholism—a "cause" that remains heavily implicated in his bad debts—is suppressed by the Dubliners surrounding Kernan, and therefore remains "pervasive and invisible" (130). Mrs. Kernan's acceptance of her husband's drinking as "part of the climate" echoes the universality and generality of the status of the "fall" and "fallen man" in Catholic theology: that moral frailty too is "part of the climate." The religious tendency of both the institutional Church and its believers to communalize morality is an important issue in this story. It is seen particularly in the collective form of the "retreat" that submerges Kernan's specific problems in the absolution of "a nice collection of scoundrels" who are going "to wash the pot together" (163). This foregrounding of the submersion of morality into collectivity allows us to track the story's interrogation of the construction of morally meliorative discourses. Put differently, I hope to read "Grace" as a parable about the danger of parable, a story that both calls for and aborts the possibility of meaningful moral confession.

This difference between moral specificity and generality produced by my reading of Kernan's fall as an act of social violence can also be glossed in relation to the difference between *actual* and *sanctifying* grace—theological concepts of major intellectual interest to the young Joyce, according to Stanislaus. Donald Torchiana lucidly explains the difference of these two forms of grace that share a spiritual economy as "a gratuitous gift awarded without regard for natural merit or fitness" (206). However, *actual grace* is a temporary and circumstantial divine assistance that helps human beings to perform a good act or avoid a sinful act in specific instances. *Sanctifying grace*, in contrast, is a "permanent, supernatural quality of the soul" (206), a habit or disposition to be good, that "resembles that grace bestowed on children baptized" (206). Both forms of grace are functions of divine mercy and charity rather than human virtue, and are therefore exempt from any human agency except passive response. The moral "paralysis" that Joyce intended to dramatize in *Dubliners* may therefore be theologically constitutive—less a matter of Irish human or cultural failing than of religious ideology and liturgical practices that blunt existential assumptions of moral responsibility for human acts and behaviors. "Grace" exposes the institutional forces that prevent moral reform with the very mechanisms designed to promote it.[6]

My project of exploring the self-implication, or self-criticism, of "Grace" as an ethical discourse is greatly aided by Joyce's willingness to represent its outcome in *Ulysses*. Indeed, by underlining a peculiar affectation of Tom Kernan's—his fondness for the phrase "retrospective arrangement" ("When you look back on it all now in a kind of retrospective arrangement" [10: 783])—*Ulysses* prods us to look back on "Grace" from its own later vantage. That perspective on Tom Kernan and his cronies from a later time makes it clear that their attempts at reform have failed to come to fruition. If we read "Grace" as a dilation of Molly Bloom's identification of "Tom Kernan that drunken little barrelly man that bit his tongue off falling down the mens W C drunk in some place or other" (18: 1264), the story's comic discursive meandering takes on a much darker coloring. We realize, in retrospective arrangement, that the reform of Tom Kernan's alcoholism is not merely a matter of his eternal salvation but, more immediately and literally, a matter of life and death. We meet Kernan again, after all, at the funeral of Paddy Dignam, whose friends pretend he died of a heart attack ("Breakdown, Martin Cunningham said. Heart" [6.305]) although, like Bloom, they know that the cause was drink ("Blazing face: redhot. Too much John Barleycorn" [6: 307]). Kernan seeks no caution for himself in Dignam's death ("Went out in a puff" [10: 771]). He critiques the style of the service ("The service of the Irish church used in Mount Jerome is simpler, more impressive I must say" [6: 665]) without recognizing the moral and medical lesson the occasion offers him. Kernan's bad example as a critic and reader who fails to read the parable of Dignam's death in favor of diverting himself with style and grace warns us in turn to read "Grace" carefully for parables of moral escapism.

The most sinister failure of "Grace" revealed in the retrospective arrangement of *Ulysses* concerns the fate of Mr. Fogarty, the carefully marked exemplar of "grace" in the *Dubliners* story. If the sublimity of divine grace resides in its gratuity, its economy as an excess of charity, then Mr. Fogarty—the "modest" grocer who brings a special gift to an unreliable and delinquent creditor who is ailing—is the sublime opposite of the figure of the usurer. The narrator bestows on Mr. Fogarty a stylistic "grace"—"He bore himself with a certain grace" (166)—that fails to mark itself as the function of his *act* rather than his *manner*. The distinction is critical because Mr. Kernan too has *grace* of manner, and *grace* of style, and a trace of culture. But Kernan rewards Fogarty's costly kindness in giving the family much needed credit at his small grocery store, and doubling it with the gratuity of a gift, by heartlessly stiffing him, as we learn in *Ulysses*:

> —I wonder how is our friend Fogarty getting on, Mr Power said.
> —Better ask Tom Kernan, Mr Dedalus said.
> —How is that? Martin Cunningham said. Left him weeping, I suppose? (6: 454)

Don Gifford glosses this exchange as implying that the "small account for groceries unsettled" at the time of Kernan's accident "has grown" by the time of Paddy Dignam's funeral, and that "Kernan has left Fogarty 'weeping at the church door,' that is, has not paid him and avoids him" (114). Tom Kernan's egregious *un-graciousness*—his ruination of a charitable benefactor—discredits the spiritual accounting of the Church, which fails to reform the Dubliners. But it also discredits the story's narration, with its attention to style over action.

Tom Kernan's defrauding of the kind and modest grocer ("modest" of means as well as comportment) is a behavior that tends to go morally unreckoned for reasons Joyce illustrates by replicating it in "Hades." There we learn that the drunken Paddy Dignam did provide a life insurance policy for his widow, but mortgaged it before his death. Mrs. Dignam and her five children would therefore be destitute. However, Dignam's friends, including Martin Cunningham and Leopold Bloom, intend to exploit a technicality in order to defraud the mortgagee and get Mrs. Dignam her Scottish Widow's insurance. "You see, he, Dignam, I mean, didn't serve any notice of the assignment on the company at the time and nominally under the act the mortgagee can't recover on the policy" (12: 762). Bloom promises to talk to the insurance company ("Must call to those Scottish Widows as I promised" [13: 1227]), although Mrs. Dignam would be unlikely to prevail in court, according to Gifford. Gifford notes, "This legal loophole was the source of considerable litigation, but attempts to void a mortgage based on the fact that the insuring company had not been notified of the mortgaging of its policy were rarely successful in the courts" (339). Joyce uses this plot to overturn anti-Semitic stereotypes of the Jew as usurer ("that's a good one if old Shylock is landed" [12.765])—a typology rife in high modernist poetry of the twenties. When Cunningham enters Barney Kiernan's and asks where Bloom is, Lenehan quips "Defrauding widows and orphans" (12.1622). But it is, of course, Dignam's widow and her orphans who will be doing the defrauding, with Bloom's help. Joyce replicates this turnaround earlier when the narrator of "Cyclops" reports trying to collect payment from Michael Geraghty who has defrauded his creditor, the Jewish small merchant Moses Herzog—"*He drink me my teas. He eat me my sugars. Because he no pay me my moneys?*" (12.31). Defrauding creditors—the twin of usury—escapes usury's opprobrium for cultural reasons, Joyce suggests: our sympathy for debtors rather than creditors, our assumption that debtors are more deserving of sympathy than creditors, is itself bolstered by the biased assumption that creditors, are either Jews or their types, "Irish Jews."

Embedded in these asymmetrical, illogical, and culturally biased ways of reckoning economic moralities is a form of sentimentality that Stephen Dedalus excoriates even as he practices it. Critics have long pointed out the ironic counterpoint between sentiment and practice in Stephen's moralistic transmission of the Meredith quotation to Mulligan, "*The sentimentalist is he who would enjoy without incurring the immense debtorship for a thing done*" (9: 550). AE Russell—objecting to "Peeping and prying into . . . the poet's drinking, the poet's debts" (9: 187)—causes Stephen to peer into the mirror of his own debt to Russell ("Do you intend to pay it back? O, yes. When? Now? Well. . . . No. When, then? . . . A.E.I.O.U." [9: 198–213]) only to dismiss the monetary debt as easily as he dismisses his plagiarisms, his discursive and literary debts to Wilde, Professor McHugh, and Meredith himself ("Cribbed out of Meredith" [14: 1486]). Stephen's telegram is a moral boomerang in two respects: it strikes its sender, and it does so by springing the economic trope back to its materialist referent. Stephen's performance of "the poet's debts" serves a parabolic function that illuminates the hypocrisy that attends moralizing—whether by poets or by priests.

This digression into Stephen Dedalus's poetic and monetary "sentimentalities"—as he would be obliged to call them—provides the retrospective arrangement for revisiting Father Purdon's sermon at the end of "Grace." Father Purdon uses the New Testament parable of the unjust steward (Luke 16: 8–9) to ground his sermon for the businessmen's retreat. Scott Klein calls the text chosen by Purdon "a radically odd passage" (121). Its enormous hermeneutical difficulties are conceded even by the preacher, according to the narration—"It was one of the most difficult texts in all the Scriptures, he said, to interpret properly" (173):

There was a certain rich man, which had a steward; and the same was accused unto him that he had wasted his goods. And he called him and said unto him, How is it that I hear this of thee? give an account of thy stewardship; for thou mayest no longer be steward. Then the steward said within himself, What shall I do? . . . I am resolved what to do, that, when I am put out of the stewardship, they may receive me into their houses. So he called every one of his lord's debtors unto him, and said unto the first, How much owest thou unto my Lord? And he said, An hundred measures of oil. And he said unto him, Take thy bill, and sit down quickly, and write fifty. Then said he to another, And how much owest thou? And he said, An hundred measures of wheat. And he said unto him, Take thy bill, and write fourscore. And the lord commended the unjust steward, because he had done wisely. (Gifford 110)

"Grace" itself—like Father Purdon—reproduces only the lesson of this parable ("*For the children of this world are wiser in their generation than the children of light. Wherefore make unto yourselves friends out of the mammon of iniquity so that when you die they may receive you into everlasting dwellings*" [173]), and it is unclear to what extent Father Purdon glosses the parable's perverse commendation of venality when he "developed the text with resonant assurance" (173).[7] But if Father Purdon narrated the whole parable to the group that includes the money-lender Mr. Harford and his client Tom Kernan, his sermon resonates with ironies. Creditors who are defrauded by delinquent borrowers rely in "Grace" not on moral suasion from the pulpit, but on secular and physical enforcement. The parabolic discourse is either completely morally irrelevant in a society that replaces the priest with "muscle" for its moral stewardship, or downright pernicious—if Tom Kernan heeded it by providing for his own security at the expense of defrauding his grocer and creditor, Mr Fogarty.

As a silent intertext glossing the retreat congregation, the parable of the unjust steward reveals unjust stewardship as endemic to Dublin's commercial and political culture. The church is peopled by usurers and pawnbrokers ("Mr Harford, the moneylender . . . old Michael Grimes, the owner of three pawnbroker's shops" [172]). The congregation includes dubious, corrupt, or nepotistic politicians, "Mr Fanning, the registration agent and mayor maker of the city, who was sitting . . . beside one of the newly elected councillors of the ward . . . and Dan Hogan's nephew, who was up for the job in the Town Clerk's office" (172).[8] Tom Kernan's own circle of friends, there for the purpose of "washing the pot," themselves constitute a rogue's gallery of financial derelictions and moral ineptitudes. Mr Power is both a borrower ("His inexplicable debts were a byword in his circle" [154]) and a lender ("Mrs Kernan, remembering . . . many small, but opportune loans" [155]) whose debts may be explained in *Ulysses* by the mistress he keeps ("Who knows is that true about the woman he keeps? Not pleasant for the wife. . . . Yes, it was Crofton met him one evening bringing her a pound of rumpsteak. What is this she was? Barmaid in Jury's. Or the Moira, was it?" [6: 234]). Mr. Cunningham, who impresses Kernan "as a judge of character and as a reader of faces" (164) and who is considered "the very man for such a case," is decidedly neither. He is married to "an unpresentable woman who was an incurable drunkard. He had set up house for her six times; and each time she had pawned the furniture on him" (157). The marriage reveals him to have been a dreadful judge of character, and a complete failure at trying to reform a drunkard. He is precisely the wrong man to be entrusted with the reformation of Tom Kernan. Mr. M'Coy, often forced "to live by his wits," goes Mrs. Cunningham one better by pawning not his own furniture, but the fraudulently acquired valises and portmanteaus of his friends—borrowed "to enable Mrs M'Coy to fulfil imaginary engagements in the country" (160). Profligate stewardship is compounded by petty fraud, bribery ("I suppose you squared the constable, Jack, said Mr M'Coy" [160]), and hypocrisy. Father Purdon's "bad" parable—with its seeming commendation of reckless stewardship rectified with fraud and injustice—functions as both mirror and moral model for these men who survive commercial failure by shrewdly manipulating loans, debts, favors, bribes, and other exchange transactions.

Father Purdon's sermon, manipulating the perverse and ambiguous meaning of the gospel text to preach just reckoning and honest accounting, ironically reenacts the very strategy of the parable's unjust steward. Instead of rendering to God a "straight and manly" accounting of his pastoral stewardship, Father Purdon (like the steward in the parable) ingratiates himself with his penitents ("Fine jolly fellow! He's a man of the world like ourselves" [164]) by offering leniency toward their moral failings and debts ("He won't be too hard on us, Tom, said Mr Power persuasively. . . . It's not exactly a sermon, you know. It's just a kind of a friendly talk, you know, in a common-sense way" (165). This lax retreat, which inspires moral evasiveness and self-justification ("I'll just tell him my little tale of woe. I'm not such a bad fellow" [171]) in its adult male clients,[9] is the dramatically soft obverse of the hellfire and brimstone aimed at the sexual temptations and transgressions of adolescent boys in *Portrait*. Cheryl Herr reads the pastoral strategy quite cynically: "As Joyce's story presents it, the church is not distinct from any secular institution. . . . it seeks to enlarge its membership and to preempt other institutions in the struggle for social control" (239). The Church's lack of moral "muscle," its inability and unwillingness to enforce a stringent moral economy,[10] allows Tom Kernan to taunt the priest who will hear his confession in advance—"If he doesn't like it, he said bluntly, he can . . . do the other thing" (171). We can fill in the ellipsis—presumably "go to hell," or what *Ulysses* calls "K.M.A."

If the Church renders to God a corrupt moral stewardship that "forgives" moral debts in the interest of allying itself with the mammon of iniquity rather than the children of light[11]—then who audits the Church? This question is at the heart of the theological discussion in Tom Kernan's bedroom, when he inveighs against "some of those secular priests, ignorant, bumptious" (164) and Popes "not exactly . . . you know . . . up to the knocker" (168). One answer is that with the doctrine of papal infallibility the Church has, in a sense, removed itself from doctrinal, if not pastoral, audit. But an implicit second answer is sounded in Joyce's moral tropes with respect to *Dubliners*—"My intention was to write a chapter of the moral history of my country" (Letter to Grant Richards, May 5, 1906; *Dubliners* 269)—and the Dantean frame Stanislaus Joyce imputed specifically to "Grace." It suggests that it is Art like that of Dante and Joyce that bears responsibility for auditing the moral stewardship of the Church (as well as that of other social institutions). In that role, does "Grace" dispense justice or mercy? These lines of inquiry raise other questions. To whom is Art answerable, and who audits Art's stewardship of social responsibility? Such questions quickly evoke the historical urgency with which they were debated by Joyce and Grant Richards while the publication of *Dubliners* itself hung in the balance. In Joyce's shocking answer to Richards' s fears of scandal and prosecution in the face of the text's moral profligacy, he conjures with the perversity of "Grace" 's parable and its injunction to "make unto yourself friends out of the mammon of inquity"—

My bag of suggestions is nearly empty but I present you with this last one. Buy two critics. If you could do this with tact you could easily withstand a campaign. Two just and strong men, each armed with seven newspapers—*quis sustinebit*? I speak in parables. (Letter to Grant Richards, June 10, 1906; *Dubliners* 279)[12]

In Joyce's perverse parable, the critic (bought and bribed) becomes Art's "muscle" or enforcer of righteousness against the public's day of the rabblement.

To further explore these questions of artistic stewardship in "Grace," I find it useful to treat the story's narrator as a proxy for Art—its spokesman (gendered male by his homosocial function, I would argue) and vehicle for its values. Although I will not gloss the gender ideology embedded in the story's moral economy except in passing, I would extend the men's plot—whose aim, according to Garry Leonard, is "to reconfirm the existing patriarchal order" (273)—to the narratorial strategy as well. But I do not consider the narrator identical with the text since the narration's speech is supplemented by the text's "body language" or semiological symptoms that modify, correct, ironize, and contradict the narrator's message and rhetoric.[13] Treating the narrator as proxy for Art, and the text as its audit, makes Art's stewardship available to critical and moral scrutiny. In this way, the story can be judged in the double register of its simultaneous capacity for moral subversion (for ingratiation, aesthetic simony, prostitution, and the like) and for self-criticism, atonement, self-correction, if not outright salvation. The narrator of "Grace" demonstrates (I hope to show) how Art forms an alliance with the children of the world and the mammon of iniquity. It does so by reenacting Father Purdon's ingratiating lenience in forgiving debts that are not his to forgive because they leave creditors weeping, as Martin Cunningham might put it. The story, as the narrator tells it, lets the scoundrels of Dublin off the hook. It treats Kernan, Power, Cunningham, M'Coy, and even Father Purdon with the same "gruff charity" (163) they treat themselves, as not such bad fellows, whose "little failings" the reader, like the Christ of Father Purdon's sermon, is expected to "understand." The text, on the other hand, like the "muscle" that makes Kernan bite his tongue, gnaws at Art's power to create shibboleths of complacency—Power's truism that "all's well that ends well," Fogarty's misquotation of Dryden, and Cunningham's fiction that the mutilated tongue can regenerate and fill in again. The narration appears to rehabilitate Tom Kernan, his tongue, and his hat so that they again "pass muster" with the reader, while the text lets us see that they are mended with empty "style" or "grace" that lacks moral fiber.

The narrator's opening gambit is to affect a rigorous objectivity in reporting a scene as though it were essentially opaque. "Two gentlemen who were in the lavatory at the time tried to lift him up: but he was quite helpless" (150). The narrator affects not to know who the gentlemen are, who the unconscious man is, what has happened—a situation that, when seen in a retrospective arrangement, turns out to be spurious, for the narrator knows and eventually tells us a great deal about Tom Kernan. But initially the narrator appears merely to offer us commentary, in real time, on a scene as strange to him as it is to us—what Senn describes as a "dumbshow" (121). The mysterious fallen man is first named by Mr. Power ("Hallo, Tom, old man! What's the trouble?" [152]). Mr. Power himself is first recognized when he is literally saluted as a figure of *Power* or Authority ("It's all right, constable. I'll see him home. The constable touched his helmet and answered:—All right, Mr Power!" [152]). It is not until Mr. Power is taking Tom Kernan home in the carriage that the narrator opens up his store of knowledge which retrospectively makes some of the events in the pub more transparent. "Mr Power, a much younger man, was employed in the Royal Irish Constabulary Office in Dublin Castle" (154), we now learn. The narrator does not dilate the significance of a connection that, if explored, would help us understand why the constable is so deferential to Mr. Power. The constable is one of the provincial bumpkins of the Dublin metropolitan police later cruelly lampooned in Cunningham's anecdote about "65, catch your cabbage!" Mr. Power, on the other hand, works for the R.I.C., the armed, "semi-military po-lice" charged with "the control and suppression of Irish dissidents" (Gifford 101). "To an extent the R.I.C. modeled itself after Scotland Yard," Gifford ex-plains, "but the R.I.C.'s function was much more political than the Yard's" (101).

What motive might prompt the narrator to pretend ignorance at the story's beginning, and to dole information out to us selectively when he finally does fill us in on some of the figures in the story? Why are we never told the identity of the two companions who were drinking with Kernan, or the name of the good Samaritan in the cycling suit? Why are we not given the significance of the information we are told? The narrator refuses to betray, for example, just what Mr. Power does for the Royal Irish Constabulary. And we might also won-der if Mr. Power's debts ("His inexplicable debts were a byword in his circle" [154]) are *really* inexplicable to the narrator, who possibly knows what Bloom knows—that Mr. Power keeps a woman on the side. If the narrator knows this, why does he refuse to tell us? These questions, while unanswerable, are useful for drawing our attention to an aspect of the narrator's comportment—namely that the narrator functions as one of the Dubliners, as their friend. He flatters the men ("he was a debonair young man" [154]) and cites their respect for each other ("Everyone had respect for poor Martin Cunningham" [157]). He mini-mizes their failures ("Mr Kernan's decline was mitigated by the fact that certain of those friends who had known him at his highest point of success still es-teemed him as a character" [154]). And he finds reasons to exonerate them, or to report their exoneration, sometimes with less than faint praise ("There were worse husbands" [156]). The narrator, in short, acts as a double of Father Pur-don in approaching these Dubliners as a man of the world who "understands" them. He further uses the authority gained by his objectivity and his urbanity to transmit his implicit judgment, that they are not such bad fellows, to us. Indeed, he works hard to present them in their best light. During his narration of the amply flawed and foolish Papal discussion in Tom Kernan's bedroom, the nar-rator either fails to detect the numerous small mistakes that are made, or refuses to betray them to us.[14] He is on the side of these men, and disinclined to criti-cize, demean, or betray them.

But the narrator's authority derives from style and rhetoric as much as from the substance of his information and his discretion of its management. In a curiously pathic transference (of the kind Hugh Kenner has termed "the Uncle Charles Principle" in *Joyce's Voices* [15–38]), the narrator appears to favor Tom

Kernan's own orotund style of speech during the early section of the story.[15] While Kernan is unable to speak for himself, the narrator tells us that "A dark medal of blood had formed itself near the man's head on the tesselated floor" (151). This narrative rhetoric—which "tesselates" the lavatory floor rather than merely "tiling" it—functions to compensate for Kernan's inability to speak because of his unconsciousness or his mutilated tongue, by speaking of him in both the style and sentiment in which he would speak of himself.[16] The narrative functions as the regenerated tongue of Tom Kernan. It mimics Kernan's own toadying admiration of worldly class, and his vanity—betrayed when he looks at himself in a mirror in *Ulysses*—that he looks like an officer returned from India ("Mr Kernan glanced in farewell at his image. High colour, of course. Grizzled moustache. Returned Indian officer" [10: 755]). The narrator's metaphor of the "medal" of blood is the first of numerous martial tropes by which he invests Kernan and his "accident"—albeit a bit mockingly—with unearned resonances of valor and heroism. These include such locutions as "a man could always pass muster" (154), "the tradition of his Napoleon, the great Blackwhite" (154), "a little leaden battalion of canisters," (154), "looked at them a little proudly, with a veteran's pride" (157), and "He felt completely outgeneralled" (171). The narrator has discursively transformed Tom Kernan into the image of his own desire: his drunken facial flush transformed into the sunburn of a returned Indian officer. This compliment is revealed, retrospectively, to be excruciatingly ironic. *Ulysses* shows Kernan to be exceptionally cowardly—afraid of cemeteries ("This cemetery is a treacherous place" [6.657]) and unattended carriages ("Damn dangerous thing. Some Tipperary bosthoon endangering the lives of the citizens. Runaway horse" [10: 776]). Conversely, Kernan's cowardice might have been produced by the violence and vulnerability attendant to his "accident" in "Grace."

If the narrator functions as Art's proxy, the homage paid to Power and Prestige—the Military, the Church, the State—marks Art's alliance with worldliness and bourgeois snobbery. The narration assumes that our prejudices are those of Tom Kernan, and therefore appeals to them—in imitation of Martin Cunningham's strategy for handling Kernan, and Father Purdon's for handling his congregation of worldlings. With respect to Tom Kernan's weaknesses, Cunningham acquits himself as a superb judge of character.[17] He plays to Kernan's social pretensions by aggrandizing Jesuit prestige—"They're the grandest order in the Church, Tom, said Mr Cunningham, with enthusiasm. The General of the Jesuits stands next to the Pope" (163)—a conceit seconded by M'Coy's "The Jesuits cater for the upper classes" (164). Cunningham singles out the cultural superiority of Pope Leo XIII—"Pope Leo, you know, was a great scholar and a poet" (167).[18] But he takes a firm stand against ecumenicism by asserting, virtually ex cathedra, the originary singularity and authenticity of the Catholic Church—"But, of course, said Mr Cunningham quietly and effectively, our religion is *the* religion, the old, original faith" (166). He further neutralizes Kernan's cynicism about corrupt popes by invoking the doctrine of papal infallibility. Ironically, he does this through a historical recreation that highlights the rhetorical circularity of infallibility as product of simple affirmation, an act of verbal fiat or rhetorical assertion—"at last the Pope himself stood up and declared infallibility a dogma of the Church *ex cathedra*" (169). The story self-reflexively becomes a parable of the power of rhetoric—"Mr Cunningham's words had built up the vast image of the Church in the minds of his hearers. His deep raucous voice had thrilled them as it uttered the word of belief and submission" (170). Tom Kernan, a lover of oratory—"Upon my word it was magnificent, the style of the oratory. And his voice! God! hadn't he a voice" (165)—is invariably moved more deeply by oratory than by theology—a proclivity Martin Cunningham deftly exploits. The narration of "Grace" produces a dramatic version of the Church's consolidation of authority and power through theological, political, and rhetorical means—the Church at its most awesome for a man of Kernan's sensibilities. But the moral stewardship that "Grace" purports to demonstrate comes up deficient in its textual audit. Father Purdon's retreat sermon is revealed to function as a theatrical performance whose oratory will thrill the unrepentant sinners in "the pit," as Tom Kernan calls it, without lifting them from their moral pit.

The sophistication and urbanity of "Grace" 's narrator gives Tom Kernan a great deal of "grace" or moral credit by protecting him rhetorically from the disgraces that would attend the full disclosure of his class slippage or *Deklassierung*. But by the narrative time of *Ulysses* Kernan's credit has run out. The unblinking "gaze" of "Wandering Rocks"—which penetrates Kernan's thoughts and discloses his vanities and pretensions directly and fully—enacts the hawk's eye Kernan ascribed to John MacHale, Archbishop of Tuam. "I never saw such an eye in a man's head. It was as much as to say: *I have you properly taped, my lad*" (170). Kernan's sartorial idiom drawn from the tailor's trade (Gifford reads "taped" as meaning "measured" or literally "sized up" [108]) is cleverly self-reflexive. Kernan uses clothes as a signifier of class and worth. Yet when he himself is properly "taped" or sized up, his second-hand frockcoat and shabby stratagems for respectability are made available to scrutiny. To Kernan, clothes make the gentleman, and he therefore overdresses (according to Gifford, *"Ulysses" Annotated* 273) to impress—"Saw him looking at my frockcoat. Dress does it. Nothing like a dressy appearance. Bowls them over" (10.738). But his frockcoat is second-hand, though his fancy endows it with the pedigree of the fashionable Anglo-Irish Kildare Street Club ("Fits me down to the ground. Some Kildare street club toff had it probably. John Mulligan, the manager of the Hiberian bank, gave me a very sharp eye yesterday on Carlisle bridge as if he remembered me" (10.745). Kernan's anachronistic name for O'Connell bridge as "Carlisle bridge" may conceal a reference to Thomas Carlyle, whose *Sartor Resartus* uses the trope of clothes to conduct a philosophical critique of social symbols and institutions. It doesn't occur to Kernan that John Mulligan may have recognized the coat as his own, or as an outdated affectation of Victorian costume, and with his "very sharp eye" penetrated the lack, hollowness, and poverty behind Kernan's pretensions. Gifford further reads Kernan's slip about Carlisle bridge as symptom of his West Briton sympathies (a suppression of the name of O'Connell) that are elaborated in his reflections on an Irish history dominated by class considerations ("Fine dashing young nobleman. Good stock, of course." [10.788]). Kernan's heroes tend to be Anglo-Irish Protestants like Robert Emmet and Edward Fitzgerald whose revolutionary heroisms he forgives even though "they were on the wrong side" because "They were gentlemen" (10.791). Fitzgerald's betrayer is contemptuously dismissed as "That ruffian, that sham squire, with his violet gloves gave him away" (10.788), without Kernan recognizing that he himself is very much such a "sham squire" dressed in lavender trousers, if not violet gloves, at his wedding. Kernan's aristocratic sycophancy has him literally running after the viceregal cavalcade, entranced by the smart outfits of the outriders—"Frockcoats. Cream sunshades. Mr Kernan hurried forward, blowing pursily. His Excellency! Too bad! Just missed that by a hair. Damn it! What a pity" (10.795). But while Kernan passes the narrator's (and our) muster in "Grace," the narrator of "Wandering Rocks" refuses to overlook Kernan's "fat strut" (10.763). The concept of *grace* itself suffers a decline in the course of the story, as Fritz Senn has argued—"From grace to demeanor, clothing, rhetorical convenience" (122)—and by the time of *Ulysses*, Tom Kernan has, unbeknownst to himself, run out of grace.

Words are Kernan's rhetorical equivalent to clothes as instruments of making an impression, and his words resemble his clothes in several respects. When his thoughts in *Ulysses* review the sale he has made to Mr. Crimmins, his style of speech, like his frockcoat, is shown to be an overdressed and archaic imitation of what he takes to be gentleman's diction—"Lovely weather we're having. Yes, indeed. . . . And now, Mr Crimmins, may we have the honour of your custom again, sir. The cup that cheers but not inebriates, as the old saying has it" (10.723–51). Kernan's diction may amuse his listeners as much as his outlandish frockcoat, if we judge by his cronies' reaction. "—Tom Kernan was immense last night, he said. And Paddy Leonard taking him off to his face. . . .—Immense, Martin Cunningham said pompously. *His singing of that simple ballad, Martin, is the most trenchant rendering I ever heard in the whole course of my experience. —*

*Trenchant,* Mr. Power said laughing. He's dead nuts on that. And the *retrospective arrangement*" (6.142). But Kernan's mannered, personal approach and flowery language in transacting business also illustrates his obsolescence. In a twentieth-century commerce increasingly dependent on modern advertising methods, Kernan is an anachronism. "Modern business methods had spared him only so far as to allow him a little office in Crowe Street on the window blind of which was written the name of his firm with the address" (154). More disturbingly, Kernan's salesman's patter in chatting Mr. Crimmins into a sale reveals a darker use of rhetoric. He exploits the *General Slocum* disaster—the June 16, 1904 explosion of an American steamer on a Sunday school excursion in which over five hundred children were killed—to portray himself as simultaneously sentimental ("Terrible affair that *General Slocum* explosion. Terrible, terrible! A thousand casualties. And heartrending scenes" [10: 725]) and cynical ("Graft, my dear sir" [10: 736]). In retrospective memory of the conversation, he lovingly quotes the rhetorical triumph of his heartless summation of the disaster—"I smiled at him. *America,* I said quietly, just like that. *What is it? The sweepings of every country including our own. Isn't that true?* That's a fact" (10: 734). Although the analogy is imperfect, Kernan's talk of the *General Slocum* comes close to enacting a form of verbal or rhetorical usury—an exploitation of the hardship or suffering of others to yield an advantage or interest far in excess of one's emotional investment. Kernan's language reveals him as a gentleman in style only: in sensibility he is very much a "sham squire."

Kernan's sentimental rhetorical exploitation of the American ship disaster exposes an even greater irony that—in further retrospective arrangement—helps us to identify the unpaid debt of "Grace": "Terrible affair that *General Slocum* explosion. Terrible, terrible! A thousand casualties. And heartrending scenes. Men trampling down women and children. Most brutal thing" (10: 725). Kernan dwells little on those trampled women and children, preferring to speculate about the "palm oil" of bribery and graft that let the unseaworthy craft, with its dysfunctional lifeboats and rotten fire hoses, go out to sea.[19] But Kernan's own account of the disaster—particularly his ostensible horror at men trampling women and children to save themselves—could have functioned nearly as a parable for him and his Dublin friends, if he were only willing to see the beam in his own eye. The Dublin of "Grace" and *Ulysses* is also a site of corruption in which safety devices to protect women and children—the life boats and fire hoses of life insurance policies, for example—are consumed by husbands willing to mortgage them for drink. And many of the men in *Dubliners* and *Ulysses* metaphorically trample their wives and children to put themselves first. Dublin widows and orphans are readily turned into objects of male sentimentality ("Her grave is over there, Jack, Mr Dedalus said. I'll soon be stretched

beside her. Let Him take me whenever He likes. / Breaking down, he began to
weep to himself quietly, stumbling a little in his walk" [6.645]). But at home
they are left to starve ("Wait awhile, Mr Dedalus said threateningly. You're like
the rest of them, are you? An insolent pack of little bitches since your poor
mother died. But wait awhile. You'll all get a short shrift and a long day from
me. Low blackguardism! I'm going to get rid of you" [10: 681]). When Tom Kernan is brought home after his "accident," Mrs. Kernan presides over an empty
larder: "I've nothing in the house to offer you," she tells Mr. Power. "We were
waiting for him to come home with the money. He never seems to think he has
a home at all" (155). She is right, alas; the penetrating "gaze" of *Ulysses* reveals
that Kernan expends much loving thought on his frockcoat, but none at all on
his wife, children, or home.

The absence of wife and children from Kernan's private thoughts and public life in *Ulysses*—in dramatic contrast to, say, Bloom's uxoriousness—prompts
us to reconsider, in retrospective arrangement, the narrator's commentary on
Mrs. Kernan and her children in "Grace." If we were to bring some of Kernan's
own skepticism and cynicism to bear on the narration, we would quickly notice
a series of curious disjunctions, contradictions, and ellipses in the relatively flattering account given of both husband and wife by the narrator. The commentary on Kernan's domestic life seems to establish Mrs. Kernan as a sensible and
credible judge of her husband. She is (indirectly) described as exonerating him
with double and inverted negatives ("a not ungallant figure"; "There were worse
husbands" [156]) that suggest that Tom Kernan has charms and virtues to balance his perfectly commonplace faults. Indeed, some critics are sufficiently
swayed by this narration to declare, "Nor are we to consider Kernan a moral
reprobate, for his wife mentions that Kernan is a fairly responsible husband and
provider" (Cunningham 222). But it is the narrator, not Mrs. Kernan, who
speaks of Kernan, and the narrative thrust continually presses against and over
curious resistances that should give us pause. What is behind Mr. Power's curious defensiveness in being "careful to explain to her that he was not responsible" [155]) for Kernan's disheveled and disgraced condition? When Mrs. Kernan
is allowed to speak for herself rather than in the narrator's indirect discourse,
she is bitter and angry—"I know you're a friend of his not like some of those
others he does be with. They're all right so long as he has money in his pocket to
keep him out from his wife and family. Nice friends!" (155). Then, what were
"Mr Power's good offices during domestic quarrels" that Mrs. Kernan gratefully
remembers? What kind of domestic quarrels require the intervention of an outsider, particularly an outsider who works for the Royal Irish Constabulary and
has influence with local constables? Had these good offices anything to do with
the violence Mrs. Kernan remembers only in negation—"He had never been

violent since the boys had grown up" (156)? The narrator treats us to the romantic image of Mrs. Kernan renewing "her intimacy with her husband by waltzing with him to Mr Power's accompaniment" (156) on her twenty-fifth wedding anniversary. But he fails to tell us why she found "a wife's life irksome" after only three weeks of marriage, and why "later on . . . she was beginning to find it unbearable" (156). We are told that the "part of mother presented to her no insuperable difficulties" but are left to imagine the difficulties that the part of wife might present to her. It is not difficult, given Kernan's "frequent intemperance" and the improvidence that leaves her only the change emptied from his trouser pockets to run her household after one of his benders. The narrator has her emphasize as a virtue that Kernan "would walk to the end of Thomas Street and back again to book even a small order" (156). Yet her own speech bitterly complains of his failure to bring the proceeds of those small orders home to her ("We were waiting for him to come home with the money" [155]). The narrator's resolute embrace of Kernan's perspective and interest is most tellingly betrayed in his description of Mrs. Kernan's memory of her wedding day. She appears to recall in vivid detail Mr. Kernan's wedding outfit—"dressed smartly in a frock-coat and lavender trousers . . . a silk hat gracefully balanced upon his other arm" [156]) while she herself and whatever bridal dress she wore are totally effaced and erased in their balance upon his other arm. Mr. Kernan appears to have married his silk hat as much as he married his wife, and given the affection and attention he still lavishes on his hats twenty-five years later, his sartorial marriage appears to have been the more enduring and successful.

The narrator's depiction of Kernan's domestic life screens and conceals his *Deklassierung* as resolutely as it protects the middle-class standing and reputation of the Dublin menfolk at large. The narrator grants this "grace" by means of Kernan's silk hat and his gaiters—"By grace of these two articles of clothing, he said, a man could always pass muster" (154). But he suppresses the symptoms of his "disgrace," the ill-educated and ill-mannered children whose behavior and condition alarm Mr. Power sufficiently ("He was surprised at their manners and at their accents and his brow grew thoughtful" [154]) to decide to intervene in Kernan's downward slide. We are given details of the success of the two eldest sons ("One was in a draper's shop in Glasgow and the other was a clerk to a tea-merchant in Belfast" [156]). But the misbehavior of the three younger children ("two girls and a boy, conscious of their father's helplessness and of their mother's absence, began some horseplay with him" [154]) is mentioned only briefly, without detail or illustration. We hear of their horseplay, but neither see nor hear it. Narrator and text give us two conflicting versions of the Kernan household in "Grace," with the narrator's functioning as the bourgeois, class-conscious commentary intent on putting a good face on things. According to this, Kernan works hard in spite of his drinking and dresses well enough to still romance his wife of twenty-five years with his gallant figure. He has managed to raise two sons to respectable adulthood, and uses style and charm in bearing and speech to inspire the loyalty and good offices of friends and customers. In these terms, the narrator's "Grace" functions as an example—or parable—of the triumph of bourgeois virtues over the temptations and trials that create temporary economic setbacks and occasional moral lapses. But when the narrative silences, contradictions, and disjunctions are pressed for meaning, the Kernan home emerges as a mess. The foppish and pompous paterfamilias is a hopeless drunkard whose brutalized older sons moved from Dublin once they were grown. His disruptive quarrels with his wife require intervention. He drinks up what little money the rare small order wrung from his obsolete sales-pitch brings in—leaving the wife to feed the family on credit squeezed from the local small grocer whose precarious business will in time be bankrupted by the Kernan derelictions. We may add to this the mounting debts, and occasional violence, incurred by Kernan's custom to loan sharks and gombeen men.

The text takes the joke out of the narrator's depiction of Mrs. Kernan as "tempted to see a curious appropriateness in his accident and, but that she did not wish to seem bloody-minded, she would have told the gentlemen that Mr Kernan's tongue would not suffer by being shortened" (158). However ambiguous, oblique, and repressed, Mrs. Kernan's sense of the justice ("a curious appropriateness in his accident") of the invisible incident before the story opens is one we might wish to share. We could even see Kernan as having received his due, his just reward externalized in the destruction of his style and grace, in a mired frockcoat, a crumpled silk hat, a mutilated tongue unable to utter its florid and orotund phrases, and a thorax clotted with phlegm. Mrs. Kernan's aggressive impulses press against the complacency in which the narrator enshrouds her, to express that her home stinks, metaphorically as well as literally ("She brought them up to his bedroom, the air of which was impregnated with a personal odour" [156]). Fine phrases, ecclesiastical history, culture, and flaccid religious retreats cannot meaningfully sanitize it. It is Mrs. Kernan and her children whose debts the narrator unjustly forgives, like the steward of the parable, in order to ingratiate himself with the Dublin men of the world and the interlocutors who resemble them. She is likely to receive justice only from another woman—from Molly Bloom, who has Kernan and his ilk properly taped and delivers unflinching judgment on them:

yes they were all in great style at the grand funeral in the paper . . . Tom Kernan that drunken little barrelly man that bit his tongue off falling down the mens W C drunk in some place or other and Martin Cunningham and the two Dedaluses and Fanny MCoys husband . . . and they call that friendship killing and then burying one another and they all with their wives and families at home more especially Jack Power keeping that barmaid he does. . . . well theyre not going to get my husband again into their clutches if I can help it making fun of him then behind his back . . . because he has sense enough not to squander every penny piece he earns down their gullets and looks after his wife and family goodfornothings poor Paddy Dignam all the same Im sorry in a way for him what are his wife and 5 children going to do unless he was insured. (18: 1261–81)

Like a usurer, or Paddy Dignam himself, the narrative of "Grace" proleptically defrauds widows and orphans, the Mrs. Dignams and Mrs. Kernans and their children with their debts and deprivations and mortgaged insurance policies. Art forgives the debt it has no right to forgive, and aborts the justice that Theodor Adorno describes as "One of the basic human rights possessed by those who pick up the tab for the progress of civilization is the right to be remembered" (72). Only the fuller text of "Grace"—the narration challenged, supplemented, and corrected by the resistant reader—can provide the audit that will right Art's accounts. The high modernists like Pound and Eliot excoriated usury, poverty, and the masses as Arnoldian threats to Art and Culture. Joyce followed Ibsen in excoriating Art and Culture itself as the usurer, sentimentalist, and unjust steward of the representation of the moral economies of the poor.

## Chapter 15

# *The Politics of Gender and Art in "The Dead"*

Although the first sentence of "The Dead" tells us that "Lily, the caretaker's daughter, was literally run off her feet" (175), Lily does not complain about her lot. Indeed, that is why she gets on so well with her mistresses, as we learn a little later—"But Lily seldom made a mistake in the orders so that she got on well with her three mistresses. They were fussy, that was all. But the only thing they would not stand was back answers" (176). The bourgeois agenda of the narrative voice[1] at this moment can be read as an intention to offer a politically complacent representation of the Morkans, one that neutralizes the master-servant relationship at the outset as benign. But once we decode this agenda, we can read in this description of Lily as a pleasing domestic fixture its suppressed truth: the orders are scrupulously checked to make sure that Lily does not steal.[2] She is further valued because she has stifled her "back answers" and does not protest the exacting demands made on her by the fussy ladies, even when she is asked to do too much, when she is run off her feet. The narration of "The Dead," promoting the Philistine ideals of the beautiful, the good, and the true (Adorno 138) in its representation of bourgeois society, successfully stifles a series of back answers that it cannot prevent from erupting in the text. Back answers repeatedly disrupt the pretty picture of prosperous and happy domesticity, of social harmony, and of refined culture in the story. Their repressed force echoes in our ears even after they have been silenced by a gold coin, an after-dinner speech, or a change of topic. "The men that is now is only all palaver and what they can get out of you" (178); "West Briton!" (190); "There's a nice husband for you, Mrs Malins" (191); "And if I were in Julia's place I'd tell that Father Healy straight up to his face. . ." (195); "And why couldn't he have a voice too? . . . Is it because he's only a black?" (198). Joyce dramatizes in "The Dead" the politics of art's determination to conceal its own politically oppressive functions by raveling a primary narrative text, Gabriel's story told in what we might call the audible or "loud" text, with a largely silent but disruptive feminist countertext.

Joyce uses Gabriel's altercation with Miss Ivors to raise the central question of the text: whether or not art serves a political function.[3] The moment is cleverly double for while the couple's words concern the politics of nationalism, their engagement, as intellectual and social equals, concerns the politics of gender—"He wanted to say that literature was above politics. But they were friends of many years' standing and their careers had been parallel, first at the University and then as teachers: he could not risk a grandiose phrase with her. He continued blinking his eyes and trying to smile and murmured lamely that he saw nothing political in writing reviews of books" (188). Interpretations of "The Dead" have traditionally assumed that Gabriel is right, and that, given Joyce's quarrels with the propagandistic aims of the Irish revival, he too would have held art above politics.[4] But this critical stance colludes with the story's endorsement of an ideology that holds nationalism to be more properly or *literally* political than feminism—thereby making Miss Ivors's "West Briton!" the only back answer taken seriously in, and by, the story. But Joyce's politics in "The Dead" are not literalized into the form of a polemic, but are rather implicit in the skepticism that the text creates in us toward the "grandiose" phrases and ideological assumptions of its own aestheticist narrative. We must be especially careful, like the women in "The Dead," not to be seduced by the story's exceptionally beautiful prose, for its lyrical narrative voice is not "innocent" but rather produces a fair share of male palaver. It effectively promotes a cultural ideology that is especially inimical to the female subject and to the female artist. Joyce therefore repeatedly nudges us to think against the ideological grain of the narration by genderizing ourselves not merely as subjectively female, but as politically feminist, as resisting readers, critics, and skeptics of the text.

"The Dead," composed while Joyce was writing *Stephen Hero*, internalizes the submerged socially critical influence of Ibsen, who is here overtly replaced by Browning as he will be replaced by Byron in *Portrait*. But it is still Ibsen who functions as the critical leaven that ferments the sweet optimistic narration in which Gabriel's story is told.[5] "The Dead" is Joyce's inverted *Doll's House*—"The purpose of *The Doll's House* . . . was the emancipation of women" (Power 35)—the husband's version of Ibsen's plot of a New Year's party that ends in a devastating marital exchange. The wife's revolt is less activist but psychologically subtler in Joyce's version, as she takes revenge for a denied trip to Galway by revisiting it spiritually and romantically in a way that displaces her husband forever from the passional center of her life and marginalizes him in his own self-image. Joyce further shifts the locus of feminist critique from the institutions of law and economics to those of art and culture. He can thereby dramatize male hegemony over art and culture as tacit denial of just that power, and

as faith in the apoliticism of an art exposed not by a cumulative historical political women's movement, but by a series of disruptive, stifled, choked female
outbursts and protests. Joyce thereby juxtaposes and intermeshes not only a
series of analogous political problems in the story (national self-figurations,
artistic and cultural desires and idealizations, bourgeois patriarchalism and
parochialism, etc.), but a series of generic functions as well. Following Ibsen's
own generic reversions and play, Joyce overlaps drama and fiction in "The
Dead" (while interpolating painting, picture, sculpture, and music as well) by
giving the narration itself, the story's "telling," a performative function. I will
therefore treat the narration of "The Dead" as a mise en scène of artistic patriarchy that requires us to be skeptical of Gabriel's romanticizing infantilization
of his wife. But we must, at the same time, be equally skeptical of the narrator's
romanticizing infantilization of the story, and particularly of the story's treatment of the marginalized Morkan women. Not only is Gabriel Conroy Joyce's
Torvald Helmer, but the narration, the story itself as narrated, is Joyce's Torvald
Helmer. Ibsen is the intertextual instrument personified in my reading by what
I've called the stifled back answer—by which both Gabriel and the narration
can be critically penetrated and ideologically dismantled. If this imputes more
political and feminist acumen to Ibsen than has traditionally been allowed, reference to Joan Templeton's 1989 *PMLA* article, in which she persuasively argues
that Ibsen was systematically defanged by his male critics, suggests the urgent
need to revisit the critical construction of Ibsen.

By being largely female, the back answers in "The Dead" suggest that Joyce
uses the politics of gender to conduct his self-critique of art in the story. But he
does this by having the story's art replicate the problems of sexual politics in society by twisting its plot in such a way that the ubiquitous oppression of woman
is both blatant and discounted, unmistakable and invisible at the same time.
The narrative maneuvers its emphasis in such a way that Irish nationalist political issues eclipse sexual politics, and the story's donnée emerges as the tragedy
of the would-be male artist, his failure of sensibility and its recuperation, rather
than the tragedy of the would-be female artist, her silencing, protest, and silencing yet again by art itself. Art's self-critique requires Joyce to dramatize that art's
representation of woman is inherently oppressive, and thereby obliges him to
specularize his own role as male artist for the purpose of critique:

He stood still in the gloom of the hall, trying to catch the air that the voice was singing
and gazing up at his wife. There was grace and mystery in her attitude as if she were a
symbol of something. He asked himself what is a woman standing on the stairs in the
shadow, listening to distant music, a symbol of. (210)

In this superb staging of the aestheticizing act,[6] Joyce displays his acute awareness that in their genderized form, in the male artist's representation of the female, the politics of representation are expressed in doubly brutal gestures of occlusion, oppression, and exploitation: doubly brutal, because these acts are masked as love. The very form of Gabriel's gesture toward woman—the rhetorical question ("He asked himself what is a woman . . . a symbol of") that proclaims its disinterest in what woman is in favor of parading its own profundity—masks artistic conceit as gyneolatry. The generality of the question implies an answer of indeterminacy and overdetermination, that woman is a symbol of anything and everything man wants her to represent—except her own sense of who or what she is. By staging Gabriel's thoughts in this way, the text of "The Dead" offers a silent second answer, a tacit back answer, to Gabriel's rhetorical question. The text tacitly responds that when woman is transformed into a symbol by man, woman becomes a symbol of her social decontextualization, her silencing, the occlusion of her suffering, and the suppression of her feeling.

To give us purchase on the irony or internal self-criticism of "The Dead" Joyce first manipulates Gabriel's literary influences. Notwithstanding Gabriel's interest in literature and especially in Continental language, and presumably art, it is not Ibsen but the English poet Browning he touts. Yet Joyce pairs Browning and Ibsen, I believe, to ironize the romantic climax of the story. Joyce uses Browning's "My Last Duchess" against Ibsen's *Doll's House* in a way that deromanticizes Gabriel's balcony scene with Gretta on the stair to reveal the oppressive sexual and aesthetic ideology that propels it. To examine these oppressive maneuvers both in love and in art more minutely, I will resort to a modification of the psychoanalytic theories of Jacques Lacan and the aesthetic theories of Theodor Adorno—strange bedfellows, perhaps, but useful for linking the problem of desire to the problem of representation. My overall thesis will be to argue that Joyce uses the events of "The Dead" to dramatize that art is not above politics at all, but that, on the contrary, art is produced by, and embodies, the social conditions of class, gender, age, and race relations. He then doubles this insight by having the narrative voice of the story act out the same disavowals of art's oppressiveness that the characters themselves act out in "The Dead." The feminist strategy I impute to Joyce is therefore less a politically correct representation of woman, than a representation of the occlusional practices that contort the representation of the female according to the ideological requirements of a patriarchal agenda. I further reckon Joyce's feminist strategy as a "cost," or at least a "risk," to his own art. The young Joyce was learning through the painful experience of rejection and censorship that it was his aesthetic effects, his lyricism, his romanticism, but not his social critique, that would earn him publication and acclaim. In "The Dead" and in *Portrait* he polishes these effects to a commercially marketable gloss, but not without covertly ironizing his lyrical language to let us see it as an exquisite form with a hypocritical soul: a paradigm for establishment aestheticism.[7]

Joyce weaves Browning and Ibsen as intertexts into Gabriel's romancing of his wife in "The Dead" because he finds in these writers a grasp of the brutalization that the idealization of female beauty can produce and conceal. By overdetermining and layering his intertexts, Joyce can generalize the argument, that the female is aestheticized in the service of a disavowed violence and that male discourse in tribute to female beauty must be scrutinized critically as symptom and mask of murder and rape. Joyce carefully weaves variations of a phrase that alludes to Browning in and out of Gabriel's thoughts and the narration—"He repeated to himself a phrase he had written in his review: *One feels that one is listening to a thought-tormented music*" (192). The text's obsession with the phrase, like Gabriel's, is with its quotability, the aesthetic ring that invites reiteration and repetition. Indeed, Gabriel rhetorically asks permission from himself to borrow part of his own phrase for his after-dinner speech. "But we are living in a sceptical and, if I may use the phrase, a thought-tormented age," (203) he says. He saves the rest of it for the title and description of the mental portrait he paints, frames, and titles, of his wife—"He asked himself what is a woman standing on the stairs in the shadow, listening to distant music, a symbol of. If he were a painter he would paint her in that attitude. . . . *Distant Music* he would call the picture if he were a painter" (210). But the distant music that Gabriel hears is, according to the narrator, the quotability and lyricism of his own prose. He repeats also the form of the rhetorical question ("*Is it because there is no word tender enough to be your name?*" [214]) with which, like Joyce himself in a letter of September 26, 1904 (*SL* 31), Gabriel graced his love letters to his wife—"Like distant music these words that he had written years before were borne towards him from the past" (214). Gabriel's wife is occluded and displaced in his memory by the grandiose phrases he can risk with this unskeptical woman. And he caresses his own words in his mind in a masturbatory gesture initiated by his caress of the written form of his own name upon the heliotrope envelope sent him by Gretta: "A heliotrope envelope was lying beside his breakfast-cup and he was caressing it with his hand" (213).

By carefully focusing our attention on Gabriel's self-displaying discourse in relation to Browning, Joyce sets up an implicit analogy between Gabriel's presentation of Gretta as a painting called *Distant Music* and Browning's dramatic monologue in "My Last Duchess."[8] The analogy produces the theme of marriage as a connoisseurship of a *female objet d'art*, an appreciation of female

beauty that resents the life and living feeling of the subject, and therefore proceeds to murder the living woman in order that she might perdure as she is desired, as pure representation, as "as if" alive rather than "as" alive—"That's my
last Duchess painted on the wall, / Looking as if she were alive." But not only is
the woman displaced by a painting in Browning's poem: the painting is displaced by the perverse discourse of the Duke of Ferrara—perverse because it
disavows the horror of what it narrates by masking itself as art history.

The Gothic elements of Browning's poem are tempered in Gabriel's aesthetic appreciation of his wife by the mediation of the bourgeois intertext of Ibsen's *Doll's House*—"A woman was standing near the top of the first flight. . . . It
was his wife" (209). That Gabriel appears, or pretends, not to recognize his wife
immediately as she stands at the top of the stair, that he is excited by her in her
guise as a beautiful and mysterious stranger, recalls Torvald Helmer's strange seduction fantasy of his wife Nora:

Do you realize—when I'm out at a party like this with you—do you know why I talk to
you so little, and keep such a distance away? . . . It's because I'm imagining then that
you're my secret darling, my secret young bride-to-be, and that no one suspects there's
anything between us. (Ibsen 183)

Gabriel, upon the couple's arrival at the Gresham after the party, has a similar
elopement fantasy about his wife—"as they stood at the hotel door, he felt that
they had escaped from their lives and duties, escaped from home and friends
and run away together with wild and radiant hearts to a new adventure" (215).
The painful irony of both Gabriel and Torvald's erotic fantasies is, of course,
their hidden truth: their wives are mysterious strangers with great secrets of their
own, and these men scarcely know the women with whom they live in such intimacy. Furthermore, it is precisely the secrets that animate the women, making them remote and strange, that excite the men. This produces the double
horror—the man's unwitting excitation by the female's hidden pain inciting
him to contemplate her seduction and rape—that ends each of these aborted
conjugal encounters. Torvald is excited by the wild desperation of Nora's taran-
tella, a desperation in which he is unknowingly implicated. His erotic stimulation by his wife's suicidal dance of death is therefore inadvertently and ironically
macabre. His anger when the distraught wife rebuffs his seduction—an anger
shadowed by conjugal enforcement ("You will, won't you? Aren't I your husband?" [Ibsen 183]—is enacted also by Gabriel—"A dull anger began to gather
again at the back of his mind and the dull fires of his lust began to glow angrily
in his veins" (218). Ruth Bauerle's essay first drew critical attention to the sinister threat of mate rape hanging over this romantic scene, as she argues that

Gabriel unwittingly begins to act out for Gretta the date rape thematized in "The Lass of Aughrim" (118).

Both Ibsen and Joyce make of the irony of aesthetic creativity a political point. Torvald and Gabriel are excited by what eludes them in their wives, by what is mysterious and strange in the women, and both impute this mysteriousness and strangeness to their own imaginations, their own powers of aesthetic and erotic sensibility. They imagine themselves Pygmalion, as it were, creating the objects of their own lust. Both imagine their wives weak and helpless in order to create gallant poses for themselves, and thereby discount the women's great strength. "She seemed to him so frail that he longed to defend her against something and then to be alone with her" (213), Gabriel thinks of the woman who had nursed a disapproving and ungrateful mother-in-law through her dying illness. Torvald makes a similar pledge to his wife, who successfully and secretly secured a life-saving therapy for his critical illness while contending with the terminus of her first pregnancy and the death of her father. "You know what, Nora—time and again I've wished you were in some terrible danger, just so I could stake my life and soul and everything for your sake" (Ibsen 186). She has done just that for him, while he ignominiously abandons her in the face of a real threat.

Both Ibsen and Joyce transform this fatuity of husbands into a poignant irony. The men do create the mysteriousness of their wives—not with art, but with a rigorous social and personal suppression. Both Torvald and Gabriel, ashamed for different reasons of their provincial wives, go to enormous lengths to alienate them from their origins, isolate them from families and friends, and silence their memories and feelings. Through this suppression, they make their wives strangers to their husbands, and estrange the women from themselves. Ibsen makes a careful point of dramatizing that Torvald knows nothing of Mrs. Linde while Dr. Rank instantly greets her as Nora's old friend—"Torvald loves me beyond words, and, as he puts it, he'd like to keep me all to himself. For a long time he'd almost be jealous if I even mentioned any of my old friends back home. So of course I dropped that" (157). Gretta's little dance of joy at the prospect of a trip to Galway ("His wife clasped her hands excitedly and gave a little jump") suggests that she has not returned to her home since her marriage—" 'O, do go, Gabriel, she cried. I'd love to see Galway again" (191). Gabriel's coldness toward her home might explain Gretta's secrecy about Michael Furey as the result of his own interdiction. Gabriel's desire to control Gretta's memory and attention serves the interest of suppressing the social reality of their marriage and their lives in order that the idealized forms of a socially stripped union, like the fantasy encounter of Torvald and his mystery

bride, might be distilled from their lives—"He longed to recall to her those moments, to make her forget the years of their dull existence together and remember only their moments of ecstasy. . . . Their children, his writing, her household
cares had not quenched all their souls' tender fire" (213). The glimpses we get
of these household cares at the beginning of the story is one of petty paternal tyrannies masked as solicitude and practiced on the bodies of wife and
children—"He's really an awful bother, what with green shades for Tom's eyes at
night and making him do the dumb-bells, and forcing Eva to eat the stirabout.
The poor child! And she simply hates the sight of it! . . . O, but you'll never guess
what he makes me wear now!" (180). Gabriel's forcing his family to eat and wear
and do what he prescribes is anticipated in Torvald Helmer's infantilizing ban
on macaroons for Nora. Indeed, Gretta's playful joke about Gabriel's solicitude,
"The next thing he'll buy me will be a diving suit" (180), nicely pinpoints
Gabriel's strategy. He makes his family feel as though the world in which they
live is an alien and dangerous element from which only his prescribed devices
and appliances will save them. Both Ibsen and Joyce create female protagonists
who bear enormous family responsibilities. They nurse sick and dying friends
and relatives, and bear and raise children with coercive interference from their
fathers. They repress their own identities and society of origin in order to maintain their husbands' social standings. They are obliged to endure a variety of
personal interdictions and domestic prohibitions, patronized in private and
sometimes insulted in public. And, it is hinted, they may on occasion be subjected to the enforcement of unwanted conjugal duties. These are women with
complex and oppressive social realities first produced, then disavowed, by their
husbands before the men can love them. The representational logic of this
situation is that, like the Duke of Ferrara, who is happiest praising the beauty of
a murdered bride, these bourgeois husbands are ultimately most excited by
their double power to oppress but disavow their oppression of the female. This
is the perversity of a particular species of uxorious bourgeois love Ibsen and
Joyce take pains to expose.

   In the critique of bourgeois love and marriage he conducts in "The Dead,"
Joyce, like Ibsen, was careful to choose a happy, prosperous family with a model
paterfamilias at its head. Gabriel is the antipode to the shiftless, ineffective, and
sometimes brutal family men who people Joyce's texts: the senior Dedalus, Martin Cunningham, Jack Power, Paddy Dignam, Farrington, Tom Kernan, and so
on. Like Ibsen, Joyce chose a best-case bourgeois scenario to expose inherent
problems in conjugal sexuality and love. Joyce goes on to elaborate Ibsen's social
analysis by giving it an aesthetic dimension, by transforming love into aesthetic
creation, and by critiquing the homologous oppressions that constitute both. To

provide a theoretical explanation for these twin pathologies whose symptom is idealization in love and art, I find a modification of the theories of Jacques Lacan and Theodor Adorno[9] especially useful. Although these theorists operate with different philosophical etiologies, they nonetheless share a common anti-essentialism and a perception that idealization is the product of complex perceptual structures. In their thinking, the structures of displacement, repression, extrusion, and the like, that produce both sexual desire and the concept of beauty, give to love and beauty political mechanisms and political ends. Lacan retrieves from Freud the startling implication of an inherent pathology in human sexuality. "Freud, as we know, went so far as to suggest a disturbance of human sexuality, not of a contingent, but of an essential kind" (281), Lacan writes. This disturbance derives from the role that the fear of castration plays in the original perception of sexual difference. The child learns the difference between male and female by making a fatal perceptual error, by imagining that the female is castrated, with the consequence that sexual identity is evermore fraught with anxiety and danger. The consequence of this perilous construction of sexual identity is that even in adult love relations, men and women find the pursuit of desire, the pursuit of the significance and recognition that is at stake in the sexual relationship, elusive except by a series of complex symbolic maneuvers. For women, especially, desire may be preempted by "the demand for love," as Lacan terms it, a condition that more closely resembles the longing to be nurtured. The emotional security of knowing that her physical needs will be supplied, that she is treasured as a valued and cherished object, may be easier for the woman to achieve than recognition, significance, and prestige as a subject in her own right. The difficulty is that these conditions are more proper to the parent and child relationship than to the marital relationship. Nora Helmer is a perfect example of a woman whose relationship to her husband is patterned on such a model of "demand for love," and Ibsen shrewdly metaphorizes precisely this aspect of it in the child and dollhouse tropes he deploys in his Christmas setting throughout the drama. Nora's desire for prestige and recognition from her husband is deferred until "the wonderful" is to happen, until she can lay before her husband her heroism on his behalf, her sacrifice of honor and risk of safety for his sake, that will call forth his respect. Gretta enjoys a similarly protective and oppressive nurturance from her husband without engaging his respect or esteem for her as a subject, as a person in her own right. But because the man fails to find in the woman the significance that would allow him to give her his recognition, he will, according to Lacan, seek for it in other women:

If, in effect, the man finds satisfaction for his demand for love in the relation with the woman, in as much as the signifier of the phallus constitutes her as giving in love what she does not have—conversely, his own desire for the phallus will make its signifier emerge in its persistent divergence towards "another woman" who may signify this Phallus in various ways, either as a virgin or as prostitute. (*Écrits* 290)[10]

In respectable bourgeois men like Torvald Helmer or Gabriel Conroy, for whom adultery is prohibited, this divergence toward the other woman takes the form of transforming the wife herself into another woman, into the stranger or the mysterious bride. Lacan, however, points out that since male anatomy does not exempt men from the anxiety of castration, the love of woman for man likewise produces a displacement:

Yet it should not be thought that the sort of infidelity that would appear to be constitutive of the male function is proper to it. For if one look more closely, the same redoubling is to be found in the woman, except that the Other of Love as such, that is to say, in so far as he is deprived of what he gives, finds it difficult to see himself in the retreat in which he is substituted for the being of the very man whose attributes she cherishes." (*Ecrits* 290)

Both Nora and Gretta fail to find in their husbands a freedom from anxiety in the face of the other that would give the men a mastery worthy of the women's recognition. Torvald's obsession with his respectability, his prestige, his authority, his rage at Krogstad's failure to proffer him a formal titular address, this enthrallment to the other, has its counterpart in Gabriel's extreme social nervousness. This expresses itself in a series of bodily tics, a blinking of his restless eyes, adjustments of his tie, playing with cuffs, flicking at his shoes—a fear of disapproval even by those he considers his social inferiors.[11] This ontological slavishness in the social realm prevents the woman from granting the man mastery except as "another man," either literally another man, as in the case of Gretta, or an idealized version of the man, as in the case of Nora. The Torvald Nora worships is not her human and socially real husband, the cowardly petty martinet who bullies her at home and his colleagues at work, but a man of sterling nobility and integrity, who does not, in fact, exist. It is only when Torvald fails to live up to Nora's idealization, when he makes his discrepancy from her ideal of him unmistakable, that he produces her anagnorisis, her moment of self-recognition and recognition of the truth of their relationship. This in turn causes her to leave him and to reclaim herself as a significant and signifying subject. Joyce also makes Gretta love an idealization of the man, but in an interesting gender twist, he permits the woman the sort of divergence usually practiced by the man. Gretta presumably "loves" her husband as a "generous person," that is, she is grateful to him for his nurturance, but she reserves her desire, her recognition, for the virginal male, Michael Furey, the idealist who achieves metaphysical mastery over her by his willingness to risk life.[12] Joyce beautifully draws the parallel between the husband who aborts the very endangerment from which he fantasizes heroically rescuing his wife, by making her, and himself, wear galoshes, while her tubercular lover stood in the rain mourning the loss of his love—"I think he died for me" (220).[13] Gabriel, seeing himself as he imagines Gretta seeing him, sees himself striving to surmount his social anxieties and perils. After Gretta's revealed memory of Michael Furey, "He saw himself as a ludicrous figure, acting as a pennyboy for his aunts, a nervous well-meaning sentimentalist, orating to vulgarians and idealising his own clownish lusts, the pitiable fatuous fellow he had caught a glimpse of in the mirror" (220). Gabriel ever teeters on the brink of symbolic negation while the social caste of the boy from the gasworks is neutralized by a heroic and fatal gesture. As a result, Gretta enshrines an ideal memory of him in her heart while marrying a man with enough sense to wear galoshes in the rain.

The displacements and divergences that constitute the subtle symbolic power plays behind the social drama in bourgeois love and sexuality also constitute a subtle aesthetic politics in the realm of beauty and representation. Adorno argues that the appreciation of beauty requires both the negation of the ugly and the realization of that negation: the ugly is both banished from beauty and necessary (as banished) to it. This concept is useful—particularly if the ugly is more precisely conceptualized as the particular, the material, the social real—for helping us to understanding the gender implications of Joyce's representational strategy in "The Dead." The aesthetic "truth" of the Joycean text is simultaneously a political "truth" for it must be sought in the way the beautiful displaces the ugly, the way art displaces social reality, and the way male creativity displaces female labor. Love and art share a homologous constitutive repression, a similar idealism produced by the disavowal and repression of the social real. Both consequently practice a kind of essentialism, a conceptual faith in love or beauty as intrinsic to the subject and object, rather than as a historical and social product. In "The Dead" love and art therefore mirror each other in a reciprocal mimesis. The figure who unwittingly exemplifies the victimization of this bourgeois essentialism of love and art is, I will suggest, Julia Morkan. She is marginalized in the periphery of the story as an infantilized, toddling, moribund old maid, robbed of a unique identity by her relational title as "Aunt Julia" and by being invariably treated as a twin or a triplet with sister and niece. Yet she is, I will argue, perhaps the truest and greatest artist in "The Dead," whose art has been suppressed, and ultimately extinguished, on purely gender grounds. And her sister Kate's "back answer" on behalf of Julia Morkan is stifled not only by their patronizing niece and nephew, by Mary Jane impatient with her aunts' peeving and their old fashioned ways and by Gabriel who considers his aunts merely "two ignorant old women" (192). The narration itself, notwithstanding all the nice little things it says about them at the beginning, also treats them as two ignorant old women. Yet Joyce embeds in "The Dead" itself a kind of shadow text, the ghost of a counter-narrative that provides a "back answer" or articulation of Julia's grievances, a complaint necessary for the critique of the social function of art in the story to be heard.

On the Morkans' wall Gabriel notices two pictures of scenes from Shakespeare's plays that serve to foreshadow two intertextual moments at the climax of the story. When Gabriel watches Gretta listening on the stair, both will mentally enact the balcony scene from Romeo and Juliet, while the song Gretta hears and remembers, "The Lass of Aughrim," repeats a version of the theme of infanticide or murdered innocence, "my babe lies cold . . . ," the infant killed by exposure to prevent it from claiming a noble or royal birthright, like the murdered princes in the Tower. However it is more than a symbolic adumbration that these pictures accomplish. They function also to exemplify the bourgeois domestication of tragedy. The use of an art whose violence is neutralized and whose ugliness is expelled becomes "kitsch" in Adorno's sense of purified beauty whose expulsion of the ugly makes itself ugly (74). Shakespeare serves, in bourgeois homes, to adorn and enhance property rather than to communicate his violent message:

A picture of the balcony scene in *Romeo and Juliet* hung there and beside it was a picture of the two murdered princes in the Tower which Aunt Julia had worked in red, blue and brown wools when she was a girl. Probably in the school they had gone to as girls that kind of work had been taught, for one year his mother had worked for him a birthday present a waistcoat of purple tabinet, with little foxes' heads upon it, lined with brown satin and having round mulberry buttons. (186)

Woman's relation to art is here historicized as a product of education, and is defined as essentially reproductive rather than productive. Shakespeare is "worked" in wools, mindlessly copied without comprehension of his textual or poetic meaning, reduced to cultural pretension or kitsch as home decor. Even Gabriel's mother, for all of her ambition and family pride, is a mere family *brains carrier* (emphasis mine), according to her sister (186), a producer of intellectual sons, and of distaff adornments for them, such as the embroidered waistcoat.[14] It is these domesticated versions of Shakespearean romance that Gabriel and Gretta both enact when their emotional passions are stirred. As Gabriel looks up at Gretta standing atop the stair, he silently plays the balcony scene with her, only first veiling his Juliet's face ("He could not see her face") in order to preserve the illusion of her beauty. The artistic act requires the suppression of the social particularity of the model ("A woman was standing. . .") and the particularity of

the face, its age, the specificity of its features, the inscription of fatigue or sadness. When the apparition of the aestheticized Gretta is dispelled, Gabriel must
reconceptualize her in a series of gentle negatives, as a tempered version of the
expelled ugly. "She had no longer any grace of attitude" (213) once she has
descended the stairs, and in sleep, Gretta's half-open mouth and adumbrated
snore can no longer be aestheticized. "He did not like to say even to himself that
her face was no longer beautiful but he knew that it was no longer the face for
which Michael Furey had braved death" (222).

Gabriel plays Romeo and Juliet with Gretta for the joy of producing the
lyricism of the poetic language that his vision of her stimulates, a poetry of
stars and sunlight and singing birds. Gabriel's narrator has him remember the
warm touch of a glove—"he was placing a ticket inside the warm palm of her
glove" (213), in echo of Romeo's "O, that I were a glove upon that hand / That I
might touch that cheek!" (11.2). But as Gabriel produces musical love lyrics under the spell of his Juliet, his Juliet is spinning her own version of Romeo and
Juliet in her imagination, which she plays back to him in their bedroom in the
Gresham. Only her Romeo is Michael Furey standing under the dripping tree
that is the synecdoche of the Capulet orchard, throwing gravel at Gretta's window to protest their fatal separation. Gretta grasps in Romeo and Juliet not the
lyricism of the language but the idealism of the gestures, of lovers willing to die
for love.

Gretta's version of Romeo and Juliet is curiously inspired by the ballad
narrative of "The Lass of Aughrim" that is, in a sense, an anti-*Romeo and Juliet*.
Romeo braving Juliet's hostile home to declare his love has a sinister mirror in
Lord Gregory raping the lass in the sanctuary of her own home—

> Oh Gregory, don't you remember,
> In my father's hall.
> When you had your will of me?
> And that was the worst of all.[15]

The nobleman's brutal violation of hospitality is cruelly iterated in his refusal to
give the girl and her babe admission on a cold and rainy night. Finally, Lord
Gregory's demand of a password to challenge the woman's identity ("Oh if you
be the lass of Aughrim / As I suppose you not to be / Come tell me the last token /
Between you and me" [Bauerle 124]) refigures the treatment of the wife as
stranger. Here again we find the man's transformation of his woman into another woman, here too for the purpose of disavowing the social real in order to
elude responsibility for her oppression. This discursive strategy within the bal-

lad reiterates the double oppression, the discursive violence of the disavowal of violence that I have pointed to earlier in Browning's Duke.

In its structure of an alternating male disavowal of sexual predation and a female "back answer," the girl's complaint of having been exploited in the ballad of "The Lass of Aughrim" recapitulates in melodramatic form the scene between Gabriel and Lily in the pantry at the beginning of the story. Joyce borrows Ibsen's technique of using a small unremarked moment in the play to indicate that hidden behind the bourgeois tragedy, and repressed and discredited by it, lie the far more egregious sufferings and oppressions of the servant class. While Ibsen's audience, actors, and critics transformed into censorship their shock at Nora's abandoning her children, they failed to bring similar outrage to Ibsen's depiction of servants quite routinely deprived of illegitimate offspring.[16] Joyce makes the story of Lily a similarly unremarked and unremarkable gap or absence in "The Dead." The male critics largely ignore this gap by treating Lily as Gabriel treats Gretta, wondering what she is a symbol of, and deciding, for example, that she could be the Easter Lily (Torchiana 253). In suppressing Lily's social reality as a servant, critics collude with the narration's promotion of Lily's willing sufferance in the stifling of her back answers. Thus her "back answer" to Gabriel is all the more remarkable, and invites us to explore the circumstantial context that links Lily subtly, proleptically, to the "Lass of Aughrim," and Gabriel, by implication, to the cruel Lord Gregory. Lily's work at the party takes the form of an isolated service as valet to the gentlemen arriving at the party. Alone in the pantry with her employers' nephew, helping him off with his coat, she is not unreasonable to interpret his pleasant allusion to her marriagability as a favorable comment on her sexual maturation. The narrative voice prods us to think of Lily as a little hysterical in construing Gabriel's pleasantries as a sexual advance, but the narrative events by no means totally preclude a repressed sexual interest as Gabriel's motive. "He looked up at the pantry ceiling, which was shaking with the stamping and shuffling of feet on the floor above, listened for a moment to the piano and then glanced at the girl, who was folding his overcoat carefully at the end of a shelf" (177). One could infer from this sequence of ocular gestures that Gabriel ventures upon a flirtation with Lily only after assuring himself that goings-on in the pantry would not be heard over the noise of dancing and the piano upstairs. If so, then we have here a possible answer to his later question, "He wondered at his riot of emotions of an hour before. From what had it proceeded?" (222). It may have been the surprise of Lily's slim prettiness that inspired his lust, its frustration later displaced onto the more sexually tractable wife. Gabriel's romanticizing of Gretta might thus be construed as having far more cynically hypocritical depths than we imagined, and his great repentant gesture, excoriating himself for romanticizing his clownish lusts, a cowardly cover for intentions variously adulterous, exploitive, and insincere. The narrative leaves as a gap just exactly what has happened to Lily, although we are prodded to infer that she has been sweet-talked into seduction by some young man and has suffered either abandonment or the onset of pregnancy in consequence. The narrative, too, sweet-talks and abandons her, treating her essentially as a decorative fixture at the party, without inquiring further into her social reality. Only her "back answer" disrupts the narration's seductive fatuities, as it disrupts Gabriel's.

The "Lass of Aughrim," like the narration of "The Dead," is art: and art does not speak the truth of social reality. The ballad gives pleasure in its discursive form, its poetry, its play upon the ambiguous credibility of the lord and lass in dialogue. The horror of the situation, the female with her infant left homeless in the rain, is assimilated as a melodramatic type to the Celtic romanticism of the song. No wonder, then, that Gretta's remembered version of the ballad, both as sung and as enacted by a Michael Furey abandoned and pleading for admittance, like the lass in the rain, shares the romanticism of a disavowed violence. For Gretta's lyrical story with its romantic donnée ("So she had had that romance in her life: a man had died for her sake" [222]) conceals a picture of depressed and futile life in the west of Ireland. From a naturalistic perspective, Michael Furey's story is one of young people apprenticed to unwholesome jobs—"a seventeen-year old Catholic probably shoveled coal to be heated for coal-gas," Torchiana speculates (240). Any artistic ambitions were likely to be aborted ("He was going to study singing only for his health" [221]), and medical care could not prevent children and young people from dying. Concealed are the poverty and wasted lives not reflected in Molly Ivors's Gaelic League romanticizing of the West of Ireland, with its educational linguistic field trips to the Aran Isles. In the story, Molly Ivors's political nationalism too fails to recuperate the social real. Marjorie Howes notes, "The West as Molly's Aran may be that clichéd embodiment of Irishness worshipped by cultural nationalism" (69).[17]

The actual performance of "The Lass of Aughrim" that inspires the twin internalized balcony scenes of the Conroys is itself, however, narrated in a strangely dual way, almost as *langue* and *parole*, to borrow the linguistic terms for language potential and language performance. In one sense, the song functions as an ideal form in its conceptual power and effects on the memories of the Conroys. As an artistic performance at the Morkan party, however, it is a failure. "The song seemed to be in the old Irish tonality and the singer seemed uncertain both of his words and of his voice" (210). The text invites us to ask why this performance occurs at all. Why does the celebrated Bartell D'Arcy ("All

Dublin is raving about him" [184]), who resists all night the importunities of Mary Jane and Gretta to perform ("He's full of conceit, I think" [191]), sing a song he scarcely knows, to a virtually empty hall, when his voice is hoarse from a cold? Clearly this man who once kissed Molly Bloom on the choir stair, sang it to please Miss O'Callaghan—a song about seduction pressed into service as a serenade to seduction. We can only speculate about its success, as he and Miss O'Callaghan go riding off together in the horse-drawn cab after leaving the Conroys off at the Gresham. But it is possible that he will have had better romantic luck with his song than Gabriel does with the serenade he and Gretta inadvertently overhear.

Yet the text, elevating the badly sung performance of "The Lass of Aughrim" to a climactic and emotionally affective and effective moment in the story, conversely discredits another musical performance whose splendor even the narrator concedes. The narrator and the assembled company, who had earlier barely listened to Mary Jane's academy piece, listen attentively to Julia Morkan's performance of "Arrayed for the Bridal." And the narrator pays her the extraordinary compliment of reporting, "To follow the voice, without looking at the singer's face, was to feel and share the excitement of swift and secure flight" (193). The narrative voice nearly lets itself get carried away for a moment, although, in a telling gesture, the narration has closed its eyes, separating sound and sight, ear and eye, precisely in order to separate the female voice and face respectively into the beautiful and the ugly. But because the narration "sees" her largely through Gabriel's eyes, sees her as old and moribund ("Poor Aunt Julia! She, too, would soon be a shade. . . . He had caught that haggard look upon her face for a moment when she was singing *Arrayed for the Bridal*" [222]), the text colludes with dismissing Julia as insignificant and with depreciating her art. Moments after having waxed nearly ecstatic over the "excitement of swift and secure flight" produced by her singing, the narration begins to ambiguate her highly enthusiastic reception. It reports that "Gabriel applauded loudly with all the others at the close of the song and loud applause was borne in from the invisible supper-table" [193]), but by adding that the applause "sounded so genuine," it implies either that it wasn't or that Julia was skeptical about its sincerity. Further, Julia's most fulsome praise comes from the two men who are treated as a comical or clownish pair by the narration. Freddy Malins's immense, sincere praise—"I never heard you sing so well, never . . . I never heard your voice sound so fresh and so . . . so clear and fresh, never"—is canceled by Browne's facetious, "Miss Julia Morkan, my latest discovery!" (193). Why should the applause not be sincere, and why should praise of Julia's singing be undermined when there is absolutely nothing in the text to contradict the narrative account of her singing as absolutely superb? I will argue that the company at the party will not let a homely old woman be a great artist, and neither will the text. The narration, caught off guard and surprised by Julia's singing, blurts out its honestly thrilled appraisal, as does the company in its long applause. But the praise is almost instantly qualified and retracted by everyone but Freddy as soon as its implications for the social real are grasped. If her singing is as splendid as it seems to have been, the people and narrative voice would need to stop patronizing Julia Morkan, would need to revise all their prejudices and stereotypes about old women, and give her their esteem as the supreme artist among them.

This deliberate suppression of the possibility that Julia produced a singing of extraordinary beauty, a musical triumph, is carried over into the male interpretation of the text in highly consequential ways. It can be seen most dramatically in what was perhaps the most vexing of the deliberate textual misrepresentations in John Huston's film version of "The Dead." The film renders Julia's performance of "Arrayed for the Bridal" as pathetically dreadful and painfully embarrassing, though Huston seemed to find her pathos "sad." The film's rendition of Julia's song deliberately violates and contradicts the clear and unequivocal direction in Joyce's text on how Julia's song is sung. We are told, "Her voice, strong and clear in tone, attacked with great spirit the runs which embellish the air and though she sang very rapidly she did not miss even the smallest of the grace notes" (193). In the film, her voice is made thin, cracking, and quavery, and Julia sings neither in tempo nor in tune. Furthermore, the film destroyed an opportunity that the text does not possess: of demonstrating that "Arrayed for the Bridal" is a fiendishly difficult piece whose singing is an operatic *tour de force*. Compared to the simple and miniscule range of the ballad tonality of "The Lass of Aughrim," Julia tackles a major operatic challenge. The film could have dramatized what the text implies but suppresses: that as a genuine musical talent Julia is probably far superior to the celebrated Bartell d'Arcy. I urge skeptics to listen to the New Hutchinson Family Singers' performance of "Arrayed for the Bridal" (a song adapted by George Linley from the melody "Son vergin vezzosa" in Bellini's opera *I Puritani*). On hearing this version, one should ask oneself whether a performance of this song, which requires a coloratura soprano of extraordinary range and flexibility, sung very rapidly and accurately in a strong clear voice, would not represent an impressive achievement. And, as if he wanted to ensure that this point not be missed, Joyce corroborates it in *Ulysses*, using the judgment of a man who *does* know professional singing, and who has heard Julia Morkan sing: Leopold Bloom. "*There is not in this wide world a vallee*," Bloom remembers, "Great song of Julia Morkan's. Kept her voice up to the very last. Pupil of Michael Balfe's, wasn't she?" (8: 416). But the Huston film blatantly ignores the narrative descriptions of Julia Morkan's musical performance as stunning, and Bartell D'Arcy's as miserable, and reverses them to make them conform to the very gender stereotypes with respect to art that the text goes to pains to discredit. So do readers and critics let the text's retroactive skepticism influence them into depreciating Julia's talent. We wonder instead what Julia and her song are a symbol of, letting ourselves be diverted by the incongruity of its bridal motif to her aged spinsterhood, without heeding either the artistic significance of her performance or the political significance of its silencing.

Joyce's text, as art, reproduces the social ideology that devalues female talent and depreciates female art. But Joyce inscribes into the oppressive discourse of his narration a "back answer" that will be stifled, to be sure, but that at least manages to write in the clearest, most factual, historical terms a formal institutionalization of the abolition of female art. The beauty of Julia's voice is professionally silenced by a simple, authoritative act of patriarchal gender privilege. Pope Pius X's pronouncement on November 22, 1903, *In Motu Proprio*, announced that the singing of church music constituted a liturgical function for which women were ineligible.[18] Henceforth soprano and alto voices would be produced by young boys (Gifford 119). The date of this edict is significant. It allows Donald Torchiana to date the story's events as occurring in early January of 1904 (Torchiana argues for Wednesday, January 6, 1904 [225]). But it also further invites us to speculate that Julia Morkan may be a perverse martyr to art, killed by sex discrimination, the victim of a species of ecclesiastical murder. I don't claim to be able to "prove" a causal link between the church edict of November 1903 and Julia Morkan's death by June 16, 1904—that is, within months of the papal destruction of her career. But I believe the text does prod us to interrogate a "lie" the narration tells us right in the beginning, when it claims "Julia, though she was quite grey, was still the leading soprano in Adam and Eve's" (176). Kate Morkan will contradict this statement in her bitter complaint about Julia's papal ouster from the choir. "I think it's not at all honourable for the pope to turn out the women out of the choirs that have slaved there all their lives and put little whipper-snappers of boys over their heads" (194), she expostulates. If Julia sings in the choir at all any more, it is certainly not as its lead soprano. The opening narration of the story then conceals that this particular Morkan Christmas party will be different from all the others because it follows within weeks of a trauma whose dimensions for the Morkan sisters include something like personal, professional, theological, and economic violence. Julia's ouster, by papal edict, on the basis of her sex and without regard to either

her talent or her service, from the church choir after thirty years of service, may well account for what is "wrong" with her throughout the story. The dark shadows in her flaccid face, the haggard look, the way she is "out of it" throughout the evening can now be read as symptoms of a bitter crisis in the Morkan's musical household. The pre-Christmas ouster may also give Julia's performance of "Arrayed for the Bridal" on the evening of the party a particularly poignant significance. Her performance was in all probability her last, a swan song of particular humiliation, as stripped of her artistic profession she is degraded back to amateur status and relegated to parlor performance. The debasement inflicted on her by a Church she has so faithfully served is particularly cruel in light of the information adumbrated in Bloom's musings. He raises the possibility that, if Julia Morkan was indeed trained by Michael Balfe—one of Ireland's most famous musical figures—she may have sacrificed a genuinely promising career to the Church. Her rare coloratura soprano voice might have made her a prima donna like the one in Mr. Browne's story, whose carriage was unyoked by the gallery boys of the old Royal and pulled through the streets of Dublin. Instead of the concert stage where she belonged—she herself modestly owns that "Thirty years ago I hadn't a bad voice as voices go"—Julia Morkan ended up "slaving there in that choir night and day, night and day. Six o'clock on Christmas morning! And all for what?" (194), her talent wasted in marginalized and unappreciated musical labor. "I often told Julia, said Aunt Kate emphatically, that she was simply thrown away in that choir" (194). And so the Morkan sisters are left with a pompous nephew who considers them ignorant old women and a spineless niece who nearly publicly insults her aunts in the interest of toadying to her clients.

Kate Morkan's protest of the pope's politically oppressive act, and her outrage at the injustice inflicted on her sister are, I believe, Joyce's equivalent to Nora's discursive assumption of selfhood in Ibsen's *Doll's House*. But the narration takes its cue from the blatantly patronizing Mary Jane, who stifles Kate's "back answer" as an infantile tantrum ("when we are hungry we are all very quarrelsome" [195]), and treats the whole episode as silly. The narration may try to conceal from the reader an important truth about the oppression of the female artist. But Joyce nonetheless gives Kate Morkan a moment of outraged voice, whose immediate stifling should attract our notice and concern and serve as our wedge for forcing a larger critique of the narration. The pope's patent injustice to her sister, to women, shakes Kate Morkan to the point of heresy—"I suppose it is for the good of the Church if the pope does it. But it's not just, Mary Jane, and it's not right" (194). Kate virtually challenges papal infallibility (announced by the First Vatican Council in 1870, less than thirty-five years before) with this protest,[19] and her heresy alarms Mary Jane sufficiently to shame her aunt into silence by reminding her that she is "giving scandal" to the Protestant Mr. Browne. Joyce—who according to Groden's chronology in the Archive wrote "The Dead" in 1907—began the writing of *A Portrait of the Artist as a Young Man* in September of the same year. It is not impossible that he is drawing here a highly ironic parallel between two artists thwarted by religion in pursuit of their artistic vocations. In *Portrait* he semaphores the adolescent boy's traumas at the hands of the Church into epic proportions. Pandy-batted by a priest as a child, terrorized by a retreat sermon as an adolescent, upbraided for heresy in class, and beaten by his friends for defending Byron, Stephen's ecclesiastical oppressions culminate in his heroic and dramatic *Non Serviam* by novel's end. Stephen's "back answers" are treated very differently from those of women. "The Dead" offers a version of an ecclesiastical oppression much more pointed and tragic in its effects. A display of papal power nullifies a lifetime of devotion and labor and transforms Julia's sacrifice and dedication of a great talent to God and his Church as a female impertinence. An ecclesiastical act that deprives an aging single woman of her livelihood is treated as a comic triviality, and the spiritual mutiny it precipitates in her sister's heart is treated as a childish tantrum.[20]

Joyce was not blind to the cruel irony he has his texts produce, nor to the difficulty of driving it home to his readers against the grain of a disavowing narration. Knowing that we are likely to follow the text's collusion in dismissing Aunt Julia and Aunt Kate as comic relief to Gabriel's angsts, Joyce devises a second maneuver to repeat and reinforce the political point the sisters dramatize, when he has Freddy Malins rise to the defense of the negro chieftain at the Gaiety. The scholarly problems of legitimating Freddy's critical judgment are extremely vexed. It is difficult to establish whether G. H. Elliott, the presumed singer referred to, is either a tenor or black,[21] and Freddy Malins might therefore be mistaken in his comments about the singer. But there is no reason to fault Freddy Malins's judgment in acknowledging the beauty of an old woman's song or in decrying the injustice of barring black singers from the legitimate operatic stage on the basis of race. "And why couldn't he have a voice too? asked Freddy Malins sharply. Is it because he's only a black?" (198). Freddy's protest against racial discrimination is not so easily dismissed by either the company or the reader as his protest against gender and age discrimination—practices more thoroughly internalized and naturalized in his society. But Freddy's protest is stifled too. "Nobody answered this question and Mary Jane led the table back to the legitimate opera" (199).

Joyce understands perfectly, I believe, that art is produced by and reproduces political ideology and social relations. He also understands, I believe, that it is establishment art's first aim to disavow just this fact about itself, in order to disavow its reproduction of social oppressions. By eschewing using his art polemically to criticize social oppressiveness, Joyce is able to critique art's own oppressive practices. He has his text, on the one hand, maintain implicit faith in an essentialist aesthetics—a faith that art is above politics. On the other, he disrupts it with incidents that show that art is the product of social forces that operate on the same principles of privilege and exclusion that govern such categories such as gender, race, class, and age, in social and cultural life. By inscribing in his disavowing narration a series of linked and analogous "back answers" or protests that trouble the text and cause it to stifle them in collusion with characters who do the same, Joyce stages art's censorship of its own oppressiveness.

# Notes

## Introduction

1. Tanja Vesala-Varttala gives such a comprehensive summary and thoughtful critique of *Dubliners* scholarship that I felt to do so in my own introduction would be simply redundant. I would therefore refer readers to the conclusion of *Sympathy and Joyce's "Dubliners": Ethical Probing of Reading, Narrative, and Textuality*, 275–302.

2. James Buzard offers an "anthropological" exploration of early *Dubliners* criticism in his essay " 'Culture' and the Critics of *Dubliners*."

3. See Morris Beja's "One Good Look at Themselves: Epiphanies in *Dubliners*"(13–14).

4. Robert Scholes points out the texts used in an illustrative way by his theorists: Todorov used Boccaccio's *Decameron*, Genette used Proust's *À la recherche du temps perdu*, and Barthes, of course, used Balzac's *Sarrasine* (65–66).

5. Patrick McCarthy focuses the exemplarity of *Dubliners* more specifically on its role within the genre of the short story. He writes, "As a contribution to the art of the short story, *Dubliners* is noteworthy for several reasons. Its sparse yet economical style, its use of suggestive details that at times seem to have a symbolic meaning, its refusal of any sort of neat conclusion have all influenced the shape of the modern short story" (3).

6. I am here thinking particularly of some of the excellent discussions of *Dubliners* found in such studies as Vincent Cheng's *Joyce, Race, and Empire*, the essays contained in Derek Attridge and Marjorie Howes's *Semicolonial Joyce*, and James Fairhall's chapter on "The Paralyzed City" in *James Joyce and the Question of History*, among others.

7. Hugh Kenner argues the obverse of this method of reading in his 1986 essay, "Signs on a White Field." He writes, "I shall also hint at a corollary, that once we have at last really read *Dubliners* we shall find *Finnegans Wake* a great deal less strange" (209).

8. Ansgar F. Nünning's essay, "Reconceptualizing the Theory and Generic Scope of Unreliable Narration," gives an excellent summary of earlier theories of unreliable narration, followed by a proposal for a more cognitive model, one that recognizes the role of "the conceptual models or frames previously existing in the mind of the reader or the critic" (78).

9. In her intriguing discussion about the difficulties of translating Eliza's "rheumatic wheels" into other languages, Jolanta Wawrzycka proposes another possibility, that Eliza's malapropism may betray that she suffers from rheumatic fever (71).

10. Vincent Cheng reports in *Joyce, Race, and Empire* on the first airing of his postcolonial reading of "The Dead." "To my surprise, I learned from the controversial response to this paper more about the nature of the risks one takes in trying to repoliticize a highly canonical work. . . . 'Very interesting and imaginative, but I'm afraid you are doing serious violence to the story' was the vexed response of one very senior scholar, whose work I admire very much" (128).

## Chapter 1. The Gnomon of the Book: "The Sisters"

1. Carle Bonafous-Murat discusses the complexities of voluntary and involuntary memory in relation to place in both "The Sisters" and "Eveline" (361–68).

2. Wolfgang Karrer also configures the sisters into a gnomonic relationship with their brother, Father Flynn (48–53).

3. John Paul Riquelme gives a narratological explanation for why the reader might feel incriminated in the narrative ambiguity and unease: "Like the psycho-narration in *A Portrait*, the consonant self-narration in 'The Sisters,' combined with brief direct presentations of the character's thoughts, creates a sense of intimacy between reader and character" (99).

4. See Laurent Milesi's essay, "Joyce's Anamorphic Mirror in 'The Sisters,'" for a beautifully theorized discussion of the inflections of vision in the dream, and in other key moments of the story (90–113).

5. Edward Brandabur interestingly gives a chiefly psychological and moral twist to the priest's putative "perversity"—"The priest derives pleasure from a relationship in which he can inflict the double pain of his revolting presence and his Jansenistic doctrine, for both of these exercise on the boy so mysteriously strong an attraction that he feels compelled to look on the loathsome work of physical and spiritual paralysis in spite of (or perhaps because of ) his great fear" (42).

6. William Johnsen finds a series of fascinating parallels between "The Sisters" and another story that appeared in *The Irish Homestead* in 1904—Berkeley Campbell's "The Old Watchman." In this story a boy also encounters an old, disappointed man who, before dying, tells how he squandered his opportunities and ended up with a wasted life (76–77).

7. Hugh Kenner offers one of the more ingenious and compelling of the typological readings of the sisters in "The Sisters." Noting that the configuration of an active and a silent sister with a dead brother recalls St. Luke's story of Martha, Mary, and their dead brother Lazarus, who is resurrected by Christ, Kenner concludes that the trouble with the priest is indicated by the absence of Christ: in other words, that he has lost his faith ("Signs on a White Field" 210)

## Chapter 2. A Walk on the Wild(e) Side: "An Encounter"

1. To a contemporary sensibility, Joyce's gesturing toward heredity, epilepsy, and the "Anglo-Saxon college and university system with its secrecy and restrictions" (*CW* 203–4), seems a less enlightened explanation of "the strange problem of the life of Oscar Wilde" than it might have early in the century.

2. Richard Brown argues that "Joyce evidently identified with Wilde in the same kind of way that he identified with Parnell: both, for him, were Irishmen condemned for sexual crimes by an unjust, hypocritical morality" (81).

3. The narrator tends to be figured as the "boy" of the story retrospectively, but still in boyhood, telling his experience. But the narrator's "good" accent—as he himself would call it—betrays a sophisticated vocabulary and diction quite beyond even the brightest and most studious of preadolescent boys. It is a mature, eloquent voice that

produces the locutions "a spirit of unruliness diffused itself among us," "those chronicles of disorder," "we ate sedulously," "brandishing his unloaded catapult," "escaladed," "our jaded thoughts," "mimic warfare," "Lest I should betray my agitation," and so on.

4. Kershner writes, "The boy's fear of appearing overly studious to his classmates is of central significance in the ideological framework of the story. Both of the adults in the story—Father Butler and the 'old josser'—immediately invoke a culturally reified distinction between boys who are active, unthinking, and lower-class and those who are studious, responsible, and upper-middle class." (35).

5. This dialogue uncannily evokes the exchange between Mr. Cotter and the aunt in the previous story, "The Sisters": "But why do you think it's not good for children, Mr Cotter? she asked" (11). Cotter's provocative comments and ellipses likewise play with his interlocutors' registers of knowing and unknowing.

6. Bernard Benstock's discussion of *seeing* in the story extends into the powers of "divination" displayed by the old man (16).

7. Gregory W. Bredbeck, "Narcissus in the Wilde," in *The Politics and Poetics of Camp*, ed. Moe Myer (New York: Routledge, 1994), 57. I am indebted to Brian Loftus for directing me to this information in Bredbeck's essay.

8. Joseph Valente, "Thrilled by His Touch: Homosexual Panic and the Will to Artistry in *A Portrait of the Artist as a Young Man*," *James Joyce Quarterly* 31 (Spring 1994): 167–88.

9. Bernard Benstock reads the "purpose of the [boy's] narrative" as "not to find adventure, but to prove his own superiority over 'a boy named Mahoney'" (16). But I would say this interpretation depends on restrospection from the last line of the story. Mahoney's liveliness—his colorful slang, his playful aggressions chasing ragged girls and cats, and brandishing his catapult—enliven the narrative as much as they enliven the narrator's day and infuse the high spirits of both. Disparagement and contempt for Mahoney are expressed only at the end of the story, where they may serve chiefly as a screen or diversion.

## Chapter 3. Blind Streets and Seeing Houses: "Araby"

1. See R. B. Kershner's extensive discussion of the dead priest's discarded books—especially Sir Walter Scott's *The Abbot*—and their curious gloss on the adventures of the boy in "Araby." "Scott's novel is peculiarly double-voiced; the ideology of nineteenth-century realism and Evangelical admonishment coexists uneasily with romantic ideology, so that Child Roland emerges as a figure both farcical and heroic, both chastened and victorious. The boy of 'Araby,' unfortunately, is trapped in a very different sort of narrative, where the idealism that is Roland's saving grace is exactly the quality responsible for the Irish boy's failure" (54).

2. In his invaluable documentation and extensive explanation of the 1894 "Grand Oriental Fête" on which the story's bazaar is based, Heyward Ehrlich gives this promised gift the name of "a fairing, a token or keepsake traditionally brought back from a fair" (312).

3. Steven Doloff gives the chivalric motif in "Araby" a hagiographic layer by likening the boy's quest to the pilgrimage of St. Ignatius Loyala: "Loyola exhibits his sustained

interest in romance by framing aspects of his religious experience also in knightly terms" (516).

4. Warren Beck, who delicately explores "Araby" as an adolescent love story, traces its movement "through self determining events to self-realization in a Joycean epiphany" (96) although he argues that the boy does not yet appreciate what he learns. "In 'Araby' the boy has been frustrated by externality, in the guises of the tardy drunken uncle and a slow train, but he is more lastingly grieved by discovery of a universal ineradicable flaw, the gap between idealization and its confined operation. This also is epiphany, but at first sight almost too appalling for him" (109).

5. For an excellent exploration of the ideological significance of the Orient within Ireland's own cultural and literary traditions, see Vincent Cheng's *Joyce, Race, and Empire* (88–100). Drawing both on post-colonial theory and historical material, Cheng is able to dilate the function of "Araby" 's Orientalism in a highly comprehensive way. See also Ranjana Khanna's " 'Araby': Women's Time and the Time of Nation" for an exploration of the relationship between national identity, gender, and time in the story (81–101).

6. For an early detailed account of the 1894 Whitsuntide Araby bazaar to benefit the Catholic Jervis Street Hospital, see Donald Torchiana's *Backgrounds for Joyce's 'Dubliners'* (56–60). Heyward Ehrlich's account greatly augments this information by arguing that the actual, historical 1894 bazaar was an "immense, sprawling, noisy" event paradoxically in contrast with "the small, dark, quiet charity sale that the boy depicts in the story" (310). Ehrlich goes on to note that "Araby embraced thirty-seven charity stalls and forty-three entertainments, requiring a combined staff of 1,760 stallholders and performers" (313). Yet the charity function of the bazaar is elided in the story—suggesting that neither of the children, the boy or Mangan's sister, nor the boy's aunt (she "hoped it was not some Freemason affair" [32]), are aware of this purpose. As a result, the thematic, symbolic, and ironic possibilities of "charity" as the boy's destination or purpose are dissipated.

7. Garry Leonard, who produces a superb analysis of the gender-ontology in the story, argues that what the boy has always in his eye is actually "I" (74).

8. Garry Leonard takes what he calls the "unusual tack of discussing this story as though it were the story of Mangan's sister." He argues that the boy must suppress the girl's story in order to create and "believe the myth of himself." But "Mangan's sister exists alongside the boy's narration and can be glimpsed through those gaps in the text where the boy's story falters" (79).

9. Ben Collins goes on to interpret, "The bracelet may be likened to Judas' silver, the rope to the crucifixion, the death of the illusion" (97). Harry Stone associates her silver bracelet with "the harlotry associations of Mary Magdalene," allowing him to assimilate the story to an overarching theme that "All women for Joyce, are Eves: they tempt and they betray" (313). Wolfgang Karrer, in contrast, restores the representation of the girl to the culturally conditioned imagination of the boy—"the aesthetic image the boy forms in his mind of Mangan's sister (bracelet, neck, hair, hem) owes something to the pre-Raphaelites pictorially" (56).

10. The MURGE group's rigorous analysis eschews the kind of dreadful allegorizing of the girl produced by Collins and Stone. But their Chatman-inspired method does

not allow them to treat Mangan's sister as a "character" at all, but only as a part of the setting or an "event" that happens to the boy. (240) Their methodological positivism prevents precisely the sort of problematizing of determinate gaps and absences that the various post-structuralist critical methodologies make possible.

11. Pound's succinct praise of "Araby" has nothing to do with ideology, however, and everything to do with craft—"Joyce's *Araby*, for instance, is much better than a 'story', it is a vivid waiting" (400).

12. Gifford cites the Baedeker description of Paris coffeehouses as "a cut below the music halls" (48). But Heyward Ehrlich gives a much more opulent description of the historical Café Chantant of the 1894 Araby bazaar: "The Café Chantant was actually located on the Grounds, where it featured French, German, Italian, Spanish, English and Irish songs, piano and violin solos, recitations, dances, and many other attractions." (317). Ehrlich also points out that the historical Café Chantant would have been neither closed nor empty at the time of the boy's arrival—"At 9:50 P.M., the actual Café Chantant was still in operation, with two more lively shows, said always to be full, still to come at 10:00 and 10:30 P.M." (319). Joyce's deliberate creation of frustrated expectation therefore seems particularly significant.

13. Torchiana suggests a plausible explanation for the aunt's suspicion, namely that the first charity bazaar in Dublin was the Masonic Bazaar held there in 1892 (56). See also Gifford 47.

14. Jim LeBlanc conducts an interesting Sartrean exploration of the strange reversals between work and play in the story (229–33)

15. Curiously, Bernard Benstock invokes the Chapel Perilous in his discussion of "An Encounter" rather than of "Araby"—"Not only is the Chapel Perilous never broached, leaving them vulnerable to the monster they never anticipated, but the purpose of the narrative has never been honestly apprehended—not to find adventure, but to prove his own superiority over 'a boy named Mahoney' " (16).

16. Considered in this light, the vivid role that commercial and communicative exchange plays in *Ulysses* could be regarded as the antidote to the moribund aestheticism in "Araby."

## Chapter 4. The Perils of "Eveline"

1. Katherine Mullin historically identifies three types of emigration propaganda a young, single, literate female in turn-of-the-century Ireland might have had to adjudicate. The first promised successful pioneering in Argentina, the second exposed the plight of misled Irish immigrants, and the third conjured the prostitution in the white slave trade as the lurid fate of the single, unprotected female émigré. "Eveline is the propagandist's sitting target," Mullin writes (197).

2. Benoit Tadie has a particularly interesting analysis of the locutions of Eveline's memory in the story (379).

3. Brenda Maddox reports that Nora Joyce's father, Tom Barnacle, was a drunkard, like Mr. Hill, who could also be very nice with the children at times. Like Eveline, Nora and her sisters "remember how he told them ghost stories before the fire" (14).

4. Darwin's voyage to Tierra del Fuego on the *Beagle* had stimulated general European interest in Patagonians. Sidney Feshbach writes, "In 1830, three aborigines 'were abducted' from Patagonia or Tierra del Fuego 'and brought to England' for exhibition and education" (224). Katherine Mullin, however, points out that "Frank's tales of the terrible Patagonians are tall because the Patagonians became extinct many years before his birth" (176).

5. The Pulitzer Prize-winning 1996 chronicle tells of the McCourt family returning to the slums of Limerick after failing to make a go of it in Brooklyn in the Depression, and enduring extreme poverty, near-starvation, typhoid, and the death of several of the children. The memoir begins with the sentence, "My father and mother should have stayed in New York where they had met and married, and where I was born. Instead, they returned to Ireland" (11).

6. Mullin notes that Joyce bought and owned a copy of Olive Mac Kirdy's *The White Slave Market*, which was published in 1912. But while Joyce wrote "Eveline" many years prior to acquiring this book, Mullen points out that "By 1904 the city [Buenos Ayres] was perceived to be the international capital of the White Slave Trade" (189).

7. Luke Gibbons fills in the broader historical and social conditions that are thought to have contributed to the dysfunctionality in post-Famine colonial Ireland (168). These include, in addition to the absence of an urban manufacturing base, the absence of a social reform agenda on the part of the Catholic Church and lack of legal protection afforded to women against domestic violence.

8. Benoit Tadie describes Eveline's dilemma as better appreciated in terms of verbal tense, than of time, and calls it a "verbal deadlock which can account for the aphasic collapse of the central character at the end of the story" (379).

9. The discrepancy between the "house" of Kenner's account, and the "home" of the 1967 and 1996 Penguin editions—edited by Scholes and Litz—that I have been using, may be an editorial one. In his original "Molly's Masterstroke" article in the Fall 1972 *James Joyce Quarterly*, Hugh Kenner explicitly "quotes" *house* as the word used in the text of "Eveline." Kenner writes, "And he had come to Dublin, it seems, to obtain a bride, and take her back to Buenos Aires, where (to quote again) 'he had a house waiting for her.' " (20). But the article has no footnote, and it is unclear which edition Kenner might have been using. Kenner's 1978 *Joyce's Voices*, which again mentions Frank's "house," has no bibliography so that the edition of *Dubliners* to which he refers is once again indeterminate.

10. Torchiana writes of Frank, "I shall even be bold enough to liken him to the Christ who revealed Himself to Margaret Mary" (73).

11. David Weir points out that the story elides all of the actions Eveline takes to prepare for her journey—"packing her baggage, writing a farewell note to her father, catching a tram, walking briskly to the North Wall" (345). The effect of this elision, he argues, is to have the narrative replace "passage" with representations of the "passive" (345).

12. J. C. Beckett argues that the Great Famine of 1846 altered the emigration practices of the Irish. "Emigration, formerly a last desperate remedy, was now the first thing thought of; and there was an almost hysterical rush to leave the country, to escape, at all costs, from 'the doomed and starving island,' and find safety elsewhere," he writes. He goes on to say that "In earlier years, emigrant sailings had been confined to spring and summer; and intending emigrants had made their preparations carefully. But, from the latter half of 1846 onwards, the panic-stricken crowds were clamorous to be off without delay; the traffic continued throughout the year; and thousands of helpless refugees put

to sea with only the scantiest supply of provisions for the voyage, and without either means of subsistence or prospect of employment on their arrival" (344).

## Chapter 5. Masculinity Games in "After the Race"

1. I am indebted to H. K. Riikonen of the University of Helsinki for pointing this letter out to me.

2. Joyce troubled to verify the plausibility of Mr. Doyle's police contract by asking his brother Stanislaus to check on the matter: "Dear Stannie Please send me the information I ask you for as follows: . . . *After the Race*—Are the police supplied with provisions by government or by private contracts?" (*SL* 75). Richard Ellmann's note to this query says that "This detail does not appear in the published story," although it patently does.

3. James Fairhall, after researching a number of *Irish Times* articles and editorials on Dublin's hosting of the Gordon Bennett Cup Race in 1903, concludes, "We can see why Joyce chose the Gordon Bennett Cup auto race as the backdrop for this glimpse into the lives of Dublin's *nouveaux riches*. It provided an opportunity to show Ireland as the victim not just of England, but of the international imperialist and capitalist order, and a somewhat willing victim at that" (395).

4. A number of critics have suggested that the card game may have been "rigged" including Vincent Cheng (108), Seamus Deane (23), and Robert M. Adams (101). An alternate scenario of fraud is suggested by Harold Mosher, who posits a far more sinister and professional confidence game in progress in the story. Mosher believes that the card game, and other games of the young Continentals, are intended to divert Jimmy's attention from the actual fraud, which is the bogus financial investment (407–28).

5. Garry Leonard makes this interesting observation about the Doyle father-son relationship: "He is performing the role of cavalier youthfulness for the sake of his father, who amassed his fortune by never acting cavalier or youthful" (113).

6. Patrick Parrinder reads "After the Race" allegorically. "The story is a political and economic allegory in which the game of cards stands for the 'great game' [D 51] of European diplomacy and high finance. The American foots the bill, and the outcome lies between the French and the English. Jimmy Doyle, the Irishman, gets cleaned out" (62). I find this reading nearly irresistible, but still feel there is benefit in attending to the way social and gender politics are manipulated within the story.

7. See Tanja Vesala-Varttala for one of the most thorough and interesting meditations on the function of Villona in the story (211–12).

8. For Tanja Vesala-Varttala, the reader's "oppositional sympathy," as she calls it, is in itself a worthy outcome of the story. "In other words, the textual function of the narration demands respect for the kind of paralyzed otherness the satiric narrative function of the same narration presents as the butt of its critique" (212).

9. Garry Leonard makes this astute observation about the story's readers: "they are told several times that Jimmy has spoken, but they never actually hear anything that he says" (115). This suggests that the reader's extrusions are even deeper than I have been suggesting.

*Chapter 6. Gambling with Gambles in "Two Gallants"*

1. See Robert Spoo's " 'Una Piccola Nuvoletta': Ferrero's *Young Europe* and Joyce's Mature *Dubliners* Stories" (401–10).

2. Epstein's point is that "In 'Two Gallants' Joyce has written the ultimate ironic end of romance, a perambulating penis with attendant 'hanger-on,' wandering through the mild Irish twilight, pursuing its infrahuman desires and finally producing, after much grim effort, a drop of gold" (370).

3. Don Gifford reads a curious line in the story—"he aspirated the first letter of his name after the manner of the Florentines"—in a way that supports my notion that Joyce may be pointing to the "two gallants" as whores. "The Florentines aspirate *c* as *h*, thus *casa* becomes *hasa* and Corely, Horley or Whorely' " (57). Claire Culleton also sounds the prostitution motif when, referring to Lenehan's favorite expression, she explains that " 'biscuit,' like 'cookie,' 'cake,' and 'tart,' is early twentieth-century slang for a prostitute" (111).

4. In a September 25, 1906 letter to Stanislaus, Joyce mentions his publishing difficulties with "Two Gallants" in a passage that also discusses Ibsen's difficult reception (*SL* 110).

5. Claire Culleton takes Lenehan's phrase and elaborates it as a technique in evidence throughout *Dubliners* for breaking into narration or into other characters' stories. "Lenehan's characteristic phrase, 'that takes the biscuit,' signals his own entry into the narrative discourse of the story and prefaces his attempts to break into the narrative" (111).

6. Garry Leonard supplies a motive for Lenehan's interest in the project out of knowledge of the drinking habits of young Dublin men as we see them later in *Ulysses*. "Because a free bout of all-night drinking depends upon it, Lenehan is particularly anxious about whether or not he has made himself sufficiently important to Corley" (120), he suggests.

7. Many of the stories can be dated by internal evidence, or by references in *Ulysses*. For example, the date of the municipal elections, combined with references to Edward VII, can be used to set "Ivy Day in the Committee Room" on 6 October 1902. The date of Pope Pius X's *In Motu Proprio* in November 1903 is helpful for setting "The Dead" in January 1904. *Ulysses* gives the date of Mrs. Sinico's death as 14 October 1903, thereby dating "A Painful Case." The *Dubliners* stories thus dated appear to fall between 1899 and 1905.

8. There is internal evidence in "Grace" that Tom Kernan doesn't fall down the lavatory steps but is rather worked over by his moneylender and the enforcer of the moneylender—Mr. Harford, and his 'muscle.' I discuss the consequences of Dublin money-lending in greater detail in my analysis of "Grace."

9. The story economically illustrates the code that gambling winnings must be shared as "stood" drinks (a convention Bloom is wrongly thought to have violated in "Cyclops") in Lenehan's idle exchange with two friends on St. George's Street. "One said that he had seen Mac an hour before in Westmoreland Street. At this Lenehan said that he had been with Mac the night before in Egan's. The young man who had seen Mac in Westmoreland Street asked was it true that Mac had won a bit over a billiard match. Lenehan said he did not know: he said that Holohan had stood them drinks in Egan's" (58).

10. Gifford points out the damaging nature of this information: "A conviction that would not only have been a disgrace but could have had serious social and economic consequences such as ostracism and loss of employment, particularly if the offender belonged to the middle class" (538).

11. For a post-colonial reading of the story, see Jim Haughey's "Joyce and Trevor's *Dubliners*: The Legacy of Colonialism" (355–65).

## Chapter 7. Narrative Bread Pudding: "The Boarding House"

1. Warren Beck's treatment of "The Boarding House" is one of the subtlest and most interesting pieces of criticism on the text. But I disagree with his admonition (148) against letting the *Ulysses* sequel of the story modify a reading of the *Dubliners* text: "A noting of the characters' recurrence from one book to the next may sometimes be illustrative and even supplementary, but such considerations should never eclipse the substantive autonomy and uniquely fit mode in each work." My argument is that the inverted style of the revisitation of the story is intended to draw attention to certain limitations and poverties of the original that can be used to interrogate the exoneration of Bob Doran as the product of a certain implicated narrative rhetoric.

2. Michel Foucault's *The History of Sexuality* (vol. 1) particularly stresses the institutional deployment of the confession in the ecclesiastical and medical control of sexuality.

3. In his essay " 'The Boarding House' Seen as a Tale of Misdirection," Fritz Senn makes a similar point. He writes, "Its misdirection involves readers by leaving them largely out of the main events. We realize how we are cut off from the crucial events, both of them; we are detained by moments in between; the actions are off stage" (405).

4. Brewster Ghiselin remarks the static setting and centralized geography of this story in the boarding house on Hardwick Street by noting, "There the soul is arrested, virtually at the center of Dublin" (74).

5. Garry Leonard points out a startling aspect of the story: "It is worth noting, then, that the text of the story nowhere records direct dialogue except in the closing lines when Polly answers her mother's call to come downstairs, 'Mr. Doran wants to speak to you' " (132). One is tempted to remark on the irony of this single line of "direct" dialogue in the story, namely, that Bob Doran desperately *does not want to speak* to Polly at this moment.

6. R. B. Kershner describes "The Boarding House" as written in the rhetoric of the oxymoron, and gives the function of this rhetoric a different emphasis—namely, the de-essentializing of the characters and situations in the story. "There is no 'essence' to these people. All are afloat in a sea of conflicting ideological currents and opposed rhetorical systems, all of which are socially affirmed" (92).

7. Because the story does not represent Polly's reverie, critics are obliged to imagine and fill in this and what Senn calls the other 'narrative vacuums" in the story (413). One of these supplements is an extension of the "sin" at the heart of "The Boarding House" into a putative pregancy. Donald Torchiana uses this elaboration to produce one of the fullest and most interesting of the symbolic readings of the story. "At the risk of being called an academic Christologist," he writes, "I would venture that Joyce is quietly representing a very human version of the Annunciation, feather pillows and all, in its total

calming joy. Polly cannot be called full of grace. She is not blessed among women, though she *will* be married. For the moment, amazingly enough, she is transported beyond the pillows before her and beyond the exigencies of her troubling pregnancy. Her visions and hopes, transport and trance beyond seeing and remembering, may well be delusions. But Joyce delicately hints that she shares them in common with at least one other *enceinte* Mary and her supposedly celibate spouse" (115). But Fritz Senn astutely points out that "If the marriage was indeed forced by such a pregnancy, it is odd that the well-cued narrator of 'Cyclops' later on fails to take up the fact for rhetorical embroidery" (413).

8. Tanja Vesala-Varrtala usefully theorizes the function of gossip in "The Boarding House." She writes, "Gossip is working as Mrs Mooney's ally in the affair at hand, for it reinforces, conveniently for her purposes, the conventional (cultural, religious, moral) ideologies and thought-patterns which have the power to direct action in the Dublin society in question" (244).

9. Torchiana notes that " 'cleave' is also one of the few words to contain their own antonym" (111).

10. Garry Leonard makes an excellent point, however, when he gives Mrs. Mooney credit for what he calls "her clear-sighted attitude about the fragile structure of the Phallic Order." Because Mrs. Mooney understands how women may be victimized, Leonard argues she is able "to protect Polly from the grim life being led by the slavey in 'Two Gallants' (and other young women who are 'on the turf')" (134). Young women without mothers in *Dubliners* are clearly in greater peril than Polly Mooney and Kathleen Kearney.

11. Bernard Benstock gives one of the strongest readings of Bob Doran as a total victim—"He spends the Sunday morning within the walls of his room in the house, a caged animal that will only be released when it is time for him to enter the arena to confront the gladitorial presence of Mrs. Mooney" (124)

12. Garry Leonard's sympathetic Lacanian reading allows him to give a beautifully nuanced analysis of the way Polly's performance or masquerade is conditioned by the gender politics of the Symbolic order. He can therefore read Polly's threat to put an end to herself as both melodrama and genuine anguish. "In front of an audience, this scenario would seem painfully contrived, but before the specific audience of Bob Doran, Polly is able to feel genuine and honestly suicidal because this 'self' she would 'do away with' has been constructed and authorized by his desire" (141).

13. In my plenary address at the 2002 Joyce Symposium in Trieste, I speculated that we may be getting Polly Mooney's thoughts in *Ulysses* in the letters of Martha Clifford. If Martha Clifford were indeed a pseudonym, Polly Doran—a typist with faulty grammar, trapped in a loveless marriage—could plausibly be Bloom's secret correspondent.

## Chapter 8. Men Under a Cloud in "A Little Cloud"

1. One of the most intriguing elaborations of the story's title is found in John Gordon's essay, " 'A Little Cloud' as A Little Cloud." He suggests, "consider the possibility that Little Chandler might actually *be* a little cloud, on something close to a literal level" (168), a proposal that he elaborates by drawing out the meteorological as an important

metaphor in the story. Harold Mosher Jr., on the other hand, interestingly elaborates the title as a cliché—"every cloud has a silver lining"—in his essay on clichés and repetitions in "A Little Cloud" (56).

2. Bernard Benstock also emphasizes that Chandler constructs a version of Gallaher, and gives this construction an interesting and plausible motive—"Chandler prefers to write his own version of various aspects of Ignatius Gallaher, especially the version that would fit his own flight" (133). In other words, Benstock suggests that Chandler would like to trade places with Gallaher, and therefore constructs a Gallaher worth trading places with.

3. According to Jacques Lacan, both males and females achieve their gender identification by coming to terms with "the unconscious castration complex." He then points out the strange paradox, that males assume their masculine identity by first unconsciously fearing its phantasmal loss. Lacan states, "There is an antimony, here, that is internal to the assumption by man (*Mensch*) of his sex: why must he assume the attributes of that sex only through a threat—the threat, indeed, of their privation" (*Ecrits* 281).

4. Garry Leonard focuses brilliantly on the reciprocal maneuvers of the two "friends" in their competition for symbolic ascendancy. "In both cases, the two subjects are poised to destroy each other to verify themselves," he writes. "Gallaher must belittle little Chandler (who must *be little* if he is to accommodate him) to exalt himself. Little Chandler has the more difficult task because he has already valorized Gallaher's point of view as representative of the 'the other'. . . . Gallaher's double bind, however, is that the more successfully he ridicules Little Chandler, the less value he can attach to the envy of his diminutive 'friend' " (152). I wish to enlarge the dynamic of this competition, however, by triangulating it with the third subjectivity of the *narrator*.

5. Thomas O'Grady, in his look at Blakean allusions in the story, pays particular attention to the figure of the infant, and the infant as figure, in "A Little Cloud" (401). Although David Lloyd focuses his discussion of drinking and masculinity chiefly on "Counterparts," his discussion of the stereotype of "the famous 'femininity' of the Celt"—which he traces to Matthew Arnold's 1867 "On the Study of Celtic Literature"—may also be relevant to the portrayal of "Little Chandler" in "A Little Cloud" (133).

6. John Paul Riquelme opts for a clear separation of Chandler and the narrator in these passages. He argues that "the interest of the walk for the reader is not what passes through the character's mind but the narrator's style for presenting what does *not* occur to the character. Here is one of those brilliant passages in these middle stories exhibiting sharply the opposition between teller and character. While Little Chandler ignores his present physical surroundings and their past, the narrator turns them both into striking, rhythmical language" (114).

7. See Kenner's *Joyce's Voices*, 15–38.

8. Bullfinch narrates the myth of the hunter-princess in footraces with her aspiring suitors, whom she outran until Hippomenes distracted her by throwing golden apples on the ground. His language conjures the scene as the "Little Cloud" narrator presents it: "At that moment he threw down one of the golden apples. The virgin was all amazement. She stopped to pick it up" (179).

9. Cheng's ideological analysis argues also for an internalization of dominant cultural values. "In his desire for cultural superiority over the madding crowd of Dublin, Chandler is in his mind-set basically very little different from Ignatius Gallaher," Cheng

writes: "both are products of a consensual acceptance of imperial hegemonic norms, values, and hierarchies" (118).

10. Kershner says of Gallaher, "there is little difference between his conversation and the yellow press he represents" (99).

11. Both Suzette Henke and Joseph Kelly see the Chandler home in much grimmer terms than I will propose. Kelly stresses its poverty: "He and his wife are too poor to afford a servant, which indicates the distance between the Chandlers and the middle class (82). In a cut-rate attempt to raise their living conditions, the Chandlers fill their house with rent-to-own furniture (83)" (369). Henke stresses the oppressions of domestic work for Annie Chandler, "who must stay indoors, cook, clean, and tend her baby," and is therefore "even more trapped and beleaguered than her timorous mate" (30). But by the domestic standards of other *Dubliners* households—for example, those of the Hills or the Farringtons—the Chandler home, while not opulent, strikes me as well-functioning for a young marriage not long past its first year ("I was married last May twelve months" [79]).

12. Joseph Kelly intriguingly interjects an excerpt from one of Joyce's letters to his Aunt Josephine, which betrays a feeling of being "fettered by domestic obligations": "I am not a very domestic animal—after all, I suppose I am an artist" (370). The question, of course, is whether "A Little Cloud" is intended to represent such frustrations or parody them.

### Chapter 9. Farrington, the Scrivener, Revisited: "Counterparts"

1. See particularly Kershner (100); Leonard (170); Scholes (384); Schloss (184).

2. David Lloyd adds another interpretation to Farrington's task of copying. He writes, "In this scene, Farrington is copying a document known in legal parlance as a *counterpart*: a copy torn off from the original in such a way that, when the two are brought together, the copy authenticates the original" (145).

3. Robert Scholes notes that an effect of the narration "which is worked for us without our being especially aware of how it is managed—is to give us a keen sense of the dull routine of Farrington's existence: of the extent to which he is in his work merely a replaceable cog in a mechanical operation" (97).

4. Florence Walzl notes that during the period preceding the onset of the first *Dubliners* stories, the only wage earner in the Joyce family was Stanislaus, "who, as a clerk at Apothecary Hall, worked long, dull hours for paltry wages." In " 'Eveline,' 'A Little Cloud,' and 'Counterparts,' Joyce's scorn and perhaps fear of Dublin clerkships are evident in his pictures of men and women doing demanding, dehumanizing work under tyrannical bosses for a pittance" (Bowen and Carens 160), Walzl suggests.

5. Carol Schloss points to W. S. Jevons's 1871 *The Theory of Political Economy* as an example of one of the first British attempts "to divorce economics from a larger sense of the well-being of the *polis* and to place it on a purely utilitarian basis" (186).

6. Donald Torchiana finds that Farrington's physiognomy and even his name disqualify him from the clerical profession: "I believe that Joyce is portraying the typical hellish day of all too many Dubliners who have no choice of jobs. Even Farrington's

name, along with his bulk, points to a country or farming life that should be his as far-rier, farmer, or pigbreeder" (141).

7. "All his family supplies him, besides a lair to retreat to, is a field for vengeance he is otherwise impotent to deal out," Warren Beck writes (188).

8. In spite of the lack of proof, I find it tempting to wonder if Joyce could have derived the idea for calling the chief clerk in the offices of Crosbie & Alleyne by the name of "Mr. Shelley" from Melville's figurative interpolation of Byron into the law office of "Bartleby."

9. Garry Leonard produces an illuminating anatomy of the mechanizing effects of Alleyne's verbal practice: "Another effect of this conversational tactic is that Mr. Alleyne reduces Farrington to the level of a malfunctioning machine that must be adjusted rather than a subject who must be listened to. Mr. Alleyne listens to Farrington only long enough to hear a phrase that he can co-opt into his own discourse and designate as the nonsense that makes his own meaning sensical" (173).

10. Appealing to Juhani Rudanko's notion of "pragmatic nastiness," which " 'con-sists of adding something gratuitously to offend the hearer' " (237), Vesala-Varttala draws attention to the excess of nastiness that makes Alleyne's speech exceed the authority needed to get jobs done. Alleyne's "pragmatic nastiness" works by cannibalizing Farring-ton's own words and then spitting them back in his face.

11. Earl Ingersoll raises the intriguing possibility that the Delacour correspondence "holds letters written to her, perhaps by Alleyne, who appears to have been mixing busi-ness with pleasure in her 'case' " (100). But it is unclear why private letters would need to be hand-copied, since handwritten copies were required specifically for legal documents.

12. Although we don't learn Farrington's fate in *Ulysses*, Bloom does worry that a "Peake" listed in the June 16, 1904 obituary is "the chap was in Crosbie and Alleyne's" (6.158). But apparently the little clerk hounded out of the law firm by Mr. Alleyne to make room for his own nephew is still alive, because Bloom decides "no"—meaning that he decides the man in the obituary is a different Peake.

13. Lloyd calls the pub "a crucial site of countermodernity," calling it "a site which preserves and transforms according to its own spaces and rhythms long-standing popu-lar practices that will not be incorporated by discipline: treating or the round system; oral performance of song, story, and rumor; conversation itself, which becomes increas-ingly a value in a society ever more subject to the individuation and alienation of the worker within the system of production" (139). Paul Lin concurs when he writes of "Counterparts": "Rather than pathologize drink as symptomatic of violence, I would ar-gue that Joyce distinguishes drinking as an alternative practice to the totalizing force of modernity" (46).

14. Trevor Williams, however, links the British Weathers and the Englishwoman to the Ulsterman Alleyne as codes for the British presence in Dublin, that "underscore the the inequality inscribed within the colonial relationship" (95).

15. By the time we read *Ulysses*, we learn that Paddy Leonard, Farrington's friend, is quite capable of mockingly mimicking his own drinking buddies ("Tom Kernan was im-mense last night, he said. And Paddy Leonard taking him off to his face" [6: 142]) and that Farrington is perhaps no safer from mocking imitation by his friends than he is from Alleyne, or Alleyne is from him, at the office.

16. Joyce's early draft, censored by Grant Richards's printer, gave the young woman "bold glances" to make her far more openly flirtatious. Farrington's censored notice that she "changed the position of her legs often" (*SL* 82) would have echoed his similar attention to the semiotics of Alleyne's jauntily crossed leg in the office.

## Chapter 10. Narration Under the Blindfold in "Clay"

1. Although I first noticed this small error in my own reading of Tindall, I later discovered that Warren Beck had mentioned it in his book (370).

2. For a detailed study of folkloric motifs in "Clay," see Coilin Owens's essay in the Winter 1990 *James Joyce Quarterly* (337–52). Another extremely interesting discussion of the function of Halloween in the story may be found in Luke Gibbons's section "James Joyce and the Suburban Supernatural" in his essay on "The Politics of Paralysis" (160–64).

3. Garry Leonard suggests an interesting alternative formulation of the issue of Maria's insignificance. He writes, "I wish to argue that *what Maria promotes is her insignificance!* Her naïve, childlike dependence on people is what makes her indispensable to them" (185). In other words, it may be worth asking "What if her helplessness is in part a masquerade . . . ?" (185).

4. The theory of desire I am invoking here can be called *onto-psychological*. It refers both to a metaphysical concept of *being*, and to the psychological dimension of how human beings think of themselves, and the way they are situated both in the world—both in the abstract, and in their specific social world. This model evolves from an elaboration of the theory of the master-slave dialectic in Hegel's *Phenomenology of Being* by psychoanalyst Jacques Lacan.

5. Edward Brandabur states bluntly: "Though 'mature,' Maria had failed to choose life" (71). Instead of seeing Maria as victimized by her internalization of class and gender ideologies, as I do, Brandabur produces an existential reading of "Clay" in which Maria is held responsible, and faulted, for her life choices. "She had long-ago repressed her real desires as an evil, rather than an unrepressed, sacrifice of the good implicit in sincere virginity; repression has left her smug but unsatisfied" (71).

6. R. B. Kershner provocatively calls the narration "a single extended character zone which asymptotically approaches *style indirect libre*" (104).

7. Tanja Vesala-Varttala makes the interesting point that "Nobody, it would seem, really bothers to speak to Maria with the purpose of asking her opinion" (188).

8. Vesala-Varttala takes a much kinder view of Maria's efforts in this case: "Maria also has a topic for conversation which she wants to take up; she wants to talk about the relationship of the two brothers Joe and Alphy. This is not the kind of topic Joe has planned for the evening" (188). Her point is that Maria is not given the opportunity to speak of the things that matter to her, and is not given attention when she does. "In order to keep everybody happy, she 'has to' conform to her molded role as a pathetic old simpleton" (189).

9. Donald Torchiana gives an example of the Protestant rhetoric of the *Twenty-Fifth Annual Report of Dublin by Lamplight*, and cites the institution's motto as "That they may recover themselves out of the snare of the devil, who are taken captive by him

at his will" (2 Timothy 2:26)" (156). I propose we may assume that this is one of the tracts on the wall to which Maria and the narrator allude.

10. Attridge makes a striking, contrasting argument. He writes, "There seems to be general complicity in the trick, even though 'one of the older next-door girls' is eventually blamed: the adults make no attempt to prevent the substitution from being effected, and are presumably watching Maria during the pause and scuffling, until 'at last'—when it is evident that Maria is not going to respond—Mrs. Donnelly raises her voice" (50, n.19). This scenario makes the Donnellys out to be much more deliberately or inadvertently cruel than in my scenario, which posits imperfect attention on the part of the adults. But it allows Attridge to accord to Maria a measure of victory by simply refusing or failing to have the trick work, and by not responding to the soft, wet substance.

11. Attridge points out that there are other places in the story when the narrative consciousness supplies the reader with information about something that Maria fails to perceive. Since the narrative voice does not identify the "soft, wet substance" for us, Attridge concludes that "the name is being withheld from us by the author as well as by the narrator" (37).

12. Derek Attridge has a different interpretation of the function of the substance in the story and Maria's response to it. He writes, "The trick fails, and it fails because Maria refrains from interpreting conceptually what she experiences by touch alone; she resists any temptation to transform the substance she knows through the most unverbal of senses into that curious thing that only language can bring into existence, a 'referent' . . . her non-conceptualization actually produces for her a small victory, perhaps her only triumph over the many people she interacts with during this evening." He urges against naming or interpreting the substance in order "to respect the other as other" (51).

13. *The Bohemian Girl* is a light opera with libretto by Alfred Bunn and music by Michael William Balfe. See Gifford (50) for a synopsis of the plot. This second stanza, which Maria misses in her rendition, is

> I dreamt that suitors sought my hand,
> That knights on bended knee,
> And with vows no maiden heart could withstand,
> They pledged their faith to me. (Gifford 80)

## Chapter 11. Shocking the Reader in "A Painful Case"

1. Tanja Vesala-Varttala's fine discussion of "A Painful Case" argues that "The painful case is contagious in several senses" and that "the idea of a painful case radiates even beyond James Duffy, pointing unrelentingly at the reader" (108). She makes the argument for readerly implication ("the reader's 'moral nature' becomes problematic and problematized in the process of re-reading Joyce's story" [80]) by keeping her focus on "the textual entanglement [that] never allows the reader to break all bonds to Duffy" (109).

2. Wolfgang Wicht writes, "Female subjectivity is occluded from the narrative. But since its absence from the male-dominated and conventional newspaper report and from Duffy's dismissive perspective is made conspicuously present by the text, the reader

is urged to criticize these reactions" (136). I concur but go further to argue that the female feelings occluded on the representational level are retrieved on a performative level—in the act of reading.

3. Tanja Vesala-Varttala invokes Ross Chambers's notion of the oppositional character of the narrative function and the textual function of fictional writing (*Room for Maneuver: Reading (the) Oppositional (in) Narrative* [1991]) in her examination of the problems of ethical reading in *Dubliners* (6–12). Wolfgang Wicht also registers this oppositionality in "A Painful Case": "Rather, the 'story' represents a person who constructs himself as subject of his ego, whereas the 'text' deconstructs this self-reflexive construct of the 'I.' This was a paradigmatic innovation in fiction. By 1906, Joyce was far from being a traditional short story writer" (131).

4. See Girard 153–75 and 266. Barbara Sloan in a 1971 essay on the narrator in "A Painful Case" finds in Gabriel D'Annunzio, among others, Joyce's model for the isolated figure of the artist as superman. "D'Annunzio belonged to the group of great nineteenth century egotists of whom Wagner (another of Joyce's favorites) was also one," she writes (29). Joseph Voelker in 1980 revisits the intertextual analogues for Duffy's isolation by adding Yeats's "The Tables of the Law" to the works of Nietzsche and Hauptmann as sources of the *Uebermensch* type that Duffy represents (23–34).

5. Don Gifford writes, "some Irish versions of the Tristan and Iseult story say that it was here that they consummated their ill-fated love" (81). Donald Torchiana gives the topographical significance of the Tristan and Isolde legend for the landscape of James Duffy's and Emily Sinico's relationship a full and interesting explication in *Backgrounds for Joyce's "Dubliners"* (165–75).

6. Wolfgang Wicht notes that "Joyce criticism has perhaps not noticed that the triangle involving Mrs. Sinico, Mr Duffy and Captain Sinico parallels the situation of Kitty O'Shea, Parnell, and Captain O'Shea." Wicht draws this point from the allusion: "Unlike Parnell, who went ahead and married at the cost of his career, Mr Duffy is a coward, an egocentric neurotic, a nothing" (137). I will take this parallel much further in the direction of exploring Joyce's generic play with the adultery narrative, only to then complicate it by layering it with another scandal narrative.

7. Garry Leonard writes of this scene, "Their conversations, held in a 'dark discreet room' are described as though the act of rhetorical intercourse was equivalent to the act of sexual intercourse" (221).

8. See Mary Lowe-Evans's "Who Killed Mrs Sinico?" for a comprehensive discussion of scholarly dissent with Duffy's judgment, that he had "sentenced her to death" (117). Lowe-Evans makes the fascinating argument that it is Mary Sinico, Emily Sinico's daughter, who is "the proximate cause of her mother's demise" (398).

9. Significantly, one of the few conversations between James Duffy and Emily Sinico we are given to hear concerns Duffy's disenchantment with the Irish Socialist Party—"The workmen's discussions, he said, were too timorous . . . they resented an exactitude which was the product of a leisure not within their reach" (111). After the abolition of the Land League, Parnell too seems to have shared his disenchantments with Kitty O'Shea—"It is certainly true that he was tired of a mass movement which—in a moment of exasperation—he described to Mrs O'Shea as hollow and wanting in solidarity" (Bew 60). Parnell, however, overcame his discouragement and went on to become leader of the Irish National League, while Duffy abandoned the ISP.

10. Discussions of Duffy's possible homosexuality have only recently reappeared,

since my first presentations and drafts of this argument. Prior to the appearance of both her and my essays on homosexuality in "A Painful Case" in the Fall 1999/Winter 2000 issue of *James Joyce Quarterly*, Roberta Jackson reports, "Just two articles note that Joyce's story is about homosexuality—a 1963 psychoanalytic study by Stephen Reid and David Norris's 1994 survey, 'The 'unhappy mania' and Mr. Bloom's Cigar: Homosexuality in the Works of James Joyce' " (87). Her footnotes indicate that Reid's article appeared in *American Imago* 20 (1963): 221–39. David Norris's essay appeared in the Spring 1994 issue of the *James Joyce Quarterly* 31: 357–73. I have since noted that Thomas Connolly in the Clive Hart collection of essays on *Dubliners*, mentions Reid's argument, and notes that "With his homosexual and heterosexual fears, James Duffy appears to be an adult version of the young boy of the first three stories, especially the boy as he is depicted in 'An Encounter', who is so fearful in the presence of the old paederast" (114). At the time Jackson's essay was in press, Colleen Lamos's superb theoretical analysis, "Duffy's Subjectivation: The Psychic Life of 'A Painful Case'," appeared in *Masculinities in Joyce*. Lamos uses Judith Butler's theory of the construction of the subject to argue that "Duffy's is a case of foreclosure that, as Butler explains, entails 'a double disavowal, a never having loved, and a never having lost' " (63). The consequence of this double disavowal for Duffy is that "the foreclosure of same-sex love coincides with the foreclosure of other-sex love; he disavows *both* homosexuality and heterosexuality" (66). This foreclosure consequently ensures that "Duffy's position is off the hetero/homo binary grid that Butler's theory maps for subjectivation" (66). This reading is an extremely significant supplement to the critical tradition of diagnosing Duffy's failing as one of narcissism, because it engages in a psychoanalytically sophisticated discourse the roles of the foreclosure of both homosexual and heterosexual desire in the story.

11. Indeed, knowledge that Joyce "stole" Duffy's aphorism from his brother Stanislaus's diary militates against our reading it as a veiled expression of homosexual desire, or attributing anything other than a stylistic significance to it. Warren Beck writes, "As for the other sentence, Joyce's cribbing it suggests the deplorable fact that people sometimes steal things they don't really need" (223)—as though this epigram baldly announcing society's homosexual taboo were an excrescence in "A Painful Case."

12. David Wright's interesting discussion of the dates in the story concludes: "Emily Sinico's death obviously occurs late in 1903. Since the story covers a four-year period, its action therefore must, according to the data in *Ulysses*, begin in late 1899, which might or might not be significant" (111). Yet I would argue that an important possible significance for setting the story in 1899 is its temporal proximity to the imprisonment of Oscar Wilde in 1895, and his release from prison to an unforgiving public in 1897. Joyce's description of Wilde's plight upon his release from prison elaborates its pathos: "One after another drove him from the door, refusing him food and shelter, and at nightfall he finally ended up under the windows of his brother, weeping and babbling like a child" (*CW* 203).

13. Suzette Henke draws our attention to the combined maternal and platonic attraction of Emily Sinico for Duffy—"Because the narcissistic Duffy wants a matriarchal muse rather than a flesh-and-blood lover, he strategically represses the amorous dimensions of their simmering liaison" (35). Henke's indictment of Duffy for narcissism and solipsism is widespread in the critical responses to the story and is perfectly legitimate, given the narrative prompts that point the reader toward just this conclusion. I

argue only that, on one level at least, these prompts might also function as an ethical reader trap.

14. In her analysis of Joyce's draft revisions of "A Painful Case," Jana Giles notes that "Joyce rewrites '. . . Mrs. Sinico threw her arms around forward into his lap and seemed to faint' to read '. . . Mrs. Sinico caught up his hand passionately and pressed it to her cheek' " (202). Although I agree with Giles that the final version is "less melodramatic, less sexual, and more poignant," I find that it concurrently makes Duffy's response *more* melodramatic, sexual, and tinged with hysteria. By changing Emily Sinico's movement from one that thrusts her arms into Duffy's lap (in what could justifiably be misconstrued as a vulgar gesture) to one of extreme emotional tenderness, the focus on sexual expression is shifted from the woman to the man.

15. Although an earlier draft copy (*JJA* 4, 129) gives Duffy's retroactive contemplation of his choices an amplitude more in tune with thoughts of an adulterous elopement, I would argue that even this passage remains ambiguous and equivocal:

The ~~thought~~ fact discomposed him because his own statement of it to himself seemed something of an accusation. He asked himself what else could he have done—carried ~~on~~ a ~~comedy of~~ furtive comedy which must have ended in mutual disgust or gone away with her out of Ireland. Either course would have been ~~ridiculous He thought of the pain~~ impossible the one of an undignified intrigue the other a ridiculous elopement. He had acted for the best: ~~and yet her death had revealed to him her loneliness. He too would be lonely now.~~ (quoted in Giles 208)

These contemplated choices rule out neither an uncomprehending latency of homosexual feeling nor Duffy's entertaining the kind of personally complex domestic arrangement (like Wilde's own marriage and household) that were not uncommon among British homosexuals, lesbians, and bisexuals in Duffy's day.

16. Roberta Jackson's excellent essay discusses the historical context of homosexual censorship and repression, including particularly the gloss on the "medicalization of same-sex desire" in the story's title (89), along with the delayed advent of queer critical readings of the story.

17. In *Quare Joyce* Joseph Valente writes that "the fact that Joyce apprehended social persecution as the price of such exceptionalism cannot only be traced, as it most often is, to the childhood trauma wrought by the ruin of the political hero, Charles Stewart Parnell, but also to the commotion created by Wilde's three trials" (8).

18. On August 12, 1906, Joyce wrote to Stanislaus, "I am thinking of rewriting *A Painful Case* so you might send me the MS along with the book of notes I had in Paris and the Latin quotations from the prophecies of the Abbot Joachim of Flora" (*SL* 94). Four days later, on August 16, 1906, he tells Stanislaus, "I am reading *The Picture of Dorian Grey* [sic] in Italian" (*SL* 95). Three days later, on August 19, 1906, Joyce writes Stannie that he has finished *Dorian Gray*—

I can imagine the capital which Wilde's prosecuting counsel made out of certain parts of it. It is not very difficult to read between the lines. Wilde seems to have had some good intentions in writing it—some wish to put himself before the world—but the book is rather crowded with lies and epigrams. If he had had the courage to develop the allusions in the book it might have been better. I suspect he has done this in some privately-printed books. (*SL* 96)

There is no evidence that the Wilde novella conditioned Joyce's desire to revise "A Painful Case," but a link is not impossible.

19. Sedgwick offers an important antidote to the kind of constructions of Nietzsche that allowed John William Corrington to read Duffy's acquision of Nietzsche as suggesting an intensification of his fascist predispositions. He writes, "The total effect cannot but put us in mind of the similarities between Duffy and certain Nazi functionaries whose whole study was to reduce the animate world to a collection of things, to bring the 'order' of death and silence from the 'chaos' of brawling undirected humanity" (134).

20. Captain Sinico's testimony at the inquest allows us to reconstruct his absence on the day of his wife's death. Although "he had arrived only that morning from Rotterdam," he "was not in Dublin at the time of the accident" (114). Emily Sinico died at ten o'clock at night. Where was Sinico if he was back from Rotterdam, but was not in Dublin that night?

21. Colleen Lamos produces a fascinating analysis of Duffy that concludes that "he stands in a melancholic (non)relation to the world." She therefore rejects the notion that James Duffy mourns for Emily Sinico at all. "Having refused both love and the deprivation of it, Duffy does not mourn; precisely his inability to grieve—his pain*less*ness, as it were—marks him as a melancholic, in Butler's sense of the term" (63).

## Chapter 12. Genres in Dispute: "Ivy Day in the Committee Room"

1. Warren Beck discusses the assorted evidence of Joyce's great fondness for this story, but notes that "Ivy Day" 's status as his favorite preceded the writing of "The Dead," and the inclusion of "A Little Cloud" in the volume (237).

2. Edward Brandabur makes the same connection between "Ivy Day" and "Aeolus" in *A Scrupulous Meanness* (111).

3. See James Fairhall's excellent essay on James Connolly, the Irish socialist leader who may have provided the model for the Labor candidate Colgan in "Ivy Day in the Committee Room." *James Joyce Quarterly* 25, 3 (Spring 1988): 289–304.

4. Vincent Cheng writes, "Fanon's description of the internecine conflict among the colonized, what Sartre refers to as the betrayal of one's brothers, was indelibly reenacted in Ireland at the national level by the drama of Parnell" (123).

5. Seamus Deane designates Mr. Henchy in the story as "the Pilate figure who is forever rubbing his hands 'as if he intended to produce a spark from them' " (29).

6. See Joseph Blotner, Susan Huntley Horowitz, and Michael Brian for a range of Christian and allegorical readings of the story.

7. Claire Culleton construes this lack of narrative intrusion in the story as the function of a weak narrator who has little control over the information in the story. "In 'Ivy Day in the Committee Room,' for example, the narrator can only describe the incoming characters and cannot identify them by name until one of the canvassers salutes them" (113).

8. My reference to "the class of ordinary Dublin men" of course begs the question of just what *class* that is. See Fairhall's essay for a superb discussion of the relationship between class and politics at the time of the 1902 municipal election, that argues that in

spite of Joyce's socialist interests, "he saw Dublin through middle-class eyes" (301). But we might also assume that the class of the canvassers in "Ivy Day" may have been to some extent determined by their qualification to vote at a time when the franchise had an economic criterion.

9. Fairhall cites Mary Daly's *Dublin: The Deposed Capital* (Cork: Cork University Press, 1985) as the source of this information.

10. Mr. Henchy certainly invokes social heredity as a criterion of character judgment, for example, recalling Tierney's little old bootlegging father as marker of a corrupt politician and publican scion, and "Poor old Larry Hynes" (124) as the decent, respectable father by whom Joe Hynes might be measured.

11. David Hayman is one of many critics who is hard on the men for their "quest of insignificant and half-earned rewards," and he does not hesitate to characterize the men of both "Ivy Day" and "A Mother" as "lenders in the temple, symptoms of a degraded culture." He also says "Paradoxically, it is to the worst parasites that payment is or seems likely to be made, to those facesavers whom Joyce would probably qualify as betrayers" (123).

12. Margery Brady reports of Parnell's death—"The cause of death was given as rheumatic fever, with a rider that the heart was weak—there was no post mortem. Later suggestions include a sudden infection, lobar pneumonia, kidney failure (Bright's disease), or cancer, while the painful left arm would have been rheumatic" (127). However, she too repeats the story of the wet shoes and clothes ("After his last speech he had remained in his damp clothes and footwear, as his famous little bag had been taken in error by one of his hosts" [126]).

13. Fairhall discusses the Dublin Corporation's responsibility for the city's "noxious tenements": "The Dublin Housing Inquiry of 1913 revealed sensationally what Connolly [the historical counterpart of the Labor candidate Colgan in the story] had been charging for years. Sixteen members of the Municipal Council (only one a Unionist) turned out to be owners of eighty-nine tenements and second-class houses. Three Home Rulers possessed the bulk of these properties; almost all were in poor repair, some being classed as unfit for human habitation, even though rebates of rates had been granted, supposedly for making improvements" (298).

14. Seamus Deane marks "the inferior quality of the world and the people surrounding this dozy fire" by describing the men as "people whose political commitment and wealth is measured in bottles of porter" (27).

15. Don Gifford notes that no Richard Tierney was listed as a publican in *Thom's*, but goes on to say that "the alderman for the Royal Exchange Ward in the early twentieth century was a publican, Joseph Delahunt" (89). Gifford's comments further concur with Fairhall's discussion of the political and economic relationship of public office and the liquor industry. "A publican who became a member of the Dublin Corporation was assumed to have a considerable business advantage because, presumably, his public house would be frequented by those in search of public favors and influence" (89).

16. Don Gifford identifies the Lord Mayor of Dublin in 1902 as "Timothy Charles Harrington. . . . He came from a lower-class background and was well-known for his simple tastes" (94).

*Chapter 13. Critical Judgment and Gender Prejudice in "A Mother"*

1. See Miller, Leonard, Ingersoll, and Sherill Grace's "Rediscovering Mrs. Kearney: An Other Reading of 'A Mother' " for particulary interesting feminist readings of the story. However, not all feminist criticism of the story rehabilitates Mrs. Kearney. In *The Politics of Desire*, for example, Suzette Henke treats Mrs. Kearney's strategy—if not Mrs. Kearney herself—unsympathetically: "This strong-willed mother mistakenly assumes that the tyrannical tactics she uses to manipulate her henpecked husband will prove successful in the dominant world of patriarchal politics" (40). Linda Rohrer Paige also excoriates "what, most assuredly, must be the inner repulsiveness of Mrs. Kearney's character" (332).

2. Fritz Senn raises the larger question about narrative time management in *Dubliners* when he asks, "How is anteriority introduced?" ("Dynamic Adjustments" 20).

3. Joyce notes "the fierce, hysterical power of Strindberg" (*CW* 71) in his essay on modern drama, "The Day of the Rabblement."

4. If gender is defined not essentially—as a nature—but as a position in relation to the Symbolic Order, then to my mind the implied gender of the narrator in "A Mother" is not undecidable ("he or she"). Given the narrative arrogation of the right to judgment, and even pre-judgment, of Mrs. Kearney, I believe we are justified in gendering the narrative voice of "A Mother" as not only male, but also as masculinist.

5. Jane Miller also notes the importance of Mr. Kearney's exemption from this norm: "It may sound dull and bourgeois, but in a world filled with alcoholic husbands, downtrodden wives, and abused children, the Kearneys' marriage is an achievement" (414).

6. Earl Ingersoll treats O'Madden Burke as "the ultimate 'insider' " endowed with considerable power: "Burke is clearly the authority here" (141). But Mary Power notes that "[n]o one bothers to ask O'Madden Burke for his credentials" (226). Jane Miller inverts the emphasis of the narrator by pointing out that "Although 'widely respected,' he has a problem with his finances. Indeed, he is based upon an actual Dubliner, O'Leary Curtis, who had a reputation for leaving a bar whenever it was his turn to buy a round of drinks" (421).

7. The story tells us that "a contract was drawn up by which Kathleen was to receive eight guineas for her services as accompanist at the four grand concerts" (138). I find it presumptuous of Gifford to construe this narrative sentence to mean that "the contract indicates Mrs. Kearney's pretension for her daughter in both the amount itself (eight pounds, eight shillings) and the fact that it is expressed in the fashionable 'guinea' rather than flatly as eight pounds" (99). There is nothing in the story to indicate that Mrs. Kearney had haggled to secure a professional salary for her inexperienced daughter. Nor is there any evidence that Mrs. Kearney—rather than Mr. Holohan, or whoever wrote the contract, or even the narrator himself—was responsible for calling the payment eight guineas rather than expressing it "flatly as eight pounds." Furthermore, as Gifford himself makes clear, four guineas are *not* "flatly" eight pounds. They are eight pounds and eight shillings, and the discrepancy plays a small but important role in the story. It illustrates the management's lack of punctiliousness about the amount of the money and, arguably, its petty willingness to use the substitution of pounds for guineas to cheat Kathleen out of the shillings.

8. Earl Ingersoll makes a shrewd observation about the way all of Mrs. Kearney's

questions and concerns are shunted off to "the Committee"—"More important here is the ominous phrase 'the Committee,' which represents an unidentified power insulated from the pleas of Mrs. Kearney for justice" (141). He also finds a significant connection between the resonance of committees and committee rooms in "Ivy Day" and in "A Mother." Bernard Benstock also makes some interesting observations about the Committee, saying "a committee is an entity that hides behind itself" (157).

9. For an interesting but somewhat Derridean reading of the story that pays particular attention to the figure of Holohan, see Marie-Dominique Garnier's " From Paralysis to Para-Lire: Another Reading of 'A Mother' " (231–46). Garnier draws attention to the repetition in these lines of Holohan's, noting, "The last words uttered by Holohan are an instance of repetitiveness, of dub-ling—or of what Heidegger terms 'dublette.' Beyond the paralysis and staleness of neurotic repetition, looms a differential repetition" (235).

## Chapter 14. Setting Critical Accounts Aright in "Grace"

1. Stanislaus Joyce reports that "the accident with which the story begins happened to my father" (*My Brother's Keeper* 226), but he does not elaborate its probable cause.

2. It is, of course, tempting to read the anonymous young man in the cycling suit as an introduction of the parable of the Good Samaritan—a dispenser of gratuitous assistance or grace—into this parabolic story. However, Earl Ingersoll has an interesting alternative interpretation which focuses on the freedom to "travel" implied in cycling (107). My own wild speculation on the charitable young cyclist's identity points to W. E. Wylie, the older brother of Gerty MacDowell's hearththrob, Reggy Wylie. We learn in "Nausicaa" that Reggy was "going to go to Trinity College to study for a doctor when he left high school like his brother W. E. Wylie who was racing in the bicycle races in Trinity college university" (13.138). The young man in "Grace" acts with the assurance of a doctor when he ministers to Kernan, and the "cycling-suit" suggests a more than casual commitment to cycling. If Joyce were prompting a "retrospective arrangement" with these clues, we would need to ponder the significance of his making the Good Samaritan a professional class Protestant.

3. Warren Beck suggests that "Kernan tries to evade the fact that Harford had deserted him in his need, and wants it thought the two of them had 'missed each other' by 'some mistake' " (285). I find it less plausible that Kernan would protect Harford out of some sense of chivalry than out of the fear implied in "His friends, who knew quite well Mr Harford's manners in drinking, were silent" (160). Interestingly, Father Robert Boyle, in a very early allegorical reading of "Grace," gives both Harford and the "sandy-haired chap" the sinister identities of Judas and Satan, respectively (18–19). In another allegorical reading of "Grace" as a version of the Book of Job, Robert A. Gates writes, "One may certainly wonder whether or not the two gentlemen who seem to be connected in some way to Kernan's downfall are not indeed reflective of the two figures that cast afflictions on Job—God and the Devil" (277). Scott Klein, on the other hand, takes my suggestion that Kernan was worked over by a loan shark, but elaborates it into a slightly different plot. "Kernan had an appointment with Harford to negotiate a loan, and for any number of potential reasons, including his failure to pay appropriate interest for earlier moneys,

was threatened and beaten up for his pains" (117). In this reading, Klein is able to account for a number of otherwise obscure details, such as why Kernan is unknown in the bar, and what happened to his paycheck.

4. In *My Brother's Keeper*, Stanislaus Joyce described his brother's first use of a "pattern" in his writing: "It is a simple pattern not new and not requiring any great hermeneutical acumen to discover—inferno, purgatorio, paradiso. Mr. Kernan's fall down the steps of the lavatory is his descent into hell, the sickroom is purgatory, and the Church in which he and his friends listen to the sermon is paradise at last" (228).

5. For example, Torchiana reads "Grace" as a parable of the marriage of drink, bad business, and religion; Kershner reads it as a parable of denial and evasion; and Leonard as a parable of the perils of masculinity.

6. Cheryl Herr frames Joyce's critical aim in "Grace" even more sharply and specifically. She writes, "Readers who find here primarily a critique of the church rather than an anatomy of its cultural function attribute to Joyce an underlying belief in religion as the vessel of truth; they ignore his identification of the church as an economic institution" (245).

7. Catholic Bibles often add such explanatory notes to the parable as "The unjust behavior of the steward is not commended, but the master admires his worldly wisdom in providing for his future" (*New Catholic Edition of the Holy Bible*, 1957 102). See also Scott Klein's excellent discussion of the hermeneutical difficulties posed to biblical scholarship by the passage (121–22).

8. The retreat congregation encompasses a number of figures from the earlier *Dubliners* stories whose imperfections have already been disclosed to the reader. These include Fanning, possibly involved in a suspect financial deal with the suspect, possibly defrocked priest, Father Keon in the Municipal Elections in "Ivy Day." The newly elected councillor who sits beside him could certainly be "Tricky Dicky Tierney" from "Ivy Day," who by the ending of the story has still not paid his campaign workers. And the group also includes "Mr Hendrick, the chief reporter of *The Freeman's Journal*" (172), whom we last saw basking in the flattery and flirtation of Miss Healy in "A Mother" ("He was pleasantly conscious that the bosom which he saw rise and fall slowly beneath him rose and fell at the moment for him, that the laughter and fragrance and wilful glances were his tribute" [145]). Since Hendrick will not be writing the review of Miss Healy she hopes to inspire for good notices, he may also be seen as a species of cheating bribe-taker.

9. Stanislaus Joyce reports the upshot of the Gardiner Street Church retreat's effects on his father—"On Sunday evening after an outing with his friends, my father came home only moderately drunk with the aforesaid 'Mr Cunningham', to whom he explained many times over that in confession the priest had told him that 'he wasn't such a bad fellow after all', which authoritative and consoling information caused him both to laugh and to weep" (*My Brother's Keeper* 226).

10. Scott Klein intriguingly arrives at the opposite conclusion, even though he builds his argument on my own premises. In his view, "Religion is another form of violence in Kernan's Dublin" (123). And "God is simply another form of strongarm man, who extorts repayment of a spiritual debt through means no less victimizing than those met in the barroom" (123).

11. Stanislaus Joyce described the prototype for Father Purdon as Father Bernard Vaughan, "a very popular evangelist in those days, whose name was frequently in the newspapers . . . a vulgarian priest in search of publicity" (*My Brother's Keeper* 228).

Cheryl Herr elaborates Vaughan's strategies for broadening his secular appeal, and points specifically to his alliance with commercial business practices: "he also published an address given to a group of businessmen and entitled 'The Uses of Advertisement.' . . . Asserting that 'expediency' is more important than 'taste' where religion is concerned, Vaughan defends himself against those 'superior-minded people' who 'object to modern methods of advertisement' and who believe that the preacher should not 'turn the House of God into a sort of theatre' " (239).

12. Richards's reply suggests that, however earnest and bitter their correspondence over *Dubliners*, he took Joyce's suggestion to have been made facetiously—"Unfortunately as things stand at present you cannot buy one critic of importance, to say nothing of two; sometimes I wish one could! Also, the habit of multiple reviewing has gone out" (letter to James Joyce, June 14, 1906, *Dubliner* 208).

13. There are many ways of schematizing the textual heteroglossia of "Grace." I find my narrator/text distinction useful for giving the narrative voice a social agenda and identity (bourgeois, homosocial, complacent) that becomes the object of the story's satire and moral criticism. Garry Leonard identifies the multiple "stories" of "Grace" with onto-psychological differences: "By having the reader learn who Mr. Kernan is at the same time that his friends convene to reconfirm who he was, Joyce forces the reader to read two stories: the one he wrote and the one the friends of Mr. Kernan are writing. This, of course, invites the reader to examine the third version of the story, that Joyce has not written—the assertion of the readers' own transcendent subjectivity as they interpret the story" (274).

14. Frank O'Connor humorously pairs Cunningham's account of ecclesiastical history with Father Purdon's interpretation of the parable—"Father Purdon assumes it to be 'a text for business men and professional men,' but, whatever it may be, it is quite clear that Father Purdon knows precisely as much about it as Mr. Cunningham does about church history, which is sweet damn all" (299). My point is that it is *not* the narrator or the narration that makes this clear.

15. Richard M. Kain also remarks on the significance of style in the story—"For the alert reader of Joyce a special delight is the adroit manipulation of tone through language. In 'Grace' false elegance is prominent. Here it is not so much that the style is appropriate to the subject; rather, it becomes the subject" (137).

16. In my discussion of "Clay," I term the phenomenon by which the narrative voice articulates the protagonist's optimal self-image as "the language of desire."

17. Hope Howell Hodgkins offers an excellent discussion of the intersection of class in religion in "Grace" in her essay " 'Just a little . . . spiritual matter': Joyce's 'Grace' and the Modern Protestant Gentleman."

18. Cunningham may be appealing to not one, but two, prejudices of Tom Kernan's in touting Pope Leo XIII as "one of the lights of the age" (167). Donald Torchiana mentions that Pope Leo XIII showed "public irritation with the Irish peasantry's violent physical reaction against their landlords, like Captain Boycott" (215), thus adding the Pope's pro-English sympathies to his "flowery sermons" as a merit in Kernan's view.

19. Gifford writes that news stories on June 16, 1904 did not yet announce the scandalous corruption that later reports of the *General Slocum* disaster brought to light: "the fire hoses on the ship were so rotten that they had been condemned and the ship immo-

bilized by a $1000 lien. Mysteriously, though, that lien was reduced to $25 on June 14 and promptly discharged so that the *Slocum* could sail (rotten hoses and all) on 15 June" (*"Ulysses" Annotated* 273). Kernan's cynicism is therefore disturbingly prescient.

## Chapter 15. The Politics of Gender and Art in "The Dead"

1. While I draw on Hugh Kenner's 'Uncle Charles Principle' (*Joyce's Voices* 15–18) for my construction of this narrative voice, I draw a very different class inference from the stylistic pretensions of the story's opening. In my views, the social interests of the opening narrative are not Lily's interests, but Morkan interests. They may even be construed as Morkan and Conroy constructions of what they would *like* Lily's views to be, what Lily *ought* to be saying and thinking about herself and about them.

2. Joyce represents the vulnerability of servants to charges of theft in the rather shameful way the Blooms treat Mary Driscoll, who is dismissed, presumably without references, on suspicion that she stole some oysters—a charge presumably trumped up by Molly to mask her real suspicion of a flirtation between her servant and her husband.

3. Michael Levenson generalizes this issue to Gabriel Conroy's larger problem with national identity. "The colonized consciousness has all its vulnerabilities heightened, and the sharp pathos in the life of Gabriel Conroy is that he aims to construct an emancipated personal identity, cultured and cosmopolitan, within an unemancipated milieu. Naively believing that he can liberate himself from inside the colonial constraint, he repeatedly aspires to a condition of self-ratifying autonomy, only to meet a failure that appears structurally inevitable" (174).

4. Vincent Cheng describes the canonization process of "The Dead" as one "that has, in large measure, managed to defang 'Joyce' as an apolitical, stylistic innovator" (128).

5. Peter Rabinowitz notes possible intertextual allusions to two other Ibsen plays as well, *When We Dead Awaken*—which he finds glossed in the title—and *The Wild Duck*, glossed by the cooked goose served for dinner (145). Patrick Parrinder adds a fourth, when he hears an echo of Ibsen's *Ghosts* in the title as well (66).

6. R. B. Kershner offers a superb analysis of this scene as a *tableau*—"that staple of popular nineteenth-century entertainment"—and its implications for Gabriel's aesthetic sensibility (144–45).

7. I am here separating the aestheticized narrative from the totality of the text, with its series of gestures that produce a critique of just that aestheticization. Seamus Deane, however, finds that in "The Dead" Joyce "surrenders critique for aesthetics and, in doing so, becomes a characteristically modernist writer" (34). Deane is particularly critical of the role of repetition in the story, especially at its end. "In all the stories in *Dubliners* other than 'The Dead,' repetition has a critical and disturbing function. It has analytic and polemical power. In this final story, all that is surrendered for lyricism" (36).

8. See Adrienne Auslander Munich's essay, " 'Dear Dead Women,' or Why Gabriel Conroy Reviews Robert Browning" for a more complex discussion of the relevance of Browning to the story. Munich is reminded of Browning's "A Toccata of Galuppi's" by Gabriel's imagined title *Distant Music* (132). See also John Freely's interesting discussion of the Browning quotation's transmogrification in Gabiel's after-dinner speech (87–96).

9. I draw chiefly on Lacan's essay, "The Signification of the Phallus" in *Écrits* (281–91) and Adorno's *Aesthetic Theory* in this discussion.

10. Lacan here provides a complex psycho-philosophical explanation of the operation of the virgin-whore dichotomy so often remarked in Joyce's work—that, I would maintain, Joyce deploys strategically, rather than naïvely, in his texts.

11. Daniel Schwarz gives a finely nuanced and highly sympathetic reading of Gabriel Conroy that convincingly foregrounds Gabriel's own vulnerabilities and their disregard by Gretta when she tells him the story of Michael Furey. "Why does she not realize that her words will hurt Gabriel and that this hyperconscious, insecure, anxious, and guilt-ridden man—her husband—will be upset and troubled? Is she not somewhat insensitive and inconsiderate to her husband?" (119). This reading is perfectly justified and consistent with the narrative temper of the story, which makes the women's assaults on Gabriel's composure and equanimity appear insensitive and ungenerous. Yet it still permits of a counter-reading, like Kershner's remark that "Gretta's response to his advances is, considering her own state of stress and romantic nostalgia, a model of tact" (141).

12. The willingness to risk life, to consider some abstract, nonmaterial value as more important than life itself, is the cornerstone of idealism in Hegelian philosophy, as interpreted by Alexandre Kojève. Lacanian desire is informed by this concept, but he gives desire a sexual etiology by replacing the fear of the loss of life with the fear of castration as a central impulse in social and intersubjective relationships. Joyce neatly distributes these ontological imperatives between Gretta's lovers. He makes Michael Furey, with his willingness to risk life, the more archaic figure of mastery. Gabriel, with his social and sexual insecurities and strategies to overcome them, becomes the psychologically and socially modern man.

13. Michael Finney's hilarious discussion of "The Dead" makes many commonsensical points that make many of our labored attempts to account for the nuances of the story look a little silly. One of Finney's better questions asks *"Why does [Gretta] say she believes Michael Furey died for her when she knows perfectly well he was a dead duck anyway?"* (478).

14. Joyce may have included these references to female domestic sewing skills because Ibsen also reflects on them in *A Doll's House*. Torvald Helmer, for example, considers a woman embroidering a much more graceful picture than a woman knitting (Ibsen 182).

15. As a folk ballad, "The Lass of Aughrim" has many versions. I took this stanza from the one Ruth Bauerle reproduces in her essay (124–25), which is also the one sung by the New Hutchinson Family's cassette of "The Joyce of Music" (University of Illinois Press, 1983).

16. At the beginning of Act II of *A Doll's House*, Nora asks her nurse Anne-Marie how she could have given her child to a stranger. She answers that she could not forgo the possibility of a good domestic place—"A girl who's poor and who's gotten in trouble is glad enough for that" (155).

17. See also Elizabeth Butler Cullingford's excellent discussion of the conflicting interpretations that the representation of Molly Ivors in the story invites (225–29).

18. Jack Morgan's comprehensive historical and cultural background for the *Motu Proprio* argues that the pronouncement was part of a much larger "conservative counterattack against modernity" by the Catholic Church. "Symbolically the legislation defined a deeper political sea change in the Church, announcing the ascendancy of a surveillant

and repressive ecclesiastical regime in Rome—the coming to the fore of a reactionary Vatican element that had been mustering its forces for a long time on the continent" (130).

19. Morgan makes an even stronger historical link between "the inerrancy doctrine established by the Vatican Council of 1817" and the *Motu Proprio*. "Pius X issued the choir document extraordinarily aggressively, a mere three-and-a-half months into his reign; it was to serve as notice of the broader repression forthcoming" (130). Given the discussion of the papal infallibility doctrine in "Grace"—the story preceding "The Dead"—Joyce may have intended readers to notice a similar historical link.

20. Vincent Pecora also finds in the story an implicit critique of the Church. He argues that Gabriel's "imitation of Christ" is made suspect as a posture of transcendence, and with it a Church that creates the structures for such transcendent desires. "For if we question Gabriel's motives here, far more is at stake than simply the interpretation of a particular character's behavior; the very institutions that produce and maintain the viability of those motives are held up for scrutiny" (243).

21. John Scarry was one of the earliest scholars to identify the "negro chieftain singing in the second part of the Gaiety pantomime" (183) as G. H. Elliott. See my *Joyce's Web* 219, note 12 for a fuller discussion of the problem of identifying Elliott's voice and race.

# Works Cited

Adams, Robert M. "A Study in Weakness and Humiliation." In *James Joyce's "Dubliners": A Critical Handbook*, ed. James R. Baker and Thomas F. Staley. Belmont, Calif.: Wadsworth, 1969. 101–4.

Adorno, Theodor. *Aesthetic Theory*. Trans. C. Lenhardt, ed. Gretel Adorno and Rolf Tiedemann. London: Routledge, 1986.

Albert, Leonard. "Gnomonology: Joyce's 'The Sisters.'" *James Joyce Quarterly* 27, 2 (Winter 1990): 355–46.

Attridge, Derek. *Joyce Effects: On Language, Theory, and History*. Cambridge: Cambridge University Press, 2000.

Attridge, Derek, and Daniel Ferrer, eds. *Post-Stucturalist Joyce: Essays from the French*. Cambridge: Cambridge University Press, 1984.

Baccolini, Raffaella. " 'She Had Become a Memory': Women as Memory in James Joyce's *Dubliners*." In *ReJoycing: New Readings of "Dubliners"*, ed. Rosa M. Bollettieri Bosinelli and Harold F. Mosher, Jr. Lexington: University Press of Kentucky, 1998. 146–64.

Baker, Joseph E. "The Trinity in Joyce's 'Grace.'" *James Joyce Quarterly* 2, 4 (Summer 1965): 299–303.

Barthes, Roland. *Sade/Fourier/Loyola*. Trans. Richard Miller. New York: Hill and Wang, 1976.

———. *S/Z: An Essay*. Trans. Richard Miller. New York: Hill and Wang, 1974.

Bašić, Sonia. "A Book of Many Uncertainties: Joyce's 'Dubliners.'" In *ReJoycing: New Readings of "Dubliners"*, ed. Rosa M. Bollettieri Bosinelli and Harold F. Mosher, Jr. Lexington: University Press of Kentucky, 1998. 14–40.

Bauerle, Ruth. "Date Rape, Mate Rape: A Liturgical Interpretation of 'The Dead.'" In *New Alliances in Joyce Studies*, ed. Bonnie Kime Scott. Newark: University of Delaware Press, 1988. 113–25.

Beck, Warren. *Joyce's "Dubliners": Substance, Vision, and Art*. Durham, N.C.: Duke University Press, 1969.

Beckett, J. C. *The Making of Modern Ireland, 1603–1923*. London: Faber and Faber, 1981.

Beja, Morris. "Farrington the Scrivener: A Story of Dame Street." In *Coping with Joyce: Essays from the Copenhagen Symposium*, ed. Morris Beja and Shari Benstock. Columbus: Ohio State University Press, 1989.

———. "One Good Look at Themselves: Epiphanies in *Dubliners*." In *Work in Progress: Joyce Centenary Essays*, ed. Richard F. Peterson, Alan M. Cohn, and Edmund L. Epstein. Carbondale: Southern Illinois University Press, 1983. 1–14.

Benstock, Bernard. *Narrative Con/Texts in "Dubliners"*. Urbana: University of Illinois Press, 1994.

Bew, Paul. *Charles Stewart Parnell*. Dublin: McGill Macmillan, 1991.

Black, Martha Fodaski. *Shaw and Joyce: The Last Word in Stolentelling.* Gainesville: University Press of Florida, 1995.

Blotner, Joseph L. " 'Ivy Day in the Committee Room': Death Without Resurrection." In *James Joyce's "Dubliners": A Critical Handbook,* ed. James R. Baker and Thomas F. Staley. Belmont, Calif.: Wadsworth, 1969. 139–46.

Boheemen-Saaf, Christine Van. "Deconstruction After Joyce." In *New Alliances in Joyce Studies,* ed. Bonnie Kime Scott. Newark: University of Delaware Press, 1988. 29–47.

Bonafous-Murat, Carle. "Disposition and Pre-disposition: The Art of Involuntary Memory in *Dubliners.*" In *Classic Joyce: Papers from the XVI International James Joyce Symposium,* ed. Franca Ruggieri. Joyce Studies in Italy 6. Rome: Bulzone Editore, 1999. 361–71.

Boyle, Robert, S.J. " 'Two Gallants' and 'Ivy Day in the Committee Room'." In *Twentieth Century Interpretations of "Dubliners",* ed. Peter K. Garrett. Englewood Cliffs, N.J.: Prentice-Hall, 1968. 100–106.

———. "Swiftian Allegory and Dantean Parody in Joyce's 'Grace'." *James Joyce Quarterly* 7, 1 (Fall 1969): 11–19.

Brady, Margery. *The Love Story of Parnell and Katharine O'Shea.* Dublin: Mercier Press, 1991.

Brandabur, Edward. *A Scrupulous Meanness: A Study of Joyce's Early Work.* Urbana: University of Illinois Press, 1971.

Bredbeck, Gregory W. "Narcissus in the Wilde." In *The Politics and Poetics of Camp,* ed. Moe Myer. New York: Routledge, 1994. 51–74.

Bremen, Brian A. " 'He Was Too Scrupulous Always': A Re-examination of Joyce's 'The Sisters'." *James Joyce Quarterly* 22, 1 (Fall 1984): 55–66.

Brian, Michael. " 'A Very Fine Piece of Writing': An Etymological, Dantean, and Gnostic Reading of Joyce's 'Ivy Day in the Committee Room'." In *ReJoycing: New Readings of "Dubliners",* ed. Rosa M. Bollettieri Bosinelli and Harold F. Mosher, Jr. Lexington: University Press of Kentucky, 1998. 207–27.

Brown, Richard. *James Joyce and Sexuality.* New York: Cambridge University, 1985.

Buerger, Peter. *Theory of the Avant-Garde.* Minneapolis: University of Minnesota Press, 1984.

Bullfinch, Thomas. *The Age of Fable or Beauties of Mythology.* New York: New American Library, 1962.

Buzard, James. " 'Culture' and the Critics of *Dubliners.*" *James Joyce Quarterly* 37, 1/2 (Fall 1999/Winter 2000): 43–61.

Chambers, Ross. *Room for Maneuver: Reading (the) Oppositional (in) Narrative.* Chicago: University of Chicago Press, 1991.

Cheng, Vincent. *Joyce, Race, and Empire.* Cambridge: Cambridge University Press, 1995.

Ciniglio, Ada V. " 'Two Gallants': Joyce's Wedding Guests." *James Joyce Quarterly* 10, 2 (Winter 1973): 264.

Collins, Ben L. " 'Araby' and the 'Extended Simile'." In *Twentieth Century Interpretations of "Dubliners",* ed. Peter K. Garrett. Englewood Cliffs, N.J.: Prentice-Hall, 1968. 93–99.

Connolly, Thomas E. "A Painful Case." In *James Joyce's "Dubliners": Critical Essays,* ed. Clive Hart. New York: Viking Press, 1969. 107–21.

Corrington, John William. "Isolation as Motif in 'A Painful Case'." In *James Joyce's "Dubliners": A Critical Handbook*, ed. James R. Baker and Thomas F. Staley. Belmont, Calif.: Wadsworth, 1969. 130-39.

Culleton, Claire A. " 'Taking the Biscuit': Narrative Cheekiness in *Dubliners*." In *ReJoycing: New Readings of "Dubliners"*, ed. Rosa M. Bollettieri Bosinelli and Harold F. Mosher, Jr. Lexington: UniversityPress of Kentucky, 1998. 110-22.

Cullingford, Elizabeth Butler. "Phoenician Genealogies and Oriental Geographies: Joyce, Language, and Race." In *Semicolonial Joyce*, ed. Derek Attridge and Marjorie Howes. Cambridge: Cambridge University Press, 2000. 219-39.

Cunningham, Frank R. "Joyce's 'Grace': Gracelessness in a Lost Paradise." *James Joyce Quarterly* 6, 3 (Spring 1969), 219-23.

Deane, Seamus. "Dead Ends: Joyce's Finest Moments." In *Semicolonial Joyce*, ed. Derek Attridge and Marjorie Howes. Cambridge: Cambridge University Press, 2000. 21-36.

De Lauretis, Teresa. *Technologies of Gender: Essays on Theory, Film, and Fiction*. Bloomington: Indiana University Press, 1987.

Deleuze, Gilles. *Masochism*. Trans. Jean McNeil. New York: George Braziller, 1971.

Doloff, Steven. "On the Road with Loyola: St. Ignatius' Pilgrimage as Model for James Joyce's 'Araby'." *James Joyce Quarterly* 28, 2 (Winter 1991): 515-17.

Ehrlich, Heyward. " 'Araby' in Context: The 'Splendid Bazaar,' Irish Orientalism, and James Clarence Mangan." *James Joyce Quarterly* 35, 2/3 (Winter/Spring 1998): 309-31.

Ellmann, Richard. *James Joyce*. Rev. ed. Oxford: Oxford University Press, 1982.

Epstein, E. L. "Hidden Imagery in James Joyce's 'Two Gallants'." *James Joyce Quarterly* 7, 4 (Summer 1970): 369-70.

Fairhall, James. "Big-Power Politics and Colonial Economics: The Gordon Bennett Cup Race and 'After the Race'." *James Joyce Quarterly* 28, 2 (Winter 1991): 387-97.

———. "Colgan-Connolly: Another Look at the Politics of 'Ivy Day in the Committee Room'." *James Joyce Quarterly* 25, 3 (Spring 1988): 289-304.

———. *James Joyce and the Question of History*. Cambridge: Cambridge University Press, 1993.

Feshbach, Sidney. " 'Fallen on His Feet in Buenos Ayres' (D 30): Frank in 'Eveline'." *James Joyce Quarterly* 202 (Winter 1983): 223-26.

Finney, Michael. "Why Gretta Falls Asleep: A Postmodern Sugarplum." *Studies in Short Fiction*, special *Dubliners* issue 32, 3 (Summer 1995): 475-81.

Foucault, Michel. *History of Sexuality*. Vol. 1, *An Introduction*. Trans. Robert Hurley. New York: Vintage, 1980.

Freely, John. "Joyce's 'The Dead' and the Browning Quotation." *James Joyce Quarterly* 20, 1 (Fall 1982): 87-96.

Fuss, Diana. *Essentially Speaking: Feminism, Nature, and Difference*. New York: Routledge, 1989.

Garnier, Marie-Dominique. "From Paralysis to Para-lire: Another Reading of 'A Mother'." In *New Perspectives on "Dubliners"*, ed. Mary Power and Ulrich Schneider. European Joyce Studies 7. Amsterdam: Rodopi, 1997. 230-46.

Gates, David A. "Tom Kernan and Job." *James Joyce Quarterly* 19, 3 (Spring 1982): 275-87.

Ghiselin, Brewster. "The Unity of 'Dubliners.'" In *Twentieth Century Interpretations of "Dubliners": A Collection of Critical Essays*, ed. Peter K. Garrett. Englewood Cliffs, N.J.: Prentice-Hall, 1968. 57–85.

Gibbons, Luke. " 'Have you no homes to go to?': James Joyce and the Politics of Paralysis." In *Semicolonial Joyce*, ed. Derek Attridge and Marjorie Howes. Cambridge: Cambridge University Press, 2000. 150–71.

Gifford, Don. *Notes for "Dubliners" and "A Portrait of the Artist as a Young Man"*. 2nd ed. Berkeley: University of California Press, 1982.

Gifford, Don, and Robert J. Seidman. *"Ulysses" Annotated: Notes for James Joyce's "Ulysses"*. 2nd ed. Berkeley: University of California Press, 1988.

Giles, Jana. "The Craft of 'A Painful Case': A Study of Revisions." In *New Perspectives on "Dubliners"*, ed. Mary Power and Ulrich Schneider. European Joyce Studies 7. Amsterdam: Rodopi, 1997.

Girard, René. *Deceit, Desire, and the Novel*. Trans. Yvonne Freccero. Baltimore: Johns Hopkins University Press, 1965.

Gordon, John. " 'A Little Cloud' as a Little Cloud." In *New Perspectives on "Dubliners"*, ed. Mary Power and Ulrich Schneider. European Joyce Studies 7. Amsterdam: Rodopi, 1997. 167–80.

Grace, Sherill E. "Rediscovering Mrs. Kearney: An Other Reading of 'A Mother.'" In *James Joyce: The Augmented Ninth*, ed. Bernard Benstock. Syracuse, N.Y.: Syracuse University Press, 1988.

Haughey, Jim. "Joyce and Trevor's Dubliners: The Legacy of Colonialism." *Studies in Short Fiction*, special *Dubliners* issue 32, 3 (Summer 1995): 355–65.

Hayman, David. "A Mother." In *James Joyce's "Dubliners": Critical Essays*, ed. Clive Hart. New York: Viking, 1969. 122–33.

Henke, Suzette A. *James Joyce and the Politics of Desire*. New York: Routledge, 1990.

Herr, Cheryl. *Joyce's Anatomy of Culture*. Urbana: University of Illinois Press, 1986.

Hodgkins, Hope Howell. " 'Just a little . . . spiritual matter': Joyce's 'Grace' and the Modern Protestant Gentleman." *Studies in Short Fiction*, special *Dubliners* issue 32, 3 (Summer 1995): 423–34.

Horowitz, Sylvia Huntley. "More Christian Allegory in 'Ivy Day in the Committee Room.'" *James Joyce Quarterly* 21, 2 (Winter 1984): 145–54.

Howes, Marjorie. " 'Goodbye Ireland I'm going to Gort': Geography, Scale, and Narrating the Nation." In *Semicolonial Joyce*, ed. Derek Attridge and Marjorie Howes. Cambridge: Cambridge University Press, 2000. 58–77.

Ibsen, Henrik. *The Complete Major Prose Plays*. Trans. Rolf Fjelde. New York: Farrar, Straus, Giroux, 1978.

Ingersoll, Earl. *Engendered Trope in Joyce's "Dubliners"*. Carbondale: Southern Illinois University Press, 1996.

Jackson, Roberta. "The Open Closet in *Dubliners*: James Duffy's Painful Case." *James Joyce Quarterly* 37, 1/2 (Fall 1999/Winter 2000): 83–97.

Johnsen, William A. "Joyce's *Dubliners* and the Futility of Modernism." In *James Joyce and Modern Literature*, ed. W. J. McCormack and Alistair Stead. London: Routledge and Kegan Paul. 5–21.

———. "Joyce's Many Sisters and the Demodernization of *Dubliners*." In *New Perspectives on "Dubliners"*, ed. Mary Power and Ulrich Schneider. European Joyce Studies 7. Amsterdam: Rodopi, 1997. 69–90.

Joyce, James. *The Critical Writings.* Ed. Ellsworth Mason and Richard Ellmann. Ithaca, N.Y.: Cornell University Press, 1989.

*Dubliners: A Facsimile of Drafts and Manuscripts.* Arr. Hans Walter Gabler. New York: Garland, 1978.

―――. *Dubliners: Text and Criticism.* Ed. Robert Scholes and A. Walton Litz. New York: Penguin, 1989.

―――. *Ulysses.* Ed. Hans Walter Gabler. New York: Random House, 1986.

Joyce, Stanislaus. *My Brother's Keeper: James Joyce's Early Years.* Ed. Richard Ellmann. New York: Viking, 1958.

―――. *The Complete Dublin Diary of Stanislaus Joyce.* Ed. George H. Healy. Ithaca, N.Y.: Cornell University Press, 1971.

―――. Kain, Richard M. "Grace." In *James Joyce's "Dubliners": Critical Essays,* ed. Clive Hart. New York: Viking, 1969. 134–52.

Karrer, Wolfgang. "Gnomon and Triangulation: The Stories of Childhood in *Dubliners.*" In *New Perspectives on "Dubliners",* ed. Mary Power and Ulrich Schneider. European Joyce Studies 7. Amsterdam: Rodopi, 1997. 45–68.

Kelly, Joseph. "Joyce's Marriage Cycle." *Studies in Short Fiction,* special *Dubliners* issue 32, 3 (Summer 1995): 367–78.

Kenner, Hugh. *Joyce's Voices.* Berkeley: University of California Press, 1978.

―――. "Molly's Masterstroke." *James Joyce Quarterly* 10, 1 (Fall 1972): 19–28.

―――. *The Pound Era.* Berkeley: University of California Press, 1971.

―――. "Signs on a White Field." In *James Joyce: The Centenary Symposium,* ed. Morris Beja, Phillip Herring, Maurice Harmon, and David Norris. Urbana: University of Illinois Press, 1986. 209–19.

Kershner, R. B. *Joyce, Bakhtin, and Popular Literature: Chronicles of Disorder.* Chapel Hill: University of North Carolina Press, 1989.

Khanna, Ranjana. " 'Araby': Women's Time and the Time of the Nation." In *Joyce: Feminism/Post/Colonialism,* ed. Ellen Carol Jones. European Joyce Studies 8. Amsterdam: Rodopi, 1998. 81–101.

Klein, Scott W. "Strongarming 'Grace.'" *James Joyce Quarterly* 37, 1/2 (Fall 1999/Winter 2000): 113–26.

Lacan, Jacques. *Écrits: A Selection.* Trans. Alan Sheridan. New York: W.W. Norton, 1977.

―――. "Of the Gaze as *Objet Petit a.*" In *The Four Fundamental Concepts of Psycho-Analysis.* Ed. Jacques-Alain Miller. Trans. Alan Sheridan. New York: W.W. Norton, 1978.

Lamos, Colleen. "Duffy's Subjectivation: The Psychic Life of 'A Painful Case.'" In *Masculinities in Joyce/ Postcolonial Constructions,* ed. Christine Van Boheemen-Saaf and Colleen Lamos. European Joyce Studies 10. Amsterdam: Rodopi, 2001. 59–71.

LeBlanc, Jim. "All Work, No Play: The Refusal of Freedom in 'Araby.'" *James Joyce Quarterly* 37, 1/ 2 (Fall 1999/Winter 2000): 229–33.

Leonard, Garry. *Reading "Dubliners" Again: A Lacanian Perspective.* Syracuse, N.Y.: Syracuse University Press, 1993.

Levenson, Michael. "Living History in 'The Dead.'" In *James Joyce's "The Dead": Case Studies in Contemporary Criticism,* ed. Daniel R. Schwarz. Boston: Bedford Books, 1994. 163–77.

Lin, Paul. "Standing the Empire: Drinking, Masculinity, and Modernity in 'Counterparts.'" In *Masculinities in Joyce: Postcolonial Constructions,* ed. Christine van

Boheemen-Saaf and Colleen Lamos. European Joyce Studies 10. Amsterdam: Rodopi, 2001. 33–57.

Lloyd, David. "Counterparts: " 'Dubliners,' Masculinity, and Temperance Nationalism." In *Semicolonial Joyce*, ed. Derek Attridge and Marjorie Howes. Cambridge: Cambridge University Press, 2000. 128–49.

Lowe-Evans, Mary. "Who Killed Mrs. Sinico?" *Studies in Short Fiction*, special *Dubliners* issue 32, 3 (Summer 1995): 395–402.

Lyotard, Jean-François. *The Differend: Phrases in Dispute*. Trans. Georges Van Den Abbeele. Minneapolis: University of Minnesota Press, 1988.

Lyotard, Jean-François, and Jean-Loup Thebaud. *Just Gaming*. Trans. Wlad Godzich. Minneapolis: University of Minnesota Press, 1985.

Maddox, Brenda. *Nora*. Boston: Houghton Mifflin, 1988.

Marcuse, Herbert. *Negations: Essays in Critical Theory*. Trans. J. J. Shapiro. Boston: Beacon Press, 1968.

McCarthy, Patrick A. "Introduction." In *ReJoycing: New Readings of "Dubliners"*, ed. Rosa M. Bollettieri Bosinelli and Harold F. Mosher, Jr. Lexington: University Press of Kentucky, 1998. 1–9.

McCourt, Frank. *Angela's Ashes: A Memoir*. New York: Scribner, 1996.

McLean, Barbara. " 'The (Boar)ding House': Mrs. Mooney as Circe and Sow." *James Joyce Quarterly* 28, 2 (Winter 1991): 520–22.

Melzer, Sondra. "In the Beginning There Was 'Eveline'." *James Joyce Quarterly* 16, 4 (Summer 1979): 479–85.

Miami University Research Group Experiment (MURGE). "Analyzing 'Araby' as Story and Discourse: A Summary of the MURGE Project." *James Joyce Quarterly* 18, 3 (Spring 1981): 267–76.

Mill, John Stuart. *The Subjection of Women*. Ed. Susan Moller Okin. Indianapolis: Hackett, 1988.

Miller, Jane. " 'O, she's a nice lady!: A Rereading of 'A Mother'." *James Joyce Quarterly*. 28, 2 (Winter 1991): 407–26.

Miller, J. Hillis. *The Ethics of Reading*. New York: Columbia University Press, 1987.

Morgan, Jack. "Queer Choirs: Sacred Music, Joyce's 'The Dead,' and the Sexual Politics of Victorian Aestheticism." *James Joyce Quarterly* 37, 1/2 (Fall 1999/Winter 2000): 127–51.

Mosher, Harold F., Jr. 1993. "Clichés and Repetitions in *Dubliners*: The Example of 'A Little Cloud'." In *ReJoycing: New Readings of "Dubliners"*, ed. Rosa M. Bollettieri Bosinelli and Harold F. Mosher, Jr. Lexington: University Press of Kentucky, 1998. 52–67.

———. "The Narrated and Its Negatives: The Nonnarrated and Disnarrated in Joyce's *Dubliners*." *Style* (Fall 1993): 407–28.

Mullin, Katherine. " 'Don't cry for me, Argentina': 'Eveline' and the Seductions of Immigration Propaganda." In *Semicolonial Joyce*, ed. Derek Attridge and Marjorie Howes. Cambridge: Cambridge University Press, 2000. 172–200.

Munich, Adrienne Auslander. " 'Dear Dead Women,' or Why Gabriel Conroy Reviews Browning." In *New Alliances in Joyce Studies*, ed. Bonnie Kime Scott. Newark: University of Delaware Press, 1988. 126–34.

Newman, F. X. "The Land of Ooze: Joyce's 'Grace' and the Book of Job." *Studies in Short Fiction* 4 (Fall 1966): 70–79.

Niemeyer, Carl. " 'Grace' and Joyce's Method of Parody." *College English* 27 (December 1969): 196–201.

Norris, Margot. *Joyce's Web: The Social Unraveling of Modernism.* Austin: University of Texas Press, 1992.

Nünning, Ansgar F. "Reconceptualizing the Theory and Generic Scope of Unreliable Narration." In *Recent Trends in Narratological Research*, ed. John Pier. GRAAT 21. Tours: Université de Tours, 1999.

O'Connor, Frank. "Work in Progress." In *Twentieth Century Interpretations of "Dubliners"*, ed. Peter K. Garrett. Englewood Cliffs, N.J.: Prentice-Hall, 1968.

O'Grady, Thomas B. "Little Chandler's Song of Experience." *James Joyce Quarterly* 28, 2 (Winter 1991): 399–405.

Owens, Coilin. " 'Clay' [I]: Irish Folklore." *James Joyce Quarterly* 27, 2 (Winter 1990): 337–52.

*The Oxford Companion to English Literature.* 5th ed. Ed. Margaret Drabble. Oxford: Oxford University Press, 1985.

Paige, Linda Rohrer. "James Joyce's Darkly Colored Portraits of 'Mother' in 'Dubliners.'" *Studies in Short Fiction*, special *Dubliners* issue 32, 3 (Summer 1995): 329–40.

Parrinder, Patrick. *James Joyce.* Cambridge: Cambridge University Press, 1984.

Pecora, Vincent P. "The 'Dead' and the Generosity of the Word." *PMLA* 101 (1987): 206–15.

Pound, Ezra. "Dubliners and Mr James Joyce." In *Literary Essays of Ezra Pound.* Ed. T. S. Eliot. New York: New Directions, 1968. 399–402.

Power, Arthur. *Conversations with James Joyce.* Ed. Clive Hart. Chicago: University of Chicago Press, 1975.

Power, Mary. "The Stories of Public Life." In *New Perspectives on "Dubliners"*, ed. Mary Power and Ulrich Schneider. European Joyce Studies 7. Amsterdam: Rodopi, 1997.

Power, Mary, and Ulrich Schneider, eds. *New Perspectives on "Dubliners".* European Joyce Studies 7. Amsterdam: Rodopi, 1997.

Rabaté, Jean-Michel. "Silence in *Dubliners.*" In *James Joyce: New Perspectives*, ed. Colin MacCabe. Bloomington: Indiana University Press, 1982.

Rabinowitz, Peter J. " 'A Symbol of Something': Interpretive Vertigo in 'The Dead.'" In *James Joyce's "The Dead": Case Studies in Contemporary Criticism*, ed. Daniel R. Schwarz. Boston: Bedford Books, 1994. 137–49.

*Random House Dictionary of the English Language.* Unabridged ed. Ed. Jess Stein. New York: Random House, 1969.

Reynolds, Mary T. *Joyce and Dante: The Shaping Imagination.* Princeton, N.J.: Princeton University Press, 1981.

Riquelme, John Paul. *Teller and Tale in Joyce's Fictions: Oscillating Perspectives.* Baltimore: Johns Hopkins University Press, 1983.

Schloss, Carol. "Money and Other Rates of Exchange: Commercial Relations and 'Counterparts.'" In *New Perspectives on "Dubliners"*, ed. Mary Power and Ulrich Schneider. European Joyce Studies 7. Amsterdam: Rodopi, 1997.

Scholes, Robert. " 'Counterparts' and the Method of *Dubliners.*" In James Joyce, *"Dubliners": Text, Criticism, and Notes.* Ed. Robert Scholes and A. Walton Litz. New York: Viking, 1969.

———. "Semiotic Approaches to a Fictional Text: Joyce's 'Eveline.'" *James Joyce Quarterly* 16, 12 (Fall 1978/Winter 1979): 65–80.

Schwarz, Daniel R. "Gabriel Conroy's Psyche: Character as Concept in Joyce's 'The Dead.'" In *James Joyce's "The Dead": Case Studies in Contemporary Criticism*, ed. Daniel R. Schwarz. Boston: Bedford Books, 1994. 102–24.

Sedgwick, Eve Kosofsky. *Epistemology of the Closet*. Berkeley: University of California Press, 1990.

Senn, Fritz. "Dubliners: 'Renewed Time After Time.'" In *New Perspectives on "Dubliners"*, ed. Mary Power and Ulrich Schneider. European Joyce Studies 7. Amsterdam: Rodopi, 1997.

———. "Dynamic Adjustments in *Dubliners*." In *New Perspectives on "Dubliners"*, ed. Mary Power and Ulrich Schneider. European Joyce Studies 7. Amsterdam: Rodopi, 1997. 1–18.

———. " 'The Boarding House' Seen as a Tale of Misdirection." *James Joyce Quarterly* 23, 4 (Summer 1986): 405–13.

———. "A Rhetorical Analysis of James Joyce's 'Grace.' " *Moderna Sprak* 74 (1980): 121–28.

Sloan, Barbara L. "The D'Annunzian Narrator in 'A Painful Case': Silent, Exiled, and Cunning." *James Joyce Quarterly* 9, 1 (Fall 1971): 26–36.

Spoo, Robert. " 'Una Piccola Nuvoletta': Ferrero's *Young Europe* and Joyce's Mature *Dubliners* Stories." *James Joyce Quarterly* 24, 4 (Summer 1987): 401–10.

Staley, Thomas F. "A Beginning: Signification, Story, and Discourse in Joyce's 'The Sisters.'" In *Critical Essays on James Joyce*, ed. Bernard Benstock. Boston: G.K. Hall, 1985. 176–90.

Stone, Harry. " 'Araby' and the Writings of James Joyce." In Joyce, *Dubliners: Text and Criticism*, ed. Robert Scholes and A. Walton Litz. New York: Penguin, 1996. 304–26.

Strindberg, August. *"The Father," A Tragedy in Three Acts, and "A Dream Play"*. Trans. and ed. Valborg Anderson. Northbrook, Ill.: AHM, 1967.

Tadie, Benoit. "Memory and and Narrative Deadlock in 'Dubliners.'" In *Classic Joyce*, ed. Franca Ruggieri. Studies in Italy 6. Rome: Bulzone Editore, 1999. 373–80.

Templeton, Joan. "The *Doll House* Backlash: Criticism, Feminism, and Ibsen." *PMLA* 104 (1989): 28–39.

Tindall, William York. *A Reader's Guide to James Joyce*. New York; Noonday Press, 1959.

Tolstoy, Leo. *Anna Karenina*. Trans. Constance Garnett. New York: Modern Library, 1950.

Torchiana, Donald T. *Backgrounds for Joyce's "Dubliners"*. Boston: Allen and Unwin, 1986.

Valente, Joseph. *James Joyce and the Problem of Justice: Negotiating Sexual and Colonial Difference*. Cambridge: Cambridge University Press, 1995.

———. "Joyce's (Sexual) Choices: A Historical Overview." In *Quare Joyce*, ed. Joseph Valente. Ann Arbor: University of Michigan Press, 2000. 1–16.

———. "Joyce's Sexual Differend: An Example from *Dubliners*." *James Joyce Quarterly* 28, 2 (Winter 1991): 427–43.

———, ed, *Quare Joyce*. Ann Arbor: University of Michigan Press, 1998.

———. "Thrilled by His Touch: Homosexual Panic and the Will to Artistry in *A Portrait of the Artist as a Young Man*." *James Joyce Quarterly* 31, 3 (Spring 1994): 167–88.

Vesala-Varttala, Tanja. *Sympathy and Joyce's "Dubliners": Ethical Probings of Reading, Narrative, and Textuality*. Tampere: Tampere University Press, 1999.

Walzl, Florence L., "Dubliners." In *A Companion to Joyce Studies*, ed. Zack Bowen and James F. Carens. Westport, Conn.: Greenwood Press, 1984. 158–228.

———. "*Dubliners*: Women in Irish Society." In *Women in Joyce*, ed. Suzette Henke and Elaine Unkeless. Urbana: University of Illinois Press, 1982. 30–56.

————. "Joyce's 'The Sisters': A Development." *James Joyce Quarterly* 10, 4 (Summer 1973): 375–421.

Wawrzycka, Jolanta W. "Text at the Crossroads: Multilingual Transformations in James Joyce's *Dubliners*." In *ReJoycing: New Readings of "Dubliners"*, ed. Rosa M. Bollettieri Bosinelli and Harold Mosher, Jr. Lexington: University Press of Kentucky, 1998. 68–84.

Weir, David. "Gnomon Is an Island: Euclid and Bruno in Joyce's Narrative Practice." *James Joyce Quarterly* 28, 2 (Winter 1991): 343–60.

Werner, Craig Hansen. *"Dubliners": A Pluralistic World*. Boston: Twayne, 1988.

Wicht, Wolfgang. " 'Eveline,' and/as 'A Painful Case': Paralysis, Desire, Signifiers." In *New Perspectives on "Dubliners"*, ed. Mary Power and Ulrich Schneider. Amsterdam: Rodopi, 1997. 115–42.

Williams, Trevor L. "No Cheer for 'the Gratefully Oppressed': Ideology in Joyce's *Dubliners*." In *ReJoycing: New Readings of "Dubliners"*, ed. Rosa M. Bollettieri Bosinelli and Harold F. Mosher, Jr. Lexington: University Press of Kentucky, 1998. 87–109.

Wohlpart, A. James. "Laughing in the Confession-Box: Vows of Silence in Joyce's 'The Sisters'." *James Joyce Quarterly* 30, 3 (Spring 1993): 409–17.

Wright, David G. "The Secret Life of Leopold Bloom and Emily Sinico." *James Joyce Quarterly* 37, 1/2 (Fall 1999/Winter 2000): 99–112.

# Index

# Acknowledgments

Some of the chapters in this book were first written as conference papers and eventually published in volumes growing out of Joyce conferences or in special issues of journals devoted to *Dubliners*. Although I have expanded and revised everything in this book, I nonetheless wish to thank presses and journals that printed earlier versions of some of the pieces for permission to revise and use them in these pages. The first printed version of the "Clay" essay appeared as an article in the March 1987 issue of *PMLA*. Versions of my essay on "The Dead" were earlier printed in *Modern Fiction Studies* and in *James Joyce, "The Dead": Case Studies in Contemporary Criticism*. I thank Johns Hopkins University Press and Bedford Books of St. Martin's Press, respectively, for permission to reproduce this essay in revised form here. Other journals that have given permission to publish revised versions of essays previously appearing in their publications include *Studies in Short Fiction* (Summer 1995) ("Blind Streets and Seeing Houses: 'Araby''s Dim Glass Revisited") and *Novel* (Fall 1995) ("Gambling with Gambles in 'Two Gallants' "). Rodopi, the publisher of *European Joyce Studies*, has granted permission to reproduce my essays appearing in *European Joyce Studies* 7 (1997) ("Narrative Bread Pudding: Joyce's 'The Boarding House' "), *European Joyce Studies* 10 (2001) ("Masculinity Games in 'After the Race' "), and *European Joyce Studies* 11 (2002) ("Critical Judgment and Gender Prejudice in 'A Mother' "). *James Joyce Quarterly* has also kindly granted permission to reprint an essay appearing in the Fall 1999/Winter 2000 issue ("Shocking the Reader in James Joyce's 'A Painful Case' "). And the following collections of essays have included versions of chapters in this book: *Quare Joyce*, edited by Joseph Valente ("A Walk on the Wilde(e) Side: The Doubled Reading of 'An Encounter' ") and *A Collideorscape of Joyce: Festschrift for Fritz Senn*, edited by Ruth Frehner and Ursula Zeller ("Setting Critical Accounts Right: Tom Kernan, Usury, and Unjust Stewardship"). I thank University of Michigan Press and Lilliput Press of Dublin, respectively, for permission to reprint revised versions of these pieces.